Clashing Views on Controversial

Economic Issues

TENTH EDITION

Selected, Edited, and with Introductions by

Thomas R. Swartz
University of Notre Dame

and

Frank J. Bonello
University of Notre Dame

McGraw-Hill/Dushkin
A Division of The McGraw-Hill Companies

This book is dedicated to the thousands of students who have persevered in the "Bonello/Swartz (B.S.)" introductory economics course sequence at the University of Notre Dame. It is also dedicated to our children and grandchildren. In order of their birth dates they are Mary Elizabeth, Karen Ann, Jennifer Lynne, John Anthony, Anne Marie, Rebecca Jourdan, David Joseph, Stephen Thomas, Chelsea Margaret, Kevin Joseph, Meghan Claire, Maureen Keating, Michael Thomas, Thomas Jourdan, and Amanda Marie.

Cover image: © 2002 by PhotoDisc, Inc.

Cover Art Acknowledgment
Charles Vitelli

Copyright © 2002 by McGraw-Hill/Dushkin,
A Division of The McGraw-Hill Companies, Inc., Guilford, Connecticut 06437

Manufactured in the United States of America

Tenth Edition

123456789BAHBAH5432

Library of Congress Cataloging-in-Publication Data
Main entry under title:
Taking sides: clashing views on controversial economic issues/selected, edited, and with introductions by Thomas R. Swartz and Frank J. Bonello.—10th ed.
Includes bibliographical references and index.
1. United States—Economic policy—1971–1981. 2. United States—Economic policy—1981–1993. 3. United States—Economic policy—1993–. I. Swartz, Thomas R., comp. II. Bonello, Frank J., comp.
338.9'22
0-07-248420-9
ISSN: 1094-7612

Printed on Recycled Paper

Preface

Where there is much desire to learn, there of necessity will be much arguing.

— John Milton (1608–1674), English poet and essayist

Presented here are 17 debates on important and compelling economic issues, which are designed to stimulate critical thinking skills and initiate lively and informed discussion. These debates take economic theory and show how it is applied to current, real-world public policy decisions, the outcomes of which will have an immediate and personal impact. How these debates are resolved will affect our taxes, jobs, wages, educational system, and so on; in short, they will shape the society in which we live.

It has been our intent throughout each of the 10 editions of *Taking Sides: Clashing Views on Controversial Economic Issues* to select issues that reveal something about the nature of economics itself and something about how it relates to current, everyday newspaper headlines and television news stories on public policy concerns. To assist the reader, we begin each issue with an *issue introduction*, which sets the stage for the debate as it is argued in the "yes" and "no" selections. Each issue concludes with a *postscript* that briefly reviews the arguments and makes some final observations. The introduction and postscript do not preempt what is the reader's own task: to achieve a critical and informed view of the economic issue at stake. Certainly, the reader should not feel confined to adopt one or the other of the positions presented. The views presented should be used as starting points, and the suggestions for further reading that appear in each issue postscript offer additional resources on the topic. Internet site addresses (URLs) have been provided at the beginning of each part, which should also prove useful as resources for further research. At the back of the book is a listing of all the *contributors to this volume,* which provides information on the economists, policymakers, political leaders, and commentators whose views are debated here.

Changes to this edition This new edition of *Taking Sides* represents a considerable revision to this book. Fourteen of the 34 selections are new, and of the 17 issues, 6 are completely new and 2 have been revised. Thus, as we continue our journey into the new millennium, this substantially revised book will help us to understand the implications of a changing set of economic issues that were not part of our world just a few years ago. The new issues are *Should California's Electric Utility Industry Be Deregulated?* (Issue 5); *Should Markets Be Allowed to Solve the Shortage in Body Parts?* (Issue 6); *Should Social Security Be Privatized?* (Issue 8); *Is President George W. Bush's Tax Cut Plan Good Economic Policy?*

102748

(Issue 10); *Is the New Economy Really New?* (Issue 11); and *Should We Sweat About Sweatshops?* (Issue 14). In addition, the question for Issue 9 on the Consumer Price Index has been revised, and the "no" sides for both Issue 9 and Issue 16 on putting pollution to the market test have been replaced with new selections.

As with all of the previous editions, the issues in the 10th edition can be used in any sequence. Although the general organization of the book loosely parallels the sequence of topics found in a standard introductory economics textbook, you can pick and choose which issues to read first, since they are designed to stand alone. Note that we have retained the modification to Part 3 introduced in the seventh edition. That part, "The World Around Us," allows us to more fully represent the host of problems our society faces in this ever-changing world in which we live.

A word to the instructor An *Instructor's Manual With Test Questions* (multiple-choice and essay) is available through the publisher. A general guidebook, *Using Taking Sides in the Classroom,* which discusses methods and techniques for integrating the pro-con approach into any classroom setting, is also available. An online version of *Using Taking Sides in the Classroom* and a correspondence service for *Taking Sides* adopters can be found at http://www.dushkin.com/usingts/.

Taking Sides: Clashing Views on Controversial Economic Issues is only one title in the Taking Sides series. If you are interested in seeing the table of contents for any of the other titles, please visit the Taking Sides Web site at http://www.dushkin.com/takingsides/.

Acknowledgments We have received many helpful comments and suggestions from our friends and readers across the United States and Canada. As always, their suggestions were very welcome and have markedly enhanced the quality of this edition of *Taking Sides.* If as you read this book you are reminded of an essay that could be included in a future edition, we hope that you will drop us a note. We very much appreciate your interest and help, and we are always pleased to hear from you.

Our special thanks go to those who responded with suggestions for the 10th edition:

Tony Barrett
College of St. Scholastica

Victoria Beyer
Morehead State University

Robert Brownlee
Centre College of Kentucky

Joan Buccino
Florida Southern College

Glenn Clayman
Columbus State Community College

Nirmalendu Debnath
Lane College

Demetrios Giannaros
University of Hartford

Jac C. Heckelman
Wake Forest University

Stephen Jones
College of the Ozarks

William Marker
Lewis University

Brian McKenna
St. Xavier University

Kim Smith
St. Francis College

Scott Morris
Southern Nazarene University

Lynn M. Smith
University of Houston

Joe Mullin
Columbus State Community College

Debbie Thorsen
Palm Beach Community College

Anatasios Papathanasis
Central Connecticut State University

John Trebnik
Marian College

Rose Rubin
University of Memphis

Michael H. Truscott
University of Tampa

Reuben Slesinger
University of Pittsburgh–Pittsburgh

Darlene Voeltz
Rochester Community College

Harlan Smith
University of Minnesota–Minneapolis

Nazma Zaman
Providence College

We also offer our special thanks to Floyd Werntz, CEO of Werntz Supply, Inc., who has helped us repeatedly to keep sight of how the "real world" actually works. Additionally, we are most appreciative of the encouragement and the effort that Theodore Knight, list manager of the Taking Sides and Sources series at McGraw-Hill/Dushkin, has expended on our behalf in expediting this edition of *Taking Sides*. The one soul who has suffered most in the preparation of this manuscript was Cheryl Reed, who had to read and transcribe Swartz's tortured handwriting.

To all those mentioned above, we owe a huge debt, many thanks, and none of the blame for any shortcomings that remain in this edition of *Taking Sides*.

Thomas R. Swartz
University of Notre Dame

Frank J. Bonello
University of Notre Dame

Contents In Brief

Contents

A. Baade argues that although one might justify a sports subsidy on the basis of "image" or "enhanced quality of life," one cannot justify spending limited development dollars on the economic returns that come from sports venues.

Free-market economists Charles T. Carlstrom and Christy D. Rollow argue that the simple use of market incentives can go a long way to solving the shortage of transplantable organs. They contend that although some people may have "qualms about the buying and selling of organs, the cost of our current approach is that shortages will remain endemic, and ultimately, more lives will be lost." Professor of anthropology Nancy Scheper-Hughes acknowledges that markets in and of themselves are not evil. But she asserts that "by their very nature markets are indiscriminate, promiscuous and inclined to reduce everything, including human beings, their labor and even their reproductive capacity to the status of commodities, to things that can be bought, sold, traded, and stolen."

Social critic and policy analyst Adrian T. Moore maintains that there is extensive evidence to suggest that private sector prisons provide quality correctional services at a lower cost to taxpayers. Columnist Eric Bates contends that "privatizing prisons is really about privatizing tax dollars [and] about transforming public money into private profits."

Michael Tanner, director of health and welfare studies at the Cato Institute, argues that Social Security needs to be replaced with a retirement system based on individually owned, privately invested accounts. He maintains that Social Security fails as it is currently structured both as an antipoverty program and as a retirement program, that it is unfair, and that it makes workers dependent on politicians for their retirement incomes. Catherine Hill, a study director at the Institute for Women's Policy Research, contends that privatization of Social Security is a bad idea because it would create significant transition and administrative costs, create a void with respect to disability and life insurance, and lower the retirement income of women.

Economist Michael J. Boskin and his colleagues argue that the Consumer Price Index (CPI) suffers from quality and new product bias, which means that the CPI overstates inflation and increases in the cost of living. Professor of economics James Devine counters that the Consumer Price Index understates inflation and changes in the cost of living because it fails to account for all pertinent changes in the quality of life.

Issue 10.   Is President George W. Bush's Tax Cut Plan Good Economic Policy?   216

Associate professor of law Peter J. Ferrara argues that President George W. Bush's tax cut plan will stimulate longer-term economic growth and provide a needed antidote to the current economic slowdown. Moreover, the tax plan is fair because it is tilted toward lower- and moderate-income taxpayers. Isaac Shapiro and Robert Greenstein, staff members at the Center on Budget and Policy Priorities, oppose President Bush's tax cut plan because "it would be likely to absorb the entire non–Social Security surplus that is realistically available" and because it would benefit the rich more than low- and middle-income groups.

Issue 11.   Is the New Economy Really New?   232

Professor of business administration William A. Sahlman contends that the development and rapid spread of a new business model, increasing admiration of entrepreneurs, increasing tolerance of failure, easy access to capital, and globalization have combined to create a new economy that is strong and resilient. Economist Dean Baker argues that until the economy proves it can continue to generate rapid output and productivity growth in the face of a stock market crash, it cannot really be considered new.

Issue 12.   Is It Time to Abolish the Minimum Wage?   252

Orthodox neoclassical economist Thomas Rustici asserts that the effects of the minimum wage are clear: it creates unemployment among the least-skilled workers. Labor economist Charles Craypo argues that a high minimum wage is good for workers, employers, and consumers alike and that it is therefore good for the economy as a whole.

designed to halt emissions of chemicals such as chlorofluorocarbons, which deplete the ozone, before irreparable damage is done to world agriculture, marine life, and human health. Professor of economics Lester B. Lave warns against drastic solutions that could themselves be harmful or, at a minimum, "costly if the greenhouse consequences are more benign than predicted."

Alan S. Blinder, a former member of the Board of Governors of the Federal Reserve System, urges policymakers to use the energy of the market to solve America's environmental problems. Economist Frank Ackerman and environmental policy analyst Kevin Gallagher contend that there is an important distinction between using market forces as a "tool" and using competitive markets as a "blueprint" to solve environmental problems. They argue that environmental goals should be set through the use of "public deliberation" and that at times those goals "may have no inherent relationship to the market."

Joe Cobb, president of the Trade Policy Institute in Washington, D.C., asserts that the North American Free Trade Agreement (NAFTA) has been a success. He cites evidence that the average living standards of American workers have improved; that U.S. exports have increased; and that the average annual growth rates of the United States, Canada, and Mexico are greater than they otherwise would have been. Researcher Alan Tonelson negatively assesses NAFTA based on his contentions that the real winners were large U.S. multinational corporations, that median wages in the United States and Mexico have declined, and that the flows of illegal immigrants and drugs into the United States from Mexico are high.

Introduction

Economics and Economists: The Basis for Controversy

Thomas R. Swartz

Frank J. Bonello

I think that Capitalism, wisely managed, can probably be more efficient for attaining economic ends than any alternative system yet in sight, but that in itself it is in many ways extremely objectionable.

— Lord John Maynard Keynes, *The End of Laissez-Faire* (1926)

Although more than 70 years have passed since Lord Keynes (1883–1946) penned these lines, many economists still struggle with the basic dilemma he outlined. The paradox rests in the fact that a free-market system is extremely efficient. It is purported to produce more at a lower cost than any other economic system. But in producing this wide array of low-cost goods and services, problems arise. These problems—most notably a lack of economic equity and economic stability—concern some economists.

If the problems raised and analyzed in this book were merely the product of intellectual gymnastics undertaken by eggheaded economists, we could sit back and enjoy these confrontations as theoretical exercises. The essays contained in this book, however, touch each and every one of us in tangible ways. They are real-world issues. Some focus upon macroeconomic topics, such as the minimum wage and the "new economy." Another set of issues deals with microeconomic topics. We refer to these issues as micro problems not because they are small problems but because they deal with small economic units, such as households, firms, or individual industries. A third set of issues deals with matters that do not fall neatly into the macroeconomic or microeconomic classifications. This set includes three issues relating to the international aspects of economic activity and two involving pollution.

The range of issues and disagreements raises a fundamental question: Why do economists disagree? One explanation is suggested by Lord Keynes's 1926 remark. How various economists will react to the strengths and weaknesses found in an economic system will depend upon how they view the relative importance of efficiency, equity, and stability. These are central terms, and we will define them in detail in the following pages. For now the important point is that some economists may view efficiency as overriding. In other cases, the same economists may be willing to sacrifice the efficiency generated by the market to ensure increased economic equity and/or increased economic stability.

Given the extent of conflict, controversy, and diversity, it might appear that economists rarely, if ever, agree on any economic issue. We would be most misleading if we left the reader with this impression. Economists rarely challenge the internal logic of the theoretical models that have been developed and articulated by their colleagues. Rather, they will challenge either the validity of the assumptions used in these models or the value of the ends these models seek to achieve. For example, it is most difficult to discredit the internal logic of the microeconomic models employed by the free-market economist. These models are elegant, and their logical development is most persuasive. However, these models are challenged. The challenges typically focus upon such issues as the assumption of functioning, competitive markets, and the desirability of perpetuating the existing distribution of income. In this case, those who support and those who challenge the operation of the market agree on a large number of issues. But they disagree most assuredly on a few issues that have dramatic implications.

This same phenomenon of agreeing more often than disagreeing is also true in the area of economic policy. In this area, where the public is most acutely aware of differences among economists, these differences are not generally over the kinds of changes that will be brought about by a particular policy. The differences more typically concern the timing of the change, the specific characteristics of the policy, and the size of the resulting effect or effects.

Economists: What Do They Represent?

Newspaper, magazine, and TV commentators all use handy labels to describe certain members of the economics profession. What do the headlines mean when they refer to the Chicago School, the Keynesians, the institutional economists, or the radical economists? What do these individuals stand for? Since we too use our own labels throughout this book, we feel obliged to identify the principal groups, or camps, in our profession. Let us warn you that this can be a misleading venture. Some economists—perhaps most of them—defy classification. They drift from one camp to another, selecting a gem of wisdom here and another there. These are practical men and women who believe that no one camp has all the answers to all the economic problems confronting society.

Recognizing this limitation, four major groups of economists can be identified. These groups are differentiated on the basis of two basic criteria: how they view efficiency relative to equity and stability, and what significance they attach to imperfectly competitive market structures. Before describing the four groups' views on these criteria, it is essential to understand the meaning of certain terms to be used in this description.

Efficiency, equity, and stability represent goals for an economic system. An economy is efficient when it produces those goods and services that people want without wasting scarce resources. Equity in an economic sense has several dimensions. It means that income and wealth are distributed according to accepted principles of fairness, that those who are unable to care for themselves receive adequate care, and that mainstream economic activity is open to all people. Stability is viewed as the absence of sharp ups and downs in business activity, in prices, and in employment. In other words, stability is marked by steady increases in output, little inflation, and low unemployment.

When the term *market structures* is used, it refers to the number of buyers and sellers in the market and the amount of control they exercise over price. At one extreme is a perfectly competitive market where there are so many buyers and sellers that no one has any ability to influence market price. One seller or buyer obviously could have great control over price. This extreme market structure, which we call pure monopoly, and other market structures that result in some control over price are grouped under the broad label of imperfectly competitive markets. That is, imperfect competition is a situation where the number of market participants is limited and, as a consequence, the participants have the ability to influence price. With these terms in mind, we can begin to examine the various schools of economic thought.

Free-Market Economists

One of the most visible groups of economists and perhaps the easiest group to identify and classify is the *free-market economists*. These economists believe that the market, operating freely without interferences from government or labor unions, will generate the greatest amount of well-being for the greatest number of people.

Economic efficiency is one of the priorities for free-market economists. In their well-developed models, *consumer sovereignty*—consumer demand for goods and services—guides the system by directly influencing market prices. The distribution of economic resources caused by these market prices not only results in the production of an array of goods and services that are demanded by consumers, but this production is undertaken in the most cost-effective fashion. The free-market economists hold that, at any point, some individuals must earn incomes that are substantially greater than those of other individuals. They contend that these higher incomes are a reward for greater efficiency or productivity and that this reward-induced efficiency will result in rapid economic growth that will benefit all people in the society. They might also admit that a system driven by these freely operating markets will be subject to occasional bouts of instability (slow growth, inflation, and unemployment). They maintain, however, that government action to eliminate or reduce this periodic instability will only make matters worse. Consequently, government, according to the free-market economist, should play a minor role in the economic affairs of society.

Although the models of free-market economists are dependent upon functioning, competitive markets, the lack of such markets in the real world does not seriously jeopardize their position. First, they assert that large firms are necessary to achieve low per-unit costs; that is, a single large firm may be able to produce a given level of output with fewer scarce resources than a large number of small firms. Second, they suggest that the benefits associated with the free operation of markets are so great compared to government intervention that even a second-best solution of imperfectly competitive markets still yields benefits far in excess of government intervention.

These advocates of the free market have been given various labels over time. The oldest and most persistent label is *classical economists*. This is because the classical economists of the eighteenth century, particularly Adam Smith, were the first to point out the virtues of the market. In *The Wealth of Nations* (1776), Smith captured the essence of the system with the following words:

> Every individual endeavors to employ his capital so that its produce may be of greatest value. He generally neither intends to promote the public interest nor knows how much he is promoting it. He intends only his own security, only his own gain. And he is in this led by an invisible hand to promote an end which was no part of his intention. By pursuing his own interest he frequently promotes that of society more effectively than when he really intends to promote it.

Liberal Economists

Another significant group of economists in the United States can be classified as *liberal economists*. Liberal here refers to the willingness to intervene in the free operation of the market. These economists share with the free-market economists a great respect for the market. The liberal economist, however, does not believe that the explicit and implicit costs of a freely operating market should or can be ignored. Rather, the liberal maintains that the costs of an uncontrolled marketplace are often borne by those in society who are least capable of bearing them: the poor, the elderly, and the infirm. Additionally, liberal economists maintain that the freely operating market sometimes results in economic instability and the resultant bouts of inflation, unemployment, and slow or negative growth.

Consider for a moment the differences between free-market economists and liberal economists at the microeconomic level. Liberal economists take exception to the free market on two grounds. First, these economists find a basic problem with fairness in the marketplace. Since the market is driven by the forces of consumer spending, there are those who through no fault of their own (they may be aged, young, infirm, or physically or mentally handicapped) may not have the wherewithal to participate in the economic system. Second, the unfettered marketplace does not and cannot handle spillover effects, or what are known as externalities. These are the third-party effects that may occur as a result of some action. Will a firm willingly compensate its neighbors for the pollutants it pours into the nearby lake? Will a truck driver willingly drive at the speed limit and in the process reduce the highway accident rate? Liberal economists think not. These economists are therefore willing to have the government intervene in these and other, similar cases.

The liberal economists' role in macroeconomics is more readily apparent. Ever since the failure of free-market economics during the Great Depression of the 1930s, Keynesianism (still another label for liberal economics) has become widely known. In his 1935 book *The General Theory of Employment, Interest, and Money,* Lord John Maynard Keynes laid the basic groundwork for this school of thought. Keynes argued that the history of freely operating market economies was marked by periods of recurring recessions, sometimes very deep recessions, which we call depressions. He maintained that government intervention through its fiscal policy—government tax and spending power—could eliminate, or at least soften, these sharp reductions in economic activity and as a result move the economy along a more stable growth path. Thus, for the Keynesians, or liberal economists, one of the extremely objectionable aspects of a free-market economy is its inherent instability.

Liberal economists are also far more concerned about the existence of imperfections in the marketplace than are their free-market counterparts. They reject the notion that imperfect competition is an acceptable substitute for competitive markets. They may agree that the imperfectly competitive firms can achieve some savings because of their large size and efficiency, but they assert that since there is little or no competition the firms are not forced to pass these cost savings on to consumers. Thus, liberal economists, who in some circles are labeled antitrusters, are willing to intervene in the market in two ways: They are prepared to allow some monopolies, such as public utilities, to exist, but they contend that these must be regulated by government. In other cases they maintain that there is no justification for monopolies, and they are prepared to invoke the powers of antitrust legislation to break up existing monopolies and/or prevent the formation of new ones.

Mainstream Critics and Radical Reform Economists

There are two other groups of economists we must identify. One group can be called *mainstream critics.* Included in this group are individuals like Thorstein Veblen (1857–1929), with his critique of conspicuous consumption, and John Kenneth Galbraith (b. 1908), with his views on industrial structure. One reasonably cohesive subgroup of mainstream critics are the post-Keynesians. They are post-Keynesians because they believe that as the principal economic institutions have changed over time, they have remained closer to the spirit of Keynes than have the liberal economists. As some have suggested, the key aspect of Keynes as far as the post-Keynesians are concerned is his assertion that "expectations of the future are not necessarily certain." On a more practical level post-Keynesians assert, among other things, that the productivity of the economic system is not significantly affected by changes in income distribution, that the system can still be efficient without competitive markets, that conventional fiscal policies cannot control inflation, and that "incomes policies" are the means to an effective and equitable answer to the inflationary dilemma. This characterization of post-Keynesianism is drawn from Alfred S. Eichner's introduction in *A Guide to Post-Keynesian Economics* (M. E. Sharpe, 1978).

The fourth and last group can be called *radical reform economists.* Many in this group trace their ideas back to the nineteenth-century philosopher-economist Karl Marx and his most impressive work, the three volumes of *Das*

Kapital. As with the other three groups of economists, there are subgroups of radical reform economists. One subgroup, which may be labeled contemporary Marxists, is best represented by those who have published their research results over the years in the *Review of Radical Political Economics*. These economists examine issues that have been largely ignored by mainstream economists, such as war, sexism, racism, imperialism, and civil rights. In their analyses of these issues they borrow from and refine the work of Marx. In the process, they emphasize the role of class in shaping society and the role of the economy in determining class structures. Moreover, they see a need to encourage explicitly the development of some form of democratic socialism, for only then will the greatest good for the greatest number be ensured.

In concluding this section, we must warn you to use these labels with extreme care. Our categories are not hard and fast. There is much grayness around the edges and little that is black and white in these classifications. This does not mean, however, that they have no value. It is important to understand the philosophical background of the individual authors. This background does indeed color or shade their work.

Summary

It is clear that there is no shortage of economic problems that demand solutions. At the same time there is no shortage of proposed solutions. In fact, the problem is often one of oversupply. The 17 issues included in this volume will acquaint you—or, more accurately, reacquaint you—with some of these problems. And, of course, there are at least two proposed solutions for each of the problems. Here we hope to provide new insights regarding the available alternatives and the differences and similarities of these alternative remedies.

If this introduction has served its purpose, you will be able to identify common elements in the proposed solutions to the different problems. For example, you will be able to identify the reliance on the forces of the market advocated by free-market economists as the remedy for several economic ills. This introduction should also help you to understand why there are at least two proposed solutions for every economic problem; each group of economists tends to interpret a problem from its own philosophical position and to advance a solution that is grounded in that philosophical framework.

Our intention, of course, is not to connect individuals to one philosophic position or another. We hope instead to generate discussion and promote understanding. To do this, not only must each of us see a proposed solution, we must also be aware of the foundation that supports that solution. With greater understanding, meaningful progress in addressing economic problems can be achieved.

On the Internet ...

The Dismal Scientist

The Dismal Scientist provides free economic data, analysis, and forecasts on a variety of topics.

http://www.dismal.com

The Economist

The Web edition of *The Economist* is available free to subscribers of the print edition or for an annual fee to those who wish to subscribe online. A selection of articles is available free to those who want to dip into the journal.

http://www.economist.com

Electronic Policy Network

This site offers timely information and ideas about national policy on economics and politics, welfare and families, education, civic participation, and health policy in the form of a virtual magazine.

http://epn.org

Resources for Economists on the Internet

This is the table of contents for Resources for Economists on the Internet. This resource of the WWW Virtual Library on Economics is an excellent starting point for any research in economics by academic and practicing economists and anyone interested in economics. It has many Web links.

http://rfe.wustl.edu/sc.html

Statistical Resources on the Web: Comprehensive Economics

Here is an excellent source of statistics collated from federal bureaus, economic indicators (both historical and current), the Federal Reserve Board, economic sources, federal statistical tables, and a consumer price inflator/deflator, plus many links to other sources.

http://www.lib.umich.edu/libhome/Documents.center/stecon.html

WebEc: WWW Resources in Economics

This is a complete virtual library of economics facts, figures, and thoughts.

http://netec.wustl.edu/webec.html

PART 1

Microeconomic Issues

*O*ur lives are profoundly affected by economic decisions made at the microeconomic level. Some important decisions are those regarding profit motives of businesses, gun ownership, city subsidies for sports venues, discrimination in labor markets, deregulation of public utilities, the health care industry, and the need for more prison space.

- Are Profits the Only Business of Business?

- Should We Encourage the Private Ownership of Guns?

- Should Cities Subsidize Sports and Sports Venues?

- Is There Discrimination in U.S. Labor Markets?

- Should California's Electric Utility Industry Be Deregulated?

- Should Markets Be Allowed to Solve the Shortage in Body Parts?

- Do Private Prisons Pay?

ISSUE 1

Are Profits the Only Business of Business?

YES: Milton Friedman, from "The Social Responsibility of Business Is to Increase Its Profits," *The New York Times Magazine* (September 13, 1970)

NO: Robert Almeder, from "Morality in the Marketplace," in Milton Snoeyenbos, Robert Almeder, and James Humber, eds., *Business Ethics*, rev. ed. (Prometheus Press, 1998)

ISSUE SUMMARY

YES: Free-market economist Milton Friedman contends that the sole responsibility of business is to increase its profits.

NO: Philosopher Robert Almeder maintains that if capitalism is to survive, it must act in socially responsible ways that go beyond profit making.

Every economic society—whether it is a traditional society in Central Africa, a fossilized planned economy such as Cuba's, or a wealthy capitalist society such as those found in North America, Western Europe, and the Pacific Rim— must address the basic economic problem of resource allocation. These societies must determine *what* goods and services they can and will produce, *how* these goods and services will be produced, and *for whom* these goods and services will be produced.

The *what, how,* and *for whom* questions must be answered because of the problem of scarcity. Even if a given society were indescribably rich, it would still confront the problem of scarcity—in the case of a rich society, "relative scarcity." It might have all the resources it needs to produce all the goods and services it would ever want, but it could not produce all these things simultaneously. Thus, even a very rich society must set priorities and produce first those goods and services with the highest priority and postpone the production of those goods and services with lower priorities. If time is of the essence, this society would determine *how* these goods and services should be produced. And since this wealthy society cannot produce all it wants instantly, it must also determine *for whom* the first bundle of goods and services will be produced.

Few, if any, economic societies are indescribably rich. On the other hand, there are many examples of economic societies that face grinding deprivation daily. In these societies and in all the societies that fall between poverty and great affluence, the *what, how,* and *for whom* questions are immediately apparent. Somehow these questions must be answered.

In some societies, such as the Amish communities of North America, the answers to these questions are found in tradition: Sons and daughters follow in their parents' footsteps. Younger generations produce *what* older generations produced before them. The methods of production—the horsedrawn plow, the hand-held scythe, the use of natural fertilizers—remain unchanged; thus, the *how* question is answered in the same way that the *for whom* question is answered—by following historic patterns. In other societies, such as self-sustaining religious communities, there is a different pattern of responses to these questions. In these communities, the "elder" of the community determines *what* will be produced, *how* it will be produced, and *for whom* it will be produced. If there is a well-defined hierarchical system, it is similar to one of the former stereotypical command economies of Eastern Europe.

Although elements of tradition and command are found in the industrialized societies of Western Europe, North America, and Japan, the basic answers to the three questions of resource allocation in these countries are determined by profit. In these economic societies, *what* will be produced is determined by what will yield the greatest profit. Consumers, in their search for maximum satisfaction, will bid for those goods and services that they want most. This consumer action drives the prices of these goods and services up, which, in turn, increases producers' profits. The higher profits attract new firms into the industry and encourage existing firms to increase their output. Thus, profits are the mechanism that ensures that consumers get what they want. Similarly, the profit-seeking behavior of business firms determines *how* the goods and services that consumers want will be produced. Since firms attempt to maximize their profits, they select those means of production that are economically most efficient. Lastly, the *for whom* question is also linked to profits. Wherever there is a shortage of goods and services, profits will be high. In the producers' attempts to increase their output, they must attract factors of production (land, labor, and capital) away from other economic activities. This bidding increases factor prices or factor incomes and ensures that these factors will be able to buy goods and services in the open marketplace.

Both Milton Friedman and Robert Almeder recognize the merits of a profit-driven economic system. They do not quarrel over the importance of profits. But they do quarrel over whether or not business firms have obligations beyond making profits. In the following selection, Friedman holds that the *only* responsibility of business is to make profits and that anyone who maintains otherwise is "preaching pure and unadulterated socialism." In the second selection, Almeder, who is clearly not a "socialist," contends that business must act in socially responsible ways "if capitalism is to survive."

Milton Friedman

 **YES**

The Social Responsibility of Business Is to Increase Its Profits

If they didn't do these things, how would they maintain business?

W hen I hear businessmen speak eloquently about the "social responsibilities of business in a free-enterprise system," I am reminded of the wonderful line about the Frenchman who discovered at the age of 70 that he had been speaking prose all his life. The businessmen believe that they are defending free enterprise when they declaim that business is not concerned "merely" with profit but also with promoting desirable "social ends; that business has a social conscience" and takes seriously its responsibilities for providing employment, eliminating discrimination, avoiding pollution and whatever else may be the catchwords of the contemporary crop of reformers. In fact they are—or would be if they or anyone else took them seriously—preaching pure and unadulterated socialism. Businessmen who talk this way are unwitting puppets of the intellectual forces that have been undermining the basis of a free society these past decades. *Selfish*

The discussions of the "social responsibilities of business" are notable for their analytical looseness and lack of rigor. What does it mean to say that "business" has responsibilities? Only people can have responsibilities. A corporation is an artificial person and in this sense may have artificial responsibilities, but "business" as a whole cannot be said to have responsibilities, even in this vague sense. The first step toward clarity in examining the doctrine of the social responsibility of business is to ask precisely what it implies for whom.

Presumably, the individuals who are to be responsible are businessmen, which means individual proprietors or corporate executives. Most of the discussion of social responsibility is directed at corporations, so in what follows I shall mostly neglect the individual proprietor and speak of corporate executives.

In a free-enterprise, private-property system, a corporate executive is an employee of the owners of the business. He has direct responsibility to his employers. That responsibility is to conduct the business in accordance with their desires, which generally will be to make as much money as possible while conforming to the basic rules of the society, both those embodied in law and those embodied in ethical custom. Of course, in some cases his employers may have a different objective. A group of persons might establish a corporation for an eleemosynary purpose—for example, a hospital or a school. The manager of such a corporation will not have money profit as his objective but the rendering of certain services.

In either case, the key point is that, in his capacity as a corporate executive, the manager is the agent of the individuals who own the corporation or establish the eleemosynary institution, and his primary responsibility is to them.

Needless to say, this does not mean that it is easy to judge how well he is performing his task. But at least the criterion of performance is straightforward, and the persons among whom a voluntary contractual arrangement exists are clearly defined.

Of course, the corporate executive is also a person in his own right. As a person, he may have many other responsibilities that he recognizes or assumes voluntarily—to his family, his conscience, his feelings of charity, his church, his clubs, his city, his country. He may feel impelled by these responsibilities to devote part of his income to causes he regards as worthy, to refuse to work for particular corporations, even to leave his job, for example, to join his country's armed forces. If we wish, we may refer to some of these responsibilities as "social responsibilities." But in these respects he is acting as a principal, not an agent; he is spending his own money or time or energy, not the money of his employers or the time or energy he has contracted to devote to their purposes. If these are "social responsibilities," they are the social responsibilities of individuals, not of business.

What does it mean to say that the corporate executive has a "social responsibility" in his capacity as businessman? If this statement is not pure rhetoric, it must mean that he is to act in some way that is not in the interest of his employers. For example, that he is to refrain from increasing the price of the product in order to contribute to the social objective of preventing inflation, even though a price increase would be in the best interests of the corporation. Or that he is to make expenditures on reducing pollution beyond the amount that is in the best interests of the corporation or that is required by law in order to contribute to the social objective of improving the environment. Or that, at the expense of corporate profits, he is to hire "hard-core" unemployed instead of better-qualified available workmen to contribute to the social objective of reducing poverty.

In each of these cases, the corporate executive would be spending someone else's money for a general social interest. Insofar as his actions in accord with his "social responsibility" reduce returns to stockholders, he is spending their money. Insofar as his actions raise the price to customers, he is spending the customers' money. Insofar as his actions lower the wages of some employees, he is spending their money.

The stockholders or the customers or the employees could separately spend their own money on the particular action if they wished to do so. The executive is exercising a distinct "social responsibility," rather than serving as an agent of the stockholders or the customers or the employees, only if he spends the money in a different way than they would have spent it.

But if he does this, he is in effect imposing taxes, on the one hand, and deciding how the tax proceeds shall be spent, on the other.

This process raises political questions on two levels: principle and consequences. On the level of political principle, the imposition of taxes and the expenditure of tax proceeds are governmental functions. We have established elaborate constitutional, parliamentary and judicial provisions to control these functions, to assure that taxes are imposed so far as possible in accordance with the preferences and desires of the public—after all, "taxation without representation" was one of the battle cries of the American Revolution. We have a system of checks and balances to separate the legislative function of imposing taxes and enacting expenditures from the executive function of collecting taxes and administering expenditure programs and from the judicial function of mediating disputes and interpreting the law.

Here the businessman—self-selected or appointed directly or indirectly by stockholders—is to be simultaneously legislator, executive and jurist. He is to decide whom to tax by how much and for what purpose, and he is to spend the proceeds—all this guided only by general exhortations from on high to restrain inflation, improve the environment, fight poverty and so on and on.

The whole justification for permitting the corporate executive to be selected by the stockholders is that the executive is an agent serving the interests of his principal. This justification disappears when the corporate executive imposes taxes and spends the proceeds for "social" purposes. He becomes in effect a public employee, a civil servant, even though he remains in name an employee of a private enterprise. On grounds of political principle, it is intolerable that such civil servants—insofar as their actions in the name of social responsibility are real and not just window-dressing—should be selected as they are now. If they are to be civil servants, then they must be selected through a political process. If they are to impose taxes and make expenditures to foster "social" objectives, then political machinery must be set up to guide the assessment of taxes and to determine through a political process the objectives to be served.

This is the basic reason why the doctrine of "social responsibility" involves the acceptance of the socialist view that political mechanisms, not market mechanisms, are the appropriate way to determine the allocation of scarce resources to alternative uses.

On the grounds of consequences, can the corporate executive in fact discharge his alleged "social responsibilities"? On the one hand, suppose he could get away with spending the stockholders' or customers' or employees' money. How is he to know how to spend it? He is told that he must contribute to fighting inflation. How is he to know what action of his will contribute to that end? He is presumably an expert in running his company—in producing a product or selling it or financing it. But nothing about his selection makes him an expert on inflation. Will his holding down the price of his product reduce inflationary pressure? Or, by leaving more spending power in the hands of his customers, simply divert it elsewhere? Or, by forcing him to produce less because of the lower price, will it simply contribute to shortages? Even if he could answer these questions, how much cost is he justified in imposing on his stockholders, customers and employees for this social purpose? What is the appropriate share and what is the appropriate share of others?

And, whether he wants to or not, can he get away with spending his stock-holders', customers' or employees' money? Will not the stockholders fire him? (Either the present ones or those who take over when his actions in the name of social responsibility have reduced the corporation's profits and the price of its stock.) His customers and his employees can desert him for other producers and employers less scrupulous in exercising their social responsibilities.

This facet of "social responsibility" doctrine is brought into sharp relief when the doctrine is used to justify wage restraint by trade unions. The conflict of interest is naked and clear when union officials are asked to subordinate the interest of their members to some more general social purpose. If the union officials try to enforce wage restraint, the consequence is likely to be wild-cat strikes, rank-and-file revolts and the emergence of strong competitors for their jobs. We thus have the ironic phenomenon that union leaders—at least in the U.S.—have objected to Government interference with the market far more consistently and courageously than have business leaders.

The difficulty of exercising "social responsibility" illustrates, of course, the great virtue of private competitive enterprise—it forces people to be respon-sible for their own actions and makes it difficult for them to "exploit" other people for either selfish or unselfish purposes. They can do good—but only at their own expense.

Many a reader who has followed the argument this far may be tempted to remonstrate that it is all well and good to speak of government's having the responsibility to impose taxes and determine expenditures for such "social" purposes as controlling pollution or training the hard-core unemployed, but that the problems are too urgent to wait on the slow course of political pro-cesses, that the exercise of social responsibility by businessmen is a quicker and surer way to solve pressing current problems.

Aside from the question of fact—I share Adam Smith's skepticism about the benefits that can be expected from "those who affected to trade for the public good"—this argument must be rejected on grounds of principle. What it amounts to is an assertion that those who favor the taxes and expenditures in question have failed to persuade a majority of their fellow citizens to be of like mind and that they are seeking to attain by undemocratic procedures what they cannot attain by democratic procedures. In a free society, it is hard for "good" people to do "good," but that is a small price to pay for making it hard for "evil" people to do "evil," especially since one man's good is another's evil.

I have, for simplicity, concentrated on the special case of the corporate ex-ecutive, except only for the brief digression on trade unions. But precisely the same argument applies to the newer phenomenon of calling upon stockholders to require corporations to exercise social responsibility (the recent G.M. cru-sade, for example). In most of these cases, what is in effect involved is some stockholders trying to get other stockholders (or customers or employees) to contribute against their will to "social" causes favored by the activists. Insofar as they succeed, they are again imposing taxes and spending the proceeds.

The situation of the individual proprietor is somewhat different. If he acts to reduce the returns of his enterprise in order to exercise his "social respon-sibility," he is spending his own money, not someone else's. If he wishes to spend his money on such purposes, that is his right, and I cannot see that there is any objection to his doing so. In the process, he, too, may impose costs on employees and customers. However, because he is far less likely than a large corporation or union to have monopolistic power, any such side effects will tend to be minor.

Of course, in practice the doctrine of social responsibility is frequently a cloak for actions that are justified on other grounds rather than a reason for those actions.

To illustrate, it may well be in the long-run interest of a corporation that is a major employer in a small community to devote resources to providing amenities to that community or to improving its government. That may make it easier to attract desirable employees, it may reduce the wage bill or lessen losses from pilferage and sabotage or have other worthwhile effects. Or it may be that, given the laws about the deductibility of corporate charitable contributions, the stockholders can contribute more to charities they favor by having the corporation make the gift than by doing it themselves, since they can in that way contribute an amount that would otherwise have been paid as corporate taxes.

In each of these—and many similar—cases, there is a strong temptation to rationalize these actions as an exercise of "social responsibility." In the present climate of opinion, with its widespread aversion to "capitalism," "profits," the "soulless corporation" and so on, this is one way for a corporation to generate goodwill as a by-product of expenditures that are entirely justified in its own self-interest.

It would be inconsistent of me to call on corporate executives to refrain from this hypocritical window-dressing because it harms the foundations of a free society. That would be to call on them to exercise a "social responsibility"! If our institutions, and the attitudes of the public make it in their self-interest to cloak their actions in this way, I cannot summon much indignation to denounce them. At the same time, I can express admiration for those individual proprietors or owners of closely held corporations or stockholders of more broadly held corporations who disdain such tactics as approaching fraud.

Whether blameworthy or not, the use of the cloak of social responsibility, and the nonsense spoken in its name by influential and prestigious businessmen, does clearly harm the foundations of a free society. I have been impressed time and again by the schizophrenic character of many businessmen. They are capable of being extremely far-sighted and clear-headed in matters that are internal to their businesses. They are incredibly short-sighted and muddle-headed in matters that are outside their businesses but affect the possible survival of business in general. This short-sightedness is strikingly exemplified in the calls from many businessmen for wage and price guidelines or controls or income policies. There is nothing that could do more in a brief period to destroy a market system and replace it by a centrally controlled system than effective governmental control of prices and wages.

The short-sightedness is also exemplified in speeches by businessmen on social responsibility. This may gain them kudos in the short run. But it helps to strengthen the already too prevalent view that the pursuit of profits is wicked and immoral and must be curbed and controlled by external forces. Once this view is adopted, the external forces that curb the market will not be the social consciences, however highly developed, of the pontificating executives; it will be the iron fist of Government bureaucrats. Here, as with price and wage controls, businessmen seem to me to reveal a suicidal impulse.

The political principle that underlies the market mechanism is unanimity. In an ideal free market resting on private property, no individual can coerce any other, all cooperation is voluntary, all parties to such cooperation benefit or they need not participate. There are no "social" values, no "social" responsibilities in any sense other than the shared values and responsibilities of individuals. Society is a collection of individuals and of the various groups they voluntarily form.

The political principle that underlies the political mechanism is conformity. The individual must serve a more general social interest—whether that be determined by a church or a dictator or a majority. The individual may have a vote and a say in what is to be done, but if he is overruled, he must conform. It is appropriate for some to require others to contribute to a general social purpose whether they wish to or not.

Unfortunately, unanimity is not always feasible. There are some respects in which conformity appears unavoidable, so I do not see how one can avoid the use of the political mechanism altogether.

But the doctrine of "social responsibility" taken seriously would extend the scope of the political mechanism to every human activity. It does not differ in philosophy from the most explicitly collectivist doctrine. It differs only by professing to believe that collectivist ends can be attained without collectivist means. That is why, in my book "Capitalism and Freedom," I have called it a "fundamentally subversive doctrine" in a free society, and have said that in such a society, "there is one and only one social responsibility of business—to use its resources and engage in activities designed to increase its profits so long as it stays within the rules of the game, which is to say, engages in open and free competition without deception or fraud."

Are these the only 2 values given?

← NO

Morality in the Marketplace: Reflections on the Friedman Doctrine

Introduction

In seeking to create a climate more favorable for corporate activity, International Telephone and Telegraph allegedly contributed large sums of money to "destabilize" the duly elected government of Chile. Even though advised by the scientific community that the practice is lethal, major chemical companies reportedly continue to dump large amounts of carcinogens and mutagens into the water supply of various areas and, at the same time, lobby strongly to prevent legislation against such practices. General Motors Corporation, other automobile manufacturers, and Firestone Tire and Rubber Corporation have frequently defended themselves against the charge that they knowingly and willingly marketed a product that, owing to defective design, had been reliably predicted to kill a certain percentage of its users and, moreover, refused to recall promptly the product even when government agencies documented the large incidence of death as a result of the defective product. Finally, people often say that numerous advertising companies happily accept, and earnestly solicit, accounts to advertise cigarettes knowing full well that as a direct result of their advertising activities a certain number of people will die considerably prematurely and painfully. Most recently, of course, American Tobacco Companies have been charged with knowingly marketing a very addictive product known to kill untold numbers in slow, painful and costly deaths while the price of the stock of these companies has made fortunes for the shareholders. We need not concern ourselves with whether these and other similar charges are true because our primary concern here is with what might count as a justification for such corporate conduct were it to occur. There can be no question that such corporate behavior sometimes occurs and is frequently legal, or at least not illegal. The question is whether corporate behavior should be constrained by nonlegal or moral considerations. If so, to what extent and how could it be done? As things presently stand, it seems to be a dogma of contemporary capitalism rapidly emerging throughout the world that the sole responsibility of business

From Robert Almeder, "Morality in the Marketplace: Reflections on the Friedman Doctrine." Copyright © 1997 by Robert Almeder. Revised and expanded from "Morality in the Marketplace," in Milton Snoeyenbos, Robert Almeder, and James Humber, eds., *Business Ethics*, rev. ed. (Prometheus Press, 1992). Reprinted by permission of Robert Almeder.

is to make as much money as is *legally* possible. But the interesting question is whether this view is rationally defensible.

Sometimes, although not very frequently, corporate executives will admit to the sort of behavior depicted above and then proceed proximately to justify such behavior in the name of their responsibility to the shareholders or owners (if the shareholders are not the owners) to make as much profit as is legally possible. Thereafter, less proximately and more generally, they will proceed to urge the more general utilitarian point that the increase in profit engendered by such corporate behavior begets such an unquestionable overall good for society that the behavior in question is morally acceptable if not quite praiseworthy. More specifically, the justification in question can, and usually does, take two forms.

The first and most common form of justification consists in urging that, as long as one's corporate behavior is not illegal, the behavior will be morally acceptable because the sole purpose of being in business is to make a profit; and the rules of the marketplace are somewhat different from those in other places and must be followed if one is to make a profit. Moreover, proponents of this view hasten to add that, as Adam Smith has claimed, the greatest good for society in the long run is achieved not by corporations seeking to act morally, or with a sense of social responsibility in their pursuit of profit, but rather by each corporation seeking to maximize its own profit, unregulated in that endeavor except by the laws of supply and demand along with whatever other laws are inherent to the competition process. This, they say, is what has made capitalist societies the envy of the world while ideological socialisms sooner or later fail miserably to meet deep human needs. Smith's view, that there is an invisible hand, as it were, directing an economy governed solely by the profit motive to the greatest good for society in the long run,[1] is still the dominant motivation and justification for those who would want an economy unregulated by any moral concern that would, or could, tend to decrease profits for some *alleged* social or moral good.

Milton Friedman, for example, has frequently asserted that the sole moral responsibility of business is to make as much profit as is legally possible; and by that he means to assert that attempts to regulate or restrain the pursuit of profit in accordance with what some people believe to be socially desirable ends are in fact *subversive* of the common good because the greatest good for the greatest number is achieved by an economy maximally competitive and unregulated by moral rules in its pursuit of profit.[2] So, on Friedman's view, the greatest good for society is achieved by corporations acting legally, but with no further regard for what may be morally desirable; and this view begets the paradox that, *in business,* the greatest good for society can be achieved only by acting without regard for morality, at least in so far as moral rules are not reflected in the legal code. Moreover, adoption of this position constitutes a fairly conscious commitment to the view that while one's personal life may well need moral governance beyond the law, when pursuing profit, it is necessary that one's corporate behavior be unregulated by any moral concern other than that of making as much money as is legally possible; curiously enough, it is only in this way that society achieves the greatest good. So viewed, it is not difficult to see how a corporate executive could sincerely and consistently adopt rigorous standards of morality in his or her personal life and yet feel quite comfortable in abandoning those standards in the pursuit of profit. Albert Carr, for example, likens the conduct of business to that of playing poker.[3] As Carr would have it, moral busybodies who insist on corporations acting morally might do just as well to censure a good bluffer in poker for being deceitful. Society, of course, lacking a perspective such as Friedman's and Carr's is only too willing to view such behavior as strongly hypocritical and fostered by an unwholesome avarice.

The second way of justifying, or defending, corporate practices that may appear morally questionable consists in urging that even if corporations were to take seriously the idea of limiting profits because of a desire to be moral or more responsible to social needs, then corporations would be involved in the unwholesome business of selecting and implementing moral values that may not be shared by a large number of people. Besides, there is the overwhelming question of whether there can be any non-questionable moral values or non-controversial list of social priorities for corporations to adopt. After all, if ethical relativism is true, or if ethical nihilism is true (and philosophers can be counted upon to argue agressively for both positions), then it would be fairly silly of corporations to limit profits for what may be a quite dubious reason, namely, for being moral, when there are no clear grounds for doing it, and when it is not too clear what would count for doing it. In short, business corporations could argue (as Friedman has done)[4] that corporate actions in behalf of society's interests would require of corporations an ability to clearly determine and rank in noncontroversial ways the major needs of society; and it would not appear that this could be done successfully.

Perhaps another, and somewhat easier, way of formulating this second argument consists in urging that because moralists and philosophers generally fail to agree on what are the proper moral rules (if any), as well as on whether we should be moral, it would be imprudent to sacrifice a clear profit for a dubious or controversial moral gain. To authorize such a sacrifice would be to abandon a clear responsibility for one that is unclear or questionable.

If there are any other basic ways of justifying the sort of corporate behavior noted at the outset, I cannot imagine what they might be. So, let us examine these two modes of justification. In doing this, I hope to show that neither argument is sound and, moreover, that corporate behavior of the sort in question is clearly immoral if anything is immoral—and if nothing is immoral, then such corporate behavior is clearly contrary to the long-term interest of a corporation. In the end, we will reflect on ways to prevent such behavior, and on what is philosophically implied by corporate willingness to act in clearly immoral ways.

The "Invisible Hand"

Essentially, the first argument is that the greatest good for the greatest number will be, and can only be, achieved by corporations acting legally but unregulated by any moral concern in the pursuit of profit. As we saw earlier, the evidence for this argument rests on a fairly classical and unquestioning acceptance of Adam Smith's view that society achieves a greater good when each person is allowed to pursue her or his own self-interested ends than when each person's pursuit of self-interested ends is regulated in some way or another by moral rules or concern. But I know of no evidence Smith ever offered for this latter claim, although it seems clear that those who adopt it generally do so out of respect for the perceived good that has emerged for various modern societies as a direct result of the free enterprise system and its ability to raise the overall standard of living of all those under it.

However, there is nothing inevitable about the greatest good occurring in an unregulated economy. Indeed, we have good inductive evidence from the age of the Robber Barons that unless the profit motive is regulated in various ways (by statute or otherwise) untold social evil can, and *will*, occur because of the natural tendency of the system to place ever-increasing sums of money in ever-decreasing numbers of hands as a result of the nature of competition unregulated. If all this is so, then so much the worse for all philosophical attempts to justify what would appear to be morally questionable corporate behavior on the grounds that corporate behavior, unregulated by moral concern, is necessarily or even probably productive of the greatest good for the greatest number. Moreover, a rule utilitarian would not be very hard pressed to show the many unsavory implications to society as a whole if society were to take seriously a rule to the effect that, if one acts legally, it is morally permissible to do whatever one wants to do to achieve a profit. We shall discuss some of those implications of this rule below before drawing a conclusion.

The second argument cited above asserts that even if we were to grant, for the sake of argument, that corporations have social responsibilities beyond that of making as much money as is legally possible for the shareholders, there would be no noncontroversial way for corporations to discover just what these responsibilities are in the order of their importance. Owing to the fact that even distinguished moral philosophers predictably disagree on what one's moral responsibilities are, if any, it would seem irresponsible to limit profits to satisfy dubious moral responsibilities.

For one thing, this argument unduly exaggerates our potential for moral disagreement. Admittedly, there might well be important disagreements among corporations (just as there could be among philosophers) as to a priority ranking of major social needs; but that does not mean that most of us could not, or would not, agree that certain things ought not be done in the name of profit even when there is no law prohibiting such acts. Doubtless, there will always be a few who would do most anything for a profit; but that is hardly a good argument in favor of their having the moral right to do so rather than a good argument showing that they refuse to be moral. In sum, it is difficult to see how this second argument favoring corporate moral nihilism is any better than the general argument for ethical nihilism based on the variability of ethical judgments or practices; and apart from the fact that it tacitly presupposes that morality is a matter of what we all in fact would, or should, accept, the argument is maximally counterintuitive (as I shall show) by way of suggesting that we cannot generally agree that corporations have certain clear social responsibilities to avoid certain practices. Accordingly, I would now like to argue that if anything is immoral, a certain kind of corporate behavior is quite immoral although it may not be illegal.

Murder for Profit

Without caring to enter into the reasons for the belief, I assume we all believe that it is wrong to kill an innocent human being for no other reason than that doing so would be more financially rewarding for the killer than if he were to earn his livelihood in some other way. Nor, I assume, should our moral feeling on this matter change depending on the amount of money involved. Killing an innocent baby for fifteen million dollars would not seem to be any less objectionable than killing it for twenty cents. It is possible, however, that a self-professing utilitarian might be tempted to argue that the killing of an innocent baby for fifteen million dollars would not be objectionable if the money were to be given to the poor; under these circumstances, greater good would be achieved by the killing of the innocent baby. But, I submit, if anybody were to argue in this fashion, his argument would be quite deficient because he has not established what he needs to establish to make his argument sound. What he needs is a clear, convincing argument that raising the standard of living of an indefinite number of poor persons by the killing of an innocent person is a greater good for all those affected by the act than if the standard of living were not raised by the killing of an innocent person. This is needed because part of what we mean by having a basic right to life is that a person's life cannot be taken from him or her without a good reason. If our utilitarian cannot provide a convincing justification for his claim that a greater good is served by killing an innocent person in order to raise the standard of living for a large number of poor people, then it is hard to see how he can have the good reason that he needs to deprive an innocent person of his or her life. Now, it seems clear that there will be anything but unanimity in the moral community on the question of whether there is a greater good achieved in raising the standard of living by killing an innocent baby than in leaving the standard of living alone and not killing an innocent baby. Moreover, even if everybody were to agree that the greater good is achieved by the killing of the innocent baby, how could that be shown to be true? How does one compare the moral value of a human life with the moral value of raising the standard of living by the taking of that life? Indeed, the more one thinks about it, the more difficult it is to see just what would count as objective evidence for the claim that the greater good is achieved by the killing of the innocent baby. Accordingly, I can see nothing that would justify the utilitarian who might be tempted to argue that if the sum is large enough, and if the sum were to be used for raising the standard of living for an indefinite number of poor people, then it would be morally acceptable to kill an innocent person for money.

These reflections should not be taken to imply, however, that no utilitarian argument could justify the killing of an innocent person for money. After all, if the sum were large enough to save the lives of a large number of people who would surely die if the innocent baby were not killed, then one would as a rule be justified in killing the innocent baby for the sum in question. But this situation is obviously quite different from the situation in which one would attempt to justify the killing of an innocent person in order to raise the standard of living for an indefinite number of poor people. It makes sense to kill one innocent person in order to save, say, twenty innocent persons; but it makes no sense at all to kill one innocent person to raise the standard of living of an indefinite number of people. In the latter case, but not in the former, a comparison is made between things that are incomparable.

Given these considerations, it is remarkable and somewhat perplexing that certain corporations should seek to defend practices that are in fact instances of killing innocent persons for profit. Take, for example, the corporate practice of dumping known carcinogens into rivers. On Milton Friedman's view, we should not regulate or prevent such companies from dumping their effluents into the environment. Rather we should, if we like, tax the company after the effluents are in the water and then have the tax money used to clean up the environment.[5] For Friedman, and others, the fact that so many people will die as a result of this practice seems to be just part of the cost of doing business and making a profit. If there is any moral difference between such corporate practices and murdering innocent human beings for money, it is hard to see what it is. It is even more difficult to see how anyone could justify the practice and see it as no more than a business practice not to be regulated by moral concern. And there are a host of other corporate activities that are morally equivalent to deliberate killing of innocent persons for money. Such practices number among them contributing funds to "destabilize" a foreign government, selling cigarettes while knowing that they are highly addictive killers of innocent people, advertising cigarettes, knowingly marketing children's clothing having a known cancer-causing agent, and refusing to recall (for fear of financial loss) goods known to be sufficiently defective to directly maim or kill a certain percentage of their unsuspecting users because of the defect. On this latter item, we are all familiar, for example, with convincingly documented charges that certain prominent automobile and tire manufacturers will knowingly market equipment sufficiently defective to increase the likelihood of death as a direct result of the defect, and yet refuse to recall the product because the cost of recalling and repairing would have a greater adverse impact on profit than if the product were not recalled and the company paid the projected number of predictably successful suits. Of course, if the projected cost of the predictably successful suits were to outweigh the cost of recall and repair, then the product would be recalled and repaired, but not otherwise.

In cases of this sort, the companies involved may admit to having certain marketing problems or a design problem, and they may even admit to having made a mistake; but, interestingly enough, they do not view themselves as immoral or as murderers for keeping their product in the market place when they know people are dying from it, people who would not die if the defect were corrected.

The important point is not whether in fact these practices have occurred in the past, or occur even now; there can be no doubt that such practices have occurred and continue to occur. Rather the point is that when companies act in such ways as a matter of policy, they must either not know what they do is murder (i.e., unjustifiable killing of an innocent person), or knowing that it is murder, seek to justify it in terms of profit. And I have been arguing that it is difficult to see how any corporate manager could fail to see that these policies amount to murder for money, although there may be no civil statute against such corporate behavior. If so, then where such policies exist, we can only assume that they are designed and implemented by corporate managers who either see nothing wrong with murder for money (which is implausible) or recognize that what they do is wrong but simply refuse to act morally because it is more financially rewarding to act immorally.

Of course, it is possible that corporate executives would not recognize such acts as murder. They may, after all, view murder as a legal concept involving one non-corporate person or persons deliberately killing another non-corporate person or persons and prosecutable only under existing criminal statute. If so, it is somewhat understandable how corporate executives might fail, at least psychologically, to see such corporate policies as murder rather than as, say, calculated risks, tradeoffs, or design errors. Still, for all that, the logic of the situation seems clear enough.

Conclusion

In addition to the fact that the only two plausible arguments favoring the Friedman doctrine are unsatisfactory, a strong case can be made for the claim that corporations *do* have a clear and noncontroversial moral responsibility not to design or implement, for reasons of profit, policies that they know, or have good reason to believe, will kill or otherwise seriously injure innocent persons affected by those policies. Moreover, we have said nothing about wage discrimination, sexism, discrimination in hiring, price fixing, price gouging, questionable but not unlawful competition, or other similar practices that some will think businesses should avoid by virtue of responsibility to society. My main concern has been to show that because we all agree that murder for money is generally wrong, and since there is no discernible difference between that and certain corporate policies that are not in fact illegal, then these corporate practices are clearly immoral (that is, they ought not to be done) and incapable of being morally justified by appeal to the Friedman doctrine since that doctrine does not admit of adequate evidential support. In itself, it seems sad that this argument needs to be made and, if it were not for what appears to be a fairly strong commitment within the business community to the Friedman doctrine in the name of the unquestionable success of the free enterprise system, the argument would not need to be stated.

The fact that such practices do exist—designed and implemented by corporate managers who, for all intents and purposes appear to be upright members of the moral community—only heightens the need for effective social prevention. Presumably, of course, any company willing to put human lives into the profit and loss column is not likely to respond to moral censure. Accordingly, I submit that perhaps the most effective way to deal with the problem of preventing such corporate behavior would consist in structuring legislation such that senior corporate managers who knowingly concur in practices of the sort listed above can effectively be tried, at their own expense, for murder, rather than censured and fined a sum to be paid out of corporate profits. This may seem a somewhat extreme or unrealistic proposal. However, it seems more unrealistic to think that aggressively competitive corporations will respond to what is morally necessary if failure to do so could be very or even minimally profitable. In short, unless we take strong and appropriate steps to prevent such practices, society will be reinforcing a destructive mode of behavior that is maximally disrespectful of human life, just as society will be reinforcing a value system that so emphasizes monetary gain as a standard of human success that murder for profit could be a corporate policy if the penalty for being caught at it were not too dear.

Fortunately, a number of states in America have enacted legislation that makes corporations subject to the criminal code of that state. This practice began to emerge quite strongly after the famous Pinto case in which an Indiana superior court judge refused to dismiss a homicide indictment against the Ford Motor Company. The company was indicted on charges of reckless homicide stemming from a 1978 accident involving a 1973 Pinto in which three girls died when the car burst into flames after being slammed in the rear. This was the first case in which Ford, or any other automobile manufacturer, had been charged with a criminal offense. The indictment went forward because the state of Indiana adopted in 1977 a criminal code provision permitting corporations to be charged with criminal acts. At the time, incidentally, twenty-two other states had similar codes. At any rate, the judge, in refusing to set aside the indictment, agreed with the prosecutor's argument that the charge was based not on the Pinto design fault, but rather on the fact that Ford had permitted the car "to remain on Indiana highways knowing full well its defects." The fact that the Ford Motor company was ultimately found innocent of the charges by the jury is incidental to the point that the increasing number of states that allow corporations to fall under the criminal code is an example of social regulation that could have been avoided had corporations and corporate managers not followed so ardently the Friedman doctrine.

In the long run, of course, corporate and individual willingness to do what is clearly immoral for the sake of monetary gain is a patent commitment of a certain view about the nature of human happiness and success, a view that needs to be placed in the balance with Aristotle's reasoned argument and reflections to the effect that money and all that it brings is a means to an end, and not the sort of end in itself that will justify acting immorally to attain it. What that beautiful end is and why being moral allows us to achieve it, may well be the most rewarding and profitable subject a human being can think about. Properly understood and placed in perspective, Aristotle's view on the nature and attainment of human happiness could go a long way toward alleviating the temptation to kill for money.

In the meantime, any ardent supporter of the capitalistic system will want to see the system thrive and flourish; and this it cannot do if it invites and demands government regulation in the name of the public interest. A *strong* ideological commitment to what I have described above as the Friedman doctrine is counterproductive and not in anyone's long-range interest because it is most likely to beget an ever-increasing regulatory climate. The only way to avoid such encroaching regulation is to find ways to move the business community into the long-term view of what is in its interest, and effect ways of both determining and responding to social needs before society moves to regulate business to that end. To so move the business community is to ask business to regulate its own modes of competition in ways that may seem very difficult to achieve. Indeed, if what I have been suggesting is correct, the only kind of enduring capitalism is humane capitalism, one that is at least as socially responsible as society needs. By the same token, contrary to what is sometimes felt in the business community, the Friedman doctrine, ardently adopted for the dubious reasons generally given, will most likely undermine capitalism and motivate an economic socialism by assuring an erosive regulatory climate in a society that expects the business community to be socially responsible in ways that go beyond just making legal profits.

In sum, being socially responsible in ways that go beyond legal profit making is by no means a dubious luxury for the capitalist in today's world. It is a necessity if capitalism is to survive at all; and, presumably, we shall all profit with the survival of a vibrant capitalism. If anything, then, rigid adherence to the Friedman doctrine is not only philosophically unjustified, and unjustifiable, it is also unprofitable in the long run, and therefore, downright subversive of the long-term common good. Unfortunately, taking the long-run view is difficult for everyone. After all, for each of us, tomorrow may not come. But living for today only does not seem to make much sense either, if that deprives us of any reasonable and happy tomorrow. Living for the future may not be the healthiest thing to do; but do it we must, if we have good reason to think that we will have a future. The trick is to provide for the future without living in it, and that just requires being moral.[6]

This paper is a revised and expanded version of "Morality in the Marketplace," which appears in Business Ethics *(revised edition) eds. Milton Snoeyenbos, Robert Almeder and James Humber (Buffalo, N.Y.: Prometheus Press, 1992) 82–90, and, as such, it is a revised and expanded version of an earlier piece "The Ethics of Profit: Reflections on Corporate Responsibility," which originally appeared in* Business and Society *(Winter 1980, 7–15).*

Notes

1. Adam Smith, *The Wealth of Nations,* ed. Edwin Canaan (New York: Modern Library, 1937), p. 423.
2. See Milton Friedman, "The Social Responsibility of Business Is to Increase Its Profits," in *The New York Times Magazine* (September 13, 1970), pp. 33, 122–126 and "Milton Friedman Responds," in *Business and Society Review* no. 1 (Spring 1972), p. 5ff.

3. Albert Z. Carr, "Is Business Bluffing Ethical?" *Harvard Business Review* (January–February 1968).
4. Milton Friedman in "Milton Friedman Responds," in *Business and Society Review* no. 1 (Spring 1972), p. 10.
5. Ibid
6. I would like to thank J. Humber and M. Snoeyenbos for their comments and criticisms of an earlier draft.

POSTSCRIPT

Are Profits the Only Business of Business?

$\mathbf{F}$riedman dismisses the pleas of those who argue for socially responsible business action on the grounds that these individuals do not understand the role of the corporate executive in modern society. Friedman points out that the executives are responsible to the corporate owners, and if the corporate executives take a "socially responsible" action that reduces the return on the owners' investment, they have spent the owners' money. This, Friedman maintains, violates the very foundation of the American political-economic system: individual freedom. If the corporate executives wish to take socially responsible actions, they should use their own money; they should not prevent the owners from spending their money on whatever social actions they might wish to support.

Almeder argues that some corporate behavior is immoral and that defense of this immoral behavior imposes great costs on society. He likens corporate acts such as advertising cigarettes, marketing automobiles that cannot sustain moderate rear-end collisions, and contributing funds to destabilize foreign governments to murdering innocent children for profit. He argues that society must not condone this behavior but, instead, through federal and state legislation, must continue to impose regulations upon businesses until businesses begin to regulate themselves.

Perhaps no single topic is more fundamental to microeconomics than the issue of profits. Many pages have been written in defense of profits; see, for example, Milton and Rose Friedman's *Free to Choose: A Personal Statement* (Harcourt Brace Jovanovich, 1980). A classic reference is Frank H. Knight's *Risk, Uncertainty, and Profits* (Kelly Press, 1921). Friedrich A. Hayek, the author of many journal articles and books, is a guru for many current free marketers. There are a number of other books and articles, however, that are highly critical of the Friedman-Knight-Hayek position, including Christopher D. Stone's *Where the Law Ends: Social Control of Corporate Behavior* (Harper & Row, 1975). Others who challenge the legitimacy of the notion that markets are morally free zones include Thomas Mulligan, "A Critique of Milton Friedman's Essay 'The Social Responsibility of Business Is to Increase Its Profits,'" *Journal of Business Ethics* (1986); Daniel M. Hausman, "Are Markets Morally Free Zones?" *Philosophy and Public Affairs* (Fall 1989); and Andrew Henley, "Economic Orthodoxy and the Free Market System: A Christian Critique," *International Journal of Social Economics* (vol. 14, no. 10, 1987).

ISSUE 2

Should We Encourage the Private Ownership of Guns?

YES: Daniel D. Polsby, from "The False Promise of Gun Control," *The Atlantic Monthly* (March 1994)

NO: Arthur L. Kellermann et al., from "Gun Ownership as a Risk Factor for Homicide in the Home," *The New England Journal of Medicine* (October 7, 1993)

ISSUE SUMMARY

YES: Law professor Daniel D. Polsby alleges that guns do not increase crime rates or violence in the streets but that the "proliferation of gun-control laws almost certainly does."

NO: Emergency room physician Arthur L. Kellermann and his colleagues argue that gun ownership increases an individual's risk of being murdered rather than providing that person with self-protection.

In 1992 crimes committed with handguns increased by almost 50 percent over the previous five-year annual average. In that year, handguns were used in 931,000 violent crimes. It may be because of statistics such as these that the Brady Bill—federal legislation requiring a five-day waiting period and a background check for individuals wishing to purchase guns—was passed by Congress in November 1993 after numerous attempts to pass gun-control legislation were defeated by the powerful pro-gun lobby during the previous seven years.

The pro-gun interests in the United States are well articulated by the National Rifle Association (NRA) and its members. This organization boasts a membership in excess of 3.3 million, and it claimed liquid assets of more than $90 million in 1990. Throughout its existence, the NRA has effectively blocked nearly every attempt at governmental control over private ownership of guns. Traditionally, the NRA and others have defended their position on the grounds that legislation in this area would violate the "right to bear arms," which they allege is protected by the Second Amendment to the Constitution.

However, in recent years public opinion has increasingly turned against the gun lobby. Also, society has begun to question whether or not the Second

Amendment is applicable to private gun ownership. The amendment in full states, "A well regulated Militia, being necessary to the security of a free State, the right of people to keep and bear Arms, shall not be infringed." Many argue that the NRA's constitutional argument is rendered invalid by the reference to a "well regulated Militia." Most legal scholars maintain that the Supreme Court's 1939 decision in *United States v. Miller* still stands as the appropriate interpretation of the Second Amendment. Here the Court ruled that the intent of the amendment was to ensure a collective right having "some reasonable relationship to the preservation or efficiency of a well-regulated militia." The Court did not rule that individuals have a right to keep and bear arms. Indeed, lower courts have turned to the *Miller* decision to *uphold,* not strike down, gun-control legislation.

The most recent Supreme Court ruling in this area came in 1980, when the Court reaffirmed that attempts to control the use of guns through legislative action "do not trench upon any constitutionally protected liberties." It is noteworthy that both Warren E. Burger, the chief justice at that time, and the current chief justice William H. Rehnquist, both conservatives, joined the majority of the Court in this interpretation.

If there is no constitutional prohibition against gun control, what are the costs and benefits of private ownership of handguns? The NRA has long argued that handguns are necessary for self-protection. The NRA's advertising slogan, "Refuse to Be a Victim," is directed toward getting that message across to women, who as a group have traditionally been more opposed to gun ownership than men. The arguments of those opposed to gun control go far beyond this, however. This becomes clear in the essay by Daniel D. Polsby that follows. Polsby raises fundamental economic questions about the demand for guns, the sources of the supply of guns, and the elastic characteristics of both supply and demand.

In large measure, the purpose of Polsby's selection is to respond to the medical community, which has challenged the NRA's contention that guns are an important means of self-protection. In this regard, Arthur L. Kellermann and his associates argue in the second selection that guns are more likely to result in injury to a member of a gun-owning household than they are to protect the household from intruders.

Daniel D. Polsby

 **YES**

The False Promise of Gun Control

During the 1960s and 1970s the robbery rate in the United States increased sixfold, and the murder rate doubled; the rate of handgun ownership nearly doubled in that period as well. Handguns and criminal violence grew together apace, and national opinion leaders did not fail to remark on the coincidence.

It has become a bipartisan article of faith that more handguns cause more violence. Such was the unequivocal conclusion of the National Commission on the Causes and Prevention of Violence in 1969, and such is now the editorial opinion of virtually every influential newspaper and magazine, from *The Washington Post* to *The Economist* to the *Chicago Tribune*. Members of the House and Senate who have not dared to confront the gun lobby concede the connection privately. Even if the National Rifle Association [NRA] can produce blizzards of angry calls and letters to the Capitol virtually overnight, House members one by one have been going public, often after some new firearms atrocity at a fast-food restaurant or the like. And last November they passed the Brady bill.

Alas, however well accepted, the conventional wisdom about guns and violence is mistaken. Guns don't increase national rates of crime and violence —but the continued proliferation of gun-control laws almost certainly does. Current rates of crime and violence are a bit below the peaks of the late 1970s, but because of a slight oncoming bulge in the at-risk population of males aged fifteen to thirty-four, the crime rate will soon worsen. The rising generation of criminals will have no more difficulty than their elders did in obtaining the tools of their trade. Growing violence will lead to calls for laws still more severe. Each fresh round of legislation will be followed by renewed frustration.

Gun-control laws don't work. What is worse, they act perversely. While legitimate users of firearms encounter intense regulation, scrutiny, and bureaucratic control, illicit markets easily adapt to whatever difficulties a free society throws in their way. Also, efforts to curtail the supply of firearms inflict collateral damage on freedom and privacy interests that have long been considered central to American public life. Thanks to the seemingly never-ending war on drugs and long experience attempting to suppress prostitution and pornography, we know a great deal about how illicit markets function and how costly to the public attempts to control them can be. It is essential that we make use of this experience in coming to grips with gun control.

The thousands of gun-control laws in the United States are of two general types. The older kind sought to regulate how, where, and by whom firearms could be carried. More recent laws have sought to make it more costly to buy, sell, or use firearms (or certain classes of firearms, such as assault rifles, Saturday-night specials, and so on) by imposing fees, special taxes, or surtaxes on them. The Brady bill is of both types: it has a background-check provision, and its five-day waiting period amounts to a "time tax" on acquiring handguns. All such laws can be called scarcity-inducing, because they seek to raise the cost of buying firearms, as figured in terms of money, time, nuisance, or stigmatization.

Despite the mounting number of scarcity-inducing laws, no one is very satisfied with them. Hobbyists want to get rid of them, and gun-control proponents don't think they go nearly far enough. Everyone seems to agree that gun-control laws have some effect on the distribution of firearms. But it has not been the dramatic and measurable effect their proponents desired.

Opponents of gun control have traditionally wrapped their arguments in the Second Amendment to the Constitution. Indeed, most modern scholarship affirms that so far as the drafters of the Bill of Rights were concerned the right to bear arms was to be enjoyed by everyone, not just a militia, and that one of the principal justifications for an armed populace was to secure the tranquillity and good order of the community. But most people are not dedicated antiquitarians, and would not be impressed by the argument "I admit that my behavior is very dangerous to public safety, but the Second Amendment says I have a right to do it anyway." That would be a case for repealing the Second Amendment, not respecting it.

Fighting the Demand Curve

Everyone knows that possessing a handgun makes it easier to intimidate, wound, or kill someone. But the implication of this point for social policy has not been so well understood. It is easy to count the bodies of those who have been killed or wounded with guns, but not easy to count the people who have avoided harm because they had access to weapons. Think about uniformed police officers, who carry handguns in plain view not in order to kill people but simply to daunt potential attackers. And it works. Criminals generally do not single out police officers for opportunistic attack. Though officers can expect to draw their guns from time to time, few even in big-city departments will actually fire a shot (except in target practice) in the course of a year. This observation points to an important truth: people who are armed make comparatively unattractive victims. A criminal might not know if any one civilian is armed, but if it becomes known that a large number of civilians do carry weapons, criminals will become warier.

Which weapons laws are the right kinds can be decided only after considering two related questions. First, what is the connection between civilian possession of firearms and social violence? Second, how can we expect gun-control laws to alter people's behavior? Most recent scholarship raises serious questions about the "weapons increase violence" hypothesis. The second question is emphasized here, because it is routinely overlooked and often mocked when noticed; yet it is crucial. Rational gun control requires understanding not only the relationship between weapons and violence but also the relationship between laws and people's behavior. Some things are very hard to accomplish with laws. The purpose of a law and its likely effects are not always the same thing. Many statutes are notorious for the way in which their unintended effects have swamped their intended ones.

In order to predict who will comply with gun-control laws, we should remember that guns are economic goods that are traded in markets. Consumers' interest in them varies. For religious, moral, aesthetic, or practical reasons, some people would refuse to buy firearms at any price. Other people willingly pay very high prices for them.

Handguns, so often the subject of gun-control laws, are desirable for one purpose—to allow a person tactically to dominate a hostile transaction with another person. The value of a weapon to a given person is a function of two factors: how much he or she wants to dominate a confrontation if one occurs, and how likely it is that he or she will actually be in a situation calling for a gun.

Dominating a transaction simply means getting what one wants without being hurt. Where people differ is in how likely it is that they will be involved in a situation in which a gun will be valuable. Someone who *intends* to engage in a transaction involving a gun—a criminal, for example—is obviously in the best possible position to predict that likelihood. Criminals should therefore be willing to pay more for a weapon than most other people would. Professors, politicians, and newspaper editors are, as a group, at very low risk of being involved in such transactions, and they thus systematically underrate the value of defensive handguns. (Correlative, perhaps, is their uncritical readiness to accept studies that debunk the utility of firearms for self-defense.) The class of people we wish to deprive of guns, then, is the very class with the most inelastic demand for them—criminals—whereas the people most likely to comply with gun-control laws don't value guns in the first place.

Do Guns Drive Up Crime Rates?

Which premise is true—that guns increase crime or that the fear of crime causes people to obtain guns? Most of the country's major newspapers apparently take this problem to have been solved by an article published by Arthur Kellermann and several associates in the October 7, 1993, *New England Journal of Medicine.* Kellermann is an emergency-room physician who has published a number of influential papers that he believes discredit the thesis that private ownership of firearms is a useful means of self-protection. (An indication of his wide influence is that within two months the study received almost 100 mentions in publications and broadcast transcripts indexed in the Nexis data base.) For this study Kellermann and his associates identified fifteen behavioral and fifteen environmental variables that applied to a 388-member set of homicide victims, found a "matching" control group of 388 nonhomicide victims, and then ascertained how the two groups differed in gun ownership. In interviews Kellermann made clear his belief that owning a handgun markedly increases a person's risk of being murdered.

But the study does not prove that point at all. Indeed, as Kellermann explicitly conceded in the text of the article, the causal arrow may very well point in the other direction: the threat of being killed may make people more likely to arm themselves. Many people at risk of being killed, especially people involved in the drug trade or other illegal ventures, might well rationally buy a gun as a precaution, and be willing to pay a price driven up by gun-control laws. Crime, after all, is a dangerous business. Peter Reuter and Mark Kleiman, drug-policy researchers, calculated in 1987 that the average crack dealer's risk of being killed was far greater than his risk of being sent to prison. (Their data cannot, however, support the implication that ownership of a firearm causes or exacerbates the risk of being killed.)

Defending the validity of his work, Kellermann has emphasized that the link between lung cancer and smoking was initially established by studies methodologically no different from his. Gary Kleck, a criminology professor at Florida State University, has pointed out the flaw in this comparison. No one ever thought that lung cancer causes smoking, so when the association between the two was established the direction of the causal arrow was not in doubt. Kleck wrote that it is as though Kellermann, trying to discover how diabetics differ from other people, found that they are much more likely to possess insulin than nondiabetics, and concluded that insulin is a risk factor for diabetes.

The New York Times, the *Los Angeles Times, The Washington Post, The Boston Globe,* and the *Chicago Tribune* all gave prominent coverage to Kellermann's study as soon as it appeared, but none saw fit to discuss the study's limitations. A few, in order to introduce a hint of balance, mentioned that the NRA, or some member of its staff, disagreed with the study. But readers had no way of knowing that Kellermann himself had registered a disclaimer in his text. "It is possible," he conceded, "that reverse causation accounted for some of the association we observed between gun ownership and homicide." Indeed, the point is stronger than that: "reverse causation" may account for *most* of the association between gun ownership and homicide. Kellermann's data simply do not allow one to draw any conclusion.

If firearms increased violence and crime, then rates of spousal homicide would have skyrocketed, because the stock of privately owned handguns has increased rapidly since the mid-1960s. But according to an authoritative study of spousal homicide in the *American Journal of Public Health,* by James Mercy and Linda Saltzman, rates of spousal homicide in the years 1976 to 1985 fell. If firearms increased violence and crime, the crime rate should have increased throughout the 1980s, while the national stock of privately owned handguns increased by more than a million units in every year of the decade. It did not. Nor should the rates of violence and crime in Switzerland, New Zealand, and Israel be as low as they are, since the number of firearms per civilian household is comparable to that in the United States. Conversely, gun-controlled Mexico and South Africa should be islands of peace instead of having murder rates more than twice as high as those [in the United States]. The determinants of crime and law-abidingness are, of course, complex matters, which are not fully understood and certainly not explicable in terms of a country's laws. But gun-control enthusiasts, who have made capital out of the low murder rate in England, which is largely disarmed, simply ignore the counterexamples that don't fit their theory.

If firearms increased violence and crime, Florida's murder rate should not have been falling since the introduction, seven years ago, of a law that makes it easier for ordinary citizens to get permits to carry concealed handguns. Yet the murder rate has remained the same or fallen every year since the law was enacted, and it is now lower than the national murder rate (which has been rising). As of last November 183,561 permits had been issued, and only seventeen of the permits had been revoked because the holder was involved in a firearms offense. It would be precipitate to claim that the new law has "caused" the murder rate to subside. Yet here is a situation that doesn't fit the hypothesis that weapons increase violence.

If firearms increased violence and crime, programs of induced scarcity would suppress violence and crime. But—another anomaly—they don't. Why not? A theorem, which we could call the futility theorem, explains why gun-control laws must either be ineffectual or in the long term actually provoke more violence and crime. Any theorem depends on both observable fact and assumption. An assumption that can be made with confidence is that the higher the number of victims a criminal assumes to be armed, the higher will be the risk—the price—of assaulting them. By definition, gun-control laws should make weapons scarcer and thus more expensive. By our prior reasoning about demand among various types of consumers, after the laws are enacted criminals should be better armed, compared with noncriminals, than they were before. Of course, plenty of noncriminals will remain armed. But even if many noncriminals will pay as high a price as criminals will to obtain firearms, a larger number will not.

Criminals will thus still take the same gamble they already take in assaulting a victim who might or might not be armed. But they may appreciate that the laws have given them a freer field, and that crime still pays—pays even better, in fact, than before. What will happen to the rate of violence? Only a relatively few gun-mediated transactions—currently, five percent of armed robberies committed with firearms—result in someone's actually being shot (the statistics are not broken down into encounters between armed assailants and unarmed victims, and encounters in which both parties are armed). It seems reasonable to fear that if the number of such transactions were to increase because criminals thought they faced fewer deterrents, there would be a corresponding increase in shootings. Conversely, if gun-mediated transactions declined—if criminals initiated fewer of them because they feared encountering an armed victim or an armed good Samaritan—the number of shootings would go down. The magnitude of these effects is, admittedly, uncertain. Yet it is hard to doubt the general tendency of a change in the law that imposes legal burdens on buying guns. The futility theorem suggests that gun-control laws, if effective at all, would unfavorably affect the rate of violent crime.

The futility theorem provides a lens through which to see much of the debate. It is undeniable that gun-control laws work—to an extent. Consider, for example, California's background-check law, which in the past two years has prevented about 12,000 people with a criminal record or a history of mental illness or drug abuse from buying handguns. In the same period Illinois's background-check law prevented the delivery of firearms to more than 2,000 people. Surely some of these people simply turned to an illegal market, but just as surely not all of them did. The laws of large numbers allow us to say that among the foiled thousands, some potential killers were prevented from getting a gun. We do not know whether the number is large or small, but it is implausible to think it is zero. And, as gun-control proponents are inclined to say, "If only one life is saved..."

The hypothesis that firearms increase violence does predict that if we can slow down the diffusion of guns, there will be less violence; one life, or more, *will* be saved. But the futility theorem asks that we look not simply at the gross number of bad actors prevented from getting guns but at the effect the law has on *all* the people who want to buy a gun. Suppose we succeed in piling tax burdens on the acquisition of firearms. We can safely assume that a number of people who might use guns to kill will be sufficiently discouraged not to buy them. But we cannot assume this about people who feel that they must have guns in order to survive financially and physically. A few lives might indeed be saved. But the overall rate of violent crime might not go down at all. And if guns are owned predominantly by people who have good reason to think they will use them, the rate might even go up.

Are there empirical studies that can serve to help us choose between the futility theorem and the hypothesis that guns increase violence? Unfortunately, no: the best studies of the effects of gun-control laws are quite inconclusive. Our statistical tools are too weak to allow us to identify an effect clearly enough to persuade an open-minded skeptic. But it is precisely when we are dealing with undetectable statistical effects that we have to be certain we are using the best models available of human behavior....

Administering Prohibition

Assume for the sake of argument that to a reasonable degree of criminological certainty, guns are every bit the public-health hazard they are said to be. It follows, and many journalists and a few public officials have already said, that we ought to treat guns the same way we do smallpox viruses or other critical vectors of morbidity and mortality—namely, isolate them from potential hosts and destroy them as speedily as possible. Clearly, firearms have at least one characteristic that distinguishes them from smallpox viruses: nobody wants to keep smallpox viruses in the nightstand drawer. Amazingly enough, gun-control literature seems never to have explored the problem of getting weapons away from people who very much want to keep them in the nightstand drawer.

Our existing gun-control laws are not uniformly permissive, and, indeed, in certain places are tough even by international standards. Advocacy groups seldom stress the considerable differences among American jurisdictions, and media reports regularly assert that firearms are readily available to anybody anywhere in the country. This is not the case. For example, handgun restrictions in Chicago and the District of Columbia are much less flexible than the ones in the United Kingdom. Several hundred thousand British subjects may legally buy and possess sidearms, and anyone who joins a target-shooting club is eligible to do so. But in Chicago and the District of Columbia, excepting peace officers and the like, only grandfathered registrants may legally possess handguns. Of course, tens or hundreds of thousands of people in both those cities—nobody can be sure how many—do in fact possess them illegally.

Although there is, undoubtedly, illegal handgun ownership in the United Kingdom, especially in Northern Ireland (where considerations of personal security and public safety are decidedly unlike those elsewhere in the British Isles), it is probable that Americans and Britons differ in their disposition to obey gun-control laws: there is reputed to be a marked national disparity in compliance behavior. This difference, if it exists, may have something to do with the comparatively marginal value of firearms to British consumers. Even before it had strict firearms regulation, Britain had very low rates of crimes involving guns; British criminals, unlike their American counterparts, prefer burglary (a crime of stealth) to robbery (a crime of intimidation).

Unless people are prepared to surrender their guns voluntarily, how can the U.S. government confiscate an appreciable fraction of our country's nearly 200 million privately owned firearms? We know that it is possible to set up weapons-free zones in certain locations—commercial airports and many courthouses and, lately, some troubled big-city high schools and housing projects. The sacrifices of privacy and convenience, and the costs of paying guards, have been thought worth the (perceived) gain in security. No doubt it would be possible, though it would probably not be easy, to make weapons-free zones of shopping centers, department stores, movie theaters, ball parks. But it is not obvious how one would cordon off the whole of an open society.

Voluntary programs have been ineffectual. From time to time community-action groups or police departments have sponsored "turn in your gun" days, which are nearly always disappointing. Sometimes the government offers to buy guns at some price. This approach has been endorsed by Senator Chafee and the *Los Angeles Times.* Jonathan Alter, of *Newsweek,* has suggested a variation on this theme: youngsters could exchange their guns for a handshake with Michael Jordan or some other sports hero. If the price offered exceeds that at which a gun can be bought on the street, one can expect to see plans of this kind yield some sort of harvest—as indeed they have. But it is implausible that these schemes will actually result in a less-dangerous population. Government programs to buy up surplus cheese cause more cheese to be produced without affecting the availability of cheese to people who want to buy it. So it is with guns. . . .

The solution to the problem of crime lies in improving the chances of young men. Easier said than done, to be sure. No one has yet proposed a convincing program for checking all the dislocating forces that government assistance can set in motion. One relatively straightforward change would be reform of the educational system. Nothing guarantees prudent behavior like a sense of the future, and with average skills in reading, writing, and math, young people can realistically look forward to constructive employment and the straight life that steady work makes possible.

But firearms are nowhere near the root of the problem of violence. As long as people come in unlike sizes, shapes, ages, and temperaments, as long as they diverge in their taste for risk and their willingness and capacity to prey on other people or to defend themselves from predation, and above all as long as some people have little or nothing to lose by spending their lives in crime, dispositions to violence will persist.

This is what makes the case for the right to bear arms, not the Second Amendment. It is foolish to let anything ride on hopes for effective gun control. As long as crime pays as well as it does, we will have plenty of it, and honest folk must choose between being victims and defending themselves.

Arthur L. Kellermann et al.

Gun Ownership as a Risk Factor for Homicide in the Home

Homicide claims the lives of approximately 24,000 Americans each year, making it the 11th leading cause of death among all age groups, the 2nd leading cause of death among all people 15 to 24 years old, and the leading cause of death among male African Americans 15 to 34 years old. Homicide rates declined in the United States during the early 1980s but rebounded thereafter. One category of homicide that is particularly threatening to our sense of safety is homicide in the home.

Unfortunately, the influence of individual and household characteristics on the risk of homicide in the home is poorly understood. Illicit-drug use, alcoholism, and domestic violence are widely believed to increase the risk of homicide, but the relative importance of these factors is unknown. Frequently cited options to improve home security include the installation of electronic security systems, burglar bars, and reinforced security doors. The effectiveness of these protective measures is unclear, however.

Many people also keep firearms (particularly handguns) in the home for personal protection. One recent survey determined that handgun owners are twice as likely as owners of long guns to report "protection from crime" as their single most important reason for keeping a gun in the home. It is possible, however, that the risks of keeping a firearm in the home may outweigh the potential benefits.

To clarify these issues, we conducted a population-based case-control study to determine the strength of the association between a variety of potential risk factors and the incidence of homicide in the home....

Results

Study Population

There were 1860 homicides in the three counties [from which samples were taken] during the study period. Four hundred forty-four (23.9 percent) took place in the home of the victim. After we excluded the younger victim in 19

From Arthur L. Kellermann, Frederick P. Rivara, Norman B. Rushforth, Joyce G. Banton, Donald T. Reay, Jerry T. Francisco, Ana B. Locci, Janice Prodzinski, Bela B. Hackman, and Grant Somes, "Gun Ownership as a Risk Factor for Homicide in the Home," *The New England Journal of Medicine*, vol. 329, no. 15 (October 7, 1993), pp. 1084–1091. Copyright © 1993 by The Massachusetts Medical Society. Reprinted by permission. References omitted.

double deaths, 2 homicides that were not reported to project staff, and 3 late changes to a death certificate, 420 cases (94.6 percent) were available for study.

Reports on the Scene

Most of the homicides occurred inside the victim's home. Eleven percent occurred outside the home but within the immediate property lines. Two hundred sixty-five victims (63.1 percent) were men; 36.9 percent were women. A majority of the homicides (50.9 percent) occurred in the context of a quarrel or a romantic triangle. An additional 4.5 percent of the victims were killed by a family member or an intimate acquaintance as part of a murder–suicide. Thirty-two homicides (7.6 percent) were related to drug dealing, and 92 homicides (21.9 percent) occurred during the commission of another felony, such as a robbery, rape, or burglary. No motive other than homicide could be established in 56 cases (13.3 percent).

.   The great majority of the victims (76.7 percent) were killed by a relative or someone known to them. Homicides by a stranger accounted for only 15 cases (3.6 percent). The identity of the offender could not be established in 73 cases (17.4 percent). The remaining cases involved other offenders or police acting in the line of duty.

Two hundred nine victims (49.8 percent) died from gunshot wounds. A knife or some other sharp instrument was used to kill 111 victims (26.4 percent). The remaining victims were either bludgeoned (11.7 percent), strangled (6.4 percent), or killed by other means (5.7 percent).

Evidence of forced entry was noted in 59 cases (14.0 percent). Eighteen of these involved an unidentified intruder; six involved strangers. Two involved the police. The rest involved a spouse, family member, or some other person known to the victim.

Attempted resistance was reported in 184 cases (43.8 percent). In 21 of these (5.0 percent) the victim unsuccessfully attempted to use a gun in self-defense. In 56.2 percent of the cases no specific signs of resistance were noted. Fifteen victims (3.6 percent) were killed under legally excusable circumstances. Four were shot by police acting in the line of duty. The rest were killed by another member of the household or a private citizen acting in self-defense.

Comparability of Case Subjects and Controls

... Interviews with a matching control* were obtained for 99.7 percent of the case interviews, yielding 388 matched pairs. Three hundred fifty-seven pairs were matched for all three variables, 27 for two variables, and 4 for a single variable (sex). The demographic characteristics of the victims and controls were similar, except that the case subjects were more likely to have rented their homes (70.4 percent vs. 47.3 percent) and to have lived alone (26.8 percent vs. 11.9 percent)....

---

* [Controls were matched with the case subjects according to sex, race, age, and neighborhood of residence.—Eds.]

Univariate Analysis

Alcohol was more commonly consumed by one or more members of the households of case subjects than by members of the households of controls. Alcohol was also more commonly consumed by the case subjects themselves than by their matched controls. Case subjects were reported to have manifested behavioral correlates of alcoholism (such as trouble at work due to drinking) much more often than matched controls. Illicit-drug use (by the case subject or another household member) was also reported more commonly by case households than control households.

Previous episodes of violence were reported more frequently by members of case households. When asked if anyone in the household had ever been hit or hurt in a fight in the home, 31.8 percent of the proxies [who were interviewed as representatives of] the case subjects answered affirmatively, as compared with only 5.7 percent of controls. Physical fights in the home while household members were drinking and fighting severe enough to cause injuries were reported much more commonly by case proxies than controls. One or more members of the case households were also more likely to have been arrested or to have been involved in a physical fight outside the home than members of control households.

Similar percentages of case and control households reported using deadbolt locks, window bars, or metal security doors. The case subjects were slightly less likely than the controls to have lived in a home with a burglar alarm, but they were slightly more likely to have controlled security access. Almost identical percentages of case and control households reported owning a dog.

One or more guns were reportedly kept in 45.4 percent of the homes of the case subjects, as compared with 35.8 percent of the homes of the control subjects.... Shotguns and rifles were kept by similar percentages of households, but the case households were significantly more likely to have a handgun.... Case households were also more likely than control households to contain a gun that was kept loaded or unlocked.

Multivariate Analysis

Six variables were retained in our final conditional logistic-regression model: home rented, case subject or control lived alone, any household member ever hit or hurt in a fight in the home, any household member ever arrested, any household member used illicit drugs, and one or more guns kept in the home. Each of these variables was strongly and independently associated with an increased risk of homicide in the home. No home-security measures retained significance in the final model. After matching for four characteristics and controlling for the effects of five more, we found that the presence of one or more firearms in the home was strongly associated with an increased risk of homicide in the home....

Stratified analyses with our final regression model revealed that the link between guns and homicide in the home was present among women as well as men, blacks as well as whites, and younger as well as older people. Restricting the analysis to pairs with data from case proxies who lived in the home of the victim demonstrated an even stronger association than that noted for the group overall. Gun ownership was most strongly associated with homicide at the hands of a family member or intimate acquaintance. . . . Guns were not significantly linked to an increased risk of homicide by acquaintances, unidentified intruders, or strangers. We found no evidence of a protective benefit from gun ownership in any subgroup, including one restricted to cases of homicide that followed forced entry into the home and another restricted to cases in which resistance was attempted. Not surprisingly, the link between gun ownership and homicide was due entirely to a strong association between gun ownership and homicide by firearms. Homicide by other means was not significantly linked to the presence or absence of a gun in the home.

Living in a household where someone had previously been hit or hurt in a fight in the home was also strongly and independently associated with homicide, even after we controlled for the effects of gun ownership and the other four variables in our final model. . . . Previous family violence was linked to an increased risk of homicide among men as well as women, blacks as well as whites, and younger as well as older people. Virtually all of this increased risk was due to a marked association between prior domestic violence and homicide at the hands of a family member or intimate acquaintance. . . .

Discussion

Although firearms are often kept in homes for personal protection, this study shows that the practice is counterproductive. Our data indicate that keeping a gun in the home is independently associated with an increase in the risk of homicide in the home. The use of illicit drugs and a history of physical fights in the home are also important risk factors. Efforts to increase home security have largely focused on preventing unwanted entry, but the greatest threat to the lives of household members appears to come from within.

We restricted our study to homicides that occurred in the home of the victim, because these events can be most plausibly linked to specific individual and household characteristics. If, for example, the ready availability of a gun increases the risk of homicide, this effect should be most noticeable in the immediate environment where the gun is kept. Although our case definition excluded the rare instances in which a nonresident intruder was killed by a homeowner, our methodology was capable of demonstrating significant protective effects of gun ownership as readily as any evidence of increased risk. . . .

Four limitations warrant comment. First, our study was restricted to homicides occurring in the home of the victim. The dynamics of homicides occurring in other locations (such as bars, retail establishments, or the street) may be quite different. Second, our research was conducted in three urban counties that lack a substantial percentage of Hispanic citizens. Our results may therefore not be generalizable to more rural communities or to Hispanic households. Third, it is possible that reverse causation accounted for some of the association we observed between gun ownership and homicide—i.e., in a limited numbers of cases, people may have acquired a gun in response to a specific threat. If the source of that threat subsequently caused the homicide, the link between guns in the home and homicide may be due at least in part to the failure of these weapons to provide adequate protection from the assailants. Finally, we cannot exclude the possibility that the association we observed is due to a third, unidentified factor. If, for example, people who keep guns in their homes are more psychologically prone to violence than people who do not, this could explain the link between gun ownership and homicide in the home. Although we examined several behavioral markers of violence and aggression and included two in our final logistic-regression model, "psychological confounding" of this sort is difficult to control for. "Psychological autopsies" have been used to control for psychological differences between adolescent victims of suicide and inpatient controls with psychiatric disorders, but we did not believe this approach was practical for a study of homicide victims and neighborhood controls. At any rate, a link between gun ownership and any psychological tendency toward violence or victimization would have to be extremely strong to account for an adjusted odds ratio of 2.7.

Given the univariate association we observed between alcohol and violence, it may seem odd that no alcohol-related variables were included in our final multivariate model. Although consumption of alcoholic beverages and the behavioral correlates of alcoholism were strongly associated with homicide, they were also related to other variables included in our final model. Forcing the variable "case subject or control drinks" into our model did not substantially alter the adjusted odds ratios for the other variables. Furthermore, the adjusted odds ratio for this variable was not significantly greater than 1.

Large amounts of money are spent each year on home-security systems, locks, and other measures intended to improve home security. Unfortunately, our results suggest that these efforts have little effect on the risk of homicide in the home. This finding should come as no surprise, since most homicides in the home involve disputes between family members, intimate acquaintances, friends, or others who have ready access to the home. It is important to realize, however, that these data offer no insight into the effectiveness of home-security measures against other household crimes such as burglary, robbery, or sexual assault. In a 1983 poll, Seattle homeowners feared "having someone break into your home while you are gone" most and "having someone break into your home while you are at home" 4th on a list of 16 crimes. Although homicide is the most serious of crimes, it occurs far less frequently than other types of household crime. Measures that make a home more difficult to enter are probably more effective against these crimes.

Despite the widely held belief that guns are effective for protection, our results suggest that they actually pose a substantial threat to members of the household. People who keep guns in their homes appear to be at greater risk of homicide in the home than people who do not. Most of this risk is due to a substantially greater risk of homicide at the hands of a family member or intimate acquaintance. We did not find evidence of a protective effect of keeping a gun in the home, even in the small subgroup of cases that involved forced entry.

Saltzman and colleagues recently found that assaults by family members or other intimate acquaintances with a gun are far more likely to end in death than those that involve knives or other weapons. A gun kept in the home is far more likely to be involved in the death of a member of the household than it is to be used to kill in self-defense. Cohort and interrupted time-series studies have demonstrated a strong link between availability of guns and community rates of homicide. Our study confirms this association at the level of individual households.

Previous case-control research has demonstrated a strong association between the ownership of firearms and suicide in the home. Also, unintentional shooting deaths can occur when children play with loaded guns they have found at home. In the light of these observations and our present findings, people should be strongly discouraged from keeping guns in their homes.

The observed association between battering and homicide is also important. In contrast to the money spent on firearms and home security, little has been done to improve society's capacity to respond to the problem of domestic violence. In the absence of effective intervention, battering tends to increase in frequency and severity over time. Our data strongly suggest that the risk of homicide is markedly increased in homes where a person has previously been hit or hurt in a family fight. At the very least, this observation should prompt physicians, social workers, law-enforcement officers, and the courts to work harder to identify and protect victims of battering and other forms of family violence. Early identification and effective intervention may prevent a later homicide.

POSTSCRIPT

Should We Encourage the Private Ownership of Guns?

The real issue here is whether or not the firearms industry should go unregulated. Advocates of regulation note that many consumer goods that appear to be far less dangerous than handguns are regulated. If everyday items such as children's toys, over-the-counter drugs, and small kitchen appliances are regulated, why are handguns left unregulated? Surely, more individuals are maimed and killed each year by handguns than by many of the goods that society now regulates.

The NRA would be quick to argue that regulation of the gun industry is not the answer. Indeed, they might argue that the answer is to deregulate all consumer goods. This is the position taken by Jacob Sullivan, managing editor of *Reason*. In an article in *National Review* (February 7, 1994), Sullivan takes great care to show how ineffective regulation such as the Brady Bill will be. Waiting periods and background checks, he argues, will not stop the Colin Fergusons of the world. (Ferguson shot 23 people, fatally wounding 6 of them, on a New York train running from Manhattan to Hicksville on the Long Island Railroad.) Ironically, according to Sullivan, these gun regulations would not have even stopped John Hinckley, who attempted to assassinate President Ronald Reagan and seriously wounded and permanently handicapped Reagan's press secretary James Brady, for whom the Brady Bill is named.

Polsby and other spokespersons for the NRA's position assert that gun control would disarm the law-abiding citizenry and leave the "bad guys" with a monopoly on guns. Kellermann and others within and outside of the medical field, however, find that the cost paid for gun ownership is too high: There are too many accidental shootings; there are too many successful gun-related suicides; and there are too many friends and family members shot in the heat of passion. For Kellermann, guns are too efficient in killing people.

There has been much written about the firearms industry and gun control, particularly after Congress passed the Brady Bill in November 1993. For background, see Jonathan Alter, "How America's Meanest Lobby Ran Out of Ammo," *Newsweek* (May 16, 1994); Frank Lalli, "The Cost of One Bullet: $2 Million," *Money* (February 1994); and Owen Ullmann and Douglas Harbrecht, "Talk About a Loaded Issue," *Business Week* (March 14, 1994). For a good discussion on the limitations of gun control, see David B. Kopel, "Hold Your Fire: Gun Control Won't Stop Rising Violence," *Policy Review* (Winter 1993). And to hear from another member of the medical community, read the editorial by Jerome P. Kassirer entitled "Guns in the Household," which appeared in the October 7,

1993, issue of *The New England Journal of Medicine* along with the Kellermann article.

Finally, we should call your attention to the struggle by the NRA to gain the support of women. In magazines such as *Women and Guns* (published by the Second Amendment Foundation) and in an ad campaign entitled "Refuse to Be a Victim," which has appeared in women's journals such as *Woman's Day* and *Redbook,* the NRA has urged women to "declare [their] independence from the tragic fear that has become the shameful plague of our times." For a discussion of this campaign, see Sally Chew, "The NRA Goes Courting," *Lear's* (January 1994).

ISSUE 3

Should Cities Subsidize Sports and Sports Venues?

YES: Thomas V. Chema, from "When Professional Sports Justify the Subsidy: A Reply to Robert Baade," *The Journal of Urban Affairs* (vol. 18, no. 1, 1996)

NO: Robert A. Baade, from "Stadium Subsidies Make Little Economic Sense for Cities: A Rejoinder," *The Journal of Urban Affairs* (vol. 18, no. 1, 1996)

ISSUE SUMMARY

YES: Attorney and economic development expert Thomas V. Chema asserts that a sports venue has both direct and indirect returns to invested dollars.

NO: Economics professor and urban sports facilities consultant Robert A. Baade argues that although one might justify a sports subsidy on the basis of "image" or "enhanced quality of life," one cannot justify spending limited development dollars on the economic returns that come from sports venues.

The cities of Vail, Colorado; Green Bay, Wisconsin; Cooperstown, New York; Indianapolis, Indiana; and Louisville, Kentucky, are all united by a common denominator. Each boasts a well-known sports venue or sporting event. South Bend, Indiana, may be known to most people as the home of the Fighting Irish football team of Notre Dame, but only our family and a few friends know, or for that matter care, that Bonello and Swartz live there too!

Is there an economic value to the city of South Bend that is totally separate and apart from the dollars spent by 90,000 college football fans who will search for the 80,000 tickets that are available six times each fall semester? In broader terms, is there an economic value for the "city fathers and mothers" associated with the ability to correctly connect ski lifts, a football team, a baseball hall of fame, an auto race, and a horse race with their respective cities? This is the essence of this issue. Robert A. Baade argues that too few individuals utilize sports facilities to make them worthy candidates for public investment. Thomas

V. Chema disagrees, particularly if the venues are strategically placed within the urban community.

We should first examine the impact of a few sports venues. Perhaps no single sports arena has had a longer, more lasting effect on its urban surroundings than the Coliseum in Rome, Italy. This marvelous, 2,000-year-old structure was home to some of the most gruesome "sports" events in Western history. In spite of its crumbling walls and hundreds of years of physical neglect, it still attracts thousands of visitors daily. In fact, this long-abandoned structure still anchors the economic development of the southeast corner of modern Rome.

Alternatively, consider the impact of the America's Cup challenge match to western Australia. The America's Cup is awarded to the winner of a worldwide sailing competition. Until 1986 the competition was always held off the New England coast because the U.S. team had never lost this international competition. Their first loss came at the hands of the Australians, who then had the right to host the challenge match in Fremantle, western Australia. This small, nineteenth-century port city had fallen into serious economic decline prior to the America's Cup challenge match. Although the Australians lost their treasured cup in 1986, they gained much in return. When the sleek racing ships sailed out of the mouth of the Swan River Bay on their return home, they left behind a transformed city awash with cappuccino shops, boutiques, restaurants, microbreweries, and pricey loft condos.

What part of Fremantle's rehabilitation is the direct result of the two or three dozen challenge teams that had to be housed and wined and dined in the two years leading up to the races? What part can be traced to the positive externalities or spillover effects associated with the presence of wealthy sailing teams and the hangers-on who could afford to go halfway around the world to see a sporting event?

In the following selections, Chema attributes large portions of economic development to the presence of sports teams, while Baade contends that it is necessary to carefully measure the dollar costs of sports enterprises to ensure that they do not result in the diversion of leisure dollars to absentee team owners and players.

Thomas V. Chema  **YES**

When Professional Sports Justify the Subsidy: A Reply to Robert Baade

Since virtually the dawn of recorded history the public has been digging into its collective pockets to subsidize the construction of sports venues. Granted, this has not always been a voluntary effort, but then the niceties of democracy were often lost on pharaohs, kings, emperors, and other potentates. The rationale for the public subsidy has varied over time and geography but, with relatively few exceptions, sports have consistently been subsidized.

Robert A. Baade has made a decade long career (or perhaps crusade) arguing against the subsidy. In his most recent paper, "Professional Sports as Catalysts for Metropolitan Economic Development," he purports to demonstrate, using two economic modeling formulae, that subsidy cannot be justified on the basis of economic development and job growth.

For a host of reasons, I disagree with the ultimate conclusion reached by Professor Baade that "cities should be wary of committing substantial portions of their capital budgets to building stadiums." Before cataloging areas of disagreement, let's accept that it is true that professional sports and sport venues are not a panacea for all urban problems. In fact, like Professor Baade, I believe that they are not necessarily even development tools. Their value as catalysts for economic development (job growth and the creation of wealth) depends upon where they are located and how they are integrated into a metropolitan area's growth strategy.

Cities of the future will be important and successful if they can create a critical mass of opportunities for people to socialize within their borders. Several millennia ago, Plato and Aristotle characterized human beings as social creatures. We want to come together, to interact.

For the past 500 years much of that interaction has taken place in cities as people did business and engaged in commerce. Today, with the information superhighway and advanced communications, we tend to be much more isolated in business transactions. Thus, we continually look for other ways to generate human contact and interaction. Cities which understand that cultural activities, recreations, sports and plain old socializing not only bring people together, but

From Thomas V. Chema, "When Professional Sports Justify the Subsidy: A Reply to Robert Baade," *The Journal of Urban Affairs*, vol. 18, no. 1 (1996), pp. 19–22. Copyright © 1996 by Blackwell Publishers. Reprinted by permission.

form a solid base for economic growth, will be the cities which prosper. Cleveland, Baltimore, Indianapolis, and Minneapolis are cities which recognize that sports venues and events can fit into an overall vision for strategic growth. They have integrated the facilities into the urban fabric and they are successful.

The key to sports venues being a catalyst for economic development is locating them in an urban setting and integrating them into the existing city infrastructure. It is the spin-off development generated by two million or more people visiting a specific area of a city during a concentrated time frame which is critical. The return on the public investment in a ballpark or arena, in dollar and cents terms as opposed to the intangible entertainment value comes not from the facility itself, but from the jobs created in new restaurants, taverns, retail, hotels, etc., that spring up on the periphery of the sports venue.

In Cleveland, for example, since the opening of Jacobs Field, 20 new restaurants employing nearly 900 people have opened within two blocks of second base. There are two new retail establishments on Prospect Avenue where there had been none since World War II. There are six projects to convert vacant upper stories of office and commercial buildings to market rate apartments and condominiums and the Gateway facility is only two years old.

This development is materializing because 5,000,000 visitors are coming to games and entertainment and they are spending their money outside the walls of the sports venues before and after the events. Moreover, they are discovering for the first time in 30 years, that downtown has much to offer. They are coming even when there are no sporting events.

Such success dramatizes the flaw in Professor Baade's past and current analyses and conclusions. Baade has researched essentially nonurban facilities which were not intended to be economic development tools. The multiuse stadiums that proliferated in the late 60s and early 70s were specifically designed to be apart from the city. The design characteristics give the impression more of a fort than a marketplace. Moreover, during the period surveyed most new venues were located in suburban or rural locations. The relatively few urban venues might as well have been in suburbs because they were separated from their host city by a moat of surface parking. These facilities became and continue to be isolated attractions. People drive to them, park on surface lots, enjoy the events in the building, and then go home. This is not bad, but it does not generate economic development spin-off. Contrary to Professor Baade's conclusion, however, it is not the sport activity, but the context which is key.

With the exception of Arlington, Texas, the post-1990 ballparks are in urban settings. They connect with the host city and give people an opportunity to spend money in that host city. Given that opportunity, people accept it and the city benefits. Drawing conclusions about the economic development impact from the last generation of sports facility is questionable at best. Certainly, there is no merit in extrapolating from the flying saucers of Pittsburgh, Cincinnati, Philadelphia, etc., and drawing conclusions as to the public return from investment in today's Camden Yards and Jacobs Field.

Moreover, the economic model proposed by Dr. Baade intuitively raises several questions. First, emphasis is placed on the assumption that most of the money generated by a stadium is "quickly disbursed beyond the stadium's environs." That may well be, but is that not equally true of a steel mill or auto plant? What is the point here, surely not that a business enterprise to be a growth generator must reinvest the income in the immediate surroundings?

Second, the fact that the current generation of public assembly facilities is a self-contained series of profit centers does not mean that spin-off development will not occur. Given the correct location and avoiding surrounding the venue with a sea of surface parking, entertainment related enterprises will spring up and flourish in the shadow of the stadiums. Witness Cleveland and Denver. Even in the dead times these businesses can survive once the public becomes familiar with them. Indeed in the modern facility there will be less true dead time because the facility will strive to maximize its usefulness, drawing people to its restaurants, team shops, etc., even when there is no event.

Third, the analysis totally ignores the fiscal impact sporting events and revenues have on the host public jurisdiction. Assuming the implausible circumstance where no sports-related revenues stay in the metropolis from a private sector perspective, there still would be the impact of tax revenues left behind. Virtually every host city has a wage or income tax, a sales tax, and/or admissions tax. This reality, multimillions of dollars, seems to be ignored by the models proposed by Professor Baade.

Fourth, it is difficult to accept the rather narrow definition of economic development posited in the study. What is the value in measuring the metropolitan growth vis-à-vis other cities? Moreover, it seems clear that the fully loaded cost of a stadium cannot be recovered from the stadium revenue alone. Indeed, that is why a subsidy is needed. The return on the subsidy investment must be judged not only on the revenue potential of the facility (and players) but on the spin-off as well. Of course, the subsidy is not made only because an economic return on investment is expected, but also because of the entertainment value of the sports activity or venue. This is not an exclusive analysis nor is the sale to the public of the subsidy ever exclusively based on the expected economic development return on investment.

Fifth, what is the rationale for measuring capital investment and sports revenue receipts on a per capita basis? I strongly suspect that any other entertainment-related industry would provide similar results to that which Professor Baade shows in his paper. In fact, if this type of analysis were applied to investments in steel mills, computer factories, supermarkets, or most other industries, the relative results would make stadium investments look pretty good. Contrary to the implication, using Professor Baade's Chicago example, the investment of $150 million in a stadium which equates to approximately $54.00 per capita is returned in less than three years based on $22.00 per capita in sports franchise revenue. A three year payback on investment is generally viewed favorably in the private sector. Such a return on a public sector investment that should last at least 40 years ought to be viewed very positively.

Sixth, the low wage, seasonal job argument which is typically made by opponents of sports facility investments is, frankly, offensive. Every community, but particularly major urban centers, need to have a diverse mixture of job types in their economy. Not everyone is a rocket scientist. Not everyone could become one even if there were such jobs available, which clearly there are not. Some members or potential members of the labor force need jobs as ushers, ticket takers, vendors, etc. These jobs are neither demeaning to their holders nor do they cause a city to gain "a comparative advantage in unskilled and seasonal labor." This type of reasoning is the product of effete snobbery.

Seventh, how does one measure the opportunity cost involved in public subsidies of sports? I have yet to see or hear of a single instance where the alternative to building a new stadium, for example, was something other than doing nothing. At least since 1989, there have been no proposals of schools v. stadiums or jails v. arenas! The real issue here is collective public investment or individual private expenditures. Economically, this is true of every public investment and sport is no exception.

Eighth, is it really appropriate to measure the economic contribution of an industry based on the growth of the host city rather than on the industry's contribution to the economy of that city? . . .

Finally, it is not clear what jobs are counted as having been created by professional sports in the Baade analysis. Clearly the team and the stadium direct employees, even including all event-related staff, constitute a small number. Most of the jobs created are not going to show up in SIC 794. This model is of very little utility.

It is appropriate for the public to review its investment in a sports venue as an investment in public infrastructure. Like a road, bridge, or water line, the return on the investment comes indirectly as well as directly. A proper analysis includes a review of the entertainment value of the facility and the spin-off value created by the facility. Similarly, a road is justified by transportation utility and the development that it opens on its periphery.

Just as not every road is equal in its economic impact, not every stadium will generate development that justifies a public subsidy. However, when a city establishes a development strategy that includes sports as part of a critical mass of attractions designed to lure people into the urban core, then a sport team or venue can and will provide significant economic value to the city.

Robert A. Baade

↩ **NO**

Stadium Subsidies Make Little Economic Sense for Cities: A Rejoinder

The thoughtful critiques of my research authored by Messrs. Chema and Rosentraub indicate significant agreement among us about the economic impact that professional sports teams and stadiums have on local and regional economies. The areas of alleged disagreement can be broadly characterized as either technical (those monetary benefits and costs that are generally recognized and quantified) or qualitative. Some of the technical issues can be addressed, perhaps resolved, through a clarification of the methods I employed and their outcomes. Other questions can be resolved only with additional data which will enable evaluation of the urban stadiums constructed after 1990. The purpose of this rejoinder is to help advance the stadium debate by commenting on issues raised by Mr. Chema and Dr. Rosentraub.

Before elaborating on specifics relating to these issues, several matters deserve comment. First, I do not have preconceived notions on whether cities, taken individually or collectively, should subsidize the construction of sports facilities. The persistent and ubiquitous use of an economic/investment rationale for public stadium subsidies, however, compels an evaluation of the economic contribution of commercial sport to metropolitan economies. Stadium subsidies represent a classic public finance issue involving both equity and efficiency questions. My research sounds a cautionary note for governments contemplating subsidies on economic grounds. Specifically, cities should reconsider how the stadium is integrated into the urban economy and/or reconsider using the promise of economic gain as a means of selling the subsidy to a skeptical public.

On a personal note, my research about the economic impact of professional sports teams and stadiums has been inspired by my interest in public finance issues and my lifelong experience with sports. In large part my choice to teach at a liberal arts college was conditioned by my affection for both academics and sport. Lake Forest College gave me an opportunity to coach as well as teach. I raise this point in response to Mr. Chema's reference to my "decade long career (or perhaps crusade) arguing against the subsidy." While he may have mistakenly inferred from my work that I dislike sports, to the contrary, I have valued sports as a participant, coach, educator, and fan.

From Robert A. Baade, "Stadium Subsidies Make Little Economic Sense for Cities: A Rejoinder," *The Journal of Urban Affairs*, vol. 18, no. 1 (1996), pp. 33–37. Copyright © 1996 by Blackwell Publishers. Reprinted by permission.

Given my experience, I may be in a better position than some to evaluate the intangibles so often used in discussing and defending sports. The second point I wish to make is that I have not discussed intangibles in my work except to recognize their potential importance. Because proponents of subsidies rationalize their position first and foremost on economic grounds, it is logical to evaluate first the merits of these arguments. My work focuses exclusively on the economic dimension. If we can resolve the issue as it relates to economics, then it may be necessary to move the stadium subsidy debate to the psychological arena where intangibles are properly the focus.

Third, I have chosen to do retrospective stadium analysis because I recognize that identifying and accurately measuring all the dollar inflows and outflows to an area's economy that are induced by commercial sport is a daunting task. Stadium economic impact studies are prospective in nature and are heavily dependent on the assumptions about the financial inflows and outflows to an area's economy as the consequences of professional sports activities. On a practical level, my approach has been to provide a filter through which the promises of increased economic growth for municipalities through professional sports can be evaluated. In retrospect it would appear that prospective economic impact studies in general have failed to capture all the significant inflows and outflows that are essential for even a ballpark estimate of the economic contribution of professional sports. On the other hand, retrospective analysis is limited by data availability.

In reacting to specific areas of concern, Mr. Chema notes the importance of stadium context. In referring to stadium location he observed: "Their value as catalysts for economic development... depends upon where they are located and how they are integrated into a metropolitan area's growth strategy." In noting the success of urban sports facilities constructed after 1990, he alleged a flaw in my research. "Such success dramatizes the flaw in Professor Baade's past and current analyses and conclusions." In response to this allegation I would refer him to Baade and Dye (1988, pp. 272–273) where we wrote:

> If an urban stadium is being planned, the plan should be expanded to incorporate ancillary development.... A stadium is not usually enough of a significant development to anchor an area's economy alone. Rather, in considering the revitalization of an urban neighborhood, a number of potential economic anchors should be developed simultaneously.... Commercial ventures require traffic. The stadium can provide infusions of people, but residential development incorporated with commercial development will ensure a balanced, nonseasonal clientele for business in the stadium neighborhood.

I have emphasized stadium context in public presentations and in my work with stadium planners and architects. Camden Yards and the Gateway Complex in Cleveland represent important experiments relating to stadium context. Research by a number of social scientists, including my own, has identified a stadium and team novelty effect. All else equal, a stadium and team will attract greater interest in the first few years of their existence. So while there is reason to be encouraged by some aspects of the economic performance of Camden Yards and Gateway (not all the financial news from Gateway is good),

I am sure that Mr. Chema recognizes that sound statistical analysis of these two projects requires more than a few observations of economic outcomes. As previously noted, retrospective analysis is limited by data availability.

Furthermore, in evaluating the stadium's economic contribution, a model must be constructed that is capable of separating the stadium from other parts of the development. An integrated development complicates the task for the scholar seeking to determine the stadium's economic contribution separate from other elements of the plan.

Mr. Chema's emphasis on context ignores at least one important contextual point. Many of the stadiums that are currently planned or under construction replace stadiums that have been deemed economically obsolete by a team. Boston, Cincinnati, Milwaukee, Minneapolis, New York, and Seattle currently are in the throes of debates about new stadiums for Major League baseball (MLB). Cincinnati, Minneapolis, and Seattle have facilities that are 25 years old or less. The dome in Minneapolis is 13 years old. This shorter stadium shelf life has important economic implications. One concern is how the new generation of facilities born out of economic imperative will affect the neighborhood's economy. Mr. Chema opines that "the fact that the current generation of public assembly facilities is a self-contained series of profit centers does not mean that spin-off development will not occur." Given the correct developmental context, that may be true, but many stadiums are being designed with the team's bottom line in mind, often to the detriment of the local economy. When a stadium is moved across the street (Chicago's Comiskey Park comes to mind) in the absence of a broader development plan to explicitly include the neighborhood, many of the economic activities and revenues appropriated by local entrepreneurs are appropriated by the stadium operatives seeking to maximize their share of stadium induced revenues.

In focusing on Cleveland and Camden Yards, Mr. Chema concentrates on the exceptions rather than the rule in stadium planning. The reality is that most stadium deals are signed at the midnight hour by legislators opting to do what is necessary to retain a team rather than formulating a plan that integrates the stadium and team into a broader development package. One could blame legislators alone for myopic stadium legislation, but these outcomes are inspired at least as much by the structure of professional sports leagues which serve their own economic interest by maintaining an excess demand for teams. St. Petersburg, Nashville, and Charlotte do not serve the economic interests of Chicago, Houston, and Milwaukee.

Mr. Chema raised other issues that are more technical in nature. He alleges that my "analysis totally ignores the fiscal impact sporting events and revenues have on the host public jurisdiction." Tax revenues are derived. If the tax base expands, tax revenues increase. Professional sports generate additional tax revenues to the extent that they expand the local economy. If sport is construed as part of the entertainment industry, as no less an authority than Bud Selig, MLB's current commissioner, contends, commercial sport from the perspective of the global economy is arguably a zero-sum game. If all the fans supporting a professional sports team within a city are residents of that city, that team will serve to realign economy activity within the city rather than expanding its tax base. Because taxes are derived, tax revenues do not change in such a situation. Does it matter much to the city whether it derives its revenues from sports entertainment or recreation provided by the local theater?

If we drew an imaginary circle from economic ground zero, the point at which the stadium activity occurs, the larger the circle the smaller the net change in economic activity. This reality should help focus the debate about stadium subsidies for various levels of government. For example, the State of Kentucky on purely economic grounds may not want to use its general funds to build a stadium for Louisville unless it can be demonstrated that either fans will pour across the Indiana, Ohio, West Virginia, and Tennessee borders or that Louisville is in need of urban renewal, a public goods argument that could justify an infusion of state funds. If the stadium replaces leisure and recreational spending in Danville with spending in Louisville, Danville may want to argue against the use of state funds for a stadium in Louisville.

Mr. Chema raised the question "what is the value in measuring the metropolitan growth vis-à-vis other cities?" As Professor Rosentraub has indicated in his critique, commercial sport contributes little in an absolute sense to a metropolitan economy. At present modeling the economies of each city that hosts professional sport is not possible and so an alternative technique must be devised to assess the actual contribution of professional sport relative to the economic promise articulated by boosters. Furthermore, an economist would be remiss if the question of opportunity cost was ignored. Public officials must evaluate the stadium not only on its own merit but relative to alternative uses of those funds. Both issues are considered at length in my paper. An argument can be made that in the municipal auction for professional sports franchises, like the auction for free agent players, the winning bid likely exceeds the team's marginal revenue product. It is likely that the greater the excess demand for professional sports teams, the greater the difference between the team's marginal revenue product and the price the host city pays.

Mr. Chema uses the figures I provided on per capita stadium investments and returns to argue that stadiums provide a good return on investment. The per capita returns were not computed for individual sports, but were calculated for commercial sports in general. For individual cities, I have calculated returns on taxpayer equity on the order of 1–2% for an individual sport and those calculations were based on figures provided from the economic impact studies of subsidy supporters. In football and baseball the trend is decidedly away from multipurpose facilities, a trend that is driven by economic imperatives (individual teams want exclusive control of stadium revenues). By the year 2000, it is not unreasonable to predict that baseball and football will no longer share a single facility in the United States.

With regard to Mr. Chema's claim that "at least since 1989, there have been no proposals of schools v. stadiums", I was puzzled by the use of the word proposals. With all due respect, I would encourage Mr. Chema to listen to the tapes of the 1995 Cincinnati City Council debates on the use of public funds for new stadiums for the NFL Bengals and the MLB Reds.

Mr. Chema understandably found offensive the use of the low wage job creation argument in conjunction with opposition to stadium subsidies. Most of us recognize the need for all types of employment. Rather than construing this argument as the product of "effete snobbery," I would ask him to recognize that some of us are trying to explain why sport might not contribute in absolute dollar terms as much as subsidy proponents suggest. My work should not be construed as a recipe for job creation, but rather as an explanation for why stadium subsidies may not have provided the projected economic boost.

As noted earlier, I argued that a retrospective approach to assessing the economic contribution of a stadium or team is necessary, given the complex manner in which dollar inflows and outflows may be affected. An after-the-fact audit of how a change in the professional sports industry influences a metropolitan economy tacitly includes both direct and indirect effects. Indirect changes include an altered city psyche or vision or a heightened spirit of cooperation. All these indirect changes may, indeed, alter the economic landscape. On page 274 of my 1988 article cited previously, I noted (Baade & Dye, 1988, p. 274):

> the most significant contribution of sports is likely to be in the area of intangibles. The image of a city is certainly affected by the presence of professional franchises. Professional sports serve as a focal point for group identification. Sports contests are a part of civic culture. There may well be a willingness of voters to pay taxes to subsidize this kind of activity just like there is for parks and museums.

Professor Rosentraub, in particular, has articulated the less visible ways in which a large public project translates into a more vibrant economy. Without repeating his words, I echo his sentiments.

An after-the-fact audit includes the economic impact of these laudable intangibles and, even then, commercial sport does not emerge as a statistically significant contributor to metropolitan economies. Dr. Rosentraub has emphasized the fact that the professional sports industry is too small to significantly influence a large metropolitan economy. I would only add that it is not only its small size which renders commercial sport relatively unimportant. It is a fact that sports spectating is but one leisure option available to the residents of a large diverse metropolis. Money spent on sports spectating is financed by reduced spending in other recreational venues and that fact contributes to the consistently statistically insignificant results for professional sports my research has yielded using a variety of models.

This fundamental principle is fortified by the fact that the primary beneficiaries of public stadium largesse are owners and players and fans for whom commercial sports produce substantial consumer surplus. For owners and players, particularly those who reside outside the city extending the subsidy, there may be adverse economic effects from diverting leisure dollars from locally owned entertainment centers to absentee owners and players.

In the final analysis I can only repeat what I have said so often. If cities subsidize commercial sports in the quest for an improved image or to enhance the quality of life for its citizens, then taxpayers should be allowed to decide the stadium subsidy issue on these bases. Using economics as a justification for the subsidy is a political expedient, perhaps necessity, but it is inconsonant with the statistical evidence.

Reference

Baade, R. A., & Dye, R. F. (1988). Sports stadiums and area development: a critical review. *Economic Development Quarterly, 2,* 265–275.

POSTSCRIPT

Should Cities Subsidize Sports and Sports Venues?

You probably have been directly or indirectly affected by a sports facility sometime in your life. For many of us this means being part of the crowd that shoulders its way into a baseball park or a basketball arena to watch a favorite team play. For others this means being trapped in a traffic jam as thousands of cars rush home at the end of a football game or the end of a day at the races. Are these modern-day coliseums that dominate the cityscape worth the millions of dollars that taxpayers are asked to pay to support them? Would the community be better advised to spend these dollars attracting industry that supports high-paying jobs or by stabilizing neighborhoods that are in distress?

Chema advocates attracting professional sports teams to cities by offering them substantial subsidies. He argues that Baade has biased his results by focusing his analysis on suburban facilities, which he says are surrounded by "a moat of surface parking." Chema details benefits such as spin-off development, a whole range of taxes, entertainment value, and relative rates of return in other industries. Baade contends that communities should be wary of the many promises made by prospective professional sports franchises. A city should not be intimidated by a team's threat to leave for one that is willing to build a new, more costly facility. Baade argues that most of the dollars generated by sports teams are earned by absentee team owners and players and that most of the new employment opportunities associated with operating these facilities are at the minimum wage level.

A surprising amount has been written on this topic. In part this can be traced to the fact that a few conservative journals have been persuaded by Baade's position. For example, look for two essays by Raymond J. Keating: "We Wuz Robbed! The Subsidized Stadium Scam," *Policy Review* (March/April 1977) and "Pitching Socialism: Government-Financed Stadiums Invariably Enrich Owners at Public Expense," *National Review* (April 22, 1996). There is plenty written on the other side as well. See Curt Smith, "Comeback: The Triumphant Return of Old-Style Ball Parks Show That Tradition Can Be Popular," *The American Enterprise* (March/April 1997) and, on a related topic, Joanna Cagau and Neil de Mause, "Buy the Bums Out," *In These Times* (December 9, 1996). Finally, there are many articles that examine the economic impact of the Summer Olympics in Atlanta, Georgia. See for example, Matthew Cooper, "Welcome to the Olympic Village," *The New Republic* (July 15 and 22, 1996).

ISSUE 4

Is There Discrimination in U.S. Labor Markets?

YES: William A. Darity, Jr., and Patrick L. Mason, from "Evidence on Discrimination in Employment: Codes of Color, Codes of Gender," *Journal of Economic Perspectives* (Spring 1998)

NO: James J. Heckman, from "Detecting Discrimination," *Journal of Economic Perspectives* (Spring 1998)

ISSUE SUMMARY

YES: Professor of economics William A. Darity, Jr., and associate professor of economics Patrick L. Mason assert that the lack of progress made since the mid-1970s toward establishing equality in wages between the races is evidence of persistent discrimination in U.S. labor markets.

NO: Professor of economics James J. Heckman argues that markets— driven by the profit motive of employers—will compete away any wage differentials that are not justified by differences in human capital.

O‌ver forty-five years have passed since Rosa Parks refused to give up her seat on a segregated Montgomery, Alabama, bus. America has had these years to finally overcome discrimination, but has it? Have the domestic programs of Presidents John F. Kennedy and Lyndon Johnson that were enacted after those turbulent years following Parks's act of defiance made it possible for African Americans to succeed within the powerful economic engine that drives American society? Or does racism still stain the Declaration of Independence, with its promise of equality for all?

Before we examine the economics of discrimination, perhaps we should look backward to see where America has been, what progress has been made, and what is left—if anything—to accomplish. American history, some say, reveals a world of legalized apartheid where African Americans were denied access to the social, political, and economic institutions that are the mainstays of America. Without this access, millions of American citizens were doomed to live lives on the fringes of the mainstream. Thus, the Kennedy/Johnson programs left one legacy, which few now dispute: These programs effectively dismantled the system of legalized discrimination and, for the first time since the end of slavery, allowed blacks to dream of a better life.

The dream became a reality for many. Consider the success stories that are buried in the poverty statistics that were collected and reported in the 1960s. Poverty scarred the lives of one out of every five Americans in 1959. But poverty was part of the lives of fully one-half of all African American families. Over time fewer and fewer Americans, black and white, suffered the effects of poverty; however, even though the incidence of poverty has been cut in half for black Americans, more than 25 percent of African American families still live in poverty. Even more distressing is the reality that African American children bear the brunt of this economic deprivation. In 1997, 37.2 percent of the "next generation" of African Americans lived in families whose total family income was insufficient to lift them out of poverty. (Note that although black Americans suffer the effects of poverty disproportionately, white-not-Hispanic families are the single largest identifiable group who live in poverty: white-not-Hispanic people make up 46.4 percent of the entire poor population; white-Hispanic, 22.2 percent; and black, 25.6 percent.)

The issue for economists is why so many African Americans failed to prosper and share in the great prosperity of the 1990s. Few would deny that in part the lack of success for black Americans is directly associated with a lack of "human capital": schooling, work experiences, and occupational choices. The real question, however, is whether differences between blacks and whites in terms of human capital can explain most of the current wage differentials or whether a significant portion of these wage differentials can be traced to labor market discrimination.

In the following selections, William A. Darity, Jr., and Patrick L. Mason argue that a significant part of the reason for black Americans' lack of economic success is discrimination, while James J. Heckman maintains that the issue is all human capital differences.

William A. Darity, Jr., and
Patrick L. Mason

 **YES**

Evidence on Discrimination in Employment

There is substantial racial and gender disparity in the American economy. As we will demonstrate, discriminatory treatment within the labor market is a major cause of this inequality. The evidence is ubiquitous: careful research studies which estimate wage and employment regressions, help-wanted advertisements, audit and correspondence studies, and discrimination suits which are often reported by the news media. Yet, there appear to have been periods of substantial reductions in economic disparity and discrimination. For example, Donohue and Heckman (1991) provide evidence that racial discrimination declined during the interval 1965–1975. Gottschalk (1997) has produced statistical estimates that indicate that discrimination against black males dropped most sharply between 1965 and 1975, and that discrimination against women declined during the interval 1973–1994. But some unanswered questions remain. Why did the movement toward racial equality stagnate after the mid-1970s? What factors are most responsible for the remaining gender inequality? What is the role of the competitive process in elimination or reproduction of discrimination in employment?

The Civil Rights Act of 1964 is the signal event associated with abrupt changes in the black-white earnings differential (Bound and Freeman, 1989; Card and Krueger, 1992; Donohue and Heckman, 1991; Freeman, 1973). Along with other important pieces of federal legislation, the Civil Rights Act also played a major role in reducing discrimination against women (Leonard, 1989). Prior to passage of the federal civil rights legislation of the 1960s, racial exclusion and gender-typing of employment was blatant. The adverse effects of discriminatory practices on the life chances of African Americans, in particular, during that period have been well-documented (Wilson, 1980; Myers and Spriggs, 1997, pp. 32–42; Lieberson, 1980). Cordero-Guzman (1990, p. 1) observes that "up until the early 1960s, and particularly in the south, most blacks were systematically denied equal access to opportunities [and] in many instances, individuals with adequate credentials or skills were not, legally, allowed to apply to certain positions in firms." Competitive market forces certainly did

From William A. Darity, Jr., and Patrick L. Mason, "Evidence on Discrimination in Employment: Codes of Color, Codes of Gender," *Journal of Economic Perspectives*, vol. 12, no. 2 (Spring 1998). Copyright © 1998 by The American Economic Association. Reprinted by permission. References and some notes omitted.

not eliminate these discriminatory practices in the decades leading up to the 1960s. They remained until the federal adoption of antidiscrimination laws.

Newspaper help-wanted advertisements provide vivid illustrations of the openness and visibility of such practices. We did an informal survey of the employment section of major daily newspapers from three northern cities, the *Chicago Tribune,* the *Los Angeles Times* and the *New York Times,* and from the nation's capital, *The Washington Post,* at five-year intervals from 1945 to 1965. (Examples from southern newspapers are even more dramatic.)...

With respect to gender-typing of occupations, help-wanted advertisements were structured so that whole sections of the classifieds offered job opportunities separately and explicitly for men and women. Men were requested for positions that included restaurant cooks, managers, assistant managers, auto salesmen, sales in general, accountants and junior accountants, design engineers, detailers, diemakers, drivers, and welders. Women were requested for positions that included household and domestic workers, stenographers, secretaries, typists, bookkeepers, occasionally accountants (for "girls good at figures"), and waitresses.[1] The *Washington Post* of January 3, 1960, had the most examples of racial preference, again largely for whites, in help-wanted ads of any newspaper edition we examined. Nancy Lee's employment service even ran an advertisement for a switchboard operator—presumably never actually seen by callers—requesting that all *women* applying be white! Advertisements also frequently included details about the age range desired from applicants, like men 21–30 or women 18–25. Moreover, employers also showed little compunction about specifying precise physical attributes desired in applicants.[2]

Following the passage of the Civil Rights Act of 1964, none of the newspapers carried help-wanted ads that included any explicit preference for "white" or "colored" applicants in January 1965. However, it became very common to see advertisements for "European" housekeepers (a trend that was already visible as early as 1960). While race no longer entered the help-wanted pages explicitly, national origin or ancestry seemed to function as a substitute. Especially revealing is an advertisement run by the Amity Agency in the *New York Times* on January 3, 1965, informing potential employers that "Amity Has Domestics": "Scottish Gals" at $150 a month as "mothers' helpers and housekeepers," "German Gals" at $175 a month on one-year contracts, and "Haitian Gals" at $130 a month who are "French speaking." Moreover, in the "Situations Wanted" section of the newspaper, prospective female employees still were indicating their own race in January 1965.

The case of the help-wanted pages of the *New York Times* is of special note because New York was one of the states that had a state law against discrimination and a State Commission Against Discrimination in place, long prior to the passage of the federal Civil Rights Act of 1964. However, the toothlessness of New York's State Commission Against Discrimination is well-demonstrated by the fact that employers continued to indicate their racial preferences for new hires in help-wanted ads, as well as by descriptions of personal experience like that of John A. Williams in his semi-autobiographical novel, *The Angry Ones* (1960 [1996], pp. 30–1).

Help-wanted ads were only the tip of the iceberg of the process of racial exclusion in employment. After all, there is no reason to believe that the employers who did not indicate a racial preference were entirely open-minded about their applicant pool. How successful has the passage of federal antidiscrimination legislation in the 1960s been in producing an equal opportunity environment where job applicants are now evaluated on their qualifications? To give away the answer at the outset, our response is that discrimination by race has diminished somewhat, and discrimination by gender has diminished substantially. However, neither employment discrimination by race or by gender is close to ending. The Civil Rights Act of 1964 and subsequent related legislation has purged American society of the most overt forms of discrimination. However, discriminatory practices have continued in more covert and subtle forms. Furthermore, racial discrimination is masked and rationalized by widely-held presumptions of black inferiority.

Statistical Research on Employment Discrimination

Economic research on the presence of discrimination in employment has focused largely on black-white and male-female earnings and occupational disparities. The position typically taken by economists is that some part of the racial or gender gap in earnings or occupations is due to average group differences in productivity-linked characteristics (a human capital gap) and some part is due to average group differences in treatment (a discrimination gap). The more of the gap that can be explained by human capital differences, the easier it becomes to assert that labor markets function in a nondiscriminatory manner; any remaining racial or gender inequality in employment outcomes must be due to differences between blacks and whites or between men and women that arose outside the labor market....

Regression Evidence on Racial Discrimination

When we consider economic disparities by race, a difference emerges by gender. Using a Blinder-Oaxaca approach in which women are compared by their various racial and ethnic subgroups, Darity, Guilkey and Winfrey (1996) find little systematic evidence of wage discrimination based on U.S. Census data for 1980 and 1990.[3] However, when males are examined using the same Census data a standard result emerges. A significant portion of the wage gap between black and white males in the United States cannot be explained by the variables included to control for productivity differences across members of the two racial groups.

Black women are likely to have the same school quality and omitted family background characteristics as black men (the same is true for white women and men). Hence, it strains credibility to argue that the black-white earnings gap for men is due to an omitted labor quality variable unless one also argues that black women are paid more than white women conditional on the unobservables. The findings of Darity, Guilkey and Winfrey (1996), Rodgers and

Spriggs (1996) and Gottschalk (1997) indicate that in 1980 and 1990 black men in the United States were suffering a 12 to 15 percent loss in earnings due to labor market discrimination.

.   There is a growing body of evidence that uses color or "skin shade" as a natural experiment to detect discrimination. The approach of these studies has been to look at different skin shades within a particular ethnic group at a particular place and time, which should help to control for factors of culture and ethnicity other than pure skin color. Johnson, Bienenstock, and Stoloff (1995) looked at dark-skinned and light-skinned black males from the same neighborhoods in Los Angeles, and found that the combination of a black racial identity and a dark skin tone reduces an individual's odds of working by 52 percent, after controlling for education, age, and criminal record! Since both dark-skinned and light-skinned black males in the sample were from the same neighborhoods, the study *de facto* controlled for school quality. Further evidence that lighter-complexioned blacks tend to have superior incomes and life chances than darker-skinned blacks in the United States comes from studies by Ransford (1970), Keith and Herring (1991) and Johnson and Farrell (1995).

Similar results are found by looking at skin color among Hispanics. Research conducted by Arce, Murguia, and Frisbie (1987) utilizing the University of Michigan's 1979 National Chicano Survey involved partitioning the sample along two phenotypical dimensions: skin color, ranging from Very Light to Very Dark on a five-point scale; and physical features, ranging from Very European to Very Indian on a five-point scale. Chicanos with lighter skin color and more European features had higher socioeconomic status. Using the same data set, Telles and Murguia (1990) found that 79 percent of $1,262 of the earnings differences between the dark phenotypic group and other Mexican Americans was *not* explained by the traditional variables affecting income included in their earnings regression. Further support for this finding comes from Cotton (1993) and Darity, Guilkey, and Winfrey (1996) who find using 1980 and 1990 Census data that black Hispanics suffer close to ten times the proportionate income loss due to differential treatment of given characteristics than white Hispanics. Evidently, skin shade plays a critical role in structuring social class position and life chances in American society, even between comparable individuals within minority groups.

Cross-national evidence from Brazil also is relevant here. Despite conventional beliefs in Brazil that race is irrelevant and class is the primary index for social stratification, Silva (1985) found using the 1976 national household survey that blacks and mulattos (or "browns") shared closely in a relatively depressed economic condition relative to whites, with mulattos earning slightly more than blacks. Silva estimated that the cost of being nonwhite in Brazil in 1976 was about 566 cruzeiros per month (or $104 U.S.). But Silva found slightly greater unexplained income differences for mulattos, rather than blacks vis-à-vis whites, unexplained differences he viewed as evidence of discrimination. A new study by Telles and Lim (1997), based upon a random national survey of 5000 persons conducted by the Data Folha Institute des Pesquisas, compares economic outcomes based upon whether race is self-identified or interviewer-identified. Telles and Lim view interviewer-identification as more useful for establishing social classification and treatment. They find that self-identification underestimates white income and over-estimates brown and black incomes relative to interviewer-classification.

Despite the powerful results on skin shade, some continue to argue that the extent of discrimination is overestimated by regression techniques because of missing variables. After all, it seems likely that the general pattern of unobserved variables—for example, educational quality or labor force attachment—would tend to follow the observed variables in indicating reasons for the lower productivity of black males (Ruhm, 1989, p. 157). As a result, adjusting for these factors would reduce the remaining black-white earnings differential.[4]

As one might imagine, given the framework in which economists tackle the issue of discrimination, considerable effort has been made to find measures of all imaginable dimensions of human capital that could be used to test the presence of labor market discrimination. This effort has uncovered one variable in one data set which, if inserted in an earnings regression, produces the outcome that nearly all of the black-white male wage gap is explained by human capital and none by labor market discrimination. (However, thus far no one has suggested a reasonable missing variable for the skin shade effect.) The particular variable that eliminates evidence of discrimination in earnings against black men as a group is the Armed Forces Qualifying Test (AFQT) score in the National Longitudinal Survey of Youth (NLSY).

A number of researchers have confirmed with somewhat different sample sizes and methodologies that including AFQT scores in an earnings equation virtually will eliminate racial differences in wages....

The conclusion of this body of work is that labor market discrimination against blacks is negligible or nonexistent. Using Neal and Johnson's (1996) language, the key to explaining differences in black and white labor market outcomes must instead rest with "premarket factors." These studies have led Abigail and Stephan Thernstrom (1997) in a prominent *Wall Street Journal* editorial to proclaim that "what may look like persistent employment discrimination is better described as employers rewarding workers with relatively strong cognitive skills."

But matters are not so straightforward. The essential problem is what the AFQT scores are actually measuring, and therefore what precisely is being controlled for. There is no consensus on this point. AFQT scores have been interpreted variously as providing information about school quality or academic achievement (O'Neill, 1990), about previously unmeasured skills (Ferguson, 1995; Maxwell, 1994; Neal and Johnson 1996), and even about intelligence (Herrnstein and Murray, 1994)—although the military did not design AFQT as an intelligence test (Rodgers and Spriggs, 1996).[5] The results obtained by O'Neill (1990), Maxwell (1994), Ferguson (1995), and Neal and Johnson (1996) after using the AFQT as an explanatory variable are, upon closer examination, not robust to alternative specifications and are quite difficult to interpret.

The lack of robustness can be illustrated by looking at how AFQT scores interact with other variables in the earnings equation. Neal and Johnson (1996), for example, adjust for age and AFQT score in an earnings equation, but not for years of schooling, presumably on the assumption that same-age individuals would have the same years of schooling, regardless of race. However, this assumption does not appear to be true. Rodgers, Spriggs and Waaler (1997) find that white youths had accumulated more schooling at a given age than black or Hispanic youths. When AFQT scores are both age and education-adjusted, a black-white wage gap reemerges, as the authors report (p. 3):[6]

> ... estimates from models that use our proposed age and education adjusted AFQT score [show] that sharp differences in racial and ethnic wage gaps exist. Instead of explaining three-quarters of the male black-white wage gap, the age and education adjusted score explains 40 percent of the gap. Instead of explaining the entire male Hispanic-white gap, the new score explains 50 percent of the gap... [B]lack women no longer earn more than white women do, and... Hispanic women's wage premium relative to white women is reduced by one-half.

Another specification problem arises when wage equations are estimated using both AFQT scores and the part of the NLSY sample that includes measures of psychological well-being (for "self-esteem" and "locus of control") as explanatory variables. The presence of the psychological variables restores a negative effect on wages of being African-American (Goldsmith, Veum and Darity, 1997).[7]

Yet another specification problem becomes relevant if one interprets AFQT scores as providing information about school quality. But since there is a school survey module of the NLSY which can be used to provide direct evidence on school quality, using variables like the books/pupil ratio, the percent of students classified as disadvantaged, and teacher salaries, it would surely be more helpful to use this direct data on school quality rather than the AFQT scores. In another method of controlling for school quality, Harrison (1972) compared employment and earnings outcomes for blacks and whites living in the same black ghetto communities, on grounds that school quality would not be very different between them. Harrison found sharp differences in earnings favoring whites.[8]

One severe difficulty in interpreting what differences in the AFQT actually mean is demonstrated by Rodgers and Spriggs (1996) who show that AFQT scores appear to be biased in a specific sense.... [They] create a hypothetical set of "unbiased" black scores by running the mean black characteristics through the equation with the white coefficients. When those scores replace the actual AFQT scores in a wage equation, then the adjusted AFQT scores no longer explain black-white wage differences. A similar result can be obtained if actual white scores are replaced by hypothetical scores produced by running white characteristics through the equation with black coefficients.[9] Apparently, the AFQT scores themselves are a consequence of bias in the underlying processes that generate AFQT scores for blacks and whites. Perhaps AFQT scores are a proxy for skills that do not capture all skills, and thus leave behind a bias of uncertain direction. Or there may be other predictors of the test that are correlated with race but which are left out of the AFQT explanatory equation.

To muddy the waters further, focusing on the math and verbal subcomponents of AFQT leads to inconsistent implications for discriminatory differentials. For example, while a higher performance on the verbal portion of the AFQT contributes to higher wages for black women versus black men, it apparently has little or no effect on the wages of white women versus white men (Currie and Thomas, 1995). However, white women gain in wages from higher scores on the math portion of the AFQT, but black women do not. Perhaps this says that white women are screened (directly or indirectly) for employment and pay on the basis of their math performance, while black women are screened based upon their verbal skills. Perhaps this is because white employers have a greater "comfort zone" with black women who have a greater verbal similarity to whites. Or perhaps something not fully understood and potentially quirky is going on with the link between these test results and wages.

Finally, since skill differentials have received such widespread discussion in recent years as an underlying cause of growing wage inequality in the U.S. economy—see, for example, the discussion in the Spring 1997 issue of *The Journal of Economic Perspectives*—it should be pointed out that growth in the rewards to skill does not mean that the effects of race have diminished. If the importance of race and skill increase simultaneously, then a rising skill premium will explain more of the changes in *intraracial* wage inequality, which may well leave a larger unexplained portion of interracial wage inequality. For example, when Murnane et al. (1995) ask whether test scores in math, reading, and vocabulary skills for respondents in the National Longitudinal Study of the High School Class of 1972 and High School and Beyond datasets have more explanatory power in wage equations for 1980 graduates than 1972 graduates, their answer is "yes"—the rate of return to cognitive skill (test scores) increased between 1978 and 1986. However, in these same regressions, the absolute value of the negative race coefficient is larger for the 1980 graduates than it is for the 1972 graduates! These results confirm that there are increasing returns to skills measured by standardized tests, but do not indicate that the rise in returns to skills can explain changes in the black-white earnings gap very well.

The upshot is the following. There is no doubt that blacks suffer reduced earnings in part due to inferior productivity-linked characteristics, like skill gaps or school quality gaps, relative to nonblack groups. However, evidence based on the AFQT should be treated with extreme caution. Given that this one variable in one particular data set is the only one that suggests racial discrimination is no longer operative in U.S. employment practices, it should be taken as far from convincing evidence. Blacks, especially black men, continue to suffer significantly reduced earnings due to discrimination and the extent of discrimination.

Direct Evidence on Discrimination: Court Cases and Audit Studies

One direct body of evidence of the persistence of employment discrimination, despite the presence of antidiscrimination laws, comes from the scope and dispensation of job discrimination lawsuits. A sampling of such cases from recent years... reveals [that] discriminatory practices have occurred at highly visible U.S. corporations often having multinational operations. The suits reveal racial and gender discrimination in employment, training, promotion, tenure, layoff policies, and work environment, as well as occupational segregation.

Perhaps the most notorious recent case is the $176 million settlement reached between Texaco and black employees after disclosure of taped comments of white corporate officials making demeaning remarks about blacks, remarks that revealed an outlook that translated into corresponding antiblack employment practices. Clearly, neither federal antidiscrimination laws nor the pressures of competitive markets have prevented the occurrence of discriminatory practices that have resulted in significant awards or settlements for the plaintiffs.

Another important source of direct evidence are the audit studies of the type conducted in the early 1990s by the Urban Institute (Mincy, 1993). The Urban Institute audit studies sought to examine employment outcomes for young black, Hispanic, and white males, ages 19–25, looking for entry-level jobs. Pairs of black and white males and pairs of Hispanic and non-Hispanic white males were matched as testers and sent out to apply for jobs at businesses advertising openings. Prior to application for the positions, the testers were trained for interviews to minimize dissimilarity in the quality of their self-presentation, and they were given manufactured résumés designed to put their credentials on a par. The black/white tests were conducted in Chicago and in Washington, D.C., while the Hispanic/non Hispanic tests were conducted in Chicago and in San Diego.

A finding of discrimination was confirmed if one member of the pair was offered the position and the other was not. No discrimination was confirmed if both received an offer (sequentially, since both were instructed to turn the position down) or neither received an offer. This is a fairly stringent test for discrimination, since, in the case where no offer was made to either party, there is no way to determine whether employers were open to the prospect of hiring a black or an Hispanic male, what the overall applicant pool looked like, or who was actually hired. However, the Urban Institute audits found that black males were three times as likely to be turned down for a job as white males, and Hispanic males also were three times as likely as non-Hispanic white males to experience discrimination in employment (Fix, Galster and Struyk, 1993, pp. 21–22).

Bendick, Jackson and Reinoso (1994) also report on 149 race-based (black, white) and ethnicity-based (Hispanic, non-Hispanic) job audits conducted by the Fair Employment Council of Greater Washington, Inc. in the D.C. metropolitan area in 1990 and 1991. Testers were paired by gender. The audit findings are striking. White testers were close to 10 percent more likely to receive interviews than blacks. Among those interviewed, half of the white testers received job offers versus a mere 11 percent of the black testers. When both testers received the same job offers, white testers were offered 15 cents per hour more than black testers. Black testers also were disproportionately "steered" toward lower level positions after the job offer was made, and white testers were disproportionately considered for unadvertised positions at higher levels than the originally advertised job.

Overall, the Fair Employment Council study found rates of discrimination in excess of 20 percent against blacks (in the black/white tests) and against Hispanics (in the Hispanic/non-Hispanic tests). In the Hispanic/non-Hispanic tests, Hispanic male job seekers were three times as likely to experience discrimination as Hispanic females. But, surprisingly, in the black/white tests, black females were three times as likely to encounter discrimination as black males. The racial results for women in this particular audit stand in sharp contrast with the results in the statistical studies described above.

The most severe criticisms of the audit technique have come from Heckman and Siegelman (1993). At base, their central worry is that testers cannot be paired in such a way that they will not signal a difference that legitimately can be interpreted by the prospective employer as a difference in potential to perform the job, despite interview training and doctored résumés.[10] For example, what about intangibles like a person's ability to make a first impression or the fact that certain résumés may be unintentionally superior to others?

In an audit study consciously designed to address many of the Heckman and Siegelman (1993) methodological complaints, Neumark, Bank, and Van Nort (1995) examined sex discrimination in restaurant hiring practices. Four testers (all college students, two men and two women) applied for jobs waiting tables at 65 restaurants in Philadelphia. The restaurants were separated into high, medium, and low price, according to average cost of a meal. Waiters at the high price restaurants tend to receive greater wages and tips than their counterparts in low price restaurants; specifically, the authors find that average hourly earnings for waiters were 47 and 68 percent higher in the high price restaurant than the medium and low price restaurant, respectively. One man and one woman applied for a job at each restaurant, so there were 130 attempts to obtain employment. Thirty-nine job offers were received.

One interesting twist to this methodology is that three reasonably comparable résumés were constructed, and over a three-week period each tester used a different résumé for a period of one week. This résumé-switching mitigates any differences that may have occurred because one résumé was better than another. To reduce other sources of unobserved ability—for example, the ability to make a good first impression—the testers were instructed to give their applications to the first employee they encountered when visiting a restaurant. That employee was then asked to forward the résumé to the manager. In effect, personality and appearance were eliminated as relevant variables for the interview decision, if not for the job offer decision.

Neumark et al. (1995) find that in the low-priced restaurants, the man received an offer while the woman did not 29 percent of the time. A woman never received an offer when the man did not. In the high-priced restaurants, the man received an offer while the woman did not in 43 percent of the tests, while the woman received an offer while the man did not in just 4 percent of the tests. Also, at high-priced restaurants, women had roughly a 40 percent lower probability of being interviewed and 50 percent lower probability of obtaining a job offer, and this difference is statistically significant. Hence, this audit study shows that within-occupation employment discrimination may be a contributing source to wage discrimination between men and women....

The Theoretical Backdrop

Standard neoclassical competitive models are forced by their own assumptions to the conclusion that discrimination only can be temporary. Perhaps the best-known statement of this position emerges from Becker's (1957) famous "taste for discrimination" model. If two groups share similar productivity profiles under competitive conditions where at least some employers prefer profits to prejudice, eventually all workers must be paid the same wage. The eventual result may involve segregated workforces—say, with some businesses hiring only white men and others hiring only black women—but as long as both groups have the same average productivity, they will receive the same pay. Thus, in this view, discrimination only can produce temporary racial or gender earnings gaps. Moreover, alternative forms of discrimination are separable processes; wage discrimination and employment segregation are unrelated in Becker's model.

Despite the theoretical implications of standard neoclassical competitive models, we have considerable evidence that it took the Civil Rights Act of 1964 to alter the discriminatory climate in America. It did not, by any means, eliminate either form of discrimination. Indeed, the impact of the law itself may have been temporary, since there is some evidence that the trend toward racial inequality came to a halt in the mid-1970s (even though interracial differences in human capital were continuing to close) and the momentum toward gender equality may have begun to lose steam in the early 1990s. Moreover, we believe that the forms of discrimination have altered in response to the act. Therefore, it is not useful to argue that either racial or gender discrimination is inconsistent with the operation of competitive markets, especially when it has taken antidiscrimination laws to reduce the impact of discrimination in the market. Instead, it is beneficial to uncover the market mechanisms which permit or encourage discriminatory practices.

Since Becker's work, orthodox microeconomics has been massaged in various ways to produce stories of how discrimination might sustain itself against pressures of the competitive market. The tacit assumption of these approaches has been to find a way in which discrimination can increase business profits, or to identify conditions where choosing not to discriminate might reduce profits.

In the customer discrimination story, for example, businesses discriminate not because they themselves are bigoted but because their clients are bigoted. This story works especially well where the product in question must be delivered via face-to-face contact, but it obviously does not work well when the hands that made the product are not visible to the customer possessing the "taste for discrimination." Moreover, as Madden (1975, p. 150) has pointed out, sex-typing of jobs can work in both directions: "While service occupations are more contact-oriented, sexual preference can work both ways: for example, women are preferred as Playboy bunnies, airline stewardesses, and lingerie salespeople, while men seem to be preferred as tire salespeople, stockbrokers, and truck drivers."

Obviously, group-typing of employment will lead to a different occupational distributions between group A and B, but will it lead to different earnings as well? Madden (1975, p. 150, emphasis in original) suggests not necessarily:

> ... consumer discrimination causes occupational segregation rather than wage differentials. If the female wage decreases as the amount of consumer contact required by a job increases, women seek employment in jobs where consumer contact is minimal and wages are higher. Only if there are not enough non-consumer contact jobs for working women, forcing them to seek employment in consumer-contact jobs, would consumer discrimination be responsible for wage differentials. Since most jobs do not require consumer contact, consumer discrimination would segregate women into these jobs, but not *cause* wage differentials.

Perhaps the best attempt to explain how discrimination might persist in a neoclassical framework is the statistical discrimination story, which, at base, is a story about imperfect information. The notion is that potential employers cannot observe everything they wish to know about job candidates, and in this environment, they have an incentive to seize group membership as a signal that allows them to improve their predictions of a prospective candidate's ability to perform.

However, this model of prejudicial beliefs does not ultimately wash well as a theory of why discrimination should be long-lasting. If average group differences are perceived but not real, then employers should *learn* that their beliefs are mistaken. If average group differences are real, then in a world with antidiscrimination laws, employers are likely to find methods of predicting the future performance of potential employees with sufficient accuracy that there is no need to use the additional "signal" of race or gender. It seems implausible that with all the resources that corporations put into hiring decisions, the remaining differentials are due to an inability to come up with a suitable set of questions or qualifications for potential employees.

Moreover, models of imperfect competition as explanations of discrimination do not solve the problem completely either. The reason for the immutability of the imperfection is rarely satisfactorily explained—and often not addressed at all—in models of this type (Darity and Williams, 1985). Struggle as it may, orthodox microeconomics keeps returning to the position that sustained observed differences in economic outcomes between groups must be due to an induced or inherent deficiency in the group that experiences the inferior outcomes. In the jargon, this is referred to as a deficiency in human capital. Sometimes this deficiency is associated with poor schooling opportunities, other times with culture (Sowell, 1981).[11] But the thrust of the argument is to absolve market processes, at least in a putative long run, of a role in producing the differential outcome; the induced or inherent deficiency occurs in pre-market or extra-market processes.

Certainly years of schooling, quality of education, years of work experiences and even culture can have a role in explaining racial and gender earnings differences. However, the evidence marshaled above indicates that these factors do not come close to explaining wage differentials and employment patterns observed in the economy. Instead, discrimination has been sustained both in the United States and elsewhere, for generations at a time. Such discrimination does not always even need direct legal support nor has it been eliminated by market pressures. Instead, changes in social and legal institutions have been needed to reduce it.

James Heckman (1997, p. 406) draws a similar conclusion in his examination of a specific sector of employment, the textile industry:

> ... substantial growth in Southern manufacturing had little effect on the labor-market position of blacks in Southern textiles prior to 1965. Through tight and slack labor markets, the proportion of blacks was small and stable. After 1964, and in synchronization with the 1964 Civil Rights Act, black economic progress was rapid. Only South Carolina had a Jim Crow law prohibiting employment of blacks as textile workers, and the law was never used after the 1920s. Yet the pattern of exclusion of blacks was prevalent throughout Southern textiles, and the breakthrough in black employment in the industry came in all states at the same time. Informally enforced codes and private practices, and not formally enforced apartheid, kept segregation in place, and market forces did not break them down.

Nontraditional alternatives to orthodox microeconomic analysis can lead to a logically consistent basis for a persistent gap in wage outcomes. These alternatives typically break down the line between in-market and pre-market discrimination so often drawn in conventional economics. The first of these involves a self-fulfilling prophecy mechanism. Suppose employers believe that members of group A are more productive than members of group B on average. Suppose further that they act upon their beliefs, thereby exhibiting a stronger demand for A workers, hiring them more frequently and paying them more.

Next, suppose that members of group B become less motivated and less emotionally healthy as a consequence of the employment rebuff. Notice that the original decision not to hire may have been completely unjustified on productivity grounds; nonetheless, the decision made *in* the labor market—a decision not to hire or to hire at low pay—alters the human capital characteristics of the members of group B so that they become inferior candidates for jobs. The employers' initially held mistaken beliefs become realized over time as a consequence of the employers' initial discriminatory decisions. As Elmslie and Sedo (1996, p. 474) observe in their development of this argument, "One initial bout of unemployment that is not productivity based can lay the foundation for continued future unemployment and persistently lower job status even if no future discrimination occurs."

More broadly, depressed expectations of employment opportunities also can have an adverse effect on members of group B's inclination to acquire additional human capital—say, through additional schooling or training. The effects of the past could be passed along by the disadvantaged group from generation to generation, another possibility ignored by orthodox theory. For example, Borjas (1994) writes of the ethnic intergenerational transmission of economic advantage or disadvantage. He makes no mention of discrimination in his work but a potential interpretation is that the effects of past discrimination, both negative and positive, are passed on to subsequent generations. Other evidence along these lines includes Tyree's (1991) findings on the relationship between an ethnic group's status and performance in the past and the present, and Darity's (1989) development of "the lateral mobility" hypothesis based upon ethnic group case histories.

More narrowly, the group-typed beliefs held by employers/selectors also can have a strong effect on the performance of the candidate at the interview stage. In an experiment performed in the early 1970s, psychologists Word, Zanna and Cooper (1974, pp. 109–120) found that when interviewed by "naïve" whites, trained black applicants "received (a) less immediacy, (b) higher rates of speech error, and (c) shorter amounts of interview time" than white applicants. They then trained white interviewers to replicate the behavior received by the black applicants in the first phase of their experiment, and found that "naïve" white candidates performed poorly during interviews when they were "treated like blacks." Such self-fulfilling prophecies are familiar in the psychology literature (Sibicky and Dovidio, 1986).

A second nontraditional theory that can lead to a permanent gap in intergroup outcomes is the noncompeting groups hypothesis advanced by the late W. Arthur Lewis (1979). Related arguments emerge from Krueger's (1963) extension of the trade-based version of the Becker model, Swinton's (1978) "labor force competition" model for racial differences, and Madden's (1975) male monopoly model for gender differences, but Lewis's presentation is the most straightforward. Lewis starts with an intergroup rivalry for the preferred positions in a hierarchical occupational structure. Say that group A is able to control access to the preferred positions by influencing the required credentials, manipulating opportunities to obtain the credentials, and serving a gatekeeping function over entry and promotion along job ladders. Group B is then rendered "noncompeting."

One theoretical difficulty with this argument that its proponents rarely address is that it requires group A to maintain group solidarity even when it may have subgroups with differing interests. In Krueger's (1963) model, for example, white capitalists must value racial group solidarity sufficiently to accept a lower return on their capital as the price they pay for a generally higher level of income for all whites (and higher wages for white workers). In Madden's (1975) model, male capitalists must make a similar decision on behalf of male workers.

This noncompeting group hypothesis blurs the orthodox distinction between in-market and pre-market discrimination, by inserting matters of power and social control directly into the analysis. This approach then links discrimination to racism or sexism, rather than to simple bigotry or prejudice. It leads to the proposition that discrimination—in the sense of differential treatment of those members of each group with similar productivity-linked characteristics—is an endogenous phenomenon. "In-market" discrimination need only occur when all the earlier attempts to control access to jobs, credentials, and qualifications are quavering.

One interesting implication here is that growth in skills for what we have been calling group B, the disadvantaged group, may be accompanied by a surge of in-market discrimination, because that form of discrimination has become more necessary to preserve the position of group A. There are several instances of cross-national evidence to support this notion. Darity, Dietrich and Guilkey (1997) find that while black males were making dramatic strides in acquiring literacy between 1880 and 1910 in the United States, simultaneously they were suffering increasing proportionate losses in occupational status due to disadvantageous treatment of their measured characteristics. Geographer Peggy Lovell (1993) finds very little evidence of discrimination in earnings against blacks in northern Brazil, where blacks are more numerous, but substantial evidence of discrimination against them in southern Brazil. Northern Brazil is considerably poorer than southern Brazil and the educational levels of northern black Brazilians are more depressed than in the south.[12] It is easy to argue that the exercise of discrimination is not "needed" in the north, since blacks are not generally going to compete with whites for the same sets of jobs. Indeed, there is relatively more evidence of discrimination against mulattos than blacks, the former more likely to compete directly with whites for employment. A third example, in a study using data for males based upon a survey taken in Delhi in 1970, Desi and Singh (1989) find that the most dramatic instance of discriminatory differentials in earnings was evident for Sikh men vis-à-vis Hindu high caste men. On the other hand, most of the earnings gap for Hindu middle caste, lower caste and scheduled caste men was due to inferior observed characteristics. Since these latter groups could be excluded from preferred positions because of an inadequate educational background, it would not be necessary for the upper castes to exercise discrimination against them. Sikh males, on the other hand, possessed the types of credentials that would make them viable contestants for the positions desired by the Hindu higher castes.

A final alternative approach at construction of a consistent economic theory of persistent discrimination evolves from a reconsideration of the neoclassical theory of competition. Darity and Williams (1985) argued that replacement of neoclassical competition with either classical or Marxist approaches to competition—where competition is defined by a tendency toward equalization of rates of profit and where monopoly positions are the consequence of competition rather than the antithesis of competition—eliminates the anomalies associated with the orthodox approach (Botwinick, 1993; Mason, 1995, forthcoming-b). A labor market implication of this approach is that wage diversity, different pay across firms and industries for workers within the same occupation, is the norm for competitive labor markets. In these models, remuneration is a function of the characteristics of the individual and the job. The racial-gender composition of the job affects worker bargaining power and thereby wage differentials. In turn, race and gender exclusion are used to make some workers less competitive for the higher paying positions. This approach emphasizes that the major elements for the persistence of discrimination are racial or gender differences in the access to better paying jobs within and between occupations.

Whatever alternative approach is preferred, the strong evidence of the persistence of discrimination in labor markets calls into question any theoretical apparatus that implies that the discrimination must inevitably diminish or disappear.

Notes

1. The only significant exception to the help-wanted ads pattern of maintaining a fairly strict sexual division of labor that we could detect was evident in the *Los Angeles Times* employment section of early January 1945, where we found women being sought as aircraft riveters, assemblers, and army photographers. Of course, World War II was ongoing at that stage, and the comparative absence of men produced the "Rosie the Riveter" phenomenon. However, despite wartime conditions, even this temporary breakdown in gender-typing of occupations was not evident in the help-wanted ads for the *Chicago Tribune,* the *New York Times,* or the *Washington Post* at the same time. Moreover, racial preferences also remained strongly pronounced in wartime advertisements of each of the four newspapers.

2. The C.W. Agency, advertising in the *Los Angeles Times* on January, 1, 1950, wanted a "Girl Model 38 bust, 25 waist, 36 hips"; "Several Other Types" with physical characteristics unspecified in the advertisement apparently also were acceptable.

3. The 1980 and 1990 Censuses provide only self-reported information on interviewees' race and their ancestry, which makes it possible to partition the American population into 50 different detailed ethnic and racial groups, like Asian Indian ancestry women, Mexican ancestry women, Polish ancestry women, French Canadian ancestry women, and so on. The explanatory variables were years of school, years of college, number of children, married spouse present, years of work experience, years of work experience squared, very good or fluent English, disabled, born in the United States, assimilated (that is either married to a person with a different ethnicity or having claimed two different ethnic groups in the census), location, region, and occupation. Annual earnings was the dependent variable. There was no control for the difference between potential and actual experience; hence, to the extent that the gap between potential and actual experience and the rate of return to actual experience varies by race, the results for the female regressions may be less reliable than the results for the male regression.

4. For a view that unobservable factors might favor black male productivity, thereby meaning that the regression coefficients are underestimating the degree of discrimination, see Mason (forthcoming-a).

5. Indeed, if one uses a measure that, unlike the AFQT, was explicitly designed as a measure of intelligence, it does not explain the black-white gap in wages. Mason (forthcoming-b; 1996) demonstrates this by using in a wage equation an explanatory variable that comes from a sentence completion test given to 1972 respondents to the Panel Study of Income Dynamics (PSID)—a test which was designed to assess "g," so-called general intelligence. Mason finds that the significant, negative sign on the coefficient for the race variable is unaffected by inclusion of the PSID sentence completion test score as an explanatory variable. Indeed, Mason (1997) finds that although discrimination declined during 1968 to 1973, discrimination grew by 2.0 percent annually during 1973–1991. On the other hand, the rate of return to cognitive skill (IQ) was relatively constant during 1968–1979, but had an annual growth rate of 1.6 percent during 1979–1991.

6. Mason (1997) finds a similar result when age and education-adjusted IQ scores are used.

7. Attention to the psychological measures also provides mild evidence that blacks put forth more effort than whites, a finding consistent with Mason's (forthcoming-a) speculation that there may be unobservables that favor black productivity. Mason argues that effort or motivation is a productivity-linked variable that favors

blacks, based upon his finding that blacks acquire more schooling than whites for a comparable set of resources.

8. Card and Krueger (1992) also directly control for school quality. They find that there is still a substantial wage gap left after controlling for school quality.

9. Systematic racial differences in the structural equations for the determination of standardized test scores also are evident in the General Social Survey data. Fitting equations for Wordsum scores separately for blacks and whites also yields statistically distinct structures (White, 1997).

10. Although some of their criticisms along these lines frankly strike us as ridiculous; for example, concerns about facial hair on the Hispanic male testers used by the Urban Institute.

11. To address the effects of culture, following Woodbury (1993), Darity, Guilkey, and Winfrey (1996) held color constant and varied culture by examining outcomes among blacks of differing ancestries. Unlike Sowell's expectation, black males of West Indian and non-West Indian ancestry were being confronted with the same racial penalty in U.S. labor markets by 1990.

12. The portion of the gap that can be explained by discrimination is much lower in the high black region of Brazil, the Northeast, than the rest of Brazil. We know of no evidence which suggests that this is or is not true for the U.S. south.

James J. Heckman

 **NO**

Detecting Discrimination

In the current atmosphere of race relations in America, the authors of the three main papers presented in this symposium are like persons crying "fire" in a crowded theater. They apparently vindicate the point of view that American society is riddled with racism and that discrimination by employers may account for much of the well-documented economic disparity between blacks and whites. In my judgement, this conclusion is not sustained by a careful reading of the evidence.

In this article, I make three major points. First, I want to distinguish market discrimination from the discrimination encountered by a randomly selected person or pair of persons at a randomly selected firm as identified from audit studies.

Second, I consider the evidence presented by the authors in the symposium, focusing for brevity and specificity on labor markets. It is far less decisive on the issue of market discrimination than it is claimed to be. Disparity in market outcomes does not prove discrimination in the market. A careful reading of the entire body of available evidence confirms that most of the disparity in earnings between blacks and whites in the labor market of the 1990s is due to the differences in skills they bring to the market, and not to discrimination within the labor market. This interpretation of the evidence has important consequences for social policy. While undoubtedly there are still employers and employees with discriminatory intentions, labor market discrimination is no longer a first-order quantitative problem in American society. At this time, the goal of achieving black economic progress is better served by policies that promote skill formation, like improving family environments, schools and neighborhoods, not by strengthening the content and enforcement of civil rights laws—the solution to the problem of an earlier era.

Third, I want to examine the logic and limitations of the audit pair method. All of the papers in this symposium use evidence from this version of pair matching. However, the evidence acquired from it is less compelling than is often assumed. Inferences from such studies are quite fragile to alternative assumptions about unobservable variables and the way labor markets work. The audit method can find discrimination when in fact none exists; it can also disguise discrimination when it is present. These findings are especially troubling

From James J. Heckman, "Detecting Discrimination," *Journal of Economic Perspectives*, vol. 12, no. 2 (Spring 1998). Copyright © 1998 by The American Economic Association. Reprinted by permission.

because the Equal Employment Opportunity Commission has recently authorized the use of audit pair methods to detect discrimination in labor markets (Seelye, 1997).

Discrimination Definition and Measurement

The authors of these papers focus on the question of whether society is color blind, not on the specific question of whether there is market discrimination in realized transactions. But discrimination at the individual level is different from discrimination at the group level, although these concepts are often confused in the literature on the economics of discrimination.

At the level of a potential worker or credit applicant dealing with a firm, racial discrimination is said to arise if an otherwise identical person is treated differently by virtue of that person's race or gender, and race and gender by themselves have no direct effect on productivity. Discrimination is a causal effect defined by a hypothetical *ceteris paribus* conceptual experiment—varying race but keeping all else constant. Audit studies attempt to identify racial and gender discrimination so defined for the set of firms sampled by the auditors by approximating the *ceteris paribus* condition.

It was Becker's (1957) insight to observe that finding a discriminatory effect of race or gender at a randomly selected firm does not provide an accurate measure of the discrimination that takes place in the market as a whole. At the level of the market, the causal effect of race is defined by the marginal firm or set of firms with which the marginal minority member deals. The impact of market discrimination is not determined by the most discriminatory participants in the market, or even by the average level of discrimination among firms, but rather by the level of discrimination at the firms where ethnic minorities or women actually end up buying, working and borrowing. It is at the margin that economic values are set. This point is largely ignored in the papers in this symposium.

This confusion between individual firm and market discrimination arises in particular in the audit studies. A well-designed audit study could uncover many individual firms that discriminate, while at the same time the marginal effect of discrimination on the wages of employed workers could be zero.... Purposive sorting within markets eliminates the worst forms of discrimination. There may be evil lurking in the hearts of firms that is never manifest in consummated market transactions.

Estimating the extent and degree of distribution, whether at the individual or the market level, is a difficult matter. In the labor market, for example, a worker's productivity is rarely observed directly, so the analyst must instead use available data as a proxy in controlling for the relevant productivity characteristics. The major controversies arise over whether relevant omitted characteristics differ between races and between genders, and whether certain included characteristics systematically capture productivity differences or instead are a proxy for race or gender.

How Substantial Is Labor Market Discrimination Against Blacks?

In their paper in this symposium, [William A.] Darity [Jr.] and [Patrick L.] Mason present a bleak picture of the labor market position of African-Americans in which market discrimination is ubiquitous. They present a quantitative estimate of the magnitude of estimated discrimination: 12 to 15 percent in both 1980 and 1990 using standard regressions fit on Current Population Survey and Census data. Similar regressions show that the black/white wage gap has diminished sharply over the last half century. Comparable estimates for 1940 show a black/white wage gap ranging from 30 percentage points, for men age 25–34 to 42 percentage points, men age 55–64. In 1960, the corresponding numbers would have been 21 percent and 32 percent, for the same two age groups; in 1970, 18 and 25 percent (U.S. Commission on Civil Rights, 1986, Table 6.1, p. 191). The progress was greatest in Southern states where a blatantly discriminatory system was successfully challenged by an external legal intervention (Donohue and Heckman, 1991; Heckman, 1990).

How should the residual wage gap be interpreted? As is typical of much of the literature on measuring racial wage gaps, Darity and Mason never precisely define the concept of discrimination they use. As is also typical of this literature, the phrase "human capital variable" is thrown around without a clear operational definition. The implicit definition of these terms varies across the studies they discuss. In practice, human capital in these studies has come to mean education and various combinations of age and education, based on the available Census and Current Population Survey (CPS) data. However, there is a staggering gap between the list of productivity characteristics available to economic analysts in standard data sources and what is available to personnel departments of firms. Regressions based on the Census and/or CPS data can typically explain 20 to 30 percent of the variation in wages. However, regressions based on personnel data can explain a substantially higher share of the variation in wages; 60–80 percent in professional labor markets (for example, see Abowd and Killingsworth, 1983). It is not idle speculation to claim that the standard data sets used to estimate discrimination omit many relevant characteristics actually used by firms in their hiring and promotion decisions. Nor is it idle speculation to conjecture that disparity in family, neighborhood and schooling environments may account for systematic differences in unmeasured characteristics between race groups.

Consider just one well-documented source of discrepancy between Census variables and the productivity concepts that they proxy: the measurement of high school credentials. The standard Census and CPS data sources equate recipients of a General Equivalence Degree, or GED, with high school graduates. However, black high school certificate holders are much more likely than whites to receive GEDs (Cameron and Heckman, 1993), and a substantial portion of the widely trumpeted "convergence" in measured black educational attainment has come through GED certification. Thus, in 1987 in the NLSY data that Darity and Mason discuss, and Neal and Johnson (1996) analyze, 79 percent of black males age 25 were high school certified, and 14 percent of the credential holders were

GED recipients. Among white males, 88 percent were high school certified, and only 8 percent of the white credential holders were GED certified. Given the evidence from Cameron and Heckman that GED recipients earn the same as high school dropouts, it is plausible that standard Census-based studies that use high school credentials to control for "education" will find that the wages of black high school "graduates" are lower than those of whites.

Most of the empirical literature cited by Darity and Mason takes Census variables literally and ignores these issues. The GED factor alone accounts for 1–2 percentage points of the current 12–15 percent black-white hourly wage gap. An enormous body of solid evidence on inferior inner city schools and poor neighborhoods makes the ritual of the measurement of "discrimination" using the unadjusted Census or Current Population Survey data a questionable exercise.

Darity and Mason bolster their case for rampant discrimination by appealing to audit pair evidence. They do not point out that audit pair studies have primarily been conducted for hiring in entry level jobs in certain low skill occupations using overqualified college students during summer vacations. They do not sample subsequent promotion decisions. They fail to point out that the audits undersample the main avenues through which youth get jobs, since only job openings advertised in newspapers are audited, and not jobs found through networks and friends (Heckman and Siegelman, 1993, pp. 213–215). Auditors are sometimes instructed on the "problem of discrimination in American society" prior to sampling firms, so they may have been coached to find what the audit agencies wanted to find. I have already noted that audit evidence does not translate into actual employment experiences and wages obtained by actors who purposively search markets.

Putting these objections to the side, what do the audits actually show for this unrepresentative snapshot of the American labor market? Table 1 presents evidence from three major audits in Washington, D.C., Chicago and Denver. The most remarkable feature of this evidence is the a + b column which records the percentage of audit attempts where black and white auditors were treated symmetrically (both got a job; neither got a job). In Chicago and Denver this happened about 86 percent of the time. The evidence of disparity in hiring presented in the last two columns of the table suggests only a slight preference for whites over minorities; in several pairs, minorities are favored. Only a zealot can see evidence in these data of pervasive discrimination in the U.S. labor market. And, as I will show in the next section, even this evidence on disparity has to be taken with a grain of salt, because it is based on the implicit assumption that the distribution of unobserved productivity is the same in both race groups.

Darity and Mason go on to dismiss the research of Neal and Johnson (1996) who analyze a sample of males who took an achievement or ability test in their early teens—specifically, the Armed Forces Qualifications Test (AFQT)—and ask how much of the gap in black-white wages measured a decade or so after the test was taken can be explained by the differences in the test scores.[1] It is remarkable and important that this early "premarket" measure of ability plays such a strong role in explaining wages measured a decade after the test is taken. This is as

Table 1

Outcomes From Major Audit Studies for Blacks
(outcome: get job or not)

Number of Audits	Pair	(a) Both Get Job		(b) Neither Gets a Job		Equal Treatment a + b	White Yes, Black No		White No, Black Yes	
Chicago*										
35	1	(5)	14.3%	(23)	65.7%	80.0%	(5)	14.3%	(2)	5.7%
40	2	(5)	12.5%	(25)	62.5%	75.0%	(4)	10.0%	(2)	15.0%
44	3	(3)	6.8%	(37)	84.1%	90.9%	(3)	6.8%	(1)	2.3%
36	4	(6)	16.7%	(24)	66.7%	83.4%	(6)	16.7%	(0)	0.0%
42	5	(3)	7.1%	(38)	90.5%	97.6%	(1)	2.4%	(2)	0.0%
197	Total	(22)	11.2%	(147)	74.6%	85.8%	(19)	9.6%	(9)	4.5%
Washington*										
46	1	(5)	10.9%	(26)	56.5%	67.4%	(12)	26.1%	(3)	6.5%
54	2	(11)	20.4%	(31)	57.4%	77.8%	(9)	16.7%	(3)	5.6%
62	3	(11)	17.7%	(36)	58.1%	75.8%	(11)	17.7%	(4)	6.5%
37	4	(6)	16.2%	(22)	59.5%	75.7%	(7)	18.9%	(2)	5.4%
42	5	(7)	16.7%	(26)	61.9%	77.6%	(7)	16.7%	(2)	4.8%
241	Total	(40)	16.6%	(141)	58.5%	75.1%	(46)	19.1%	(14)	5.8%
Denver**										
18	1	(2)	11.1%	(11)	61.1%	72.1%	(5)	27.8%	(0)	0.0%
53	2	(2)	3.8%	(41)	77.4%	81.2%	(0)	0.0%	(10)	18.9%
33	3	(7)	21.2%	(25)	75.8%	97.0%	(1)	3.0%	(0)	0.0%
15	4	(9)	60.0%	(3)	20.0%	80.0%	(2)	6.7%	(2)	13.3%
265	9	(3)	11.5%	(23)	88.5%	100.0%	(0)	0.0%	(0)	0.0%
145	Total	(23)	15.8%	(103)	71.1%	86.9%	(7)	4.8%	(12)	8.3%

Note: Results are percentages; figures in parentheses are the relevant number of audits.
*This study was conducted by the Urban Institute.
**Denver pair numbers are for both black and Hispanic audits. For the sake of brevity, I only consider the black audits. The Denver study was not conducted by the Urban Institute but it was conducted to conform to Urban Institute practice.
Sources: Heckman and Siegelman (1993).

true for studies of white outcomes taken in isolation as it is for black-white comparisons. Their findings are important for interpreting the sources of black-white disparity in labor market outcomes. . . .

The Neal-Johnson story is not about genetic determination. They demonstrate that schooling and environment can affect their measured test score. A huge body of evidence, to which the Neal-Johnson study contributes, documents that human abilities and motivations are formed early and have a decisive effect on lifetime outcomes; the evidence is summarized in Heckman (1995) and in Heckman, Lochner, Taber, and Smith (1997). Not only is early ability an important predictor of later success for blacks or whites, it can be manipulated. Early interventions are far more effective than late ones because early skills and motivation beget later skills and motivation. As Heckman, Lochner. Taber and Smith document, however, successful early interventions can be quite costly.

The objections raised by Darity and Mason against the Neal-Johnson study are largely specious. For example, Rodgers and Spriggs (1996) miss the point of the Neal-Johnson article by "adjusting" the test score by a later variable, such as schooling. But ability is known to be an important determinant of schooling (Cawley, Heckman and Vtylacil, 1998), so it should be no surprise that "adjusting" the score for later schooling eliminates an important component of ability and that adjusted scores play a much weaker role in explaining black-white differentials.[2]

Only one point raised by Darity and Mason concerning Neal and Johnson is potentially valid—and this is a point made by Neal and Johnson in their original article. Black achievement scores may be lower than white scores not because of the inferior environments encountered by many poor blacks, but because of expectations of discrimination in the market. If black children and their parents face a world in which they receive lower rewards for obtaining skills, they will invest less if they face the same tuition costs as whites. Poor performance in schools and low achievement test scores may thus be a proxy for discrimination to be experienced in the future.

There is solid empirical evidence that expectations about rewards in the labor market influence human capital investment decisions; for example, the reward to skills held by black workers increased following the passage of the 1964 Civil Rights Act, and a rapid rise in college enrollment of blacks followed (Donohue and Heckman, 1991). But the difficulty with the argument in this context is that it presumes that black parents and children operate under mistaken expectations about the present labor market. Although it was once true that the returns to college education were lower for blacks than for whites (Becker, 1957; U.S. Civil Rights Commission, 1986), the return to college education for blacks was higher than the return for whites by the mid-1970s, and continues to be higher today. Some parallel evidence presented by Johnson and Neal (1998) shows that the returns to (coefficient on) AFQT scores for black males in an earnings equation are now as high or higher than those for whites, although they used to be lower in the pre–Civil Rights era. Given the greater return for blacks to college education and ability, it seems implausible to argue that a rational fear of lower future returns is currently discouraging black formation of skills.

Ability as it crystallizes at an early age accounts for most of the measured gap in black and white labor market outcomes. Stricter enforcement of civil rights laws is a tenuous way to improve early childhood skills and ability.[3] The weight of the evidence suggests that this ability and early motivation is most easily influenced by enriching family and preschool learning environments and by improving the quality of the early years of schooling.

The Implicit Assumptions Behind the Audit Method

The method of audit pairs operates by controlling for systematic observed differences across pairs. It does this by attempting to create two candidates for jobs or loans who are "essentially" the same in their paper qualifications and personal characteristics, and then comparing their outcomes in their dealings with the same firm. Averaging over the outcomes at all firms for the same audit pair produces an estimate of the discrimination effect. An average is often taken over audit pairs as well to report an "overall" estimate of discrimination. More sophisticated versions of the method will allow for some heterogeneity in treatment among firms and workers or firms and applicants.

One set of difficulties arise, however, because there are sure to be many unobserved variables. As noted by Heckman and Siegelman (1993), given the current limited state of knowledge of the determinants of productivity within firms, and given the small pools of applicants from which matched pairs are constructed that are characteristic of most audit studies, it is unlikely that all characteristics that might affect productivity will be perfectly matched. Thus, the implicit assumption in the audit pair method is that controlling for some components of productivity and sending people to the same firm will reduce the bias below what it would be if random pairs of, say, whites and blacks were compared using, for example, Census data. The implicit assumption that justifies this method is that the effect of the unobserved characteristics averages out to zero across firms for the same audit pair.

However, the mean of the differences in the unobserved components need not be zero and assuming that it is begs the problem. Nowhere in the published literature on the audit pair method will you find a demonstration that matching one subset of observable variables necessarily implies that the resulting difference in audit-adjusted treatment between blacks and whites is an unbiased measure of discrimination—or indeed, that it is even necessarily a better measure of discrimination than comparing random pairs of whites and blacks applying at the same firm or even applying to different firms. . . .

Consider the following example. Suppose that the market productivity of persons is determined by the sum of two productivity components. These two productivity components are distributed independently in the population so their values are not correlated with each other. Both factors affect employer assessments of employee productivity.[4] Suppose further that average productivity of the sum is the same for both whites and blacks; however, blacks are more productive on average on one component while whites are more productive on average on the other. Now consider an audit pair study that equates only the first component of productivity and equates firm effects by sending the audit pair to the same firm. Under these conditions, the audit estimator is biased toward a finding of discrimination, since in this example, only the characteristic which makes black productivity look relatively high is being used to standardize the audit pair. The condition of zero mean of unobservable productivity differences across race groups is not especially compelling and requires a priori knowledge that is typically not available.

Now consider the case in which the observed and unobserved components of productivity are dependent. In this case, making the included components as alike as possible may accentuate the differences in the unobserved components. As a result, it can increase the bias over the case where the measured components are not aligned.

... [T]hink of pairing up black and white high jumpers to see if they can clear a bar set at a certain height. There is no discrimination, in the sense that they both use the same equipment and have the bar set at the same level. Suppose now that the chance of a jumper (of any race) clearing the bar depends on two additive factors: the person's height and their jumping technique. We can pair up black and white jumpers so that they have identical heights, but we can't directly observe their technique. Let us make the generous assumption, implicit in the entire audit literature, that the mean jumping technique is equal for the two groups. Then, if the variance of technique is also the same for white and black high-jumpers, we would find that the two racial groups are equally likely to clear the bar. On the other hand, if the variance differs, then whether the black or white pair is more likely to clear the bar will depend on how the bar is set, relative to their common height, and which racial group has a higher variance in jumping technique. If the bar is set at a low level so that most people of the given height are likely to clear the bar, then the group with the lower variance will be more likely to clear the bar. If the bar is set at a very high level relative to the given height, then the group with a higher variance in jumping technique will be more likely to clear the bar. A limitation of the audit method is readily apparent from this analogy: there is no discrimination, yet the two groups have different probabilities of clearing the bar.[5] And if there is discrimination—that is, the bar is being set higher for blacks—the differential dispersion in the unobserved component could still cause the minority group to clear the bar more often. The method could fail to detect discrimination when it does exist.

Thus, depending on the distribution of unobserved characteristics for each race group and the audit standardization level, the audit method can show reverse discrimination, or equal treatment, or discrimination, even though blacks and whites in this example are subject to the same cutoff and face no discrimination. The apparent bias depends on whether the level of qualifications set by the audit designer makes it more or less likely that the applicant will receive the job, and the distribution of variables that are unobservable to the audit design. The apparent disparity favoring Washington whites in Table 1 may be a consequence of differences in unobserved characteristics between blacks and whites when there is no discrimination.

Even more disturbing, suppose that there is discrimination against blacks, so the productivity cutoff used by firms is higher for blacks than whites. Depending on the audit designer's choice of what level of qualifications are given to the auditors, the audit study can find no discrimination at all. However, whether the qualifications make it relatively likely or unlikely to get the job is a fact rarely reported in audit studies....

Making audit pairs as alike as possible may seem an obviously useful step, but it can greatly bias the inference about average discrimination or discrimination at the margin. Intuitively, by taking out the common components that are most easily measured, differences in hiring rates as monitored by audits arise from the idiosyncratic factors, and not the main factors, that drive actual labor markets. These examples highlight the fragility of the audit method to untested and unverifiable assumptions about the distributions of unobservables. Similar points arise in more general nonlinear models that characterize other employment decision rules.

The Becker Model

The papers in this symposium make the erroneous claim that in Becker's (1957) model, market discrimination disappears in the long run. It need not. Entrepreneurs can consume their income in any way they see fit. If a bigoted employer prefers whites, the employer can indulge that taste as long as income is received from entrepreneurial activity just as a person who favors an exotic ice cream can indulge that preference by being willing to pay the price. Only if the supply of entrepreneurship is perfectly elastic in the long run at a zero price, so entrepreneurs have no income to spend to indulge their tastes, or if there are enough nonprejudiced employers to hire all blacks, will discrimination disappear from Becker's model.

However, even if the common misinterpretation of Becker's model is accepted, it is far from clear that the prediction of no or little discrimination in the U.S. labor market in the long run is false. The substantial decline over the past 50 years in wage differentials between blacks and whites may well be a manifestation of the dynamics of the Becker model. It may take decades for the effects of past discrimination in employment and schooling as it affects current endowments of workers to fade out of the labor market. But the evidence from the current U.S. labor market is that discrimination by employers alone does *not* generate large economic disparities between blacks and whites.

Appendix

Implicit Identifying Assumptions in the Audit Method

Define the productivity of a person of race $r \in \{1,0\}$ at firm f, with characteristics $\sim X = (X_1, X_2)$ as $P(\sim X, r, f)$. $r = 1$ corresponds to black; $r = 0$ corresponds to white. Assume that race does not affect productivity so we may write $P = P(\sim X, f)$. The treatment at the firm f for a person of race r and productivity P is $T(P(\sim X, f), r)$. Racial discrimination exists at firm f if

$$T(P(\sim X, f), r = 1) \neq T(P(\sim X, f), r = 0).$$

As noted in the text, audit methods monitor discrimination at randomly selected firms within the universe designated for sampling, not the firms where blacks are employed.

The most favorable case for auditing assumes that T (or some transformation of it) is linear in f and X. Assume for simplicity that $P = X_1 + X_2 + f$ and

$T(P, r) = P + \gamma r$. When $\gamma < 0$ there is discrimination against blacks. γ may vary among firms as in Heckman and Siegelman (1993). For simplicity suppose that all firms are alike. Audit methods pair racially dissimilar workers in the following way: they match some components of $\sim X$ and they sample the same firms. Let P_1^* be the standardized productivity for the black member of the pair; P_0^* is the standardized productivity for the white member. If $P_0^* = P_1^*$,

$$T(P_1^*, 1) - T(P_0^*, 0) = \gamma.$$

When averaged over firms, the average treatment estimates the average γ.

Suppose that standardization is incomplete. We can align the first coordinate of X at $\{X_1 = X_1^*\}$ but not the second coordinate, X_2, which is unobserved by the auditor but acted on by the firm. $P_1^* = X_1^* + X_2^1$ where X_2^1 is the value of X_2 for the $r = 1$ member and $P_0^* = X_1^* + X_2^1$. In this case

$$T(P_1^*, 1) - T(P_0^*, 0) = X_2^1 - X_2^0 + \gamma.$$

For averages over pairs to estimate γ without bias, it must be assumed that $E(X_2^1) = E(X_2^0)$; i.e., that the mean of the unobserved productivity traits is the same. This is the crucial identifying assumption in the conventional audit method. Suppose that this is true so $E(X_2^1 = E(X_2^0) = \mu$. Then the pair matching as in the audit method does not increase bias and in general reduces it over comparisons of two X_1-identical persons at two randomly selected firms. Under these conditions, bias is lower than if two randomly chosen auditors are selected at the same firm if $E(X_1^1) \neq E(X_1^0)$.

However, the decision rule to offer a job or extend credit often depends on whether or not the perceived productivity P exceeds a threshold c:

$$T = 1 \text{ if } P \geq T = c$$

$$T = 0 \text{ otherwise}$$

In this case, the audit pair method will still produce bias even when it does not when T is linear in $\sim X$ and f unless the *distributions* of the omitted characteristics are identical in the two race groups. Suppose that $P = X_1 + X_2.X_2$ is uncontrolled. Then assuming no discrimination ($\gamma = 0$)

$$T(P_1^*, 1) = 1 \text{ if } X_1^* + X_2^1 + f \geq c = 0 \text{ otherwise}$$

$$T(P_0^*, 0) = 1 \text{ if } X_1^* + X_2^0 + f \geq c = 0 \text{ otherwise.}$$

Even if the distributions of f are identical across pairs, and f is independent of X, unless the *distributions* of X_2^1 and X_2^0 are identical, $\Pr(T(P_1^*, 1) = 1) \neq \Pr(T(P_0^*) = 1)$ for most values of the standardization level X_1^*. The right tail area of the distribution governs the behavior of these probabilities. This implies that even if blacks and whites face the same cutoff value, and in this sense are treated without discrimination in the labor market, even if the means of the distributions of unobservables are the same across race group, if the distributions of the unobservables are different, their probabilities of being hired will differ and will depend on the level of standardization used in the audit study—something that is rarely reported. The pattern of racial disparity in Table 1 may simply be a consequence of the choice of the level of standardization in those audits, and not discrimination.

Worse yet, suppose that the cutoff $c = c_1$ for blacks is larger than the cutoff $c = c_0$ for whites so that blacks are held to a higher standard. Then depending on the right tail area of X_2^1 and X_2^0, the values of c_1 and c_0, and the level of standardization X_1^*,

$$\Pr(T(P_1^*,) = 1) \overset{>}{\underset{<}{=}} P(T(P_0^*, 0) = 1).$$

In general, only if the *distributions* of X_2^1 and X_2^0 are the same for each race group, will the evidence reported in Table 1 be informative on the level of discrimination in the universe of sampled firms.

Figure 1

Relative Hiring Rate as a Function of the Level of Standardization. Blacks Have More Dispersion. Threshold Hiring Rule: No Discrimination Against Blacks Normally Distributed Unobservables

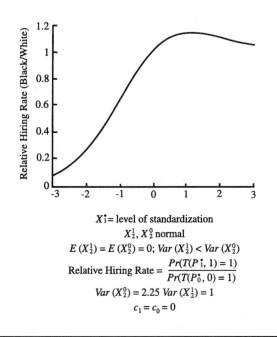

X_1^* = level of standardization

X_2^1, X_2^0 normal

$E(X_2^1) = E(X_2^0) = 0; Var(X_2^1) < Var(X_2^0)$

$$\text{Relative Hiring Rate} = \frac{Pr(T(P_1^*, 1) = 1)}{Pr(T(P_0^*, 0) = 1)}$$

$Var(X_2^0) = 2.25 \, Var(X_2^1) = 1$

$c_1 = c_0 = 0$

Figure 2

Relative Hiring Rate as a Function of the Level of Standardization. Blacks Held to Higher Standard; Blacks Have More Dispersion. Threshold Hiring Rule: No Discrimination Against Blacks Normally Distributed Unobservables

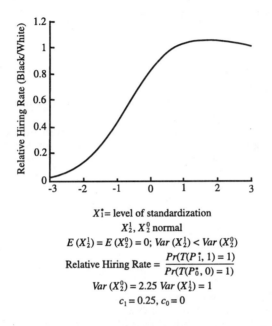

$X_1^* =$ level of standardization

X_2^1, X_2^0 normal

$E(X_2^1) = E(X_2^0) = 0;\ Var(X_2^1) < Var(X_2^0)$

$$\text{Relative Hiring Rate} = \frac{Pr(T(P_1^*, 1) = 1)}{Pr(T(P_0^*, 0) = 1)}$$

$Var(X_2^0) = 2.25\ Var(X_2^1) = 1$

$c_1 = 0.25,\ c_0 = 0$

Figures 1 and 2 illustrate these two cases for X_2^1 and X_2^0 normally distributed (and independent of each other) where X_1^* is the level of audit standardization and firms are standardized to have $f = 0$. In Figure 1 there is no discrimination in the market. Yet the black hire rate falls short of the white rate if the standardization rate is $X_1^* < 0$, and the lower the value of X_1^*, the greater the shortfall. In Figure 2, which is constructed for a hypothetical economy where there is discrimination against blacks, for high standardization rates, audits would appear to reveal discrimination *in favor* of blacks when in fact blacks are being held to a higher standard. The evidence in Table 1 is intrinsically ambiguous about the extent of discrimination in the market. For further discussion, see Heckman and Siegelman (1993).

Notes

1. Specifically, Darity and Mason write: "This effort has uncovered one variable in one data set which, if inserted in an earnings regression, produces the outcome that nearly all of the black male-white male wage gap is explained by human capital and none by labor market discrimination."

2. The Rodgers and Spriggs comment (1997) on Neal-Johnson raises other red herrings. Their confused discussion of endogeneity of AFQT, and their "solution" to the problem end up with an "adjusted" AFQT measure that is poorly correlated with the measured AFQT, and so is a poor proxy for black ability.

3. However, nothing I have said vindicates abolishing these laws. They have important symbolic value and they addressed and solved an important problem of blatant discrimination in the American South.

4. They need not be perfectly observed by employers but may only be proxied. However, it is easiest to think of both components as fully observed by the employer, but that the observing economist has less information.

5. I owe this analogy to Alan Krueger. This analogy also shows how artificial the audit studies are because one would expect to find athletes choosing their sports based on their chances of success, as in the purposive search in the labor market discussed earlier.

6. For simplicity, assume that γ is the same across all firms. Alternatively, assume that it is distributed independently of $\backsim X$ and f.

7. Allowing f to vary but assuming it is normal mean zero and variance σ_f^2 does not change the qualitative character of these calculations assuming that f is distributed independently of the characteristics.

References

Abowd, John, and Mark Killingsworth, "Sex, Discrimination, Atrophy, and the Male-Female Wage Differential," *Industrial And Labor Relations Review,* Fall 1983, *22*:3, 387–402.

Becker, Gary, *The Economics of Discrimination.* Chicago: University of Chicago Press, 1957.

Cameron, Stephen, and James Heckman, "The Nonequivalence of High School Equivalents," *Journal of Labor Economics, 1993, 11*:1, pt1, 1–47.

Cawley, John, James Heckman, and Edward Vytlacil, "Cognitive Ability and the Rising Return to Education," NBER working paper 6388, January 1998.

Donohue, John, and James Heckman, "Continuous vs. Episodic Change: The Impact of Affirmative Action and Civil Rights Policy on The Economic Status of Blacks," *Journal of Economic Literature,* December 1991. *29*:4, 1603–43.

Heckman, James, "The Central Role of the South in Accounting For The Economic Progress of Black Americans," Papers and Proceedings of The American Economic Association, May 1990.

Heckman, James, "Lessons From the Bell Curve," *Journal of Political Economy,* 1995, *103*:5, 1091–1120.

Heckman, James, and Peter Siegelman, "The Urban Institute Audit Studies: Their Methods and Findings." In M. Fix and R. Struyk, eds. *Clear and Convincing Evidence: Measurement of Discrimination in America.* Urban Institute, Fall 1993.

Heckman, James, Lance Lochner, Christopher Taber, and Jeffrey Smith, "The Effects of Government Policy on Human Capital Investment and Wage Inequality," *Chicago Policy Review,* Spring 1997, *1*:2, 1–40.

Johnson, William R., and Derek Neal, "Basic Skills and the Black-White Earnings Gaps." In Jencks, Christopher and Meredith Phillips, eds. *The Black-White Test Score Gap.* Washington, D.C. Brookings, 1998.

Neal, Derek, and William Johnson, "The Role of Premarket Factors in Black-White Wage Differences," *Journal of Political Economy, 1996, 104*:5, 869–95.

Rodgers III, William, and William Spriggs, "What Does AFQT Really Measure: Race, Wages, Schooling and the AFQT Score," *The Review of Black Political Economy,* Spring 1996, *24*:4, 13–46.

Rodgers III, William, William E. Spriggs, and Elizabeth Waaler, "The Role of Pre-market Factors in Black-White Differences: Comment," Unpublished Manuscript, College of William and Mary, May 25, 1997.

Seelye, Katherine, "Employment Panel To Send People Undercover to Detect Bias in Hiring," *New York Times,* Sunday, December 7, 1997, p. 22.

U.S. Commission on Civil Rights, *The Economic Progress of Black Men in America,* Clearinghouse Publication 91, 1986.

POSTSCRIPT

Is There Discrimination in U.S. Labor Markets?

Economists assume that markets are anonymous; that is, they assume that rational economic actors would not take race, sex, religious affiliation, or any other personal characteristic into consideration when buying or selling. Consumers are trying to maximize their consumer satisfaction, while producers are in the same marketplace trying to maximize their profits. Just as the often paraphrased axiom of Adam Smith suggests: Each acting for his or her own self-interest advances the well-being of the whole. In the world of neoclassical economics, there is simply no room for discrimination.

Yet the appearance of discrimination, if not the reality of discrimination, is all around us. Why are unemployment rates for African Americans twice those for white Americans? Why, on the average, do African American households earn 60 cents for every dollar earned by white households? Why do U.S. corporations, universities, courthouses, and even military officers' clubs have so many whites? And, more important, why do nearly 40 percent of African American children suffer the life-altering effects of poverty? Is this the product of market discrimination, or is it the consequence of deficient skill levels among African Americans?

In addition to Heckman's many contributions—he is perhaps the most prolific contributor to this debate from the neoclassical position—we suggest that you return to the source of his position, the work of Gary Becker, who in 1957 wrote *The Economics of Discrimination* (University of Chicago Press). Some of Heckman's other work is also highly recommended. See, for example, his essay "Lessons From the Bell Curve," *Journal of Political Economy* (vol. 103, 1995), pp. 1091–1120, and the book chapter he wrote with Peter Siegelman, "The Urban Institute Audit Studies: Their Methods," which appears in Michael Fix and Raymond Struyk, eds., *Clear and Convincing Evidence: Measurement of Discrimination in America* (Urban Institute Press, 1993). Finally, you might read Heckman's paper "The Value of Quantitative Evidence on the Effect of the Past on the Present," *American Economic Review* (May 1997).

Darity and Mason have also contributed extensively to this literature. See, for example, Mason's "Male Interracial Wage Differentials: Competing Explanations," *Cambridge Journal of Economics* (May 1999). You might also look for Darity and Samuel L. Myers, Jr.'s book *Persistent Disparity* (Edward Edgar, 1999). Lastly, we suggest a coauthored essay by Darity, Jason Dietrich, and David K. Guilkey, "Racial and Ethnic Inequality in the United States: A Secular Perspective," *American Economic Review* (May 1997).

ISSUE 5

Should California's Electric Utility Industry Be Deregulated?

YES: George Reisman, from "California Screaming, Under Government Blows," *Web site of the Ludwig von Mises Institute,* http://www.mises.org/articles.asp (December 22, 2000)

NO: Wenonah Hauter and Tyson Slocum, from *It's Greed Stupid! Debunking the Ten Myths of Utility Deregulation,* Report of Public Citizen's Critical Mass Energy and Environment Program (January 2001)

ISSUE SUMMARY

YES: Professor of economics George Reisman asserts that the root cause of California's power problems is not the "free market" but "destructionist government policy... inspired by environmentalist fanaticism." He goes on to argue that this inappropriate government intrusion "has increasingly restricted the supply of electric power."

NO: Wenonah Hauter and Tyson Slocum, director and senior researcher, respectively, of Public Citizen's Critical Mass Energy and Environment Program, contend that California's attempt to deregulate its electric utilities has failed miserably. They debunk what they consider to be the 10 "myths" that proponents of deregulation used to call for the original round of deregulation in California and are currently using to call for even more deregulation of California's electric power system.

During the winter of 2000–2001, banner headline after banner headline declared, "Rolling Blackouts Hit Californians," "California is Unplugged," and "The Electricity Blame Game Is On." What happened to cause this energy crisis in California and what should be done now are the focus of this issue. It is a topic of great importance because the doubling, tripling, or even greater price increases of electricity that California has experienced may well snake across the rest of America, leaving economic chaos in the wake.

Indeed, the crisis is already impacting other western U.S. states. Many of the non-Californian utilities that generate electricity in the West are less dependent on natural gas—the most significant of several energy sources that have skyrocketed in price—than California is. Nevertheless, the fact that natural gas prices have risen sharply has increased the demand for all sources of energy that serve as substitutes, particularly hydroelectricity, coal, and nuclear energy. This problem is compounded by the fact that hydroelectricity is under its own price pressures. The drought that hit the region in the summer of 2000 coupled with the light snow pack the following winter drained the reservoirs that drive the electricity-generating turbines in that industry. Electricity prices in Idaho, Washington, and Oregon soon began to soar as the whole region competed with California for the limited amount of electricity that found its way to the marketplace.

What are the root causes of this crisis? Many people would argue that the answer to that question is rooted in AB 1890, a major deregulation bill that was passed unanimously in the California state legislature in 1996. AB 1890 had several key components. One central element was the establishment of a "Power Exchange," which was intended to serve as a centralized market for electricity. The buyers in this centralized market were the utilities, who would purchase electric power and in turn sell that electricity to their residential, commercial, and public sector customers. The sellers were those who actually generated the electric power supply. In order to ensure that no producer monopolies would have an unfair competitive advantage in this centralized market, the state's investor-owned utilities (IOUs) were required to sell their electricity-generating assets. However, the IOUs were allowed to recover their "stranded costs" by placing a monthly "competitive transition charge" on their ratepayers' bills. These stranded costs were the expenditures that IOUs had made on investments in traditional and alternative sources of energy that were formerly required by law but that would no longer be competitive in a deregulated market. Californians assumed the financial burden of compensating the IOUs for their stranded costs, and in turn the IOUs were required to reduce their rates by 10 percent and to cap them at this level until all stranded costs were recovered. Next, the deregulation mandated that the utilities participate in an electric power transmission system, which was to coordinate the distribution of electric power throughout the state. One final aspect of this deregulation was that publicly owned utilities were free to act independently. They could buy and sell in the Power Exchange, or they could sell their electricity on the open market.

In the following selections, George Reisman and Wenonah Hauter and Tyson Slocum discuss what happened in California and debate what policymakers should do to get the West Coast out of this mess and to keep it from spreading east. Reisman argues that Californians simply did not go far enough in their attempted deregulation. For him, California needs even more deregulation, not less. Hauter and Slocum maintain that this call for even more deregulation is based on the same flawed arguments that were used to get California into this situation in the first place.

George Reisman  **YES**

California Screaming, Under Government Blows

The state of California is experiencing a fiasco in its electric power system. The system has repeatedly run near the overload point, necessitating brownouts and threatening rolling blackouts. Wholesale power prices in San Diego County and the southern portion of adjacent Orange County have briefly been as high as $5,000 per megawatt hour and, according to one report, as high as $11,500 per megawatt hour.

At first, the local utilities in these counties attempted to pass their greatly increased wholesale power costs on to their customers, in the form of doubled and tripled electric bills, but the state government, in response to widespread protest, soon prevented them from doing so. Now these utilities are threatened with bankruptcy, having lost approximately $6 billion dollars in the process. Out-of-state suppliers of electric power have threatened to cut off further supplies to the state, out of fear of not being paid by utilities on the verge of bankruptcy. At last report, these suppliers have been ordered by the federal government's Secretary of Energy to continue their supplies.

Incredibly, the fiasco is being blamed on deregulation and the establishment of a free market in electric power. See, for example, the disgraceful article *"California Screaming"* by Paul Krugman in *The New York Times* of December 10, 2000—on line at *The Times'* lead in to this article, which accurately conveys its tenor, is "California's blind faith in markets has led to an electricity shortage so severe that the governor has turned off the lights on the official Christmas tree."

Clearly, it is necessary to review the facts that have caused California's fiasco, in order to arrive at a rational judgment of its nature. This review will establish that the actual cause of the fiasco is not at all the free market but rather, from beginning to end, destructionist government policy, in large part inspired by environmentalist fanaticism. Assertions, such as that of *The New York Times*, which was just quoted, will be shown to constitute a literal contradiction in terms.

Destructionist government policy has increasingly restricted the supply of electric power in California and throughout the United States. It is responsible for the fact that for the last twenty years or more, there have been no new atomic power plants constructed and few or no new coal, oil, or hydro power plants built. Indeed, it has caused existing plants of these types to be dismantled. In California, in the last decade, only power plants using natural gas as their fuel have been allowed to be constructed, and such plants now account for most of the state's generating capacity.

Because power plants using natural gas are substantially more expensive to operate in comparison with the other types of power plants, and would quickly be plunged into unprofitability if exposed to the competition of other types of power plants, investors have been unwilling to invest in additional generating capacity in California, and elsewhere, to the extent they otherwise would have. At the same time, the government-caused dependence on natural gas as the source of fuel for power plants has contributed to the recent sharp rise in the price of natural gas to record levels. The rise in the price of natural gas has been especially great in California, where lack of adequate pipeline capacity has limited natural gas supplies more than in the rest of the United States.

Over the same period that the government has restricted the supply of electric power, there has been a substantial increase in the demand for electric power. The rise in demand has been brought about both by population growth and by the increase in power consumption per capita caused by economic progress. An example of this last is the increase in power consumption caused by the use of personal computers and their peripherals by tens of millions of people.

When these facts are combined with government price controls on electric power (which have existed since the early years of the industry), *shortages* of electric power are an inevitable result. This is because the government prevents not only the increase in supply that would keep pace with the increase in demand but also the rise in the price of electric power that would keep the demand for power within the limit of the supply available, however artificially restricted that supply might be as the result of government interference.

The government's responsibility for shortages of electric power, it should be realized, inescapably implies its responsibility for power brownouts and blackouts. For their immediate cause is a demand for power too great for the power system to supply, i.e., a power shortage.

It cannot be stressed too strongly that a shortage is an excess of quantity demanded over supply available. And that it is caused by a government price control, which prevents price from rising high enough to reduce quantity demanded to the supply available, which would eliminate the shortage. Of course, the more the government holds down the supply of electric power, the higher is the price that is required to prevent a shortage of power. When the government refuses to allow a price that is high enough to keep the quantity of power demanded within the limit of the supply of power available, brownouts and blackouts are the result.

It should be understood that when taken in conjunction with price controls on electric power, the government's inflation of the money supply also contributes to power shortages. This is because inflation contributes both to the increase in the demand for power and to the restriction of its supply. The former results largely from the rise in money incomes that the spending of the additional quantity of money brings about, and which gives people the financial means to afford larger quantities of any given good at any given price. The latter results from the fact that inflation drives up the costs of constructing and operating power plants and thus correspondingly reduces their profitability in the face of controlled selling prices. The process does not have to go very far before it no longer pays to construct power plants—assuming, of course, that the environmentalists did not prevent their construction in the first place.

All this is the basic context of the fiasco now existing in California and which, on the basis of a combination of ignorance and deceit, is being blamed on, of all things, "a free market" in electric power.

The so-called free market in electric power in California consists of the fact that, last summer [2000], price controls were removed from the power supplies of San Diego County and the southern portion of adjacent Orange County, while remaining in force throughout the rest of the state.

The power supplies of this relatively small part of California were suddenly opened up to the competition of power companies throughout the rest of the state and in surrounding states who were desperate for additional power to avoid the brownouts and blackouts caused by government price controls in their operating territories. Starting last summer, by offering a higher wholesale price, these power companies could bid away power generated in this area from use by the area's local residents and businesses. Locally generated power could be retained for use in the area only at a wholesale price that matched the price generated by this competition.

It should be understood that the power companies are in a position in which any customer can turn on additional power-using devices, and they are obliged to supply the additional power needed to meet that additional demand. Price controls and the government's restrictions (described above) preventing the construction of new power-generating capacity now repeatedly compel the utilities to operate close to the limit of their existing power-generating capacity.

To avoid overloading and thereby crashing their systems and causing wide-spread blackouts, they must either find the necessary additional power or induce other customers, typically large ones, to cut back on their power consumption, by such means as the offer of substantial rate concessions. Finding additional power, wherever it is available, can serve to avoid expensive rate concessions and, worse, a system crash. This is the desperate situation for which the limited power supplies of San Diego County and the southern portion of adjacent Orange County were put in the position of having to provide a remedy.

Anyone familiar with economic theory could easily have predicted that the result would be a skyrocketing of power prices in the area. For the limited power supplies of this small area were being made to bear the burden of coping with the statewide and indeed, Western-states-regionwide power shortages caused by destructionist government policies.

Now the truth is that an immediate, partial solution to the sharp rise in power prices in this limited area is the *immediate decontrol of power prices throughout the rest of California* and, indeed, throughout the whole Western-states region, which shares a more-or-less integrated power grid. The effect of such decontrol would be an immediate substantial increase in the supply of electric power available for the decontrolled market and thus, probably within days, if not hours, a sharp drop in the price of electric power in the decontrolled market.

This increase in supply, it must be stressed, would *not* come from an increase in production, though very soon there would be such an increase and thus a further increase in supply and reduction in price in the decontrolled market. No, it would come from the more or less substantial portion of *the already existing production of electric power that is presently consumed by submarginal buyers,* i.e., by buyers unable or unwilling to pay the potential free-market price, which, of course, would be higher than the controlled price still in force over the far greater part of the state. When the price control is removed, this substantial part of the supply, presently not available for the decontrolled market, is made available for the decontrolled market, where its effect is to enlarge the supply and thus correspondingly reduce the price.

Lifting price controls in the remainder of Orange County and in Los Angeles County, for example, would add supplies from these areas to the supplies presently available only from San Diego County and the southern portion of Orange County to meet urgent needs for power throughout the state and the Western-states region in general. The rise in price in these additional areas would serve to reduce the quantity of power demanded in these areas. The supply of power previously used to meet this portion of the demand would be available for the now larger decontrolled market. The effect of this larger supply in the larger decontrolled market would be to reduce the price of power in the decontrolled market.

Decontrol throughout the state and in surrounding states would still much more substantially enlarge the supply available in the decontrolled market and drive down the price there. Indeed, at the same time that larger supplies were being made available to meet urgent needs for power, decontrol would serve greatly to diminish the urgency of those needs. This is because the rise in power prices throughout the state would serve everywhere to reduce the quantity of power demanded and thus serve to reduce the amount of power needed from outside sources to prevent brownouts or blackouts.

It should be clear that decontrol limited to the territory of just one or two counties is decontrol in a very high-pressure pressure-cooker, so to speak. It is decontrol in which all the pressure of the shortages of the whole rest of the state and surrounding states come to bear on the very limited supplies of power available just in this relatively small area. Decontrol over the whole state and region would serve to eliminate all of this pumping up of the pressure that has propelled prices so high in San Diego County and south Orange County.

A further increase in supply and reduction in price that would result from state-wide and region-wide decontrol would come from existing power capacity that is presently forced off the market by price control, coming back on to the market. That there is such capacity is confirmed by the following statement in a recent newspaper report: "Natural-gas prices traded at record levels

Friday [December 8, 2000], hitting $60 per million British thermal units. *That prompted some gas-fueled generating plants to shut down* because they couldn't make a profit under the ISO's [Independent System Operator's—a state official] wholesale cap of $250 a megawatt hour." (*The Orange County Register,* December 10, 2000, News Section 1, p. 12. Italics added.)

The elimination of price control would bring such producers back into the market, increase the market supply, and reduce the market price. As matters stand, the forced withdrawal of such producers serves to further increase the pressure on the very limited supplies of the small area that is free of controls, and to further drive up their price. For buyers who might have been supplied by those producers, and now are not, must turn instead to the supplies of that small area.

The preceding makes clear that the price of a good in a fully decontrolled market is substantially less than the price of a good in an only partially decontrolled market, and is virtually certain to be very substantially less in comparison to the price in a partially decontrolled market as small as the one in California has been. Full decontrol in California would mean lower power prices both for this reason and because of the return to the market of output from existing producers that the controls had driven away by making its production unprofitable.

The following hypothetical example will serve to drive home the principle that the elimination of price control on the full supply of a good available results in a lower decontrolled price than when only a portion of the supply of a good is free of price control. Thus imagine that the full available supply of a good is 100 units and that at a fully uncontrolled, free-market price of $120, the quantity of the good demanded is also 100 units. In this case, the free-market price is $120—that is the price at which quantity demanded and supply available of the good are equal and, consequently, neither a shortage nor an unsaleable surplus of the good exists.

Now imagine that the government imposes a price control on this good of $100 per unit. At this, lower price, the quantity of the good demanded becomes greater than the 100 units of supply available. This is because now the good can be afforded by everyone who values a unit of it above the price of $100, whereas before only those who valued a unit of the good above the market price of $120 could afford it. At the free-market price, all buyers not prepared to pay at least $120 per unit would have been rendered submarginal. They would have been excluded from the market by the $120 price. Now however, as the result of the price control, a more or less substantial number of submarginal buyers become admitted to the market. They can cross the lower bar of the $100 price, while they could not have crossed the higher bar of the free-market price of $120.

Assume that as a result of the lower, controlled price, buyers are now prepared to attempt to buy 130 units of the good. Since only 100 units of the good are available, would-be buyers of 30 units must go away empty-handed. The efforts of these would-be buyers to buy 30 units that do not exist is the measure of the shortage that the price control has created.

When there is a price control and shortage, the distribution of the supply is made largely random and chaotic. That is, it becomes an essentially accidental matter *which* of the buyers seeking 130 units will be supplied and to what extent. It is entirely possible in this situation that a full 30 units of the supply could fall into the hands of buyers who at the free-market price of $120 would have been submarginal, that is, into the hands of buyers who value these units below the free-market price of $120—who value them merely above the $100 controlled price. We do not need to make such an extreme assumption, however. Assume that the effect of the price control and resulting shortage is merely to enable 10 units of the supply to fall into the hands of such submarginal buyers.

Since there are only 100 units of supply available, the diversion of 10 units into the hands of submarginal buyers, means that only 90 units of the supply remain available for buyers able and willing to pay $120 or more per unit. Thus buyers of 10 units, who value them all above $120 are excluded from the market. It is against the law—i.e., the price control—for them to outbid the submarginal buyers, as they would do in a free market. The result is that unless they are lucky, which in this case they are not, they will have to go away empty-handed.

It is entirely possible, and we will assume it to be the case, that among this group of excluded buyers are buyers who value a unit of the good far above the free-market price of $120—who would be prepared to pay as much as $1,000 for a unit of it, or even as much as $2,000. Under price controls and shortages, even buyers with the most vital and urgent need for a good, as these buyers can be assumed to be, may have to go away empty-handed, because the units they seek are obtained instead by buyers who in a free market would have been submarginal and excluded from the market by the free-market price.

Now, finally, imagine that into this situation comes the government of California, with its "blind faith in markets," as *The New York Times* has so audaciously called it. It decontrols the price of *one* unit of the hundred. What happens? The price of this unit is determined by the competition between the most desperate and second-most desperate buyer of an additional unit who have up to now been excluded from the market by the price control and resulting shortage. In the present example, it is determined at a point between the $2,000 maximum potential bid of the most desperate of these buyers and the $1,000 maximum potential bid of the second-most desperate of these buyers. Thus, the resulting price is, say, $1,500.

It should be obvious that if instead of timidly freeing just one unit of the supply from price control, the entire supply of 100 units were freed, the resulting price would be far lower—it would be the $120 free-market price.

Now although, as the above example confirms, the free-market price would be very much lower than the price prevailing in the very narrow decontrolled market of just one and a half counties, it would still be more or less substantially higher than the previously controlled price. Whatever it turned out to be, *its immediate effect would be to end the shortage of electric power and thus brownouts and blackouts.* This would be to the advantage of all consumers of power—poor consumers no less than rich ones.

The establishment of a free-market price for power means that poorer consumers are enabled to bid more for the power they need to run their one and only refrigerator, say, than many wealthier, higher-income buyers are willing to pay for the power needed to operate a second or third refrigerator. It means that they are enabled to bid more for the electric power that provides the light they need in which to read than many wealthier, higher-income buyers are able and willing to pay for power to run their pool lights or other outside lights. Retention of price control, in contrast, means that the wealthier, higher income buyer has no economic reason not to go on using power for a second or third refrigerator and for his pool lights, which serves to deprive the poorer consumer of the power for his one refrigerator or the light in which to read. A free market price guarantees the availability of electric power for the truly urgent purposes of virtually everyone who has a job.

When faced with the need to restrict consumption, a free market does so by eliminating the least important of the uses to which a good was previously devoted, i.e., its previously marginal uses. In the present case, such uses will probably turn out in large part to be power-intensive industrial uses in the production of products that are unable to bear substantially higher power costs.

To the extent that the resulting free-market price were higher than the previously controlled price, it would operate to increase the profits of power producers and thereby provide both the incentive and the means (the latter through reinvestment of the profits) to increase investment in and thus production of power. This, of course, is part of the more complete, longer-run solution to California's power fiasco. Obviously, it requires the removal of obstacles to the construction of new and additional power plants, i.e., the environmentalists must get out of the way. The freedom to construct power plants fueled by atomic energy and by coal must be restored.

The effect of stepped up investment in and production of power would be a reduction in the price of power and in the profitability of producing it. The rate of profit in power production would fall from a more or less sharply above-average rate toward the average rate. The price of electric power would gravitate toward its cost of production plus only as much profit as required to provide the average rate of profit, i.e., only enough profit to make the power industry competitive with the rest of the economic system for capital investment. While the high profits of the power industry following the removal of price controls would be temporary, what would endure is a larger-sized power industry.

Thereafter, in order for any power producer to earn a premium rate of profit, he would have become an innovator in improving power production. He would have to find ways to reduce its cost of production and/or improve what he could transmit over power lines. But these premium profits too would be temporary. They would come to an end as soon as competitors succeeded in making the improvements part of the general standard of the industry. Further high profits would have to be earned by further reductions in cost of production and/or further improvements in quality of one kind or another, and so on and on. The long-run beneficiaries would be the consumers of power, who would buy their power at progressively lower real prices.

This, indeed, is the overwhelming thrust of the free market: ever lower, not higher prices. To be sure, this result is not very obvious when prices are expressed in terms of fiat paper money, which is comparable in its cost of production to paper clips or pins, and which gets cheaper faster than businessmen can make most goods and services get cheaper, with the result that prices expressed in paper money almost always rise.

But it is very obvious when prices are expressed in terms of how many hours or minutes of labor the average worker must put in at a job in order to earn the price of something. Once prices are thought of in these terms, it is clear that the real price of almost everything has been falling for generations —precisely because of the free market and its profit motive and freedom of competition. That is the real meaning of a free market in electric power as well.

It should now be clear that the assertion of *The New York Times* that "California's blind faith in markets has led to an electricity shortage so severe that the governor has turned off the lights on the official Christmas tree" is the complete opposite of the truth, and is so by the very meaning of the terms involved.

Presenting knowledge of the actual causes of California's electric-power fiasco will prevent the enemies of the free market, such as *The New York Times* and its columnists, from getting away with blaming the free market for the consequences of the anti-free-market, destructionist policies they advocate.

In the view of writers such as Krugman, there may as well never have been any governmental restrictions on power production inspired by environmentalism. Lack of sufficient capacity is the fault of "the deregulated market." In Krugman's own words: "But in the deregulated market, where prices fluctuate constantly, companies knew that if they overinvested, prices and profits would plunge. So they were reluctant to build new plants—which is why unexpectedly strong demand has led to shortages and soaring prices."

The same gentleman knows nothing of the distorting effects of price controls on markets that are only partially decontrolled. In his eyes, the cause of the very high power prices in San Diego County and the southern portion of Orange County can only be "manipulation." To prove it, he imagines the following case:

> "Suppose that it's a hot July, with air-conditioners across the state running full blast and the power industry near the limits of its capacity. If some of that capacity suddenly went off line for whatever reason, the resulting shortage would send wholesale electricity prices sky high. So a large producer could actually increase its profits by inventing technical problems that shut down some of its generators, thereby driving up the price it gets on its remaining output."

In reality, of course, all kinds of contractual arrangements requiring delivery of specified quantities of power at specified prices would operate to prevent the kind of behavior Krugman imagines. Because of such contracts covering the greater part of their output, any rise in the price of power would go mainly to the benefit of the contract holders, rather than to the companies generating power. The amount of output on which the latter could obtain the benefit of such a short-term rise in price would be too small to make such behavior on their part worthwhile.

Putting this aside, Krugman ignores the actual, and significant, fact that in the summer of 2000, the power companies of California were operating dangerously close to the limit of their capacity, causing considerable fear of the dire consequences that would result should there be any breakdown in any of their capacity, which became all the more likely, the longer there was no down time for necessary maintenance and repairs.

Now, in the fall of 2000, when approximately twenty-five percent of California's power capacity is off line, undergoing the maintenance and repairs that could not be performed in the summer, in the face of peak demand, Krugman suggests that this too is part of a process of "manipulation." Perhaps he believes that the California utilities that have been driven to the brink of bankruptcy are growing rich in this process.

Krugman and *The New York Times* appear to suffer from the malady of substituting fantasy for knowledge of reality. The seriousness of the malady is not diminished by the fact that *The Times* is often able to pull it off with a pompousness that is exceeded only by its ignorance.

NO ←

Wenonah Hauter and Tyson Slocum

It's Greed Stupid!

Introduction

If the purpose of deregulation is really to improve the quality of people's lives by lowering the cost of a critical commodity, it is obviously failing miserably —as demonstrated in California. To understand what has happened, we must begin with the past.

Prior to "deregulation," electricity was supplied by regional monopolies that owned both the power plants and the transmission lines for the distribution of power. The California legislature set the rate of return of profit for the utilities, and the state Public Utilities Commission [CPUC] planned for future power needs and helped insure that rate increases were fair and based on the "cost of service." While this system was often abused because of the enormous political power of the electric utilities and their ability to influence policy-makers, it did keep in check the profiteering that we are now witnessing in California.

By the mid-1990s, large industrial consumers sought to escape the high costs of power in some parts of the country, like California, that came as a result of building expensive nuclear power plants. At the same time, independent power producers like Enron were actively lobbying to be able to sell power to these big consumers. Political pressure for deregulation mounted because the breakup of the $300 billion dollar utility industry meant huge amounts of money could be made. Enron, an important campaign contributor to the Republican Party and to President Bush, lobbied for deregulation not only in California, but at state legislatures across the nation and in Congress.

Despite warnings from consumer groups, deregulation has been heartily embraced by both political parties, and under the Clinton administration, the U.S. Department of Energy [DOE] wrote its own federal deregulation bill that it promoted unsuccessfully.

In California, the utilities, at first, were skeptical of deregulation, because of the high cost of power from their nuclear plants. However, they began to hunger for the profits that could be made in a speculative market. They lobbied heavily for deregulation because they knew that with their enormous political clout in the state legislature, they could shape the outcome of deregulation.

From Wenonah Hauter and Tyson Slocum, *It's Greed Stupid! Debunking the Ten Myths of Utility Deregulation,* Report of Public Citizen's Critical Mass Energy and Environment Program (January 2001). Notes omitted.

The legislation, written primarily by California's utilities, was extremely complex, a vast program for a vast state. It was wrangled over in a series of rapid-fire hearings, and rammed through the legislature at the last minute in a process that took only three weeks. It was unanimously passed and signed into law by Governor Pete Wilson in the fall of 1996.

The legislation, written and supported by utilities, privatized their profit and socialized their risks. The most glaring example of this was the $28 billion dollar consumer-funded bailout for their so-called "stranded costs." Stranded costs are essentially mortgage payments that the utilities make to cover their purchase of expensive boondoggle nuclear power plants. The utilities argued that the bailout was necessary because they would now be assuming market-place risk, and the uncertainty of their future profits made the paying off of debts they incurred under regulation too burdensome. To accomplish this bailout, rates were artificially frozen for 4 years, at what was then 50% above the national average cost of electricity. To date, ratepayers have bailed out the utilities for approximately $20 billion dollars through added costs to their electric bills.

In 1998, a coalition of consumer groups, Californians Against Utility Taxes, sponsored an initiative, Proposition 9, which would have invalidated portions of the 1996 deregulation bill, and prevented the utility bailout. The proposition would have required the utilities and their shareholders, not ratepayers, to bear the burden of the $28 billion bailout. According to energy analysts at the California Energy Commission, if Proposition 9 had passed, residential power customers would have seen their energy costs "fall between 18 to 32 percent." California's utilities spent more than $30 million defeating Proposition 9, compared to the $1 million spent by consumer advocates.

The legislation not only provided them with a bailout, but it enabled them to go on an international spending spree in which they purchased power plants. It also provided them with capital they used to invest in other industries that they had been prohibited from entering under the regulated monopoly system. California's utilities have invested in telecommunications and other types of high-growth services that they plan to sell in conjunction with their sale of electricity. Between the bailout and their forays into new industries, Wall Street applauded their moves because of their increased earnings potential.

Also, the legislation provided incentives for California's utilities to sell their power plants to unregulated companies. They sold most of their fossil fuel plants at above the book value, providing them with a significant profit. However, they retained their nuclear and hydro-power generation, along with a small amount of fossil-fuel plants.

Additionally, the deregulation bill transferred pricing of California's electricity generation to the Federal Energy Regulatory Commission by creating the Power Exchange, a private nonprofit organization that would operate the auction for wholesale power.

Most of the corporations that bought the California utilities' power plants are from out-of-state—such as Virginia-based AES, North Carolina-based Duke, and Houston-based Dynegy and Reliant. Eleven companies, not all of which own power plants in California, sell electricity into the Power Exchange, where electricity is bought and sold several times (in paper transactions) before it is actually delivered to consumers. Another new privately run entity, the Independent System Operator (CAISO), acts as a traffic cop, directing electricity to where it was needed.

Myth #1: Deregulation does not work because California did not deregulate enough.

Advocates for deregulation say that if the rate freeze was removed and consumers paid for the real cost of electricity through a free market, there would not be a problem. But they fail to mention that over the past few months, the cost of wholesale electricity has at times been almost 4,000 percent higher than before deregulation because of the speculative nature of the electricity market. *If all the costs were passed on to consumers, the average residential monthly consumer, who paid approximately $55 a month before deregulation, would have paid approximately $600 a month when prices spiked in California this winter.*

Second, the utilities agreed to assume a risk under deregulation, in return for the bailout and rate freeze. However, now that their plans have soured, they want to renege on the deal that they lobbied for in 1996. The retail rate "freeze" was designed by and for the state's electric utilities, as a way to subsidize them for their bad business decisions of the past, such as nuclear power plants.

Until the spring of 2000, the utilities greatly benefited from the artificially high rates that were "frozen" in 1996 at 50% above the national average for electricity. These outrageously high rates included: 1) reimbursement for their cost-of-service (all of the expenses associated with producing power); 2) approximately an 11.75% profit margin; and 3) the $20 billion dollar bailout for utilities' bad investments of the past. The outrageous utility bailout is listed as a "Competitive Transition Charge" (CTC) on every Californian's electric bill.

The Utility Reform Network (TURN), a consumer advocacy organization in California, explains the bailout and rate freeze:

> This opportunity [the rate freeze], however, included the explicit risk that some costs might not be collected by the end of the rate freeze. With the advent of higher-than-expected power prices in recent months, these utilities now argue that they never took a risk for the costs of power under the rate freeze and therefore should be compensated for money spent to buy power for its customers.

To make matters even worse, the utilities overestimate the cost of electricity that they claim to have "under collected" from consumers in their frozen rates. As a result of the price spikes that began in 2000, the utilities are asserting that consumers have to pick up the exorbitant cost of wholesale electricity. The utilities claim to be "owed," approximately $12 billion dollars.

In fact, this number is wildly exaggerated, because the utilities did not sell all of their power generation (they retained nuclear plants, hydra-electric facilities, and a small amount of fossil generation). Under deregulation, the electricity from all utility owned or contracted generation is resold into the Power Exchange. During periods of high energy prices, the net revenues associated with this generation can be substantial. But, instead of offsetting the costs of purchasing power for customers, under the current rules, these utility owned units provide no direct benefit to rate payers in the form of lower energy procurement prices.

For example, if it costs PG&E [Pacific Gas and Electric] approximately 1.4 cents per kilowatt hour to generate hydro-electricity and they sell this power at the Power Exchange for approximately 40 cents per kilowatt hour, they make a huge profit. This profit should be subtracted from the amount that the utilities estimate they have been overcharged for wholesale power. But, the utilities have not subtracted in their estimates of how they have been overcharged, their own substantial profits in wholesale market, which is roughly estimated at $6 billion dollars. This means that the $12 billion dollar figure that they claim to have over-paid in the wholesale market is wildly inflated by at least $6 billion.

Because of the profiteering on electricity trading at the Power Exchange, the city of San Francisco initiated a lawsuit on January 18, 2001, against a number of companies for unfair business practices. The companies being sued include Dynegy Power Marketing; Enron Power Marketing, Inc.; PG&E Energy Trading Holding Corporation; Reliant Energy Services; Sempra Energy Trading Corporation (owner of San Diego Gas and Electric); Southern Company Energy Marketing; Duke Energy Trading and Marketing; NRG Energy, Inc.; and Morgan Stanley Capital Group, Inc.

The California Public Utilities Commission comments that the pricing patterns in the Power Exchange's "day ahead" and "day of" markets raise questions about the bidding behavior of market participants that cannot be coincidental.

California is suffering today because of no regulation—not because of over-regulation.

Myth #2: Deregulation will lower costs for consumers.

Deregulation has been sold to the public as a way to lower prices. Unfortunately, the inverse is often true, with deregulation resulting in higher prices over time. When deregulation legislation sailed through the California legislature with unanimous bipartisan support in 1996, proponents claimed that consumers would see *at least* a 20 percent reduction in their electric rates eventually. Now, as wholesale prices have skyrocketed since last year, proponents argue that consumer rates will have to *increase* to encourage more competition. Long-term contracts are being promoted as the antidote for the crisis. But, the price being quoted for electricity under these contracts is at least three times more expensive than under regulation. What happened to lower rates under deregulation?

The answer is that California's power producers have no restrictions on the prices they can charge for electricity, and regulators no longer set minimum energy reserve requirements to prevent power shortages. Advocates of deregulation said that prices and reserves would be set at optimum levels by the free market. But the opposite has been true. Power marketers restrict supplies by reducing the amount of electricity that is produced, creating shortages and price spikes (see Myth 4). Predictably, gaming the system has meant skyrocketing profits for power marketers in California.

An analysis of the effects on consumer prices in another deregulated energy industry—natural gas—is a good indication of what will happen to consumers' electric bills if they are left to the vagaries of a deregulated market. Since the natural gas industry was deregulated a decade ago, wellhead, or wholesale, costs have actually fallen. But the price at which natural gas is sold to residential consumers has skyrocketed. In 1984, just prior to complete deregulation, residential prices for natural gas were 44 percent above the wellhead price. By 1987, it was 110 percent above. By 1999, it was 181 percent above. At the same time, prices to larger, industrial consumers rose, but not as much as for residential consumers. In 1984, industrial prices were 28 percent above the wholesale price of electricity. In 1987, they were 39 percent of the wellhead price. By 1999, it was 42 percent of the wholesale price. This price discrimination indicates a noncompetitive market.

Even with high natural gas prices—which according to economic theory causes sellers to increase supplies—reserves are low and there are indications that some type of market manipulation may be occurring. It seems that we have our own natural gas cartel operating in the U.S., which behaves like OPEC [Organization of Petroleum Exporting Countries]. With government regulators no longer protecting consumers and defining the rules of the road, control has been ceded to a handful of energy companies that in many cases are also [in] the business of selling electricity in places like California.

At the very least, if the market is not being manipulated, years of experience show that the natural gas market is failing for consumers. After 15 years of higher prices, it is time to reexamine natural gas deregulation.

Meanwhile, we have a very different example set by publicly owned electric power systems. While energy companies defend their high prices, California's 30 communities with municipally owned and controlled power offer the same electricity at lower prices. The City of Los Angeles' Department of Water and Power charges 20 to 25 percent less than comparable privately run utilities elsewhere in the state.

Myth #3: Prices for electricity are being driven up because the demand for electricity is increasing.

Planning for new power plants is based on the need for electricity at the time of year that maximum usage of power occurs—the time of peak demand. Indeed, California's Independent System Operator (CAISO), the traffic cop for the transmission of electricity under the deregulated market, has records showing that the state's peak demand for electricity in 2000 occurred on July 12 and was approximately 45,600 megawatts. (For comparison, a large nuclear power plant is approximately 2000 megawatts.) California uses the most electricity in the summer, when air conditioners run.

CAISO uses this information about demand to find out how much energy must be produced by various plants to meet California's energy needs. The agency records the highest amounts of demand by hour within the state of

California. The data shows that while demand did soar in May, in four out of the past six months—July, August, October and December—California saw a lower peak demand in 2000 than during the same months in 1999.

Overall, according to the California Energy Commission and confirmed by California Public Utilities Commission President, Loretta Lynch, the average amount of electricity used throughout the day grows at about 2% a year. This does not mean that peak demand is growing; it does mean that consumers use more power at midnight because they are using their computers.

In fact, recently, there have been blackouts when demand was less than 30,000 megawatts, approximately 15,600 megawatts less demand than the peak amount of electricity needed in California in the summer. Obviously, it is supplies of electricity being held back, not demand that is causing the problems with deregulation.

Myth #4: The problems are being caused because there is not enough power to supply California.

So, why are suppliers short? *Because under deregulation, power producers have no incentive to run plants at full capacity.* As noted above, California has 55,500 megawatts of power generating capacity and 4,500 megawatts of power on contract. Following is a breakdown of plant ownership:

- unregulated power suppliers: 21,231 megawatts (40%)
- public agencies: 11,934 megawatts (23%)
- qualifying facilities, large industrial consumers and others: 11,745 megawatts (22%)
- utilities: 8,245 megawatts (15%)

Of this power, the Independent System Operator has access to approximately 45,000 megawatts to provide electricity for the state. But large numbers of power plants are not running at full capacity or are down for unscheduled maintenance, keeping supplies short.

The tighter the supply, the more prices rise. As much as 13,000 MW of capacity was off-line in January for undisclosed reasons. According to *The Wall Street Journal*, on August 2000, 461% percent more capacity was off-line than a year earlier.

Because details about why these plants are off-line is confidential, the public is literally left in the dark. According to CAISO, many suppliers are not even complying with the requirement to turn in an annual plan for when they will have plants off-line for maintenance, and there are no penalties for this lack of cooperation. Regardless of whether one suspects that power producers are intentionally taking capacity off-line to hike prices, these statistics illustrate that under deregulation, the public has little control over pricing and reliability.

The fact is that today, the state of California has access to more capacity than the 45,000 MW of summertime peak demand—the maximum amount used during the highest usage time of year.

California has 55,000 megawatts of in-state electricity generating capacity through about 1,000 power plants. In addition, the state is able to import about 4,500 megawatts of electricity, which is under existing long-term contracts. These thousands of megawatts of capacity could easily meet demand if wholesaler suppliers were not manipulating the system. The situation would be even better if energy efficiency strategies were maximized. New plants are not needed; instead, stricter scrutiny of existing plant operations is needed. Even so, many new plants are *already* under construction, which will even further increase the amount of electricity that is available.

Myth #5: California's environmental laws are preventing new power plants from being built in the state.

It is untrue that California's environmental laws have prevented new plants from being built and are responsible for the current crisis. As noted earlier, there is enough existing capacity tied into the state's grid to meet even summertime peak demand. And while the state's sensible environmental laws get the blame for the lack of new construction, it is important to note that California's utilities did not want to make investments in new power plants. The state's utilities blocked decisions by the CPUC to build new capacity because under deregulation, the utilities realized they would have assumed the economic risk for bad decisions—rather than consumers—who paid for past mistakes as part of rates.

Southern California Edison (SCE) even went so far as stopping the development of 1,500 MW of new renewable energy and cogeneration (the heat from industrial processes is used to generate electricity) projects. This more environmentally friendly electricity would have been available to help meet the current crisis, and would have cost under 5.5 cents per kilowatt-hour. But, SCE's Chief Executive Officer, John Bryson, in the mid-1990s petitioned the Federal Energy Regulatory Commission (FERC) to stop the construction of these projects.

Before deregulation, California had a planning process for building the infrastructure for the energy sources to meet demand. In 1993, this Biennial Resource Planning Update (BRPU) process set a price that was below 5.5 cents per kilowatt (a much lower price than the cost of power from long-term contracts today), and a bidding process was initiated. The cost of environmental damage was taken into consideration in the bidding process. The Public Utilities Commission accepted bids and planned to build 1,500 MW of new wind, geothermal and cogeneration plants. Bryson then started a petitioning process at FERC, which resulted in none of the generation being built because he did not want to risk investments in new capacity. FERC voted to not allow the California Utilities Commission to require the new projects. Today, California is suffering from the FERC's bad decision and Bryson's efforts to stop new renewable energy capacity from being built.

Even so some power plants were built, according to the agency that permits new power plants:

> In the 1990s before the state's electricity generation industry was restructured, the California Energy Commission certified 12 new power plants. Of these, three were never built. Nine plants are now in operation producing 952 megawatts of generation.... Since April 1999, the Energy Commission has approved nine major power plant projects with a combined generation capacity of 6,278 megawatts. Six power plants, with a generation capacity of 4,308 megawatts are now under construction, with 2,368 megawatts expected to be on-line by the end of the year 2001.
>
> In addition, another 14 electricity generating projects, totaling 6,734 megawatts of generation and an estimated capital investment of more than $4.3 billion, are currently being considered for licensing by the Commission.

Although new power plants are under construction and in the planning process, the best way to address California's energy needs is through energy efficiency measures and renewable energy projects. Building more centralized plants may be a way to obtain higher profits for power producers, but it is a poor investment in light of the new technologies that are rapidly becoming available. For instance, the expanded use of distributed generation, where small amounts of generation (roof top solar power is an example) is located on a utility's distribution system to help meet energy demand.

Energy efficiency is always the cheapest and best method of lowering the demand for electricity. It cuts energy use, saves consumers money, offers predictable financial requirements, and benefits the environment by reducing energy use. Examples include: the use of compact fluorescent bulbs—which last ten times longer than conventional ones and use one quarter of the energy; double-paned windows; and more efficient appliances and industrial production lines.

According to the Center for Renewable Energy and Sustainable Technology, higher energy efficiency standards for central air conditioners (over the course of its lifetime) would save as much electricity as more than 1.2 million Californians would use. And more efficient clothes washers would save the electricity consumed by more than 700,000 Californians.

Renewable energy projects should be built to replace old, dirty generation. Renewable energy projects can now be built at the same cost as conventional facilities. Today wind turbines show great promise, tomorrow, fuel cells are likely to change the face of energy production. Renewable energy offers dependable, even fixed-cost power that is particularly important in a state that is facing blackouts and price roller coasters.

Myth #6: Deregulation is good for the environment.

While deregulation creates short-term incentives to gouge consumers by artificially ensuring low supplies of electricity, in the long run deregulation creates economic incentives for power suppliers to sell more electricity. As prices rise, suppliers push to build new plants in an attempt to maximize profit. At the same time, deregulation provides an incentive to keep cheap, dirty coal power plants running longer. The market forces driving deregulation will not shut down old plants and replace them with cleaner ones. Instead, the old plants will run, and new plants will be built as well, because deregulation encourages more energy use.

This situation means that nationally the likely environmental effects of deregulation will be sharply increasing emissions, particularly if existing coal-fueled power plants remain exempt from air pollution standards.

In addition, because a speculative electricity market is inherently volatile, and because some suppliers have an alarming amount of market power, a larger reserve margin of power is necessary. The independent power producers are using the uncertainty of the market to push for relaxing environmental regulations, to drill for natural gas in sensitive areas and to build more power plants and more transmission lines.

If utility deregulation continues on its current course, not only will air pollution increase and ecologically sensitive areas be degraded, but our global climate will be further threatened by more greenhouse gases.

Myth #7: California's energy crisis is best resolved through state, not federal, actions (as stated by President Bush).

Unfortunately, the Clinton Administration promoted electricity deregulation relentlessly, and now the new Republican Administration is supporting the same reckless deregulation scheme that we are seeing unfold in California today.

The Bush administration argues that blame for the current crisis lies with the state: allow the utilities to pass their costs on to consumers and ease the state's environmental standards to quickly build new power plants to increase supply.

The cause of California's deregulation crisis is the result of the removal of any government oversight on producing and selling electricity. With government regulators no longer present to protect the public interest, power producers and marketers are charging outrageous prices for electricity, and the utilities then attempt to pass on the cost to consumers (see Myth 3).

While the Bush administration seems content to blame the state for the problems with deregulation and to claim that raising rates and building new power plants would solve everything, the federal government is sitting on the one action that will directly address today's high prices. Under the authority of the Federal Energy Regulatory Commission (FERC), which is now chaired by Bush-appointee Curt L. Hebert, Jr., the federal government is the sole entity that can impose cost-based rates on these power producers. If the administration was willing to order power plant owners to sell their product at the cost-of-service (the cost of generating power) and a reasonable profit, California's utilities could buy the electricity needed and the pressure to raise consumer's electric rates would be removed. Meanwhile, the state could investigate the price-gouging and act thoughtfully in solving the problems caused by deregulation.

But, Enron, Reliant, and the other power producers and power marketers operating in California heavily financed the Bush administration. Bush and his new energy secretary, Spencer Abraham, who lost his recent run for the Senate and who once advocated the abolition of DOE, received more than $2.5 million from energy interests during the campaign and for the inauguration events. The new power suppliers for California are making so much money from their profiteering that they will maintain pressure on the Bush Administration to keep the current system in place.

To date, the only federal action Bush has called for is to drill in the unique and pristine coastal area of Alaska's National Arctic Wildlife Refuge to tap into a supply of oil that would amount to only a six month supply of oil and would take 10 years to bring to market. Furthermore, oil is rarely used for electric power generation today.

Myth #8: California's three big utilities were forced, against their will, to sell their power plants.

As described in the introduction, California's three big utilities lobbied intensely to pass the 1996 deregulation bill, which provided incentives for them to sell their power plants. Some nuclear and hydropower facilities were retained by the utilities. The California utilities believed that they would thrive from electric utility deregulation and become international energy companies.

The sale of the power plants, along with the infusion of consumer-funded subsidies, gave the two utilities accelerated depreciation, enabling them to build up cash on their parent companies' balance sheets to finance the stock buyback plans and pour investments into Mission Energy, the National Energy Group and other unregulated divisions. According to a report released by TURN in October 2000, the generation owned or contracted by Pacific Gas and Electric (PG&E) and Southern California Edison (SCE) produced large profits between May and August of 2000, amounting to $2.7 billion. Because the power is credited to stranded costs, the average monthly collection of stranded costs was accelerated by 79% for PG&E and 56% for SCE. Accelerated depreciation has provided large amounts of cash for the utilities.

However, now that they have been beat at their own game by bigger and meaner companies like Enron, they are crawling back to the legislature and begging for another consumer bailout.

Myth #9: California's utilities are close to bankruptcy and need to be bailed out.

California's two major utilities, Southern California Edison and Pacific Gas & Electric, claim to have racked up such significant losses under deregulation that they are threatening to file for bankruptcy. In 1996, when the promise of huge profits loomed large they agreed to assume some risk. Now that the market has failed they are demanding that the state provide direct assistance, or else (they claim) they will no longer be able to afford to supply their customers with electricity.

But their parent companies, using the money they made from selling their power plants and from the bailout have spent more than $22 billion on power plants, stock buybacks and other purchases that far exceed their alleged $12 billion debt from California operations. Edison International and PG&E have done this both through those two companies and through affiliated companies, Mission Energy (a subsidiary of Edison International) and National Energy Group (a PG&E subsidiary).

Created in 1990, Mission Energy's revenues and profits didn't take off until 1999, when expensive investments began to pay off. A recent Public Citizen analysis showed that Mission Energy, along with a few other smaller Edison International subsidiaries, spent more than $10 billion on non-California investments since December 1998—more than double the SCE's stated debt of $5 billion. In addition, Edison International has spent $2.35 billion on stock buyback programs since deregulation began.

PG&E's high-growth subsidiary, National Energy Group, hasn't been as forthcoming, electing not to disclose the purchase price of many of its recent acquisitions. Information gleaned from several news reports reveals that since 1999, PG&E's purchases outside California and the Pacific Northwest have totaled at least $9 billion. This far eclipses PG&E's alleged $6.6 billion deficit from its California operations. PG&E spent more than $1 billion on its own stock buyback plans since the onset of deregulation.

Myth #10: Electricity deregulation is working in other states.

Electricity deregulation has passed (or been adopted by a regulatory process) in 23 states plus the District of Columbia. However, because of the situation in California, Utah has repealed its deregulation bill and New Mexico has delayed implementation of its deregulation legislation. Of the states that passed bills, only a handful of them have begun changing their energy supply systems. Some places, like Washington, D.C., negotiated long-term contracts at reasonable rates, which will put off by several years the disasters of a truly deregulated market. And in almost all states, deregulation is to be phased in over a period of years. To make the legislation politically viable, price caps, mandated rate reductions and other benefits that will be sunset were included.

Also, electric utilities across the country were given huge bailouts for their bad investments in nuclear power and other items as part of the deregulation deals in their states. These so-called "stranded costs" were passed on to consumers. According to a report by the Safe Energy Communications Council, utilities in 11 of the states that have deregulated (California, Illinois, Massachusetts, Michigan, Montana, New Hampshire, New Jersey, New York, Pennsylvania, Ohio and Texas) are demanding or have already received more than $112 billion to bail out their failed investments.

States such as Massachusetts, where utilities were bailed out, have had no electricity suppliers willing to serve residential suppliers. The idea that there is competition in the market has become a joke. Power suppliers that sprang up to serve customers in New England, Pennsylvania and New Jersey are now "dumping" their customers back to the old utilities. The new suppliers simply cannot compete in the region's electricity markets.

Pennsylvania, which has been touted as a deregulation success, does not really have a deregulated market. The state's utilities went through a regulatory process to determine how much their bailout should be. The cost of the bailout was included in the price of electricity that each utility can charge. Each investor-owned utility has a regulated price of electricity; depending on how large a settlement it received for its "stranded cost" recovery. This is basically a regulated price for electricity, which depending on the utility, will be in place for as many as nine years.

This regulated price of electricity is keeping prices in check in Pennsylvania. It means that suppliers must keep their prices lower than the regulated price to be competitive. For instance, PECO Energy has a winter price of 5.57 cents per kilowatt-hour. But many of the utilities in the region retained ownership of their plants, so suppliers must buy electricity from the utilities that are still regulated. This has meant that many suppliers have gone out of business.

No matter where deregulation has occurred, problems are already arising. For the past two summers, blackouts have plagued residents and businesses in other deregulated markets where prices on the wholesale market have spiked, most notably in Chicago, New York City and northern New Jersey.

New York City is an instance in which consumers were subject to the vagaries of the market and prices skyrocketed because of the volatile, speculative market for electricity. New York used a regulatory process to deregulate. Consolidated Edison, which serves New York City, *was* allowed to pass all of its costs on to consumers. So when price spikes occurred, bills skyrocketed, raising rates 43% for residential consumers and 49% for commercial users. Obviously, passing on the cost of a speculative market for electricity will not make deregulation a success.

Additionally, deregulation is encouraging dozens of mergers and acquisitions in the electric industry. We have seen this type of consolidation in other industries, and it has meant higher prices and poorer service in most cases for consumers.

We've seen what mergers do to consumers when we look at the airline industry. The largest airlines have engaged in numerous mergers, reducing competitors at every turn. They are masters at price discrimination, forcing business travelers to pay fares several times higher than vacation travelers, who can plan for travel weeks or months in advance. They also use their ticketing computers to send price signals to each other in a game of collusion that keeps profits up. Major airlines maintain "fortress hubs" where they have a monopoly on air service, allowing them to set prices due to lack of competing airlines. Deregulation in the airline industry has also led to terrible service, which is now legendary.

Consolidation does not lead to competition, lower prices or better service. On the contrary, it allows a handful of companies to exert market power and prevent consumers from receiving good service at reasonable prices. But, unfortunately, utility analysts predict that only a handful of companies will survive deregulation, if it continues to be embraced, and that these same companies will sell any number of services. This concept, called convergence, will mean that consumers will be forced to use a single company to provide necessary services such as power, water, telecommunications and Internet access. Prices for all of these services will be "bundled" (included in a single price), which will leave little room for price comparison.

Policymakers should think seriously, and there should be a public debate, before deregulation reaches this level. The bottom line is that if deregulation doesn't help real Americans, we shouldn't continue to pursue it.

Conclusion

Electricity is an absolute necessity that should not be a speculated product. Consumers have a right to affordable energy, produced in the most environmentally sustainable fashion possible. But, when treated as a speculative commodity, the cost and supply of electricity becomes uncertain. This situation invites price-gouging and profiteering, as we are witnessing today in California.

We must critically analyze the intentionally perpetuated myths by the proponents of deregulation, because it is clear that what many pro-deregulation politicians are saying just is not true. We need to carefully look at their assertions, or we will not only continue to bailout utilities, we will [also have] higher prices, less reliability, and a threatened environment. It is time to hold policymakers accountable for the mess they have created, and roll back dangerous electric utility deregulation schemes.

POSTSCRIPT

Should California's Electric Utility Industry Be Deregulated?

Much is riding on who is right and who is wrong in this debate. In large measure, this is because many states were expected to follow California's lead by passing their own utility deregulation legislation, and a number did follow that lead in the last few years of the 1990s. Then-governor Pete Wilson aggressively pursued the passage of this legislation in California, perhaps in the hope that his vocal and active support would gain him national recognition, which he could use to pursue his political ambitions in a national arena. For whatever reason, Governor Wilson went state to state "selling" his deregulation plan to his fellow governors, and by the year 2000 four states had joined California by initiating their own legislation: Massachusetts, New York, Pennsylvania, and Rhode Island.

Pennsylvania is perhaps the most successful deregulation experiment to date. Governor Tom Ridge initiated regulatory reform in the electric power industry in December 1996, not long after the California state legislature passed its deregulation package. Unlike in California, however, Pennsylvania's deregulation was put into place in phases. It took until January 1999 to put the system into place, and another full year passed before consumers could "shop around" for electric power suppliers. There are other fundamental differences between the Pennsylvania case and the California experience. One notable difference is the fact that although consumers could search the marketplace for the most economical electricity supplier, the utilities remained regulated in the transmission of this power. Perhaps the most important difference is the fact that Pennsylvania's utilities were not obligated to divest their generating capacity. They could if they cared to divest, but their only requirement was to "unbundle" their services—that is, they were to separate their role as a source of electric power from their corporate capacity to transmit that power. See Adrian T. Moore and Lynne Kiesling, "Powering Up California: Policy Alternatives for the California Energy Crisis," *Reason Public Policy Institute Policy Study No. 280* (February 2001).

State governments were not alone in experimenting with deregulating electric power. A number of national governments moved in this direction during the waning years of the twentieth century. Deregulation was put into place in England and Wales, New Zealand, Norway, Australia, and several South American countries, including Chile. See Vernon L. Smith, "Regulatory Reform in the Electric Power Industry," *Regulation* vol. 19, no. 1, 1996.

Free-market economists are keen to deregulate all markets, including the market for electric power. Readers should take care to note this bias. There is, however, a nicely balanced essay that is very insightful. Although Severin

Borenstein's essay "The Trouble With Electricity Markets (and Some Solutions)," POWER Working Paper PWP 081 (January 2001), is more balanced, it does not in any way ignore market forces. Indeed, it provides the reader with an excellent market analysis of the root causes of the energy crisis in California and points toward some possible policy solutions. Borenstein's essay was published by the Program on Workable Energy Regulation (POWER). This program is part of the Energy Institute at the University of California, whose Web site is http://www.ucei.org.

In his essay, Borenstein asserts that there are fundamental problems with the market for electricity wherever that electricity is being provided. That is, this crisis is not unique to California. The basic problem, as Borenstein sees it, is that the demand for electricity is price inelastic, while the supply faces "strict production constraints." What he means is that this is a capital-intensive industry and that utilities are reluctant to create large amounts of expensive excess capacity to handle those rare occasions when there is an extraordinary "peak load" event—a prolonged heat spell, perhaps. This desire on the part of utilities to put in place the optimum-sized generating facility is frustrated by the fact that once electric power is produced, it is very difficult and expensive to store. The net result is that the industry is constantly faced with the potential for a mismatched supply and demand, and these sharp swings from a shortage to a surplus result in a natural volatility in prices and, therefore, in profitability. This is why the grid systems have come into being. Grids serve as a mechanism to shift the excess supplies in one area to areas that are experiencing shortages. When a whole region experiences a shortage, there is no inventory of electricity to fall back upon, and a crisis of brownouts or rolling blackouts occurs.

ISSUE 6

Should Markets Be Allowed to Solve the Shortage in Body Parts?

YES: Charles T. Carlstrom and Christy D. Rollow, from "The Rationing of Transplantable Organs: A Troubled Lineup," *The Cato Journal* (Fall 1997)

NO: Nancy Scheper-Hughes, from "The End of the Body: The Global Traffic in Organs for Transplant Surgery," http://sunsite.berkeley.edu/biotech/organswatch/pages/cadraft.html (May 14, 1998)

ISSUE SUMMARY

YES: Free-market economists Charles T. Carlstrom and Christy D. Rollow argue that the simple use of market incentives can go a long way to solving the shortage of transplantable organs. They contend that although some people may have "qualms about the buying and selling of organs, the cost of our current approach is that shortages will remain endemic, and ultimately, more lives will be lost."

NO: Professor of anthropology Nancy Scheper-Hughes acknowledges that markets in and of themselves are not evil. But she asserts that "by their very nature markets are indiscriminate, promiscuous and inclined to reduce everything, including human beings, their labor and even their reproductive capacity to the status of commodities, to things that can be bought, sold, traded, and stolen."

The first human heart transplant in the United States took place a surprisingly short time ago. Dr. Michael DeBakey performed the first successful coronary artery bypass graft in 1964, and less than four years later, on May 3, 1968, Dr. Denton Cooley and his team of surgeons shocked the world by announcing that they had successfully transplanted a heart in Everett Thomas, who lived for 204 days with a heart donated by a 15-year-old girl. Until Cooley and DeBakey achieved this revolutionary medical breakthrough, those with progressive heart failure were doomed to die. There was simply no hope of reversing the process that destroys this vital organ.

Cooley and his team performed their second operation, which was quickly followed by a series of other transplants in their Houston, Texas, operating theater. At first there was no real shortage of transplantable organs; the carnage on U.S. highways alone was enough to supply the limited number of healthy hearts that these teams of surgeons could reasonably expect to transplant. But as the word spread among those who were dying of various heart conditions, the demand for this radical surgery skyrocketed.

Any time that a shortage appears, there are several ways to mediate between those who demand and those who control the supply. In a market economy, price performs the role of the "grand allocater." In brief, whoever is willing to pay the highest price moves to the top of the waiting list. Applying this model to body parts, those who are less fortunate in terms of their resource holdings become less fortunate in terms of access to the limited supply of organs. This seemingly "cold-blooded" solution is quick to bring a chorus of protests. But what are the alternatives? Can lessons be learned from parallel situations? Should a shortage of human hearts and other transplantable organs that are needed to save lives be treated like a shortage of gasoline, which fuels our cars, or a shortage of electricity, which runs air conditioners and traffic signals? In the cases of gasoline and electricity, price controls have been used to address the shortages.

How did these market interventions work? The gasoline shortages that arose in the 1970s were a result of the Organization of Petroleum Exporting Countries' (OPEC) successful attempts to artificially restrict the world's supply of crude oil. As a result, the price of gasoline skyrocketed. Both the Nixon administration in the early 1970s and the Carter administration at the end of the 1970s responded by imposing "ceiling prices." The price of regular grade gasoline was not allowed to rise above $1.75 a gallon. Since the equilibrium price of gasoline was well above this level, a shortage resulted. A serious question arose: Who would get the limited supply? In a market arrangement, those who were willing to pay the highest price would get the gasoline. In the case of the price-controlled world of the 1970s, those who were willing to wait in long lines got the limited supply. Whoever was in line first got a chance to buy the limited quantity that was available. Is that any more "just" or "fair" than a market solution?

In the following selection, Charles T. Carlstrom and Christy D. Rollow suggest that a price-controlled world is no more just or fair than a controlled system and that, worse, this world of market controls is inefficient. They advocate the use of market incentives to solve the shortage. In their view, markets are not only a more efficient solution but a solution that will actually save more lives than the current system. In the second selection, Nancy Scheper-Hughes takes serious exception to Carlstrom and Rollow's position. She asks, Which lives will be saved? Will those who are poor be condemned to death simply because they are poor? Will the organs that are needed for transplants be "harvested" from both rich and poor equally, or will only the poor be economically blackmailed into selling their organs so that they can survive in our market-dominated world?

**Charles T. Carlstrom and
Christy D. Rollow**

 **YES**

The Rationing of Transplantable Organs: A Troubled Lineup

On June 6, 1995, baseball legend Mickey Mantle was placed on the transplant waiting list after being diagnosed with end-stage liver disease caused by hepatitis, liver cancer, and years of alcohol abuse. Two days later, he underwent surgery, despite the fact that the average liver transplant patient waits 67 days. His doctors claimed that Mantle received no preferential treatment; rather, his gravely ill status placed him at the top of the list. Yet, because of Mantle's original liver cancer, he died two months later. Given that 804 patients died in 1995 while awaiting a liver transplant, Mantle's case and others like his raise questions about which of the 7,400 liver patients on the waiting list should have received the 3,900 livers that became available that year. Society has to confront this and similar questions because of the severe shortage of transplantable organs.

Organs are not the only goods rationed in the United States—they are just the most controversial. Hunting permits, oil drilling leases, cellular telephone licenses, and radio frequencies are other examples of rationed resources. The distinguishing feature of these goods is that prices alone are not permitted to allocate the commodity; as a result, someone must determine how they will be distributed.

There are many ways that goods can be rationed, such as lotteries, first-come, first-served, and coupons. As a consequence of price controls, gasoline was rationed in the 1970s, largely on a first-come, first-served basis.[1] The result was long lines at the pumps and an effective price of gasoline that included both the direct cost of purchasing gas plus the indirect cost of queuing. Although some view such a system as equitable, its inefficiencies are obvious once we factor in the time and even the gas wasted as people waited in line. Rationing also played a role during World War II, when the government issued coupons for purchasing staples such as meat and butter. This solution was also seen as equitable in many quarters, although, like lotteries, it did not ensure that those who most needed or valued a good received it.

This conflict between equity and efficiency arises whenever goods are rationed. Determining the most equitable way to allocate gasoline and food is

From Charles T. Carlstrom and Christy D. Rollow, "The Rationing of Transplantable Organs: A Troubled Lineup," *The Cato Journal*, vol. 17, no. 2 (Fall 1997). Copyright © 1997 by The Cato Institute. Reprinted by permission. References omitted.

difficult, but deciding how to allocate transplantable organs is infinitely more complex. The complexity stems from the fact that someone must choose who receives lifesaving transplants—a decision that impacts efficiency through the number of lives lost over time. Since both equity and efficiency are paramount when rationing goods, the market for transplantable organs is an ideal case to illustrate this conflict. ⟨Are organs (lives) to be considered "goods?"⟩

Ten Americans die each day while awaiting an organ transplant, and the problem is becoming more severe. Between 1988 and 1994, the median waiting time nearly doubled (see Figure 1). It is imperative, then, that society find ways to increase the supply of organs, even through buying and selling. For most goods, prices are allowed to adjust to provide incentives, thus ensuring their most efficient allocation. While some people would understandably have qualms about the buying and selling of organs, the cost of our current approach is that shortages will remain endemic, and ultimately, more lives will be lost. Allowing monetary payments may not completely eliminate this shortage, but it will undoubtedly increase the number of organs available.

This paper examines the inherent difficulties of rationing by analyzing the market for transplantable organs. We look at the current procurement and allocation system and discuss various proposals to increase the efficiency of the market. Although the particulars of this market are unique to organ transplantation, society faces similar choices whenever prices are regulated and shortages occur. As Dr. Arthur L. Caplan, director of the Center for Bioethics at the University of Pennsylvania, notes, "It [organ transplantation] is a case study of rationing. It is of fundamental interest to every American. All of us will have to confront the decision of what is fair in the allocation of scarce resources. This is a canary in a mine that all of us will have to enter."

Rationing Organs: The Current System

In 1984, Congress passed the National Organ Transplant Act, which outlawed the buying and selling of internal organs.[2] The National Task Force on Organ Transplantation recommended to Congress in 1986 that organ donation remain purely voluntary, governed by the altruism of the donor or the donor's family. Additionally, it suggested that the "selection of patients for transplant not be subject to favoritism, discrimination on the basis of race or sex, or ability to pay" (U.S. House of Representatives 1991: 44). This nondiscriminatory clause is crucial, because when prices are regulated and shortages occur, goods must be rationed. Since discrimination is one form of rationing, it is costless when markets are not allowed to operate freely.[3] In contrast, in an unregulated market, individuals and firms must forgo profits if they wish to discriminate—that is, engage in nonprice rationing.

Another concern was that political clout would influence the allocation process; hence, an independent nonprofit organization was selected to operate the Transplantation Network under the auspices of the Department of Health and Human Services. In October 1986, the United Network for Organ Sharing (UNOS) was awarded this federal contract. The group's task is twofold: establish criteria that match donors with waiting recipients, and develop policies that

Figure 1

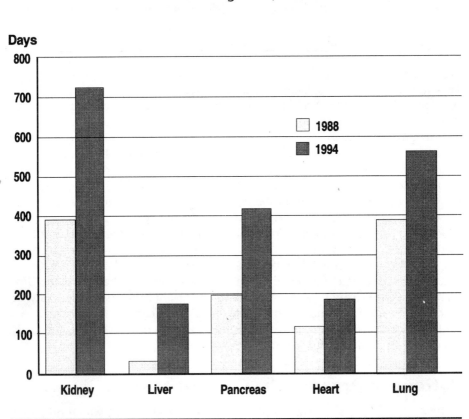

Median Waiting Times, 1988–94

Source: UNOS (1995)

facilitate the procurement of organs. Figure 2 illustrates that within the current voluntary system, UNOS has been largely unsuccessful in increasing donations; supply increases have been minimal compared to demand. The major difficulties in devising an equitable organ distribution system are summarized in Table 1.

The Sickest-First Policy

Many contend that in a fair system, organs would be given to those who "need them the most—the so-called sickest-first policy." UNOS uses this strategy in ranking liver and heart patients as part of its policy of minimizing patient deaths. The approach is myopic, however, since it ignores the impact that today's decisions have on the number of deaths over time.[4] The Mickey Mantle case is a stark example because Mantle, and hence his liver, died two months

not valid support just b/c he's famous!

Figure 2

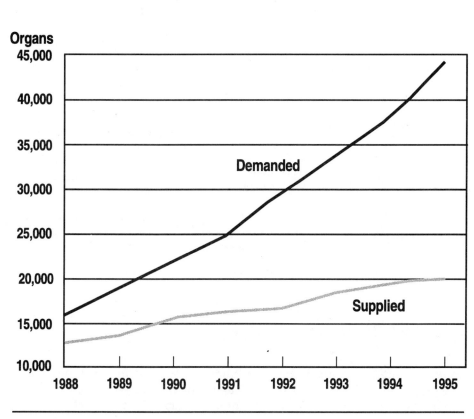

Organs Supplied and Demanded, 1988–95

Source: UNOS (1996)

after surgery. Indeed, the two-year graft (organ) survival rate for patients who are in intensive care prior to their liver transplant is approximately 50 percent, compared to 75 percent for those who are still relatively healthy. These groups' individual two-year survival rates differ by 10 to 15 percentage points.

Given the differences in two-year survival rates, the cost of transplanting 100 fewer livers into intensive-care patients today would be a loss of 85 to 90 lives versus 100 over a two-year period.[5] Since graft survival rates are higher for healthier patients, the number needing retransplantation would decline. Thus, another benefit of this one-time policy change would be to free organs for others. Another advantage is that by transplanting livers into healthier individuals, the number of critically ill patients would decrease, thereby saving additional lives. On net, this policy change would be more efficient because it would save more lives.

Table 1

Organ Rationing Schemes		
Allocation Methods	Benefits	Costs
Waiting time	Equitable	Inappropriate matching; organ wastage; no consideration of urgency
Priority to sickest first	Equitable	Higher retransplantation and death rates; less benefit overall
Priority to sickest last	Higher overall survival; less retransplantation	Sickest patients die
Best biological match	Higher overall survival; less retransplantation	Fewer transplants for certain groups, including highly sensitized patients and some minorities

Source: UNOS (1977)

The Best Biological Match

Another allocation method (the one emphasized for kidneys) is biological matching, which is measured by the quality of the antigen match between donor and patient.[6] Once a kidney becomes available, UNOS searches among waiting-list patients and ranks them according to their biological match with that organ. When four of the six most critical antigens match, the one-year graft survival rate is 13 percentage points higher than for a total antigen mismatch. Four years later, that difference increases to 20 percent.

Instead of biological matching, waiting time alone could be emphasized —the first-come, first-served approach.[7] While this may seem more equitable, the cost of such a policy change would be enormous. In the first year alone, the average biological match would decrease by nearly three antigens, and graft survival rates would fall by about 6 percentage points. Even discounting subsequent declines in graft survival rates, the number of kidney transplant candidates eventually would increase by nearly 5,600, translating into approximately 202 more waiting-list deaths each year.[8] The importance of graft survival is obvious, given that nearly one-quarter of those on the kidney waiting list have received a transplant previously.

Despite their emphasis on biological matching, UNOS distributes kidneys on a regional basis, mandating that kidneys procured within a region stay local.[9] If, on the other hand, kidneys were distributed nationally, the pool of potential recipients would increase, thereby increasing the likelihood of finding a patient with a good antigen match. Thus, distributing kidneys nationally would expand the average biological match. This policy change not only would save lives, but also would eliminate inequities caused by regional variations in waiting times.[10]

Discrimination in Kidney Allocation

Certain groups of patients wait longer than others for kidney transplants and, because of equity concerns, are given special consideration. For example, highly sensitized patients are much more likely to reject an organ transplant because of antibodies acquired from multiple blood transfusions or from rejecting a previous transplant. UNOS gives them preference when a kidney is found that will not necessarily be rejected; otherwise, they may never be transplanted. Giving highly sensitized patients preference can be extremely costly, however, because it reduces the size of the waiting-recipient pool searched. In effect, UNOS limits its search to the prioritized group unless a match outside the group is considerably higher. Thus, the likelihood of finding a well-matched kidney decreases, along with patient and graft survival rates. Since highly sensitized patients make up less than 3 percent of all kidney patients awaiting transplants, discriminating for them is likely to cost more than if the group receiving preference were larger.

An even greater preference is given to patients with type-O blood. Although organs from donors with type-O blood can potentially be transplanted into patients with any blood type, transplant candidates with O blood can receive only an organ of the same type. Thus, to ensure that these patients' waits are not substantially longer, UNOS mandates that kidneys from O donors will go only to O patients, with the exception of perfectly matched kidneys. The cost of this policy is that potentially good matches are forgone.

Other groups, such as blacks, also spend a disproportionate amount of time awaiting transplants. The median waiting time for black kidney patients is twice as long as it is for whites. This has led many to conclude that UNOS's policies are inherently racist and that blacks should receive preference similar to that given to highly sensitized patients. The longer waiting time, however, is not due to discrimination but to a disproportionate number of blacks who suffer from hypertension and diabetes—the two major causes of kidney failure.

Blacks represent 29 percent of all patients with end-stage renal disease, while they make up only 12 percent of the population and donate less than 12 percent of all kidneys. These numbers are important because the quality of the biological match is usually better when both the donor and the recipient are of the same race. The fact that blacks demand more kidney transplants as a share of their population and that the supply of kidneys from blacks is, if anything, slightly less than this figure explains the wide discrepancy between black and white waiting times.[11] Thus, a policy change giving preference to blacks not only would be more inefficient, costing additional lives, but also would violate UNOS's directive not to discriminate.

Encouraged Volunteerism: The Need for Incentives

Changes in the way UNOS rations organs can potentially decrease waiting times and save lives, but major reductions in waiting-list deaths, and thus improvements in efficiency, will require a substantial increase in organ donations. Table 2 shows the gap between the number of available organs and the number of people who need a kidney, liver, pancreas, heart, or lung transplant. Although the shortages vary, most of them are critical and have shown little response to public awareness programs, professional education efforts, or legislation. "Routine inquiry laws, for example, require hospital personnel to inform the families of potential donors about their option to donate. In fact, doctors still mention this opportunity only two-thirds of the time.[12]

increase AWARENESS!!!

Table 2

U.S. Organ Waiting List and Transplant Statistics

Organ	Quantity Demand (as of 12/25/96)	Quantity Supply (January–December 1996)
Total kidney	36, 013	11, 949
Cadaveric		8, 560
Living		3, 389
Liver	7, 467	4, 058
Pancreas	1, 786	1, 022
Heart	3, 935	2, 381
Lung	2, 546	844

Note: Multiple organ transplants are counted as more than one organ.

Source: UNOS (1997)

Trading Organs

The only way to increase the supply of organs is to increase the number of cadaveric organs, with the exception of kidneys, for which there is also the possibility of living donations.[13] More than one-quarter of the 11,700 kidneys donated each year come from living related individuals—an impressive number considering that kidney removal requires the donor to be hospitalized for five to seven days and to spend two to three months convalescing.[14]

What can be done to further increase the supply of kidneys from living donors? Currently, only 7 percent of these donations are from nonrelated individuals (primarily spouses), mainly because kidneys from nonrelated donors are usually poor matches or of the wrong blood type. To increase donations,

UNOS could facilitate the trading of kidneys, allowing patients to receive a well-matched kidney in exchange for a kidney from a spouse or close friend. This policy would increase kidney donations from both related and nonrelated sources. For instance, a patient's relative or spouse may be willing to donate a kidney, but because they have the wrong blood type, they are not suitable donors for that individual.[15]

Financial Incentives

Although altruism can be a powerful factor in motivating organ donations, it works best within families and cannot be expected to function as efficiently in the market for cadaveric organs. Individuals may sign anatomical donor cards indicating their wishes, but in practice, procurement agencies will remove organs only with familial consent. Thus, to increase supply, it is necessary to provide families with additional incentives. This is especially true given the relatively few deaths (10,000 to 12,000 annually) that occur in such a way that the deceased's organs are suitable for transplantation.

To increase donations, we need to consider financial incentives mimicking those that prices provide in a market economy. Perhaps the simplest approach is to give tax incentives to families who agree to donation. Donated organs already go to UNOS, a nonprofit organization; therefore, a monetary value would need to be assigned to organs only for tax purposes. To significantly increase the donor pool, society should also reconsider its position against the buying and selling of cadaveric organs. Allowing payments to surviving family members is another way of providing market incentives.[16]

To operate efficiently, the structure of this market would still require a centralized agency like UNOS to facilitate the matching process. Donor and recipient information is critical, since an individual's willingness to pay would depend on the quality of the antigen match with the available organ. One possible market structure would be to grant authority to buy and sell organs exclusively to the federal government, an approach suggested by Nobel laureate Gary S. Becker.

Shifting Rents

A common misperception about situations in which goods are not allowed to be bought and sold is that their market value is zero. An unintended consequence of price restrictions, however, is that the quantity supplied falls and the good becomes extremely valuable. To take advantage of the difference between the regulated price and the market's valuation, black markets tend to develop. Even if the price of the good does not rise, the actual cost may increase because of queuing costs, as in the case of gasoline price controls.

Black markets for transplantable organs have not developed in the United States, but it is possible that the price of transplants is higher, because organs cannot be legally sold. The law allows for "reasonable payments to all who participate in the organ donation process." The ambiguity of this term provides an opportunity for organ procurement organizations (OPOs) to artificially inflate prices. Currently, they receive approximately $25,000 for retrieving just the kidneys from a cadaver. An interesting, but as yet unresolved, question is how much of this $25,000 includes an implicit market price for the organ.

Other medical personnel (transplant surgeons, hospitals, etc.) also benefit financially from the organ procurement process, and are probably collecting some of these profits, also known as rents. Rents accrue whenever the quantity of a good is artificially restricted, thereby giving organizations monopolistic power. In the case of organs, the price, not the quantity per se, is restricted; however, the net effect is the same. Because of this, the shadow price (value) and hence the amount collected are likely to depend on the relative scarcity of the organ. Liver transplants are among the most expensive transplant surgeries —$300,000 on average—and as Table 2 indicates, livers are in especially short supply.

Figure 3 illustrates this concept in the market for transplantable organs, where S_c represents the supply of organs under the current system, and P_H represents the price that would clear the market.[17] This is the highest price, over and above normal fees, that a hospital can potentially charge for a transplant. Area $OP_H aO_c$ shows the maximum rents that would be collected.

It is clear, however, that all of these rents are not being collected, given current shortages. Yet, it is equally clear that some rents are being collected. For example, it is particularly telling that OPOs keep procured organs in their local area, even though UNOS's policies sometimes dictate otherwise. This is frequently true when OPOs are affiliated with hospitals' transplant centers, in which case the potential profits of keeping organs in-house can be substantial. Thus, there is an implicit market price, P, between zero and P_H that is being charged. At that price, the value of rents would be area $OPbO_c$. If P is above P^*, as shown, then selling organs would actually lower the total price of a transplant (including the equilibrium price of the organ, P^*). Similarly, if P is below the market-clearing price, the total price of a transplant would increase by less than P^*. Thus, allowing organs to be sold would increase their supply, lower their market value, and shift payments from OPOs, hospitals, and surgeons to family members.

Even if the price of transplantation did rise by the full amount of P^*, the money going to donors' families ("death benefits") would likely pale in comparison to the overall price of the operation. Consider the case where the family benefit is $5,000 and rent shifting does not occur. When allocated among two kidneys, a heart, liver, and pancreas, the extra cost per organ is probably closer to $1,000, an insignificant amount compared to the price of a transplant.

Equity Issues

Selling organs would not favor the rich at the expense of the poor, as many argue, since those receiving organ payments would likely have lower average incomes. Organ recipients, both rich and poor, would also benefit from the increased supply of organs. Currently, Medicare pays for kidney transplants,

Figure 3

The Market for Transplantable Organs

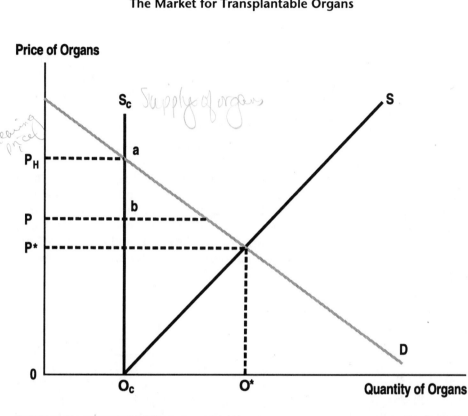

Price of Organs

while 90 percent of liver and heart transplants are covered by Medicare, Medicaid, and private insurance.[18] Each additional organ supplied benefits everyone, regardless of wealth.

Repealing the prohibition against the buying and selling of organs could lessen the disparity between black and white waiting times for kidneys. Because the antigen match is usually higher for individuals of the same race, any policy change that increases the percentage of black donors from its present level of 12 percent will decrease their waiting time. Thus, organ payments are more likely to persuade people of lower average income, including blacks, to donate, even if the payment amount is the same across all groups.

Given the higher demand for kidneys from black donors, in the absence of nondiscriminatory laws, payments to individual black families would likely be higher than payments to whites. But even without government assistance, this would not aggravate income inequality, since the extra amount paid by blacks would largely go to blacks. Given that Medicare (and frequently Medicaid) pays for kidney transplants, if anything, income inequality would be reduced by allowing organs to be sold.

Budgetary Concerns

Budgetary concerns are also misplaced. As previously noted, buying and selling organs may not increase transplantation costs at all, and even if it does, this policy change would still save Medicare money. It costs Medicare more than $40,000 annually to dialyze each kidney patient, while the cost of a transplant and subsequent medication is about $100,000 the first year and $12,000 per year thereafter. Because of this, the Health Care Financing Administration estimates that transplantation is considerably more cost effective than continued dialysis.

For example, if the average life of a transplanted kidney were only three years, the budgetary impact of organ payments would be neutral. The median graft survival rate, however, is closer to six years. Therefore, as long as the family benefit is less than $180,000 ($90,000 per kidney), the government will save money. Since the vast majority (nearly 70 percent) of all waiting-list patients are waiting for kidneys, each additional dollar spent encouraging families to donate will save taxpayer money.

Conclusion

Rationing is considered anathema to most Americans, yet it is necessary when prices are regulated. Goods are frequently rationed by simplistic methods such as lotteries or first-come, first-served. These may be more "equitable" approaches, but they are also among the most inefficient and can ultimately harm everyone involved. The inefficiencies are particularly pronounced in the market for transplantable organs, where costs are measured in human lives.

Deciding what is fair and who should be first in line for organ transplants is especially troubling and difficult. Dr. Mark Siegler, who directs the University of Chicago clinical ethics program, has stated that "all alcoholics should go to the bottom of the transplant list... yet Dr. Siegler [also] said he would exempt Mickey Mantle from his rule because the baseball legend is 'a real American hero'... [W]e have got to take them with all their warts and failures and treat them differently." It is especially important that UNOS resolve these issues given the current prohibition against the buying and selling of organs.

The cost of this prohibition is that lives are being lost. Additional incentives, including monetary, are required if cadaveric organ donations are to increase substantially. Even if these incentives do not eliminate the need for rationing, each additional organ procured will reduce the difficult, and sometimes arbitrary, decisions that UNOS must make. While many feel that the distribution of organs is too important to be left to market forces, ultimately, it is too important not to be.

Notes

1. Some states developed other rationing schemes based on license plate numbers and birthdays. These were largely ineffective in reducing queuing.

2. Specifically, the law prohibits the selling of organs if the transfer affects interstate commerce. Therefore, states may allow payments for organs, as long as the organs stay within state boundaries. However, given the current distribution system, states find it problematic to allow the selling of organs. Thus, the 1984 law has effectively prohibited a market in transplantable organs.

3. There may be social costs associated with discrimination, but it is costless for the individual firm.

4. A similar tradeoff exists during wartime with the triage of combat victims. This system maximizes overall survival by allowing the most critically ill soldiers to die.

5. This assumes that all intensive-care patients would die within two years without a transplant.

6. Biological matching is not considered for livers and hearts because of time constraints. Ordinarily, when transplanting kidneys, a patient's health status is not considered given the alternative of dialysis.

7. Currently, UNOS gives only slight priority to waiting time.

8. Estimate is based on authors' calculations.

9. The exception is if an individual with a perfect match is identified in another region.

10. There are costs involved in distributing organs nationally, because of increases in ischemic (preservation) time. These costs are small for kidneys, but large for other organs such as hearts. The feasibility of distributing livers nationally is currently being debated.

11. Nevertheless, many argue that steps should be taken to end "discrimination. As a result, the number of black transplant coordinators has been increased in an effort to ensure that blacks have equal access to transplants. Not surprisingly, these efforts have failed.

12. One reason for the law's failure is lack of enforcement. There is a remarkable belief that monitoring is unnecessary. One staff member from Oregon's Health Department expresses it this way: "In a small state one does not need to coerce people to comply, especially with a requirement that is perceived as good policy."

13. Recently, however, doctors successfully transplanted a segment (lobe) of liver from a living donor.

14. A new laparoscopic procedure could reduce the recovery time from two to three months to two to three weeks. Doctors and ethicists are divided over the ethics of allowing living kidney donations.

15. UNOS's procedures do allow for the trading of cadaveric organs. For example, when one region receives a perfectly matched kidney from outside the area, UNOS requires that the receiving region eventually reimburse the sending region with a payback kidney.

16. The extent to which payments would elicit donations is unclear. The answer will likely come from pilot programs, such as the one recently introduced in Pennsylvania. Residents are offered the opportunity to contribute one dollar to a "Donor Awareness Trust Fund" when they renew their drivers' licenses or complete their state income tax forms. Up to 10 percent of this fund (a maximum of $3,000) can be redistributed to families of deceased donors for hospital, medical, and funeral costs.

17. Actually, the notion of market-clearing in this market is ambiguous. By convention, an organ shortage is defined to occur when the quantity demanded (as measured by waiting-list patients) exceeds the annual supply. At any point in time, however, the quantity of organs demanded will exceed the available supply, even in a free market. Effectively, the relevant time frame for market-clearing should be organ-specific and should depend on the mortality rate of those awaiting transplants.

18. Medicare covers almost all kidney recipients and pays 80 percent of expenses. The remaining 20 percent is picked up by either private insurance or Medicaid.

NO ⬅

Nancy Scheper-Hughes

The End of the Body

The Global Economy and Brute Life

In a recent issue of *Atlantic Monthly* (January 1998) George Soros, best known as a world-class billionaire financier, analyzed some of the deficiencies of the global capitalist economy. It is a fairly elementary exercise, but coming from a person in his position, one tends to sit up and take notice. The benefits of world capitalism, Mr. Soros notes, are unevenly distributed. Capital is in a better position than labor. And, surely it is better to be situated at the center of the global economy than at the peripheries. Given the inherent instability of the global financial system, *busts* will inevitably follow *booms,* like night the day, and capital tends to return to its centers leaving the minor players in faraway places high and dry. Meanwhile, the rapid growth of global monopolies have compromised the authority of states and weakened their regulatory functions.

But what bothers Mr. Soros most is the erosion of social values and social cohesion in the face of the increasing dominance of anti-social market values. Not that markets are to be blamed, of course. By their very nature markets are indiscriminate, promiscuous and inclined to reduce everything, including human beings, their labor and even their reproductive capacity to the status of commodities, to things that can be bought, sold, traded, and stolen. So, while, according to Mr. Soros, a Market Economy is generally a good thing, we cannot live by markets alone. "Open" and democratic societies require strong social institutions to serve such vital goals as social justice, political freedom, bodily integrity and other human rights. The real dilemma, as Mr. Soros sees it, is one of uneven development. The evolution of the global market has outstripped the development of a mediating global society.

Indeed, amidst the neo-liberal readjustments of virtually all contemporary societies, North and South, we are experiencing today a rapid depletion, an "emptying out" even, of the traditional modernist, humanist, and pastoral ideologies and practices. But meanwhile, new mediations between capital and work, between bodies and the state, belonging and extra-territoriality, and even between, social exclusion and medical-technological inclusion are taking shape. So, rather than a conventional story of the sad decline of humanistic

From Nancy Scheper-Hughes, "The End of the Body: The Global Traffic in Organs for Transplant Surgery," http://sunsite.berkeley.edu/biotech/organswatch/pages/cadraft.html (May 14, 1998). Copyright © 1998 by Organs Watch. Reprinted by permission of the author. References omitted. An adapted version of this article was published as "The Global Traffic in Human Organs," *Current Anthropology*, vol. 41, no. 2 (April 2000).

social values and social relations, our discussion is tethered to a frank recognition that the conventional grounds on which those modernist values and practices were based have shifted beyond recognition.

Nowhere, perhaps, are these processes more transparent than in the rapid dissemination in the past decade of organ transplantation technologies and practices which under the ideal conditions of an "open," neo-liberal, global Market Economy has allowed for an unprecedented movement of, among other "things," mortally sick bodies moving in one direction and detached "healthy" organs (transported by commercial airlines in ordinary plastic beer coolers stored in the overhead luggage compartment of the economy section) in another direction, creating a bizarre "kula ring" of international trade. This essay critically explores—with particular reference to recent organ transplantation "developments" in Brazil, South Africa, India, the United States, and China—the new forms of bio-economics and bio-sociality (Rabinow 1996) that are now emerging in the wake of the internationalization of this immensely powerful, if crude, medical technology.

What is needed, then, is something akin to Donna Haraway's (1985) radical "manifesto" for the cyborg bodies and cyborg selves that we have, in fact, already become through the appearance of these strange markets, excess capital, advanced bio-technology, "surplus bodies" and human "spare parts." Together, these have allowed for a spectacularly lucrative world trade in organ transplantation which promises to certain, select individuals of reasonable economic "means" living almost anywhere in the world—from the Kalahari Desert in Botswana to the deserts of the Arab Emirate of Oman—a "miraculous" extension in what Giorgio Agamben (1998) refers to as "brute" or "bare" life, the elementary form of biological "species life." This, in turn, is made possible by the internal and domestic reorganization of neo-liberal, democratic states and their successful capture of the "cadaver" now redefined as the "state's body" and the concomitant politicization of death. By this we mean the increasing capacity of the post-transplantation State to define and determine the hour of death and to claim, unashamedly, the "first rights" (and first *rites*) to the disposal of the body's parts.

Until very recently, only highly deviant authoritarian and police states—Nazi Germany, Argentina in the late 1970s, Brazil in the 1960s and 1970s, and South Africa under apartheid—had assumed this capacity in the 20th century, this final word, as it were, over brute life, politicized death, and the creation and *maintenance* of a surplus population of "living dead," whether Black industrial workers kept in barbaric worker hostels in apartheid South Africa (see Ramphele 1994), the "disappeared" in Argentina, or those walking cadavers kept hostage in Nazi concentration camps. The "democratization" of practices bearing at least some family resemblances to these (i.e., the "living dead" maintained in intensive care units for the purpose of organ retrieval) in neo-liberal states has generally occurred in the absence of public outrage or resistance, with the possible exception of public unrest following democratic Brazils' passage of its authoritarian law of "presumed consent" to organ donation in 1997, which we shall discuss. . . .

In the face of this ultimate, late modern dilemma—this "end of the body" as we see it—the task of anthropology is relatively clear and straight forward: the recovery of our discipline's unrealized radical epistemological promise and a commitment to the "primacy of the ethical" (Scheper-Hughes 1994) while daring to risk practical, even political, involvement in the dangerous topic[1] under consideration. The need to define new ethical standards for the international practice of organ donation—especially in light of the abuses that undermine the bodily integrity of socially disadvantaged members of society and the public trust that is necessary for voluntary organ donation to continue, brought together a small international task force. The "Bellagio Task Force on Transplantation, Bodily Integrity, and the International Traffic in Organs," led by social historian, David Rothman, is comprised of a dozen international transplant surgeons, organ procurement specialists, human rights activists, and a medical anthropologist (myself, NS-H) meeting in 1995 and again in 1996 in the Rockefeller Conference Center in Bellagio, Italy. The task force is examining the ethical, social, and medical ramifications of these problems and is considering various strategies to impact them, including the creation of an international human rights body—a "Human Organs Watch," if you like—to monitor reports of any gross violations in the procurement and distribution of human organs in transplant surgery. An initial report of the Task Force was published in *Transplantation Proceedings* (Rothman et al., 1997). At the 1996 meeting, I was "delegated" by the Task Force to launch a very exploratory, ethnographic, comparative study of the social and economic context of organ transplantation, including the global and domestic traffic in organs.

The field research on which this discussion is based, therefore, derives from this "mission." It represents the preliminary findings from the early stages of the collaborative "Selling Life" project. . . .

The focus on the "commodification" of the body and body parts within the new global economy owes a particular debt to the writings and thought of Sidney Mintz, particularly his magisterial book, *Sweetness and Power.* This article is offered as a "transplanted" surrogate for the 1996 Sidney Mintz lecture which I was extremely honored to present at Johns Hopkins University.[2]

The Organs Ring and the Commodified Body

Indeed, as Arjun Appadurai has noted (1986) there is nothing fixed, stable, or sacrosanct about the "commodity candidacy" of things. Nowhere is this more dramatically illustrated than in the "booming" global and domestic markets in human organs and tissues from both living and deceased donors to supply the transplant industry, a medical business driven by the simple market calculus of "supply and demand." The very idea of organ "scarcity" is what Ivan Illich would call an artificially created need, invented by transplant technicians and dangled before the eyes of an ever expanding sick, aging, and dying population. This market is part of an impressive development and refinement of transplant technologies. These developments were facilitated historically through the medical definition of irreversible coma (at the end of the 1950s) and the new legal status of "brain death" (at the end of the 1960s) in which, as Giorgio Agamben (1998:163) notes, death became an epiphenomenon of transplant technologies. These transformations reveal the extent to which the sovereign power of postmodern states, both "democratic" and authoritarian, is operationalized through the life sciences and medical practices. These apparatuses, sciences, and technologies are globally integrated in markets which, in turn, increasingly reconfigure local states and local "cultures."

Lawrence Cohen, for example, who has worked in rural towns in various regions of India, from north to south, now reports that in a very brief period of time the idea of trading "a kidney for a dowry" has caught on and become one strategy for poor parents desperate to arrange a comfortable marriage for an "extra" daughter. In other words, a spare kidney for a spare daughter. Cohen notes that ten years ago when villagers and townspeople first heard through newspaper reports of kidney sales occurring in the cities of Bombay and Madras they responded with predictable alarm and revulsion. Today, some of these same villagers speak *matter of factly* about just when in the course of a family cycle it might be necessary to sell a "spare" organ. Some village parents say they can no longer complain about the fate of a dowry-less daughter. "Haven't you got a spare kidney?" one or another unsympathetic neighbor is likely to respond.

And in rural Brazil, over a similarly short period and in response to demands to "donate" a kidney to a family member, working class people have begun to view their bodies and body parts as comprised of unessential redundancies. "Nanci," I was challenged by a forty year old woman who had "given" a kidney (for a small compensation) to a distant relation, "Wouldn't you feel compelled to give an organ of which you yourself had two and the other 'fellow' had none?" I pointed out, rather lamely, that the Good Lord had given us two of quite a few organs and I hated to think of myself as selfish (*egoista*) for wanting to hang on to as many of the pairs as I could! It was not so long ago —1986, in fact—and in this same community when I had been invited to accompany a small procession to the graveyard where we ceremoniously buried a "fellow's" amputated foot! The folk Catholic ideology of the sacredness of the body—and the integrity of its component parts—was still then the commanding ethos. And though I felt a bit silly giving that gangrenous foot the benefit of a decade of the rosary as a "send off," Rosalva's reconceptualization in the late 1990s of her body as a mere reservoir of spare parts struck me as a troublesome turn of events.

The particular and well documented case of organ selling and, more recently, of organ stealing (see *New York Times,* May 12, 1998) in Indian villages is but one small, if well documented, link in a "booming" world market in organs and human tissues (not to mention blood, semen, ova, and babies) that links east and west, north and south. Over the past 30 years, organ transplantation has been transformed from a rare and experimental procedure performed in a few advanced medical centers in the first world to a fairly common therapeutic procedure carried out in hospitals and clinics, not all of them certified and legitimate, throughout the world. Kidney transplantation, which is the most universal form of organ transplant, is now conducted in the U.S., in most European and Asian countries, in several South American and Middle Eastern countries, and in a few African countries (in North Africa and South Africa). Survival rates for kidney transplant have increased markedly over the past decade, although these still vary by country and by quality and type of organ (living or cadaveric).

Until recently the "best" medical option for kidney transplantation was using a genetically closely related living donor (Fischel 1991). Today, however, morbidity rates from infection and hepatitis are higher in countries like Brazil, India, and China, which still rely heavily on living kidney donors than in the U.S., Canada, and the countries of Western Europe which rely more on cadaveric donation. But within some poorer countries to the South, like Brazil, survival rates for kidney transplant are still better with a matched living donor than with an "anonymous" cadaveric organ which stands a good chance of not having been adequately tested or screened.

Organ transplantation now takes place in a trans-national space with both donors and recipients following the paths of capital and technology in the global economy. In general, the movement of donor organs follows modern routes of capital: *from South to North, from third world to first world, from poor to rich bodies, from black and brown to white bodies, from young to old bodies, productive to less productive, and female to male bodies.* Residents of the Gulf States (Kuwait, Saudi Arabia, Oman, United Arab Emirates) travel primarily to India to obtain kidneys, while residents of Taiwan, Hong Kong, Korea and Singapore travel to mainland China for transplant surgery, allegedly with organs removed from executed prisoners. Japanese patients travel to North America as well as to Taiwan and Singapore for organs retrieved from brain dead donors, a definition of death only very recently and reluctantly accepted in Japan.

And, a great many people—and by no means are all of them wealthy—have shown their willingness to travel great distances to secure a transplant using both legal and illegal channels. This is so even when the survival rates in some of the more commercialized contexts is quite poor. Between 1983–1988, 131 patients from just three renal units in the United Arab Emirates and Oman traveled to Bombay, India where they purchased, through local brokers, kidneys from living donors. The donors, from urban shantytowns outside Bombay, were compensated between $2,000 and $3,000 for a kidney. News of the "organs bazaars" operating in the slums of Bombay, Calcutta and Madras appeared in Indian weeklies and in special reports by ABC and the BBC. Meanwhile, prestigious medical journals, (including *The Lancet* and *Transplant Proceedings*) published dozens of articles analyzing the medical risks and poor outcomes resulting from transplantation using "poor quality" kidneys from medically compromised "donors."[3]

A medically invented, artificial scarcity in human organs for transplantation has generated a kind of panic and a desperate international search for them and for new surgical possibilities. Bearing many similarities to the international market in adoption, those looking for transplant organs are so single minded in their quest that they are sometimes willing to put aside questions about how the organ [or "the baby" in the case of adoption] was obtained. In both instances the language of "gifts," "donations," " heroic rescues" and "saving lives" masks the extent to which ethically dubious and even illegal practices are used to obtain the desired "scarce" commodity, infant or kidney, for which foreigners (or "better off" nationals) are willing to pay what to ordinary people seems a king's ransom. With desperation built in on both sides of the equation—deathly ill "buyers" and desperately needy "sellers"—once seemingly "timeless" religious beliefs in the sanctity of the body and proscriptions against body mutilation have collapsed over night in some parts of the third world under the weight of these new market's demands. These new demands are driven by the rapid dissemination of the medical technology and expertise of transplant surgery and a new global social imagry about the possibilities of bodily rejuvenation and "repair" through organ replacement.

The gap between supply and demand that drives the new global trade in organs is exacerbated by religious sanctions and/or cultural inhibitions with respect to "brain death" and the proper handling of the dead body. Prohibitions in one country or region can stimulate an "organs market" in more secular or culturally pluralistic neighboring countries or regions. Meanwhile, the "scarcity" of organs produced in the wake of centralized "waiting lists" for transplantation has provided many incentives to physicians, hospital administrators, government officials, and blatantly commercial intermediaries to engage in ethically questionable tactics for obtaining organs. For example, heart transplantation is hardly performed at all in Japan due to deep reservations about the social definition of brain death, while most kidney transplants are gotten with living, related donors (see Lock 1996, 1997; Ohnuki-Tierney 1994).

For many years desperate Japanese nationals have resorted to intermediaries with connections to the underworld of organized crime (the so called "body mafia") to locate donor hearts or (when lacking related donors), paid unrelated kidney donors in other countries, including the United States. According to Lock (personal communication, 1997) who is engaged in a comparative study of transplant surgery in Japan and Canada (1996, 1997), a ring of Japanese *yakuza* gangsters, working on behalf of desperate Japanese transplant candidates through connections at a major medical center in Boston was uncovered by journalists and broken up by police there a decade ago. And, until recently, Japanese kidney patients also traveled to Taiwan and Singapore to purchase organs obtained (without consent) from executed prisoners, until this practice was roundly condemned by the World Medical Association in 1994 and was prohibited by new regulations.

The ban on the use of organs from executed prisoners in one part of "capitalist" Asia, opened up the possibilities for a similar practice in another part of "communist" Asia. The demand for hard currency by strapped governments recognizes no fixed ideological or political boundaries. Recently, the *New York Times* (February 24, 1998) reported on an FBI operation which led to the arrest of two Chinese citizens charged with conspiring to sell human organs of executed prisoners. The undercover "sting" operation was set up by the human rights activist, Harry Wu, who has been alerting the world since the 1980s to this alleged, covert practice in China. This particular case is still pending investigations, but its outcome may determine once and for all the veracity of Harry Wu's (and other human right activists') contested claims about the organs trade in China today, which we will discuss at greater length below.

Despite the publicity and attention to the more spectacular international traffic in human organs, an equally important though far less explored dimension of the organs trade is domestic, following the usual routes of social and economic cleavages and obeying domestic rules of class, race, gender, and geography. Dr. X, an elderly Brazilian surgeon and nephrologist, admitted during an interview in São Paulo in 1997 that "the commerce in organs has always been a reality in Brazil and among and between Brazilians.

"Those who suffer most," he said, are the usual "nobodies," mostly poor and uneducated, who are tricked into "donation" through illegal and unethical bodily transactions. The elderly doctor cited a transplantation scandal that occurred in Brazil in the late 1980s, one of several such cases exposed by local journalists and human rights activists. This particular one concerned a young accident victim, a mere girl of 12 years, from the interior town of Taubate, who while undergoing surgery on her broken leg, had a "spare" kidney removed by unscrupulous surgeons. Following a complaint lodged by her family who noticed a scar where none should have been, the local Public Defender began an investigation but it was interrupted by the Federal Police. Consequently, the Federal Board of Medicine was "compelled" to pass a verdict of "not guilty" due to lack of evidence.

But the poor and socially disadvantaged populations of Brazil and elsewhere in the world have not remained silent in the face of these threats and assaults to their health and to their bodily integrity, security, and dignity. For many years these marginal populations, living in urban shantytowns and hillside favelas, possessing little or no "symbolic capital" have announced their fears and their outrage through the idiom of seemingly "wild" rumors and urban legends ... that warn of the existence and the dangerous proximity of markets in bodies and body parts (Scheper-Hughes 1996). The circulation of the rumors and "urban legends" of organ theft have produced in their wake a climate of hostile "civil" resistance toward even legitimate and altruistic organ donation and organ transplantation in some countries to the South (such as Brazil and Argentina) where voluntary donations began to drop precipitously in the 1980s. Medical associations and governments have tried, without success, to correct the "disinformation" being disseminated by the persistent organ stealing rumors.

And, in a curious reversal, these "illiterate" rumors originating in the periphery have migrated to the comfortable and affluent "core," the comfortable middle class communities of the U.S. Despite the appointment of a full-time USIA [United States Information Agency] disinformation specialist, Todd Leventhal (see USIA 1994) who has led a long and expensive U.S. government campaign to kill the "body parts" rumor, as recently as the late fall of 1997 a variant of the organ stealing rumor carrying dire warnings about the existence of seductive female (or, less often, male) medical "agents" involved in the body parts trade was circulated among thousands of Americans via an electronic mail "chain letter." One strand of the chain was passed among a network of progressive academics, and to my amusement I was one of the recipients. The warning was followed a few days later by an apology stating that the story may have been "just a rumor."

Indeed, it would seem from this that a great many people in the world, both North and South, are uneasy. Something seems amiss or profoundly wrong about the nature of the beast that medical technology has released in the name of transplant surgery. But why now, why so many years later? Has transplant surgery opened a Pandora's Box that has resulted in a long overdue, popular backlash? Or, is there something new about the current organization of transplant surgery that has turned a once proud and altruistic moment in medical history into something unseemly and grotesque?

Dr. B., a heart transplant surgeon in Cape Town, South Africa whom I interviewed in February 1998, said he has become very *"disheartened"* about his profession's recent decline in prestige, trust, and value: "Organ transplantation has moved from an era back in 1967 when the atmosphere and public attitude was very different. . . . You know, people then still spoke about organ donation as that fantastic gift. Our first organ donor, Denise Dawer, and her family, were very much hallowed here. They were given a lot of credit for what they did and their photos are displayed in our hospital's new Transplant Museum. Society at that stage was still very positive. Now that there have been hundreds of thousands of donors throughout the world, the idea of organ donation has lost some of its luster. And, donors' families throughout the world have been put under a lot more pressure. And there have been some incidents that were unfortunate. . . . So we've begun to all of a sudden to experience a sea of backlash. In Europe there has been a strong backlash because of the state's demand, the moral requirement even, to donate. Europeans have generally had a good social conscience, they tend to believe in the better good of society, and so up until now they supported organ transplantation as a social good. But, now, suddenly objections are beginning to be raised. The Lutheran Church in Germany, for example, has started to question the idea of brain death, long after it had been generally accepted there. And so we have seen a drop of about 20% in organ donations in Europe, but especially in Germany. This is entirely new. So we are experiencing a real backlash, and what happens in Germany, unfortunately, has repercussions for South Africa." . . .

The Right to Sell and Future Markets

Despite evidence of widespread moral panic about bodily integrity and organ stealing some transplant surgeons and bioethicists, like Dr. Abdullah Daar, a member of the Bellagio Task Force, [a working group set up by Columbia University to study the use of organs for transplantations] sees the commercialization and commodification of human organs, whether one likes it or not, as a fait accompli. Labor is sold, sex is sold, sperm and ova are sold, even babies are sold in international adoption. What makes kidneys so special, so exempt? Daar has asked repeatedly. What is needed, he insists, is rigorous oversight and regulation in addition to an official Donors Bill of Rights that would both inform and protect potential donors.

But other members of the Task Force argue with Daar's reliance on western notions of contract and individual "choice." They are mindful of the social and economic context that makes the "choice" to sell a kidney anything but a "free" and "autonomous" one in an urban slum of Calcutta or a shantytown of São Paulo. Similarly, the idea of "consent" is problematic in a prison with the executioner looking over one's shoulder. In response to Daar's critique of human rights "paternalism" and his defense of the autonomy of the individual and his or her right to sell an organ, Veena Das has countered that in all notions of contract there are certain exclusions—such as in family law, labor law, and anti-trust law. There are basic assumptions concerning protected areas of life—anything that would damage social or community relations—that should be taken outside of contract theory. A market price—even a fair one—on body parts exploits the desperation of the poor. In addition, many humanists and bioethicists hold it to be self-evident that certain objects (like irreplaceable, non renewable solid organs) are fundamentally "inalienable" from the person. To ask the law to negotiate, as Daar suggests, a fair and reasonable price for a live human kidney is asking the law to go against everything that contract theory (as well as society) stands for. In addition, one has to be concerned about the effects of organ sales on the coarsening of medical practice and on doctors who are forced to inflict physical harm on one person who is not viewed as a "patient" in order to save the life of another individual who is exclusively viewed as "the patient."

Nonetheless, the movement toward commercialization is gaining ground in the United States. The AMA (American Medical Association) is currently considering the possibility of financial incentives that would enable people to bequeath organs to their heirs or to charity for a price. Dr. L.R. Cohen (no relation to anthropologist Lawrence Cohen) has proposed a "futures market" in cadaveric organs that would operate through contracts offered to the general public. These contracts would provide that at the time of the seller's death, if organs are successfully transplanted from his body, a substantial sum would be paid to his designee. He suggests $5,000 per major organ utilized. Cohen's proposal is based on the idea that a market can exist side by side with and even supplement altruism. Pure gifting can always be expected among family members, but financial inducements might be necessary to provide organs for strangers.

Dr. Charles Plows, Chair of the AMA's Committee on Ethical and Judicial Affairs agrees in principle with Cohen's proposal: "The only one who doesn't get anything out of this whole transplant transaction is the person who's deceased. The hospital makes money out of furnishing the areas where this work is done. Certainly, transplant surgeons do well for themselves. The patient gets a life-saving organ. But the man or woman who's donating the organ receives nothing." At present the AMA is exploring several options. One is a fixed price per organ. Another is to let market forces—supply and demand—set the price. The idea still makes a lot of doctors in the U.S. uncomfortable, but Dr. Plows and his colleague hope to get a pilot project off the ground in 1998.

India: Kidney Bazaar

The first inklings of a commercial market in organ trafficking appeared in 1983 when an American physician, H. Barry Jacobs, established the International Kidney Exchange in an attempt to broker kidneys from living donors in the Third

World, especially India. By the early 1990s upwards of 2,000 kidney *transplants with living donors* were performed each year in India, leading Prakash Chandra (1991) and other investigative journalists to refer to their country as the "great organ bazaar of the world." Proponents of paid living donors, such as Dr. K.C. Reddy, an Indian urologist with a thriving practice of kidney transplantation in Madras, argued that legalizing the trade would eliminate middle men who profit by exploiting paid donors.

Meanwhile, the free market in kidneys that catered through the 1980s to wealthy patients from the Middle East was forced underground following the passage of a law in 1994 that criminalizes organ sales. Recent reports by human rights activists, journalists, and medical anthropologists, including Lawrence Cohen, indicate that the law has produced in its wake an even larger *domestic* black market in kidneys. In some areas this new business is controlled by organized, cash-rich crime gangs expanding out from the heroin trade (in some cases with the backing of local political leaders). In other areas the business are controlled by ever more wealthy owners of profit hospitals.

An investigative report (*Frontline* December 26, 1997) found that a doctor-broker nexus in Bangalore and Madras still profits from the sale of kidneys by poor Indian donors to rich Indians, and to a smaller number of absolutely desperate foreigners with end-stage renal disease. A loophole in the law allows unrelated donors related to recipients by "ties of affection" to give a kidney following approval by local Medical Authorization Committees. These committees have been readily corrupted in areas where kidney sales have become an important source of local income. The result is that sales are now conducted with official seals of approval by the local Authorization Committee.

Today, Lawrence Cohen reports from the field, only the very rich can get an unrelated kidney. In addition to paying the donor, the middle men, and the hospital, now they must bribe the Authorization Committee members as well. As for the kidney sellers, recruited by brokers who get half the cost of the sale, almost all are trapped in terrible cycles of debt and caught in the clutches of money lenders. The kidney trade is another link, Cohen suggests, in an older and earlier system of debt peonage which has been reinforced by neo-liberal structural readjustment policies. Kidney sales are a key sign, says Cohen, of the sometimes bizarre effects of a global capitalism that seeks to turn everything into a commodity.

And there are hints and allegations of criminal practices within this climate of rampant commercialism. During the Berkeley conference on the commercialization of organs, Das told an NPR (National Public Radio, "Marketplace" program) reporter of a young woman she encountered in Delhi whose stomach pains were diagnosed as a bladder stone requiring surgery. But, in fact, the doctor, the woman charged, used the bladder stone as a pretext to operate and remove one of her kidneys which he delivered to a middleman for an undisclosed and confidential third party.

China: Collective Bodies

Today, China stands alone in continuing to use the organs of executed prisoners for transplant surgery. Although this practice has been documented by various international human rights organizations and investigated even by the FBI, Chinese public officials have impeded any form of inspection or verification of the executions. In October 1984, a Chinese government directive issued a document stating that "the use of corpses or organs of executed criminals *must be kept strictly secret,* and attention must be paid to avoid negative repercussions" (cited in *Human Rights Watch/Asia* 1994:7).

Following up on a report published by Human Rights Watch/Asia in August 1994 on "Organ Procurement and Judicial Execution in China," David Rothman visited major hospitals in Beijing and Shanghai in 1995 where he interviewed transplant surgeons and other medical officers about the technical and the social dimensions of transplant surgery as practiced at their respective units. While the surgeons and hospital administrators answered technical questions freely and accurately, they refused to respond to such questions as: Where do donated organs come from? How many foreigners come to the medical institutions seeking transplants? How much do the hospitals charge for various transplant operations?

While the "blank stares" of Chinese medical personnel that Rothman encountered in response to his questions are no proof of complicity or guilt, Dr. C.J. Lee, head of a transplant team in Taiwan, and member of the Bellagio Task Force, shared with the Task Force his personal knowledge and experience of transplant practices in Asia. The use of the organs of executed prisoners was practiced at his own unit in Taiwan until the country responded to the pressure of international human rights activists against it. China has held out, in part, Dr. Lee suggests, because of the need for foreign dollars and in part because there is less ethical soul-searching in China (as elsewhere in Asia) [or] "informed consent." And, an alternative social ethic interprets the practice as a kind of public service, an opportunity to pay the community back for wrongs committed and to gain merit for one's self.

Of course, not all Chinese embrace this collectivist ethos and some see the practice as a gross human rights abuse. Mr. Lin, a recent Chinese immigrant to California, reported a disturbing story (recorded for NPR's "Marketplace") during the Berkeley conference on the commercialization of organs, 1996. Just before arriving in California two years ago he visited a friend at a medical center in Shanghai. In the bed next to his friend was a wealthy and politically well situated professional man who told Mr. Lin that he was waiting for a kidney transplant later that day. His new kidney would arrive, he said, as soon as a prisoner was executed that morning. Minutes after the condemned prisoner was shot in the head, doctors present at the execution would quickly extract his kidneys and rush them to the hospital where two transplant surgery teams would be assembled and waiting. Reports by Human Rights Watch/Asia and by the Laogai Research Foundation (January 1995) have documented through Chinese informants and available medical and prison statistics that the state systematically takes kidneys, cornea, liver tissue and heart valves from executed prisoners. While these organs are sometimes given to reward politically well connected Chinese, often they are sold to medical "visitors" from Hong Kong, Taiwan, Singapore and other Pacific Rim nations who will pay as much as $30,000 for an organ.

Harry Wu, the human rights activist imprisoned in China until recently, was among the first to reveal the sale of prisoners' organs. At the Berkeley conference Wu said: "In 1992 I interviewed a doctor who routinely participated in removing kidneys from condemned prisoners. In one case she said, breaking down in the telling, that she had even participated in a surgery in which two kidneys were removed from a living, anesthetized prisoner late at night. The following morning the prisoner was executed by a bullet to the head." In this chilling case, brain death followed, rather than preceded, the harvesting of his vital organs.

Wu and other human rights activists claim that the Chinese Government takes organs from 2,000 executed prisoners each year. Moreover, that number is growing because the list of capital crimes in China has been expanded to accommodate the demand for organs. While the precise number of prisoners executed in China each year is unknown, Amnesty International has recently reported that a new "Strike Hard" anti-crime campaign has led to a sharp increase in the number of people executed, among them petty thieves and tax cheaters. In 1996 alone at least 6,100 death sentences were handed out and at least 4,367 confirmed executions took place. David Rothman, among others, is convinced that what lies behind the draconian anti-crime campaign is a "thriving medical business" that relies on prisoners' organs for raw materials. The state is sponsoring, he says, an "insatiable killing machine" driven by the rapacious "need" for fresh and healthy organs.

Recently, Wu's allegations have been bolstered following a sting operation he set up in New York City that led to the arrest of two Chinese citizens offering to sell cornea, kidneys, livers and other human organs to American doctors wanting them for transplant surgery. Posing in the undercover operation as a prospective customer from a dialysis center, Wu produced a video tape of the men, Mr. Wang Chenyong and Mr. Fu Xingqi in a Manhattan hotel room offering to sell him quality organs from a dependable source—fifty to two hundred prisoners executed on Hainan Island each year. Mr. Wang guaranteed this commitment by producing documents to Wu indicating that he had been deputy chief of criminal prosecutions in that prison. A pair of cornea would cost an exorbitant $5,000. In a taped telephone call, Wang boasted of making a 1000% profit (*Mail and Guardian* 2/27/1998; *San Jose Mercury News* 3/19/98; *New York Times* 2/24/98). Following their arrest by FBI agents the men were charged with conspiring to sell human organs and are being held without bond awaiting criminal proceedings. As a further fallout, a German company, Frenesius Medical Care A.G., based in a suburb of Frankfurt, announced that it was ending its half-interest in a kidney dialysis unit (next to a transplant clinic) in Guangzhou, China, citing the company's strong suspicions that foreign patients visiting the center may also be there to receive "kidneys harvested from executed Chinese criminals" (*New York Times* 3/7/98). [A] Frenesius spokesman stated that the company did not know anything about the "cover-up" role of the dialysis center and that the center was totally administered by Chinese medical personnel and controlled by military commands....

The Move to Primary Care and Privatization of Organ Transplantation

... As organ transplantation moves into the private sector, a creeping commercialism has necessarily taken hold. In the absence of a national policy regulating transplant surgery, and no regional, let alone national, official waiting lists, the distribution of transplantable organs is appallingly informal and subject to corruption. Public and private hospitals can hire their own transplant co-ordinators who are under pressure from competing, even warring, factions to "drop" the usable heart or kidney in a bucket rather than give it to a competitor. The situation is grave. The temptation "to accommodate" patients who are able to pay is affecting both the public and private sector hospitals. At Groote-Schurr Hospital's kidney transplant unit, a steady trickle of donor "couples" arrive from Mauritius and Nimibia. Although they claim to be related, the nurses say that many are simply paid donors, but since they arrive from across the border, the doctors look the other way. While I was in Cape Town, a very ill older business man from the Cameroons arrived at the kidney transplant unit with a paid donor the man found in Johannesburg. The donor was a young university student from Burundi who agreed to part with one of his kidneys for his expenses and a bonus of 2,000 rand (about $400). The head of the kidney unit read the international medical codes against organ sales to the pair, explained the risks and dangers of living kidney donation, but as they persisted he agreed to order the blood matching tests. When they failed to match and were turned away, the symbiotic pair begged to be transplanted in any case. Such was their almost unimaginable desperation, that they were willing to face the eventuality of almost certain organ rejection. Of course, the doctors refused their plea. Will private hospitals be as conscientious as the public ones in refusing hopeless cases among those patients willing to pay regardless of the outcome?

Meanwhile, those who live at a distance, without easy means of communication and transportation, such as in the sprawling townships of Soweto outside Johannesburg and Khayalitsha outside Cape Town have a ghost of a chance of receiving a transplant. The rule of thumb among heart and kidney transplant surgeons in Johannesburg is: "No fixed home, no phone, no organ." The ironies are striking. At the famous Chris Hani Bara Hospital on the outskirts of Soweto, I met a sprightly and playful middle aged man, flirting with nurses, during his dialysis treatment. "He's very familiar with you!" I commented to the head nurse. "And well, he might be," she replied. "He's been on the waiting list for a kidney for more than 20 years." Not a single patient at the huge Bara Hospital's kidney unit had received a transplant in the past year.

The week before I was in the splendid, suburban community of Sun Valley outside Cape Town where, in a private, gated community protected by armed guards for the comfort and security of the wealthy, white, and mostly retired residents, I met with Mr. W. Breytanbach, Ex-Deputy Minister of Defense under President P.W. Botha, still recuperating from the heart transplant he had received on his government pension and health plan in less than a month's wait. At first he was distraught on learning that he was the recipient of the heart of a young, colored nurse, and at first he blamed his difficult recovery on his "inferior woman's heart." He has since softened, he says, and he has even tried to contact the family of his donor through the hospital network so that he could thank them. The family has not responded. As we chatted about his time served on South Africa's notorious Security Committee, I had to control my rising sense of outrage. The sub-heading, "State Killer Gets New Heart" came several times to mind during the interview, prompting me, finally, to ask Mr. Breytanbach if he thought he owed the new South African government something for having given him, of all people, a new lease on life. He replied:

> "To this day I still do not know why I was given a heart transplant. I know that at the time I had only 10 or 12 days at most to live and if I did not have [the operation] I would be dead. And it is great to be alive! I look at the country and I see that there may be more people more deserving than me of a heart transplant, and many who cannot get it because of a shortage of funds or of donors with so many people waiting for hearts. But by hook or by crook, I don't know how Dr. V. does it [in the private hospital] but I have been there and I can see that there are no questions asked about whether the person can really afford it or not. If need be, [heart transplant surgeon] just goes ahead and operates."

At the venerable Groote-Schuur Hospital, however, the waiting time for all major surgical procedures has increased and a virtual moratorium has brought heart transplantation to a standstill.

Concluding Remarks

Organ transplantation depends, as Cantarovitch (1990) suggests, on a social contract and social trust, the grounds for which must be explicit. This requires national and international laws protecting the rights of both organ donors and organ recipients. At a very rudimentary level, the practice of organ transplantation requires a reasonably fair and equitable health care system. For example, the Ministry of Health in Gauteng, South Africa proposed a temporary moratorium in late 1995 on heart transplants in an effort to sort out unreliable private sector doctors performing these operations under questionable medical circumstances. The present moratorium in Cape Town is more difficult to justify.

The social ethics of transplant surgery also require a reasonably democratic state in which basic human rights, especially bodily integrity, are protected and guaranteed. Organ transplantation occurring, even in elite medical centers by the most conscientious of physicians, within the milieu of a police state or authoritarian state—as the illustrations from China, and from pre-democratic transition in Brazil and South Africa exemplify—all too readily lead to gross human rights abuses of both living and dead bodies. Similarly, where vestiges of forced labor exist (especially in "debt peonage" systems which unfairly bind workers to their "owners"), and where unjust transactions keep being "legally" and "medically" covered-up (including trade in corneas, kidneys, children and facilitation of access to care) the panic and mistrust of medicine and transplant surgery in particular will persist.

Under conditions like these the most vulnerable will continue to fight back with the only resources they have—gossip, rumors, or rebuttals and resistance to "modern laws." In this way, they settle accounts, albeit obliquely, with the "situation of emergency" that continues to exist for them in this time of economic and democratic readjustments. These subaltern lives manifest their consciousness of the real and unjust processes of social exclusion/inclusion at work in the everyday, and articulate their own ethical categories and political stances in the face of the "consuming" demands which value their bodies most at the point they can be claimed by the State as "brain dead" and therefore as a reservoir of spare parts. While to transplant surgeons and to body dealers an organ is just an organ, a heart is just a pump, and a kidney is just a filter, a thing, a commodity better used than wasted, to vast numbers of ordinary people an organ is something else—a lively, animate, spiritualized part of the self that most would still like to take with them when they die.

Notes

1. I refer to this as a "dangerous" topic advisedly. The global "organs trade" is extensive, extremely lucrative, explicitly illegal in the legal codes of most countries, unethical according to every governing body of medical, professional life, and therefore, covert. The organs trade links elite surgeons and technicians from the upper reaches of bio-medical practice to "body mafia" from the lowest reaches of the criminal world. The practice involves complicity or, at least, by-stander "passivity" from within the ranks of police, mortuary workers, pathologists, civil servants, ambulance drivers, emergency room workers, eye bank and blood bank managers, and transplant coordinators. Although I have been harassed in the field before with respect to other research projects, this is the first time when in the course of my investigations into various aspects of global traffic (organs and babies) in the interior of Brazil I was warned by a close friend of being followed by a possible "hit man" representing a local (and deeply implicated) Judge, forcing me to leave the site earlier than intended.

2. The original Sidney Mintz lecture, "Small Wars: the End of Childhood", was based on my introduction to the co-edited (with Carolyn Sargent) volume, *Small Wars: the Cultural Politics of Childhood* (University of California Press) which is slated to appear in November 1998. I gratefully acknowledge the initial critical reading of that text by Richard Fox and Sidney Mintz.

3. Saalahudeen and his colleagues (1990) noted the poor medical outcomes for the large number of patients who travelled from the Gulf States to India for organ transplants in the 1980s.

POSTSCRIPT

Should Markets Be Allowed to Solve the Shortage in Body Parts?

As Carlstrom and Rollow suggest, there are some interesting parallels between the price controls and rationing that were used to contain the surge in fuel prices after OPEC flexed its muscles in the 1970s and the initial adjustments to the current shortage of body parts. As the price of fossil fuels increased and the lines outside of filling stations lengthened, alternative sources of energy began to appear in the marketplace.

If the price of kidneys, hearts, lungs, and other transplantable organs remains high, will the development of artificial organs continue? Will the practice of transplanting organs taken from other species, such as pig hearts, into humans be perfected and more generally accepted? Will the cloning of human body parts become as widespread as the raising of antibiotic cultures in laboratories?

But even if there is a universal acceptance of "human meat markets," existing law prohibits it. In 1987 Congress revised the National Organ Transplant Act to explicitly bar the sale of human organs. Should that ban be lifted, as Carlstrom and Rollow argue? They are not alone in their attempts to legalize the sale of transplantable organs; others also support the move to create a market for body parts. Indeed, the support is widespread in the Libertarian community. Perhaps the most vocal advocate is the Cato Institute (www.cato.org), but advocacy does not end there. Former Delaware governor Pete du Pont, who serves as policy chair of the National Center for Policy Analysis, has also endorsed this position. A number of Web sites support the views of Carlstrom and Rollow. See Organ Keeper (http://www.organkeeper.com); Organ Sales.com (http://www.organsales.com); and the Organ Selling Homepage (http://web.organselling.com).

Those who are opposed to selling organs cringe at the thought of replacing the donor system with a vendor system. In another essay by Scheper-Hughes, "Theft of Life: The Globalization of Organ Stealing Rumors," *Anthropology Today* (June 1996), the author explores the possibility of organ theft as the high price of organs and a market to sell them in become ever more present. Many people assert that the inequities that currently exist between whites and ethnic minorities would increase sharply if society moved to a market system for the allocation of human organs. H. Leon Hewitt provides an extensive bibliography on this subject at the Web site, Negative Effects of Organ Transplants, sponsored by the Institute on Race, Health Care and the Law at http://www.udayton.edu/~health/03access/98hewitt.htm.

ISSUE 7

Do Private Prisons Pay?

YES: Adrian T. Moore, from "Private Prisons: Quality Corrections at a Lower Cost," *Reason Public Policy Institute Policy Study No. 240* (April 1998)

NO: Eric Bates, from "Private Prisons," *The Nation* (January 5, 1998)

ISSUE SUMMARY

YES: Social critic and policy analyst Adrian T. Moore maintains that there is extensive evidence to suggest that private sector prisons provide quality correctional services at a lower cost to taxpayers.

NO: Columnist Eric Bates contends that "privatizing prisons is really about privatizing tax dollars [and] about transforming public money into private profits."

M any people feel unsafe walking the streets of urban America or even pitching a tent in a wilderness area. Many believe that the United States is plagued by a terrifying crime rate. We are reminded of this daily by the crime reports we read in local newspapers or see in obscene detail on local and national television news programs. In 1997 the National Crime Victimization Survey reported that 34.8 million crimes were committed against U.S. residents; 74 percent (25.8 million) were property crimes, 25 percent (8.6 million) were crimes of violence, and the remaining 1 percent were personal thefts.

The most stark representation of the crime data generated by the 1997 *FBI Uniform Crime Reports* is the "Crime Clock." In terms of this clock, a criminal offense is committed every 2 seconds in the United States! There is one violent crime every 19 seconds: one murder every 27 minutes, one forcible rape every 6 minutes, one robbery every 54 seconds, and one aggravated assault every 29 seconds. Additionally, there is one property crime every 3 seconds: one burglary every 12 seconds, one larceny-theft every 4 seconds, and one motor vehicle stolen every 23 seconds.

If we took these statistics at face value, we would probably believe that the American criminal justice system is under siege, with no hope in sight. In fact, there does appear to be hope in sight, even though the electronic and print media may be slow to report it. All measures of criminal activity are down, whether we look at violent crimes or crimes against property. This is not something new. Both violent crime and property crime fell by 7 percent from 1994 to 1997, and the mid-year 1998 report suggests that the rate of decline will continue. Perhaps the best measure of criminal activity is the FBI's "crime index," which, as reported in the *FBI Uniform Crime Reports*, "fell for the 6th straight year in 1997."

The crime index, however, is only half the story. While criminal activity fell in the 1990s, America's incarceration rate continued to increase. This is a trend that began to appear in the mid-1970s. Prior to this, the nation's incarceration rate was relatively stable at about 110 prison inmates per 100,000 U.S. residents. But over time the rate climbed fourfold to its current level of 445 inmates for every 100,000 in the population. Among the adult male population the rate is much higher: 1,100 per 100,000. Thus, while the rate of violent crime in the United States has fallen by 20 percent, the number of prison inmates has risen by 50 percent.

By the end of 1996 the United States had 5.5 million people on probation or in jails and prisons. This represents 2.8 percent of all U.S. residents! Some individual states, such as California, house more prison inmates than many major countries; indeed, California's prison system alone is 40 percent larger than the whole Federal Bureau of Prisons and larger than the combined prison systems of France, Britain, Germany, Japan, Singapore, and the Netherlands.

Thus, in spite of a construction boom in the "corrections industry," prisons are more overcrowded today than they were before the crime rate began to fall. States, sometimes under federal judicial mandates requiring them to reduce overcrowding, have increasingly turned to the private sector for assistance. This has made "privatized corrections" a growth industry. Several dozen corporations have sprung into existence, in an attempt to profit from the shortage of prison beds. Two corporations, Wackenhut Corrections Corporation and Corrections Corporation of America, dominate this new industry. These two companies operate 29 minimum- and medium-security facilities, which imprison 10,000 felons. Others in the industry, like the Pricor Corporation, "rent out" underused county jail capacity—mostly in rural Texas—to any correction facility across the country, as long as it is willing to pay the going rate. Should this privatization trend in the corrections industry be encouraged? Are the economic efficiencies that Adrian T. Moore details in the following selection worth the social and private costs of which Eric Bates warns in the second selection?

 **YES**

Private Prisons: Quality
Corrections at a Lower Cost

Background: Not Enough Space or Money

Why are U.S. federal agencies and state and local governments turning to the private sector for correctional services? Because tougher crime policies and budget constraints have combined to create a problem, if not a crisis, in the nation's prisons and jails. Governments are incarcerating more criminals, but they have recently become unwilling to spend sufficient tax dollars for new prisons to house them. The prison system is increasingly characterized by overcrowding, lawsuits, and court orders. Therein lies the problem for federal, state, and local officials—expenditures on corrections have grown rapidly, but the prison population has grown faster.

Corrections is one of the fastest-growing state budget items. In the last 15 years, state spending on corrections grew more than 350 percent—compared to 250 percent growth for spending on public welfare and 140 percent growth for spending on education. More than one-third of the states devote 5 percent or more of their spending to corrections. (See Table 1.)

The Numbers Tell the Story

State spending on corrections has gone up because the number of inmates in the system has skyrocketed. Since 1984 the number of inmates has risen 100 percent in local jails, 213 percent in state prisons, and 290 percent in federal facilities. Incarceration rates are well over double what they were in 1980.

Some states have embarked upon unprecedented prison building programs. Texas and California have led the pack, spending billions of dollars in the last decade building new facilities. According to the Bureau of Justice Statistics, the capacity of state and federal prisons grew 41 percent in the first half of this decade. Local jurisdictions have felt similar pressure: over 800 jurisdictions have identified the need for new construction in the next few years.

But all the building to date has not met the need. Today many state and federal prisons are holding over 20 percent more prisoners than their capacity, and a great number of facilities—even entire state and county systems—are

From Adrian T. Moore, "Private Prisons: Quality Corrections at a Lower Cost," *Reason Public Policy Institute Policy Study No. 240* (April 1998). Copyright © 1999 by The Reason Foundation, 3415 S. Sepulveda Blvd., Suite 400, Los Angeles, CA 90034. www.rppi.org. Reprinted by permission. Notes omitted.

under court order to limit or reduce their inmate populations. Nineteen state prison systems are 25 percent or more over capacity, and at least 10 more state systems, and federal prison systems, could be considered very overcrowded. (See Table 2.) In most of these states, the situation is not getting better. Crowding in California's prison system worsened between 1994 and 1996, going from 84 percent over capacity to 96 percent over capacity.

Table 1

States With High Corrections Expenditures as a Percentage of Total Budget (1994)

State	% of Budget to Corrections	Total Annual Corrections Expenditures (in millions)
TX	10	$2,046
CA*	9	$4,042
VA	9	$651
OK	8	$274
RI	8	$130
SC	8	$299
MD	7	$509
NY	7	$2,430
OR	7	$220
TN	7	$372
WY	7	$33
KS	6	$200
NJ	6	$941
CT	5	$392
FL	5	$1,457
ID	5	$60
NM	5	$136
SD	5	$34

*1996 figures

Sources: American Correctional Association; California Department of Corrections.

With taxpayers clearly demanding that criminals be put in prison and kept in longer, there seems to be no choice but to increase the capacity of the prison system. But with popular pressure to cut government spending, funding the increase will be difficult. Legislators face a lot of pressure to hold the line on corrections spending, fewer than half of referendums to approve bond financing of new prisons are being approved by voters.

Table 2

Most Overcrowded Prison Systems (1996)

State	% of Capacity*
CA	196
IA	171
OH	171
DE	163
WA	150
MA	148
MI	146
VA	145
NJ	142
NH	140
IL	138
PA	138
OK	133
WI	133
WY	132
NE	131
NY	131
ND	127
HI	125
FEDERAL	124

---

*These figures are rough; different states calculate capacity in different ways.

Sources: U.S. Department of Justice; Camille Camp and George Camp, *The Corrections Yearbook, 1997* (South Salem, N.Y.: Criminal Justice Institute, 1997), p. 62.

Alternatives

There are alternatives to incarceration. Many states are starting to look at alternative sentencing, including community-based institutions, home confinement, and other programs. But there is a limit to how many criminals such methods can cope with. California's nonpartisan legislative analyst calculates that alternative punishments will be appropriate or possible for only a small share of future convicted criminals. The need for additional prisons and jails will not disappear, and policy makers must look in new directions for corrections policy.

This has led federal, state, and local officials to consider how the private sector can become involved in corrections. The private sector's lower costs and quality services can help cope with the growing number of prisoners without busting the budget. But what do private prisons have to offer? And what evidence is there on how they have performed?

Correctional Services Offered by the Private Sector

There are three basic types of correctional services offered by the private sector:

1. Design and construction of jails and prisons.
2. Services for offenders, such as food service or medical care, and juvenile and community correction centers.
3. Contract management of major detention facilities.

Local, state, and federal governments have contracted with the private sector for each of these types of services. The first two services have been used widely, with little controversy, for decades. The last has grown rapidly, amidst controversy, since the early 1980s.

Design and Construction

Private contractors have long designed and built jails and prisons. In a relatively new development, some governments have accelerated completion of projects by delegating more authority to, and reducing regulatory requirements on, private design-build teams. Even more recent is the appearance of prisons wholly financed and built by the private sector, which offer their bed space on a per-diem contract basis to jurisdictions experiencing an overflow of prisoners.

The per-bed cost of prison space is influenced by many factors, including the security level, location, and jurisdiction of the facility. Coming up with useful average costs for government construction is difficult. However, the Criminal Justice Institute has calculated that the average cost of government construction is $80,562 for a maximum-security cell, $50,376 for a medium-security cell, and $31,189 for a minimum-security cell.

Cost Savings
Private companies can build prisons and jails for considerably less than these figures and in less time. Firms in the industry often contend that they can cut between 10 percent and 40 percent off construction costs, with 30 percent being the most common savings estimate. Independent estimates of the cost savings show a similar range of 15 to 25 percent. In addition, private construction can shift a number of risks, including that of cost overruns, to the private sector.

Sources of Cost Savings
Since the final payment does not come until project completion, private firms have an incentive to complete construction more quickly. Construction of a prison or jail takes governments an average of two and one-half years—private firms complete the same type of project in about half the time. One company

may have set a record, constructing a new facility in less than 90 days. The firm purchased land, got zoning clearance, lined up financing, and designed, built, and opened a 100-bed maximum-security juvenile facility in just three months.

When a private firm is asked to build a new facility or expand an existing one, only one person has to approve the request—the CEO. This is in sharp contrast to the often laborious approval process and multiple contract requirements a government construction project must go through. The speediness of private construction gives public officials more flexibility in making corrections policy than does the slower-moving government construction process.

Speed of construction is only one way private firms cut building costs. They also save money because they are free of many costly rules imposed on government projects, such as purchasing restrictions and subcontracting quotas. The most extensive savings are reaped when the private firm is allowed to both design and build a facility. Public-works projects all over the world have used design-build contracts and achieved greater efficiency and cost savings—design-build contracts for corrections projects can do so as well.

Allowing private operating firms to design facilities can lead to considerable long-term operating-cost savings as well. Operating costs are 75 to 85 percent of the overall cost of a prison, and about 60 percent of the operating costs are for personnel. This means that designing a facility to require less staff, while providing the necessary security, can dramatically reduce operating costs. Innovative designs that require fewer personnel are a specialty of private corrections firms, but they have been very slow to catch on with government corrections projects.

Some people object that private prisons are authorized and built so fast that the public has little chance to weigh in on the decision. They say that although public hearings and procurement procedures take time, they are part of the democratic process that many jurisdictions have established. They accuse local officials of avoiding public debate over facility financing by entering into a lease-purchase agreement or by allowing a private firm to build a prison on its own and then contracting on a per-diem basis for each inmate it sends to the facility. Since the capital cost of the facility is embedded in the lease payment or the per-diem rate paid to the private firm, the taxpayers still pay the cost—but the structure of the deal sometimes avoids democratically established review procedures for capital expenditures. This is clearly a problem that local governments have to resolve with their citizens. Some officials that have failed to do so have found themselves facing challenges in court from local citizen groups.

Whichever way the courts come to decide this issue, public officials will continue to find that private construction cuts the cost of new facilities. This will be increasingly important not only to provide space for new prisoners, but also to replace existing aged facilities as needed. Nearly 300 prisons in the United States are over 50 years old, and more than 50 are over 100 years old. These facilities will need replacement or thorough renovation as they decay or become obsolete and inefficient to operate.

Services for Offenders

For-profit and nonprofit private organizations play a major role in providing services to correctional agencies. Most correctional institutions use some
form of privatization in such areas as medical services, mental-health services, substance-abuse counseling, educational programs, food services, and
management of prison industries.

The use of private services by correctional agencies is most extensive outside institution walls. This reflects the fact that more than 80 percent of convicted offenders in most states are in community supervision, either on parole
or on probation.

Private involvement in community corrections (low-security work-release
or halfway-house facilities) is a long-standing tradition in most states. In addition, state governments have traditionally let contracts for services such as
counseling on abuse of alcohol and other drugs; assessment and treatment of
sexual offenders; and job training and placement.

Private involvement in providing services to inmates during detention and
after release has brought a new wave of innovation. Florida legislators found the
private prisons in their state to be miles ahead of the state prisons in providing
effective rehabilitation, education, and other services. Private firms are developing efficient and effective post-release programs aimed at reintegrating inmates
into the community and reducing recidivism rates.

Providing these kinds of services does cost money. Inmates will receive
these services only if the services are included in the terms of the contract.
However, given that a contract with a private firm to house inmates saves money,
more funds may be available to pay for specialized services that can reduce
recidivism rates.

Management of Detention Facilities

A decade ago, private management of jails and prisons was almost unheard of.
The first county, state, and federal prison management contracts were awarded
in 1984 and 1985. In 1986, only a fraction of 1 percent of the nation's adult jail
and prison population was privately managed.

This has changed. According to the 1997 "Private Adult Correctional Facility Census" (PACFC), at the end of 1996 private firms operated 132 adult
facilities in the United States, holding 85,201 inmates. (See Figure 1.) This
amounts to around 4 percent of the total U.S. adult prison population and
reflects a 25 percent annual growth rate. Experts anticipate that this rate of
growth will continue for some time. The PACFC predicts that the capacity of
private adult prisons in the United States will exceed 275,000 inmates by the year
2002. Other nations are turning to private prisons as well—the United Kingdom
has four in operation and several more under construction, Australia has four
in operation, and Canada and South Africa are expected to move forward soon
with planned projects.

More states than ever are making use of private corrections—25 states, as
well as the District of Columbia and Puerto Rico, have a private facility in operation or under construction. The federal government is also turning to the

Figure 1

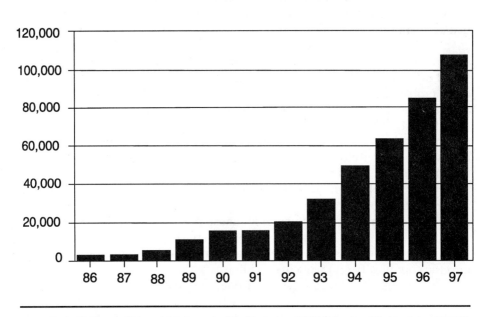

11-Year Growth in Rated Capacity of Private Prisons

Source: Charles W. Thomas, "Private Adult Correctional Facility Census, 1997," University of Florida, Gainesville 1997, and his unpublished estimated figure for 1977.

private sector for corrections services. The Immigration and Naturalization Service and the U.S. Marshals have long contracted with private firms to manage detention centers and other low-security facilities. And in mid-1997, the federal Bureau of Prisons turned a prison over to a private operator for the first time. Just a few weeks after that contract was signed, Congress passed legislation directing the Bureau of Prisons to take control of most District of Columbia correctional facilities and to place 50 percent of the District's inmates in privately operated facilities by 2003.

There are currently at least 15 firms operating adult correctional facilities in the United States. Two large firms—Corrections Corporation of America and Wackenhut Corrections Corporation—manage the majority of private prisons. Four midsize firms—Correctional Services Corporation, Cornell Correction, Management and Training Corporation, and U.S. Corrections Corporation —each manage a number of facilities and have developed a breadth of experience. Other firms in the industry manage just a few facilities each. Two British firms—Securicor and Group 4 Prison Services—operate prisons in the United Kingdom and Australia and now have subsidiaries in the United States. A key point: the size of the smaller firms belies their experience. Most of the private firms' management personnel come from careers in government prison systems, so even small private companies can draw upon a wealth of experience and expertise.

Managing major facilities has been the most controversial form of private-sector involvement, but it also has the most potential to help public officials cope with their correctional needs. The rest of this study is devoted to helping public officials and others understand the issues and controversies that surround this use of private-sector corrections—in particular the evidence that private prisons save money, yet still provide quality service.

Cost Savings of Private Prisons

There is a growing body of evidence that private prison operating costs are around 10 to 15 percent less than typical government prison operating costs. The number of detailed academic cost comparisons continues to grow, as does the first-hand experience of local officials with tangible cost savings.

Cost Comparison Studies

Any discussion of cost savings must compare private and government facilities. But it is hard to find two facilities that are exactly alike in design, age, personnel, inmate population, and other factors. So adjustments have to be made to data from different facilities to make them comparable.

Government agencies and private firms use different budgeting and accounting methods. Adjustments can help correct for most differences, but the result is a comparison of estimates, not specific expenditure data. Also, there are hidden costs that are hard to account for. A government institution's budget normally does not include various central administrative and support expenses. For example, some state prison budgets do not include the cost of some medical services, legal services, or personnel administration services, many of which are handled on a central accounting basis by other state agencies. On the other hand, a private facility's budget will include administrative and support costs but will not include the government's costs of preparing and monitoring contracts.

By making necessary adjustments, reasonable estimates and approximations can be used to compare government and private costs. The professionals who conduct comparison studies are versed in the difficulties and the adjustments needed to overcome them. They are familiar with the sometimes subjective nature of comparative analysis and point out assumptions and qualifications that readers need to understand. In most cases the authors make it clear that potential savings could be somewhat more or less than identified.

... Of the 14 studies, 12 found private prison costs to be lower than government prison costs—5 percent to 28 percent lower.

Two of the studies... deserve particular attention. The study by researchers from Louisiana State University (LSU) has been widely acclaimed for overcoming the problem of comparing "apples to oranges." It compared three facilities, two privately operated (by different firms) and one operated by the state of Louisiana. The facilities were built from the same plans and had

Table 3

Staffing and Operating-Cost Comparison: Prairie Correctional Facility (PCF) and Jackson Correctional Institution (JCI) (1995)

	Private (PCF)	Public (JCI)
Inmates	516	663
• Inmates as % of capacity	100%	108%
Staff		
• Correctional officers (C.O.s)	103	163
• Other staff	63	110
• Staff per 100 inmates	32.2	41.2
• C.O.s per 100 inmates	20.0	24.6
Estimated 1995 spending	$7,200,000	$12,000,000
1995 per diem/inmate	$38.23	$49.59
1995 spending/inmate/year	$13,953	$18,100

Local Cost Comparison: An Example. A study of Wisconsin prisons compared the costs of a private prison in Minnesota, Prairie Correctional Facility, to a similar Wisconsin state prison, Jackson Correctional Institution. The two prisons are about the same age, have similar inmate populations, and are geographically close. The study found that the daily cost per inmate in the private facility was 23 percent lower than in the government facility. A summary of the comparison is presented in the table [above]. For more details, see George Mitchell, "Controlling Prison Costs in Wisconsin," Wisconsin Policy Research Institute, December 1996.

very similar populations—as much "apples and apples" as one could reasonably hope to find. This study found both private prisons to be about 15 percent more cost-effective than their government counterpart.

While not able to directly compare identical facilities, the Arizona study went to considerable lengths to adjust and compensate for differences between the privately run prison and the government-run prisons. Careful steps were taken to account for indirect costs. The state's first private prison, a 444-bed facility, was compared to all 15 government-run prisons in the state. Some government prisons performed better than the private prison, and some performed worse, but the private prison's costs were 17 percent less than the average cost of the state prisons.

In stark contrast to these two studies is a report issued in 1996 by the General Accounting Office (GAO). The GAO examined five studies comparing government and private prison costs and concluded that it "could not draw any conclusions about cost savings or quality of service." ...

The GAO report is important because it is widely cited by privatization opponents, but its methods and conclusions are odd. Of the four studies it examined..., two found the private facilities to have significantly lower costs. The GAO argued that the results of those two studies should be ignored because they suffered from limitations, specifically: (1) the fact that some comparisons involve actual costs and "hypothetical" costs; and (2) the fact that facilities being compared might be designed differently or operated differently.

The GAO report has been widely criticized for a number of shortcomings, including:

- The GAO, without explaining why, chose to ignore a number of cost comparisons... and focus on only five studies. Among those overlooked were studies from Australia and the United Kingdom, which are not as useful in the United States (although they are certainly relevant). But why ignore the studies by the Texas Criminal Justice Policy Council, the Kentucky Auditor of Public Accounts, and the Florida Office of the Auditor General? The GAO also left out the prominent LSU study. It had not yet been published, but the GAO investigators had been made aware of it by several of the sources they contacted. Ignoring the Louisiana study was particularly egregious because it compared identical facilities—exactly the type of comparison the GAO report said was needed.

- The GAO's insistence that cost comparisons must look at identical facilities, besides being belied by their ignoring the LSU study, misses a crucial point. One of the principal advantages that private firms bring to corrections is that they do things differently. It is precisely the innovative practices of private firms—their breaking away from "the way things have always been done"—that bring about cost savings.

- The GAO report discounts the results of the Texas Comptroller's study because it compared the cost of existing private facilities to the cost of "hypothetical government facilities." Actually, the Texas study compared the cost of the private facilities to the "cost that the TDCJ [Texas Department of Criminal Justice] would incur if it *took over the operation of the four private facilities*" (emphasis added). Moreover, the GAO chose to ignore a subsequent report by the Texas Criminal Justice Policy Council (a state agency) that found the cost advantage of the private facilities to be even greater (21 percent).

- Two of the studies the GAO gave credence are in fact flawed or at least limited. The Washington report was similar to the GAO report in that it reanalyzed earlier data rather than collecting new data—so it is not surprising that it reiterated the results of the Tennessee Legislature's study. The GAO also included a report that compared community corrections facilities in California. This study should not have been included, because it compares halfway-house facilities, not real prisons, and the two "government" facilities were in fact for-profit facilities operated by special agencies of local governments to house state prisoners.

- Finally, the GAO report was not an objective survey of available information, as was requested by the House of Representatives when it asked the GAO to undertake the study. Rather, according to Dr. Charles Logan, it is "so consistently one-sided and negative that it reaches the point of dishonesty."

Other Evidence

To buttress the copious empirical evidence that the private operation of prisons saves money, there are simple commonsense observations. For one thing, why would so many states and federal agencies enter into contracts with private prison firms if not to save money? Tennessee state senator Jim Kyle points out that only the potential cost savings that private prisons offer will entice a politician to take on the battle to contract for correctional services. Indeed, the most frequent reason given for privatization is to save money. Unless we assume that the decision makers in all the governments that contract with private prison firms are willfully stupid, we have to believe that cost savings are being achieved.

This observation is buttressed by the legislation many states have passed to ensure cost savings from prison privatization. For example, Texas and Mississippi both require contracts with private prisons to cost at least 10 percent less than using the state system, Florida requires 7 percent savings, and Tennessee requires payments to private firms to be less than government facility costs. States are refining their methods of assuring savings. Several of the studies... were commissioned by state governments checking to see that cost savings were achieved. The Arizona Department of Corrections, in cooperation with the state Office of Excellence, is developing a new and sophisticated cost comparison model.

How the Private Sector Cuts Costs

Undeniably, the key to the lower costs of the private sector is competition. In order to win contracts—and keep them—a firm must be efficient. Rising costs, or cuts that lead to poor quality, would soon take a firm to where it could win no more contracts.

The private sector saves money by doing a number of things differently from government. Since their success hinges on delivering the same product as the government but at lower cost, or a better product at a cost-effective price, they turn to new management approaches, new monitoring techniques, and administrative efficiencies—in a word, innovation. Moving beyond "the way it has always been done" allows them to reduce labor costs, reduce tension between correctional officers and inmates, make full use of a facility's capacity, and make more efficient purchases.

Reducing Labor Costs
About two-thirds of correctional departments' operating budgets are devoted to personnel, so naturally that is where most of the opportunity for savings lies.

Private operating firms strive to reduce personnel costs without understaffing a facility. They do this by:

Using more efficient facility design.   If a private firm has a role in designing a facility, it is likely to use innovative new design techniques, with sight lines and technology that allow inmates to be monitored with fewer correctional personnel.

Reducing administrative levels.   Private operating firms tend to have fewer administrative personnel than the often bureaucratic structures of government correctional departments. One private prison administrator, with 14 years of experience in government corrections, says that private prisons use roughly one-third the administrative personnel government prisons use.

Minimizing the use of overtime.   Many correctional departments are understaffed, leading to the use of overtime to ensure sufficient correctional officers for each shift in each facility. Sometimes it is less expensive to use overtime than to hire more employees, but only up to a point. Overtime also increases when employees call in sick. In the public sector, sick time is considered an entitlement, not a privilege, and it is almost rebellious not to use it. With considerable success, private firms use incentives to reduce sick time and the consequent overtime expenditures. While overtime helps raise the take-home pay of existing employees, it can significantly raise operating costs. By using full staffing and more efficient personnel management, private prison firms use less overtime.

Exercising greater freedom to manage personnel.   Private operating firms are not bound by civil-service rules in managing their personnel; this significantly reduces personnel management costs. Private operating firms can use both positive and negative incentives to induce employees to perform. Civil-service rules and terms of public-employee union contracts tend to increase costs.

As a rule, private operating firms do not cut costs by cutting personnel quality. Pay for correctional officers at private firms tends to be nearly the same, or only slightly lower, than for government correctional officers. Where compensation is lower, private operating firms make up for it in part by offering opportunity for advancement based on merit rather than civil-service rules. Also, many private operating companies offer employee incentive packages that can be very lucrative. For instance, employee stock ownership plans have reaped tremendous rewards for many employees.

Reducing Incidents

Almost every incident between inmates, or between inmates and correctional officers, costs a prison money. These incidents lead to lawsuits, which also increase personnel costs. Private operating firms respond to these incentives by managing facilities in ways that minimize incidents. This means maintaining tight control of inmates and keeping them well-fed and occupied with work, education, or recreation—in short, establishing in the inmates' eyes the legitimacy of the private correctional officers' authority. Several studies have shown that privately operated facilities tend to have fewer incidents than comparable government facilities. In Florida, "get tough" policies in the state-run prisons have been accompanied by a 62 percent increase in inmate assaults on other inmates and a 250 percent increase in inmate assaults on correctional officers. In the state's private prisons, where the new policies did not apply, there has been no such increase in incidents.

Fully Using Facility Capacity

If a jurisdiction does not use all of the beds in its facility, private operating firms can often lower the per-inmate costs by contracting to hold prisoners from other jurisdictions in the excess space. This allows the local jurisdiction to reduce its share of covering the fixed costs of operating the facility.

Efficient Purchasing and Maintenance

Freedom from bureaucratic purchasing rules and procedures lets private operating firms shop locally for the lowest-cost necessary supplies and services. This saves both time and money. One private prison warden explains that if he needs some item, such as camera film, he doesn't have to order it through a complex state purchasing process or wait for it to be shipped from a distant supplier—he just goes to a store and buys it.

The story is similar for facility maintenance. Private operators and owners of prisons have incentives to make maintenance decisions that save long-run capital costs as well as current operating costs. Private firms can invest today in ways that generate savings over time, while the public sector often has difficulty getting approval or funds for such investments. For example, in one prison a private company that took over operations switched all lighting over to fluorescent bulbs and refitted the plumbing to stop rampant leaks, generating considerable savings in utility costs.

Competition, Not Private-Sector "Magic," Creates Efficiency and Innovation

When governments contract with the private sector, efficiency and innovation do not come about because private firms have some magic pixie dust, unobtainable by the public sector, to sprinkle about. It is competition that creates efficiency and innovation, because competition punishes inefficiency and inertia. That means two things: first, that the contracting process needs to be competitive in the long run for efficiency to remain, and second, that competition from the private sector makes the public sector more efficient as well. This is the great uncounted benefit of private-sector provision of correctional services. Contracts usually save money not only directly, but also indirectly, by forcing the government corrections departments to tighten up their ships.

There has been little success at quantifying the indirect benefits competition brings to the overall provision of correctional services. Perhaps the best attempt was part of the 1995 cost comparison study in Tennessee. The study compared costs at two government prisons and one private prison at the beginning and at the end of the year of study. When the facilities knew they were being compared, they strove for their best efficiency, and the cost at all three prisons declined over the year—5 and 8 percent at the two government prisons and 15 percent at the private prison.

Anecdotal evidence of competitive pressures and "cross-fertilization" abounds as well. Russ Boraas, Private Prison Administrator for the Virginia Department of Corrections, believes the cross-fertilization benefits of contracting with private firms to run some prisons may be the greatest benefits of contracting. Virginia has two new prisons designed, built, and operated by private firms. Both firms dramatically reduced capital and operating costs of the facilities by replacing expensive external guard towers with high-tech sensors and a roving patrol, and by eliminating a 30-day food storage warehouse and storing just enough food for a week.

For no reason that anyone can remember, Virginia prisons keep 30 days of food on hand in warehouses that are expensive to build, maintain, and operate. Boraas believes it is a practice going back to when prisons were remote and supplied by mule train. No one had ever bothered to question the practice until the private companies came in and did something different. He says that the rest of the state prisons are now adopting the private firms' food storage practices, and that only maximum-security prisons are likely to have external guard towers in the future.

There are plenty of similar stories:

- Responding to a perceived threat from the growth of private prison operation, the Connecticut Department of Corrections (DOC) adopted a philosophy of running its prisons more like businesses and dramatically cut annual spending. At the end of 1996, the department returned $46 million to the state treasury. Savings were realized by cutting staff and increasing revenue generated by inmates. Despite this, Connecticut still spends $65 a day for each inmate, one of the highest per-inmate cost rates in the nation.
- Carl Nink, of the Arizona DOC, explains how the state's prison wardens had never defined the measures that constitute successful performance of a prison until they had to write a contract with the operator of the state's first private prison. The result forced a lot of wardens to go back and reevaluate their own policies and practices to ensure they meet the same standards being asked of the private firm.
- According to Tim Wilson, Head of Contracts for Her Majesty's Prison Service, in the years since the lower costs at new private prisons have become public, costs at government prisons in the United Kingdom have been falling.

The existence of private prisons, and the threat of privatization, changes the incentives for government corrections officials. As long as there is a credible threat of privatization, these incentives to reduce costs and improve quality will remain. It remains to be seen what amount of competition is necessary to maintain these incentives for the public sector.

Conclusion

The evidence from comparative cost studies strongly supports the conclusion that private prisons save an average of 10 to 15 percent on operating costs. The conclusion is also supported by the experience of public officials in many states that use private prisons. Competitive pressure provides the incentive to be efficient that helps drive private-sector costs down, and the firms achieve cost savings through innovative design and management practices.

NO ↵

Eric Bates

Private Prisons

Afew hours after midnight one August evening last year, Walter Hazelwood and Richard Wilson climbed a fence topped with razor wire at the Houston Processing Center, a warehouse built to hold undocumented immigrants awaiting deportation. Once outside, the two prisoners assaulted a guard, stole his car and headed for Dallas.

When prison officials notified the Houston police that the men had escaped, local authorities were shocked. Sure, immigrants had fled the minimum-security facility near the airport a few times before. But Hazelwood and Wilson were not being detained for lacking the papers to prove their citizenship. One was serving time for sexual abuse; the other was convicted of beating and raping an 88-year-old woman. Both men, it turned out, were among some 240 sex offenders from Oregon who had been shipped to the Texas detention center months earlier—and local authorities didn't even know they were there.

The immigration center is owned and operated by Corrections Corporation of America [C.C.A.], which manages more private prisons than any other company worldwide. While C.C.A. made nearly $14,000 a day on the out-of-state inmates, the company was quick to point out that it had no legal obligation to tell the Houston police or county sheriff about their new neighbors from Oregon. "We designed and built the institution," explained Susan Hart, a company spokeswoman. "It is ours."

Yet like a well-to-do rancher who discovers a couple of valuable head of cattle missing, C.C.A. expected Texas rangers to herd the wayward animals back behind the company's fence. "It's not our function to capture them," Hart told reporters.

Catching the prisoners proved easier, however, than charging them with a crime. When authorities finally apprehended them after eleven days, they discovered they could no more punish the men for escaping than they could lock up a worker for walking off the job. Even in Texas, it seemed, it was not yet a crime to flee a private corporation.

"They have not committed the offense of escape under Texas law," said district attorney John Holmes. "The only reason at all that they're subject to being arrested and were arrested was because during their leaving the facility, they assaulted a guard and took his motor vehicle. *That* we can charge them with, and have."

The state moved quickly to pass legislation making such escapes illegal. But the Texas breakout underscores how the rapid spread of private prisons has created considerable confusion about just what the rules are when a for-profit company like Corrections Corporation seeks to cash in on incarceration. Founded in 1983 with backing from the investors behind Kentucky Fried Chicken, C.C.A. was one of the first companies to push the privatization of public services. The selling point was simple: Private companies could build and run prisons cheaper than the government. Business, after all, would be free of red tape—those inefficient procedures that waste tax dollars on things like open bidding on state contracts and job security for public employees. Unfettered American capitalism would produce a better fetter, saving cash-strapped counties and states millions of dollars each year.

Sooner or later, people realize that "the government can't do anything very well," Thomas Beasley, a co-founder of C.C.A. and a former chairman of the Tennessee Republican Party, said near the start of prison privatization. "At that point, you just sell it like you were selling cars or real estate or hamburgers."

꧁◉꧂

Not everyone is quite so enthusiastic about the prospect of selling human beings like so many pieces of meat. By privatizing prisons, government essentially auctions off inmates—many of them young black men—to the highest bidder. Opponents ranging from the American Civil Liberties Union to the National Sheriffs Association have argued that justice should not be for sale at any price. "The bottom line is a moral one," says Ira Robbins, who wrote a statement for the American Bar Association opposing private corrections. "Do we want our justice system to be operated by private interests? This is not like privatizing the post office or waste management to provide services to the community. There's something meaningful lost when an inmate looks at a guard's uniform and instead of seeing an emblem that reads 'Federal Bureau of Prisons' or 'State Department of Corrections,' he sees one that says 'Acme Prison Corporation.'"

But such moral concerns have gone largely unheeded in all the excitement over how much money the boys at Acme might save taxpayers. There's only one problem: The evidence suggests that the savings reaped from nearly fifteen years of privatizing prisons are more elusive than an Oregon convict in a Texas warehouse.

꧁◉꧂

In 1996 the General Accounting Office examined the few available reports comparing costs at private and public prisons. Its conclusion: "These studies do not offer substantial evidence that savings have occurred." The most reliable study cited by the G.A.O. found that a C.C.A.-run prison in Tennessee cost only 1 percent less to operate than two comparable state-run prisons. The track record also suggests that private prisons invite political corruption and do little to improve quality, exacerbating the conditions that lead to abuse and violence.

Although private prisons have failed to save much money for taxpayers, they generate enormous profits for the companies that own and operate them. Corrections Corporation ranks among the top five performing companies on the New York Stock Exchange over the past three years. The value of its shares has soared from $50 million when it went public in 1986 to more than $3.5 billion at its peak last October. By carefully selecting the most lucrative prison contracts, slashing labor costs and sticking taxpayers with the bill for expenses like prisoner escapes, C.C.A. has richly confirmed the title of a recent stock analysis by PaineWebber: "Crime pays."

"It's easier for private firms to innovate," says Russell Boraas, who oversees private prisons for the Virginia Department of Corrections. As he inspects a medium-security facility being built by C.C.A. outside the small town of Lawrenceville, Boraas notes that the prison has no guard towers—an "innovation" that saves the company $2.5 million in construction costs and eliminates twenty-five full-time positions. "Think about it," Boraas says. "A state corrections director who eliminates guard towers will lose his job if a prisoner escapes and molests a little old lady. The president of the company won't lose his job, as long as he's making a profit."

Although corrections officials like Boraas initially viewed the drive to privatize prisons with skepticism, many quickly became converts. The crime rate nationwide remains well below what it was twenty-five years ago, but harsher sentencing has packed prisons and jails to the bursting point. There are now 1.8 million Americans behind bars—more than twice as many as a decade ago—and the "get tough" stance has sapped public resources and sparked court orders to improve conditions.

With their promise of big savings, private prisons seemed to offer a solution. Corporate lockups can now hold an estimated 77,500 prisoners, most of them state inmates. Over the next five years, analysts expect the private share of the prison "market" to more than double.

Corrections Corporation is far and away the biggest company in the corrections business, controlling more than half of all inmates in private prisons nationwide. C.C.A. now operates the sixth-largest prison system in the country—and is moving aggressively to expand into the global market with prisons in England, Australia and Puerto Rico. That's good news for investors. *The Cabot Market Letter* compares the company to a "a hotel that's always at 100% occupancy... and booked to the end of the century." C.C.A. started taking reservations during the Reagan Administration, when Beasley founded the firm in Nashville with a former classmate from West Point. Their model was the Hospital Corporation of America [H.C.A.], then the nation's largest owner of private hospitals. "This is the home of H.C.A.," Beasley thought at the time. "The synergies are the same."

From the start, those synergies included close ties to politicians who could grant the company lucrative contracts. As former chairman of the state G.O.P., Beasley was a good friend of then-Governor Lamar Alexander. In 1985 Alexander backed a plan to hand over the entire state prison system to the fledgling company for $200 million. Among C.C.A.'s stockholders at the time were the Governor's wife, Honey, and Ned McWherter, the influential Speaker of the state House, who succeeded Alexander as governor.

Although the state legislature eventually rejected the plan as too risky, C.C.A. had established itself as a major player. It had also discovered that knowing the right people can be more important than actually saving taxpayers money. The company won its first bid to run a prison by offering to operate the Silverdale Work Farm near Chattanooga for $21 per inmate per day. At $3 less than the county was spending, it seemed like a good deal—until a crackdown on drunk drivers flooded the work farm with new inmates. Because fixed expenses were unaffected by the surge, each new prisoner cost C.C.A. about $5. But the county, stuck with a contract that required it to pay the company $21 a head, found itself $200,000 over budget. "The work farm became a gold mine," noted John Donahue, a public policy professor at Harvard University.

When the contract came up for renewal in 1986, however, county commissioners voted to stick with Corrections Corporation. Several enjoyed business ties with the company. One commissioner had a pest-control contract with the firm, and later went to work for C.C.A. as a lobbyist. Another did landscaping at the prison, and a third ran the moving company that settled the warden into his new home. C.C.A. also put the son of the county employee responsible for monitoring the Silverdale contract on the payroll at its Nashville headquarters. The following year, the U.S. Justice Department published a research report warning about such conflicts of interest in on-site monitoring—the only mechanism for insuring that prison operators abide by the contract. In addition to being a hidden and costly expense of private prisons, the report cautioned, government monitors could "be co-opted by the contractor's staff. Becoming friendly or even beholden to contract personnel could lead to the State receiving misleading reports."

But even when problems have been reported, officials often downplay them. The Justice Department noted "substantial staff turnover problems" at the Chattanooga prison, for instance, but added that "this apparently did not result in major reductions in service quality." The reason? "This special effort to do a good job," the report concluded, "is probably due to the private organizations finding themselves in the national limelight, and their desire to expand the market."

The same year that federal officials were crediting C.C.A. with "a good job" at the undermanned facility, Rosalind Bradford, a 23-year-old woman being held at Silverdale, died from an undiagnosed complication during pregnancy. A shift supervisor who later sued the company testified that Bradford suffered in agony for at least twelve hours before C.C.A. officials allowed her to be taken to a hospital. "Rosalind Bradford died out there, in my opinion, of criminal neglect," the supervisor said in a deposition.

Inspectors from the British Prison Officers Association who visited the prison that year were similarly shocked by what they witnessed. "We saw evidence of inmates being cruelly treated," the inspectors reported. "Indeed, the warden admitted that noisy and truculent prisoners are gagged with sticky tape, but this had caused a problem when an inmate almost choked to death."

The inspectors were even more blunt when they visited the C.C.A.-run immigration center in Houston, where they found inmates confined to warehouse-like dormitories for twenty-three hours a day. The private facility, inspectors concluded, demonstrated "possibly the worst conditions we have ever witnessed in terms of inmate care and supervision."

⁂

Reports of inhumane treatment of prisoners, while deeply disturbing, do not by themselves indicate that private prisons are worse than public ones. After all, state and federal lockups have never been known for their considerate attitude toward the people under their watch. Indeed, C.C.A. and other company prisons have drawn many of their wardens and guards from the ranks of public corrections officers. The guards videotaped earlier this year assaulting prisoners with stun guns at a C.C.A. competitor in Texas had been hired despite records of similar abuse when they worked for the state.

Susan Hart, the C.C.A. spokeswoman, insisted that her company would never put such people on the payroll—well, almost never. "It would be inappropriate, for certain positions, [to hire] someone who said, 'Yes, I beat a prisoner to death,'" she told *The Houston Chronicle*. "That would be a red flag for us." She did not specify for which positions the company considers murder an appropriate job qualification.

In fact, C.C.A. employs at least two wardens in Texas who were disciplined for beating prisoners while employed by the state. And David Myers, the president of the company, supervised an assault on inmates who took a guard hostage while Myers was serving as warden of a Texas prison in 1984. Fourteen guards were later found to have used "excessive force," beating subdued and handcuffed prisoners with riot batons.

The real danger of privatization is not some innate inhumanity on the part of its practitioners but rather the added financial incentives that reward inhumanity. The same economic logic that motivates companies to run prisons more efficiently also encourages them to cut corners at the expense of workers, prisoners and the public. Private prisons essentially mirror the cost-cutting practices of health maintenance organizations: Companies receive a guaranteed fee for each prisoner, regardless of the actual costs. Every dime they don't spend on food or medical care or training for guards is a dime they can pocket.

As in most industries, the biggest place to cut prison expenses is personnel. "The bulk of the cost savings enjoyed by C.C.A. is the result of lower labor costs," PaineWebber assures investors. Labor accounts for roughly 70 percent of all prison expenses, and C.C.A. prides itself on getting more from fewer employees. "With only a 36 percent increase in personnel," boasts the latest annual report, "revenues grew 41 percent, operating income grew 98 percent, and net income grew 115 percent."

Like other companies, C.C.A. prefers to design and build its own prisons so it can replace guards right from the start with video cameras and clustered cellblocks that are cheaper to monitor. "The secret to low-cost operations is having the minimum number of officers watching the maximum number of inmates," explains Russell Boraas, the private prison administrator for Virginia. "You can afford to pay damn near anything for construction if it will get you an efficient prison."

At the C.C.A. prison under construction in Lawrenceville, Boraas indicates how the design of the "control room" will enable a guard to simultaneously watch three "pods" of 250 prisoners each. Windows in the elevated room afford an unobstructed view of each cellblock below, and "vision blocks" in the floor are positioned over each entranceway so guards can visually identify anyone being admitted. The high-tech panel at the center of the room can open any door at the flick of a switch. When the prison opens next year, C.C.A. will employ five guards to supervise 750 prisoners during the day, and two guards at night.

Another way to save money on personnel is to leave positions unfilled when they come open. Speaking before a legislative panel in Tennessee in October, Boraas noted that some private prisons in Texas have made up for the low reimbursement rates they receive from the state "by leaving positions vacant a little longer than they should." Some C.C.A. employees admit privately that the company leaves positions open to boost profits. "We're always short," says one guard who asked not to be identified. "They do staff fewer positions—that's one way they save money." The company is growing so quickly, another guard explains, that "we have more slots than we have people to fill them. When they transfer officers to new facilities, we're left with skeletons."

∽⊗∾

At first glance, visitors to the South Central Correctional Center could be forgiven for mistaking the medium-security prison for a college campus. The main driveway rolls through wooded hills on the outskirts of Clifton, Tennessee, past picnic benches, a fitness track and a horse barn. But just inside the front door, a prominent bulletin board makes clear that the prison means business. At the top are the words "C.C.A. Excellence in Corrections." At the bottom is "Yesterday's Stock Closing," followed by a price.

∽⊗∾

In addition to employing fewer guards, C.C.A. saves money on labor by replacing the guaranteed pensions earned by workers at state-run prisons with a cheaper—and riskier—stock-ownership plan. Employees get a chance to invest in the company, and the company gets employees devoted to the bottom line. "Being a stockholder yourself, you monitor things closer," says Mark Staggs, standing in the segregation unit, where he oversees prisoners confined for breaking the rules. "You make sure you don't waste money on things like cleaning products. Because it's your money you're spending."

Warden Kevin Myers (not related to C.C.A. president David Myers) also looks for little places to cut costs. "I can save money on purchasing because there's no bureaucracy," he says. "If I see a truckload of white potatoes at a bargain, I can buy them. I'm always negotiating for a lower price."

But what is thriftiness to the warden is just plain miserly to those forced to eat what he dishes out. "Ooowhee! It's pitiful in that kitchen," says Antonio McCraw, who was released from South Central last March after serving three years for armed robbery. "I just thank God I'm out of there. You might get a good meal once a month. The rest was instant potatoes, vegetables out of a can and processed pizzas. C.C.A. don't care whether you eat or not. Sure they may cut corners and do it for less money, but is it healthy?"

The State of Tennessee hoped to answer that question when it turned South Central over to C.C.A. in 1992. The prison was built at roughly the same time as two state-run facilities with similar designs and inmate populations, giving officials a rare opportunity to compare daily operating costs—and quality —under privatization.

The latest state report on violence at the three prisons indicates that South Central is a much more dangerous place than its public counterparts. During the past fiscal year, the C.C.A. prison experienced violent incidents at a rate more than 50 percent higher than state facilities. The company also posted significantly worse rates for contraband, drugs and assaults on staff and prisoners.

"If that doesn't raise some eyebrows and give you some kind of indication of what the future holds, I guess those of us who are concerned just need to be quiet," says John Mark Windle, a state representative who opposes privatization.

Corrections officials note that understaffing can certainly fuel violence, which winds up costing taxpayers more money. The state legislature has heard testimony that employee turnover at South Central is more than twice the level at state prisons, and prisoners report seeing classes of new recruits every month, many of them young and inexperienced. "The turnover rate is important because it shows whether you have experienced guards who stick around and know the prisoners," says inmate Alex Friedmann, seated at a bare table in a visitation room. "If you have a high turnover rate you have less stability. New employees come in; they really don't know what's going on. That leads to conflicts with inmates."

Internal company documents tell a similar story. According to the minutes of an August 1995 meeting of shift supervisors at South Central, chief of security Danny Scott "said we all know that we have lots of new staff and are constantly in the training mode." He "added that so many employees were totally lost and had never worked in corrections."

A few months later, a company survey of staff members at the prison asked, "What is the reason for the number of people quitting C.C.A.?" Nearly 20 percent of employees cited "treatment by supervisors," and 17 percent listed "money."

Out of earshot of their supervisors, some guards also say the company contributes to violence by skimping on activities for inmates. "We don't give them anything to do," says one officer. "We give them the bare minimum we have to."

Ron Lyons agrees. "There's no meaningful programs here," says Lyons, who served time at state-run prisons before coming to South Central. "I can't get over how many people are just laying around in the pod every day. I would have thought C.C.A. would have known that inmate idleness is one of the biggest problems in prisons—too much time sitting around doing nothing. You definitely realize it's commercialized. It's a business. Their business is to feed you and count you, and that's it."

Given all the penny-pinching, it would seem that C.C.A. should easily be able to demonstrate significant savings at South Central. Instead, a study of costs conducted by the state in 1995 found that the company provided almost no savings compared with its two public rivals. The study—cited by the General Accounting Office as "the most sound and detailed comparison of operational costs"—actually showed that the C.C.A. prison cost *more* to run on a daily basis. Even after the state factored in its long-term expenses, C.C.A. still spent $35.38 a day per prisoner—only 38 cents less than the state average.

The study contradicted what is supposed to be the most compelling rationale for prison privatization: the promise of big savings. But the industry champion dismissed its defeat by insisting, much to the amazement of its challengers, that it hadn't tried very hard to save tax dollars. "When you're in a race and you can win by a few steps, that's what you do," said Doctor R. Crants, who co-founded C.C.A. and now serves as chairman and chief executive officer. "We weren't trying to win by a great deal."

⚜

The comment by Crants, as remarkable as it seems, exposes the true nature of privatization. When it comes to savings, the prison industry will beat state spending by as narrow a margin as the state will permit. To a prison company like C.C.A., "savings" are nothing but the share of profits it is required to hand over to the government—another expense that cuts into the bottom line and must therefore be kept to a minimum, like wages or the price of potatoes. At its heart, privatizing prisons is really about privatizing tax dollars, about transforming public money into private profits.

That means companies are actually looking for ways to keep public spending as high as possible, including charging taxpayers for questionable expenses. The New Mexico Corrections Department, for example, has accused C.C.A. of overcharging the state nearly $2 million over the past eight years for operating the women's prison in Grants. The company fee of $95 a day for each inmate, it turns out, includes $22 for debt service on the prison.

⚜

Last summer, a legislative committee in Tennessee calculated that state prisons contribute nearly $17.8 million each year to state agencies that provide central services like printing, payroll administration and insurance. Since company prisons usually go elsewhere for such services, states that privatize unwittingly lose money they once counted on to help pay fixed expenses.

The "chargebacks," as they are known, came to light last spring when C.C.A. once again proposed taking over the entire Tennessee prison system. This time the company offered to save $100 million a year—a staggering sum, considering that the annual budget for the system is only $270 million.

Like many claims of savings, the C.C.A. offer turned out to be based on false assumptions. Crants, the company chairman and C.E.O., said he derived the estimate from comparing the $32 daily rate the company charges for medium-security prisoners at South Central with the systemwide average of $54. But the state system includes maximum-security prisons that cost much more to operate than South Central. "It's almost like going into a rug store," says State Senator James Kyle, who chaired legislative hearings on privatization. "They're always 20 percent off. But 20 percent off what?"

Yet the sales pitch, however absurd, had the intended effect of getting Kyle and other lawmakers into the store to look around. Once there, the prison companies kept offering them bigger and better deals. Given an opportunity to submit cost estimates anonymously, firms offered fantastic savings ranging from 30 percent to 50 percent. Threatened by the competition, even the state Department of Corrections went bargain basement, offering to slash its own already low cost by $70 million a year. Despite opposition from state employees, legislators indicated after the hearings that they support a move to turn most prisoners over to private companies—a decision that delighted C.C.A. "I was pretty pleased," Crants said afterward. The governor and legislators are wrangling over the details, but both sides have agreed informally to privatize roughly two-thirds of the Tennessee system. A few prisons will be left in the hands of the state, just in case something goes wrong.

Lawmakers didn't have to look far to see how wrong things can go. South Carolina decided last February not to renew a one-year contract with C.C.A. for a juvenile detention center in the state capital. Child advocates reported hearing about horrific abuses at the facility, where some boys say they were hogtied and shackled together. "The bottom line is the staff there were inexperienced," said Robyn Zimmerman of the South Carolina Department of Juvenile Justice. "They were not trained properly."

Once again, though, such stark realities proved less influential than the political connections enjoyed by C.C.A. The chief lobbyist for the company in the Tennessee legislature is married to the Speaker of the state House. Top C.C.A. executives, board members and their spouses have contributed at least $110,000 to state candidates since 1993, including $1,350 to Senator Kyle. And five state officials—including the governor, the House Speaker and the sponsor of the privatization bill—are partners with C.C.A. co-founder Thomas Beasley in several Red Hot & Blue barbecue restaurants in Tennessee.

The political clout extends to the national level as well. On the Republican side, Corrections Corporation employs the services of J. Michael Quinlan, director of the federal Bureau of Prisons under George Bush. On the Democratic side, C.C.A. reserves a seat on its seven-member board for Joseph Johnson, former executive director of the Rainbow Coalition. The Nashville *Tennessean* points to Johnson as evidence that the company "looks like America.... Johnson is African-American," the paper observes, "as are 60% of C.C.A.'s prisoners."

Johnson played a pivotal behind-the-scenes role earlier..., using his political connections to help C.C.A. swing a deal to buy a prison from the District of Columbia for $52 million. It was the first time a government sold a prison to a private company, and C.C.A. hopes it won't be the last.... [W]ith backing from financial heavyweights like Lehman Brothers and PaineWebber, the company formed C.C.A. Prison Realty Trust to focus solely on buying prisons. The initial stock offering raised $388.5 million from investors to enable C.C.A. to speculate on prisons as real estate.

·✿·

Why would cities or states sell their prisons to the C.C.A. trust? PaineWebber cites the lure of what it calls "free money." Unlike many public bond initiatives earmarked for specific projects like schools or sewage systems, the broker explains, "the sale of an existing prison would generate proceeds that a politician could then use for initiatives that fit his or her agenda, possibly improving the chances of re-election." Companies building their own prisons certainly receive friendly treatment from officials. Russell Boraas invited companies bidding on a private prison to a meeting and asked what he could do to help. "I said, 'Guys, I know quite a bit about running construction projects, but I don't know much about private prisons. What are you looking for? What can I do to make this user-friendly for you?' They said it would be nice if they could use tax-exempt bond issues for construction, just like the state." So Boraas allowed companies to finance construction with help from taxpayers, and a local Industrial Development Authority eventually aided C.C.A. in getting $58 million in financing to build the prison.

Such deals raise concerns that private prisons may wind up costing taxpayers more in the long run. Although governments remain legally responsible for inmates guarded by public companies, firms have little trouble finding ways to skirt public oversight while pocketing public money. Instead of streamlining the system, hiring corporations to run prisons actually *adds* a layer of bureaucracy that can increase costs and reduce accountability. Prison companies have been known to jack up prices when their contracts come up for renewal, and some defer maintenance on prisons since they aren't responsible for them once their contract expires.

Even more disturbing, private prisons have the financial incentive—and financial influence—to lobby lawmakers for harsher prison sentences and other "get tough" measures. In the prison industry, after all, locking people up is good for business. "If you really want to save money you can lock prisoners in a box and feed them a slice of bread each day," says Alex Friedmann, the prisoner at South Central. "The real question is, Can you run programs in such a way that people don't commit more crime? That should be the mark of whether privatization is successful in prisons—not whether you keep them locked up but whether you keep them out."

C.C.A. officials dismiss such concerns, confident the current boom will continue of its own accord. "I don't think we have to worry about running out of product," says Kevin Myers, the warden at South Central. "It's unfortunate but true. We don't have to drum up business."

Perhaps—but Corrections Corporation and other company prisons already have enormous power to keep their current prisoners behind bars for longer stretches. Inmates generally lose accumulated credit for "good time" when they are disciplined by guards, giving the C.C.A. stockholders who serve as officers an incentive to crack the whip. A 1992 study by the New Mexico Corrections Department showed that inmates at the women's prison run by C.C.A. lost good time at a rate nearly eight times higher than their male counterparts at a state-run lockup. And every day a prisoner loses is a day of extra income for the company—and an extra expense for taxpayers.

Some C.C.A. guards in Tennessee also say privately that they are encouraged to write up prisoners for minor infractions and place them in segregation. Inmates in "seg" not only lose their good time, they also have thirty days added to their sentence—a bonus of nearly $1,000 for the company at some prisons. "We will put 'em in seg in a hurry," says a guard who works at the Davidson County Juvenile Detention Facility in Nashville.

The prison holds 100 youths—"children, really," says the guard—most of them teenage boys. "They may be young, but they understand what's going on," he adds. One day, as a 14-year-old boy was being released after serving his sentence, the guard offered him some friendly advice.

"Stay out of trouble," he said. "I don't want to see you back here."

"Why not?" the kid responded. "That's how you make your money."

POSTSCRIPT

Do Private Prisons Pay?

There are many concerns about private prisons that are not addressed in the selections by Moore and Bates. One issue that is repeatedly noted by those who write in this area concerns legality; that is, can the "state" incarcerate its inmates in a private facility? Consider the difficulties with the "rent-a-cell" business. Has a prisoner broken the law by escaping from a private prison? Can a corrections officer use "deadly force" to control prison riots? Is it "cruel and unusual punishment" to force a prisoner to serve her or his time 1,500 miles away from friends and family? Are correctional officers adequately trained in private facilities? Who is responsible for regulating private prisons? Will private prison corporations make their records open to the public?

The answers to these and other questions are found in the growing body of literature on the development of the private prison system. One source of information is the Prison Privatization Research Site at http://www.ucc.uconn.edu/~Logan/. This Internet site addresses many of these questions by looking at the more than 100,000 prison beds in the nearly 200 private corrections facilities currently under contract or under construction in the United States, the United Kingdom, and Australia as of the end of 1997. For views that agree with Moore's enthusiastic support of private prisons, see the Texas Public Policy Foundation's *Bexar County Opportunity Analysis,* which can be found online at http://www.tppf.org/ by clicking on Public Policy Research and then on Government Efficiency. On the other side, see Phil Smith's critique of private prisons entitled "Private Prisons: Profits of Crime," *Covert Action Quarterly* (Fall 1993). You can find this on the Internet at http://www.mediafilter.org/MFF/prison.html.

There are many other good sources of information. For example, in "The Prison-Industrial Complex," *The Atlantic Monthly* (December 1998), Eric Schlosser likens the developments in the corrections industry to the development of President Dwight Eisenhower's military-industrial complex. Schlosser suggests that the "confluence of special interests" has given America a "prison-industrial complex." Or you might wish to go directly to the U.S. Department of Justice and look for their Bureau of Justice Statistics, which can be found at http://www.ojp.usdoj.gov/bjs/. Finally, for a good annotated bibliography, see the Web site Cashing in on Criminality: Private Prisons, Corporate Power, and the Color of Crime, at http://speech.csun.edu/ben/news/karyl.html.

Financial Reports and the Financial Condition of the Federal Government

Available at this site is a daily treasury statement, information on the federal budget from the Office of Management and Budget, a collection of statistics on social and economic conditions in the United States, and much more.

http://www.fms.treas.gov/conditn.html

Joint Economic Committee

Start here to explore the work and opinions of the members of the Joint Economic Committee on many topics—tax reform and government spending, international economic policy, and who is benefiting from economic growth, to name just a few.

http://www.house.gov/jec/

The Public Debt Online

Here you will find links to the public debt of the United States "to the penny," historical debt, interest expense and the public debt, and frequently asked questions about the public debt.

http://www.publicdebt.treas.gov/opd/opd.htm

U.S. Macroeconomic and Regional Data

Hosted by the State University of New York, Oswego, Department of Economics, this site contains the full text of recent economic reports to the president and links to various global and regional economic indicators.

http://www.oswego.edu/~economic/mac-data.htm

U.S. Treasury Department

In addition to information about the U.S. Treasury Department itself, this site features the latest news and speeches from the Treasury Department, a calendar of important events in the department's history, and a public engagement schedule to find out where and when Treasury Department officials will speak.

http://www.ustreas.gov

PART 2

Macroeconomic Issues

*G*overnment policy and economics are tightly intertwined. Fiscal policy and monetary policy have a dramatic impact on the national economy, and the state of the economy can often lead to changes in taxes, government spending, and interest rates. Decisions regarding tax cuts, the minimum wage, and welfare reform must be made in the context of broad macroeconomic goals, and the debates on these issues are more than theoretical discussions. Each has a significant impact on our lives.

- Should Social Security Be Privatized?

- Does the Consumer Price Index Overstate Inflation and Changes in the Cost of Living?

- Is President George W. Bush's Tax Cut Plan Good Economic Policy?

- Is the New Economy Really New?

- Is It Time to Abolish the Minimum Wage?

ISSUE 8

Should Social Security Be Privatized?

YES: Michael Tanner, from " 'Saving' Social Security Is Not Enough," *Cato Institute Project on Social Security Privatization SSP No. 20* (May 25, 2000)

NO: Catherine Hill, from "Privatizing Social Security Is Bad, Particularly for Women," *Dollars and Sense* (November/December 2000)

ISSUE SUMMARY

YES: Michael Tanner, director of health and welfare studies at the Cato Institute, argues that Social Security needs to be replaced with a retirement system based on individually owned, privately invested accounts. He maintains that Social Security fails as it is currently structured both as an antipoverty program and as a retirement program, that it is unfair, and that it makes workers dependent on politicians for their retirement incomes.

NO: Catherine Hill, a study director at the Institute for Women's Policy Research, contends that privatization of Social Security is a bad idea because it would create significant transition and administrative costs, create a void with respect to disability and life insurance, and lower the retirement income of women.

S ocial Security, more formally the Old Age, Survivors, and Disability Insurance program (OASDI), was signed into law on August 14, 1935, by President Franklin D. Roosevelt. As originally designed, OASDI provided three types of benefits: retirement benefits to the elderly who were no longer working, survivor benefits to the spouses and children of people who have died, and disability benefits to people who experience non-work-related illness or injury. The Medicare portion of Social Security, which provides benefits for hospital, doctor, and medical expenses, was not created until 1965.

There are many terms used to describe OASDI. It is an entitlement program in the sense that everyone who satisfies the eligibility requirements receives benefits. Eligibility is established by employment and contributions to the system (in the form of payroll taxes) for a minimum period of time. It is also a defined benefits program; that is, the level of benefits is determined by legislation. The opposite of a defined benefits program is a defined contributions program, in which benefits are determined by contributions and whatever investment income is generated by those contributions. OASDI is also described as a pay-as-you-go system; this means that payments received by recipients are financed primarily by the contributions of current workers. Still another description of OASDI is that it is an income security program. In this context, the reference is to a whole set of government programs designed to provide minimum levels of income to various people. Finally, OASDI is described as a social insurance program to distinguish it from private insurance programs. The insurance feature rests on the fact that OASDI protects against certain unforeseen events, such as disability and early death. The social feature arises from the fact that contributions and the level of benefits are determined by legislation and that the contributions are mandatory (payroll taxes that must be paid). In a private insurance program the beneficiary and the insurance issuer voluntarily negotiate the level of contributions and the level of benefits.

With respect to the administration of OASDI, there are several components to consider. One component is the Social Security and Medicare Trustees. This six-member panel annually prepares estimates of the inflows and outflows of funds and the long-term actuarial soundness of the system. A second component is the Social Security Advisory Council. This panel is constituted every four years and reviews the projections of the trustees. In the process the council may offer suggestions for changes in the program. The third component involves both Congress and the president. They are involved because any changes to the system in terms of contributions and benefits requires the passage of legislation.

Members of the Social Security Advisory Council agree that there is currently a Social Security "crisis," which refers to the fact that with the currently legislated structure of revenues and benefits, the system will be unable to meet its financial obligations at some future date. Presently, revenues are greater than outpayments, and the excess is accumulated in a trust fund. Around the year 2015, outpayments will exceed revenues, and the difference will be covered by drawing down the trust fund. Eventually, the trust fund will be exhausted (around the year 2036), and revenues will only be sufficient to cover about two-thirds of outpayments.

A number of strategies have been developed for dealing with the Social Security crisis. They range from an increase in Social Security payroll taxes to a reduction in benefits, to an increase in the age at which a person would become eligible for benefits, to privatization. This issue focuses on the last strategy. In the following selections, Michael Tanner states that there are a number of problems with the current Social Security system—problems that could be redressed by replacing Social Security with a system of individually owned, privately invested accounts. Catherine Hill argues against privatization generally because it involves significant transition and administrative costs, entails market risk, and creates a void for disability and life insurance protection. She also argues against privatization because it would hurt women in particular by lowering their retirement income.

"Saving" Social Security Is Not Enough

Introduction

The corridors of Washington are ringing with calls to "save" Social Security. And it is certainly easy to understand why the program needs "saving." Social Security is rapidly heading for financial insolvency. By 2015 the program will begin running a deficit, paying out more in benefits than it takes in through taxes. The resulting shortfall will necessitate at least a 50 percent increase in payroll taxes, a one-third reduction in benefits, or some combination of benefit cuts and tax increases. Overall, Social Security faces a long-term funding shortfall of more than $20 trillion.[1]

As a result, there have been numerous proposals designed to shore up the program's shaky finances. Those proposals generally take one of two tracks: setting aside current Social Security surpluses in some form of "lock box" or injecting general revenue financing into the system.

There are serious flaws in both of those approaches. The lock-box proposals do not, in fact, do anything to change Social Security's financing. Currently, surplus Social Security taxes are used to purchase government bonds, which are held by the Social Security trust fund. Those bonds will eventually have to be repaid. To do so, the government will have to raise revenue. Thus the bonds represent nothing more than a claim against future tax revenues, in essence a form of IOU.[2] ...

Some proposals go beyond setting aside Social Security surpluses and would inject all or part of the current general revenue budget surpluses into the Social Security system. Aside from the fact that Social Security's liabilities far outstrip the amount of surplus available, it is impossible to prefund Social Security under the program's current structure. Any additional funds put into the system today would simply purchase more government bonds, which would have to be paid in the future from whatever tax monies were available then.

However, setting aside the important point that none of the current proposals to save Social Security actually does so, the current focus on "saving" Social Security is itself misguided. Merely finding sufficient funding to preserve Social Security fails to address the serious shortcomings of the current system. The question should be, not whether we can save Social Security, but whether we can provide the best possible retirement system for American workers. Such a system should keep seniors out of poverty as well as improve prospects for future generations. It should provide an adequate retirement income and the best possible return on an individual's money. It should be fair, treating similarly situated people equally. Certainly, it should not penalize the disadvantaged in society such as the poor and minorities. And it should allow people to own their benefits, freeing seniors from dependence on politicians and politics for retirement benefits.

On all those scores, Social Security is an abysmal failure. It fails both as an anti-poverty program and as a retirement program. It contains numerous inequities and leaves future retirement benefits to the whims of politicians. Why should the goal of public policy be to save such a program?

Instead of saving Social Security, we should begin the transition to a new and better retirement system based on individually owned, privately invested accounts. A privatized system would allow workers to accumulate real wealth that would prevent their retiring to poverty. Because a privatized system would provide a far higher rate of return, it would yield much higher retirement benefits. Because workers would own their accounts, money in them could be passed on to future generations. That would particularly benefit the poor and minorities. Finally, again because workers would own their retirement accounts, they would no longer be dependent on politicians for their retirement incomes.

Social Security as an Anti-Poverty Program

Social Security has elements of both an insurance and a welfare program. It is, in effect, both a retirement and an anti-poverty program.[3] Although people most often think of the retirement component of the program, the system's defenders often focus on its anti-poverty elements. For example, Rep. Bill Archer (R-Tex.), chairman of the House Ways and Means Committee and author of a proposal to save Social Security, calls the program "the country's greatest anti-poverty program."[4] But is it really?

There is no question that the poverty rate among the elderly has declined dramatically in the last half century. As recently as 1959, the poverty rate for seniors was 35.2 percent, more than double the 17 percent poverty rate for the general adult population.[5] Today, it has declined to approximately 11.9 percent.[6]

Clearly, Social Security has had a significant impact on that trend. A 1999 study by the Center on Budget and Policy Priorities [CBPP] found that in the absence of Social Security benefits approximately 47.6 percent of seniors would have incomes below the poverty level.[7] That suggests that receipt of Social Security benefits lifted more than 35 percent of seniors, approximately 11.4 million people, out of poverty. CBPP also points out that the percentage of elderly who would have been in poverty in the absence of Social Security has remained relatively constant over the last several decades, while the percentage of elderly in poverty after receiving Social Security benefits has been steadily declining, indicating the increased importance of Social Security as an anti-poverty remedy.[8]

The primary problem with this line of analysis is that it assumes that any loss of Social Security benefits would not be offset by income from other sources. In other words, it simply takes a retiree's current income and subtracts Social Security benefits to discover, no surprise, that total income is now lower and, indeed, frequently low enough to throw the retiree into poverty.

Social Security benefits are a substantial component of most retirees' income. Those benefits constitute more than 90 percent of retirement income for one-quarter of the elderly. Nearly half of retirees receive at least half of their income from Social Security.[9] The question, therefore, is not whether the sudden elimination of Social Security income would leave retirees worse off—clearly it would—but whether in the absence of Social Security (or an alternative mandatory savings program) retirees would have changed their behavior to provide other sources of income for their own retirement.

For example, we could ask how many seniors, in the absence of Social Security, would still be working. If they were, they would have a source of income not considered by the CBPP study. Clearly, not all seniors are able to continue working. However, many can and would. Indeed, Congress recently repealed the Social Security earnings test precisely because there are many seniors who *want* to continue working.

A more important question is whether workers, without Social Security to depend on, would have changed their behavior and saved more for their retirement. The evidence is strong that Social Security discourages individual savings. For example, Martin Feldstein of Harvard University and Anthony Pellechio of the National Bureau for Economic Research have found that households reduce their private savings by nearly one dollar for every dollar of the present value of expected future Social Security benefits.[10] Other studies have put the amount of substitution somewhat lower but still indicate a substantial offset. Even two researchers for the Social Security Administration, Dean Leimer and David Richardson, have conceded that "a dollar of Social Security wealth substitutes for about three-fifths of a dollar of fungible assets."[11]

Therefore, given that many seniors would have replaced Social Security income with income from other sources, the impact of Social Security on reducing poverty among the elderly may be overstated.

However, even taking the arguments of Social Security's defenders on their own terms, the evidence suggests that Social Security fails as an anti-poverty tool. After all, despite receiving Social Security benefits, nearly one of eight seniors still lives in poverty. In fact, the poverty rate for seniors remains slightly higher than that for the adult population as a whole.[12]

For some subgroups, the problem is far worse. For example, although the poverty rate for elderly married women is relatively low (6.4 percent), the poverty rate is far higher for elderly women who never married (21.1 percent), widowed women (21.5 percent), and divorced or separated women (29.1 percent).[13] African American seniors are also disproportionately left in poverty. Nearly 30 percent of African Americans over the age of 65 have incomes below the poverty level.[14]

Social Security's failure as an anti-poverty program is not surprising since Social Security benefits are actually quite low. A worker earning the minimum wage over his entire working life would receive only $6,301 per year in Social Security benefits, well below the poverty level of $7,990. As mentioned above, poor seniors receive nearly 80 percent of their retirement income from Social Security. Many have no other income at all. Social Security is insufficient to raise those seniors out of poverty.

This can be contrasted with what those people would have received had they been able to invest their payroll taxes in real capital assets. For example, if the minimum wage worker described above had been able to invest his payroll taxes, he would be receiving retirement benefits of $20,728 per year, nearly three times the poverty level.[15] Clearly, by forcing workers to invest in the current pay-as-you-go system, rather than in real capital assets, Social Security is actually contributing to poverty among the elderly.

Not only does Social Security contribute to poverty among current seniors, it also helps perpetuate poverty for future generations. Social Security benefits are not inheritable. A worker can pay Social Security taxes for 30 or 40 years, but, if that worker dies without children under the age of 18 or a spouse over the age of 65, none of the money paid into the system is passed on to his heirs.[16] As Jagadeesh Gokhale, an economist at the Federal Reserve Bank of Cleveland, and others have noted, Social Security essentially forces low-income workers to annuitize their wealth, preventing them from making a bequest of that wealth to their heirs.[17]

Moreover, because this forced annuitization applies to a larger portion of the wealth of low-income workers than of high-income workers, it turns inheritance into a "disequalizing force," leading to greater inequality of wealth in America. The wealthy are able to bequeath their wealth to their heirs, while the poor cannot. Indeed, Gokhale and Boston University economist Laurence Kotlikoff estimate that Social Security doubles the share of wealth owned by the richest 1 percent of Americans.[18]

Feldstein reaches a similar conclusion. He suggests that low-income workers substitute "Social Security wealth" in the form of promised future Social Security benefits for other forms of savings. As a result, a greater proportion of a high-income worker's wealth is in fungible assets. Since fungible wealth is inheritable, whereas Social Security wealth is not, a small proportion of the population holds a stable concentration of fungible wealth.[19] Feldstein's work suggests that the concentration of wealth in the United States would be reduced by as much as half if low-income workers were able to substitute real wealth for Social Security wealth. Individual accounts would allow them to do so.

Thus, far from being "the country's greatest anti-poverty program," Social Security appears to do a poor job of lifting seniors out of poverty and may in fact perpetuate their poverty while increasing inequality in this country.

Social Security as a Retirement Program

If Social Security is an inadequate anti-poverty program, does it at least meet its second goal as a retirement program? When Franklin Roosevelt proposed Social Security, he promised a program that would provide retirement benefits "at least as good as any American could buy from a private insurance company."[20] While that may have been true at one time, it certainly is no longer the case.

Social Security's rate of return has been steadily declining since the program's inception and is now far lower than the return from private capital investment. According to the Social Security Administration, workers born after 1973 will receive rates of return ranging from 3.7 percent for a low-wage, single-income couple to just 0.4 percent for a high-wage-earning single male.[21] The overall rate of return for all workers born in a given year was estimated at slightly below 3 percent for those born in 1940, 2 percent for those born in 1960, and below 1 percent for those who will be born this century.[22] Numerous private studies predict future rates of return for an average-wage earner ranging from 2 percent to a negative 3 percent.[23]

To make matters worse, the studies generally assume that Social Security will be able to pay all its promised benefits without increasing payroll taxes. However, the Social Security system is facing a long-term financial shortfall of more than $20 trillion. According to the system's own Board of Trustees, either taxes will have to be raised by at least 50 percent or benefits reduced by 25 percent. As a result, the rate of return will be even lower than the rates cited above. In many cases the return will actually be negative.[24]

By comparison, the average rate of return to the stock market since 1926 has been 7.7 percent.[25] That return has held despite a major depression, several recessions, World War II, two smaller wars, and the turbulent inflation-recession years of the 1970s. Of course, there have been ups and downs in the market, but there has been no 20-year period since 1926 during which the market was a net loser. Indeed, there has never been a 20-year period in which the market performed worse than projected future returns from Social Security.[26]

Even corporate bonds have consistently outperformed Social Security. Discounting the period 1941–51, when government price controls artificially reduced the return, corporate bonds have paid an average real annual return of more than 4 percent.[27]

Thus, because it deprives American workers of the ability to invest in private capital markets, the current Social Security system is costing American retirees hundreds of thousands of dollars. A single-earner couple, whose wage earner is 30 years old in 2000 and earning $24,000 per year, can expect to pay more than $134,000 in Social Security taxes over their lifetimes and receive $292,320 in lifetime Social Security benefits (including spousal benefits), assuming that both husband and wife live to normally expected ages.[28] However, had they been able to invest privately, they would have received $875,280.[29] That means the current Social Security system is depriving them of more than half a million dollars.

A second way to consider Social Security's adequacy as a retirement program is to look at the replacement rate, that portion of preretirement income replaced by Social Security benefits. Most financial planners say that a person will need retirement benefits equal to between 60 and 85 percent of preretirement wages in order to maintain his or her standard of living.[30]

However, Social Security provides only 42.4 percent of preretirement income for average-income workers. Because Social Security has a progressive benefit formula, low-income workers do better with a replacement rate of 57.1 percent, still below what is needed. That is especially true since low-income workers lack other forms of retirement income. The replacement rate for high-income workers is only 25.6 percent. In the future, the situation will grow even worse. Even under current law, replacement rates are scheduled to decline significantly. By 2030 Social Security will replace only 36.7 percent of an average-wage earner's preretirement income. However, because Social Security cannot pay all promised future benefits, the Congressional Research Service estimates that the replacement rate for an average worker will decline to as low as 26 percent, a 40 percent decline from the current already inadequate levels.[31] Clearly, Social Security, both now and in the future, leaves many seniors without the income necessary to maintain their standard of living.

Again, compare this with the replacement rates provided under a system of private investment. Assuming that the worker described previously were able to invest the full nondisability portion of his Social Security taxes (10.6 percent of wages), his replacement rate would be an astounding 260 percent of preretirement income! If he invested just 4 percent of wages, he would still have a replacement rate equal to 100 percent of his preretirement income.

Social Security Is Unfair

As if it were not bad enough that Social Security fails in its stated mission as an anti-poverty and retirement program, the program also contains very serious inequities that make it fundamentally unfair.

The program's most obvious unfairness is *intergenerational.* Retirees currently receiving benefits paid a relatively low payroll tax over their working lifetimes and receive a fairly high rate of return. That high return is subsidized by much higher payroll taxes on today's young workers who, in turn, can expect much lower future benefits. As Daniel Shapiro, professor of philosophy at West Virginia University, has pointed out, one of the basic precepts of social justice is the minimization of *unchosen* inequalities.[32] However, the future generations forced to bear the burden of Social Security's unfunded liabilities must do so entirely because of the time of their birth and not through any fault or choice of their own.

The program's *intragenerational* inequities are less visible but just as unfair. As we have already noted, Social Security benefits are not inheritable. Therefore, lifetime Social Security benefits depend, in part, on longevity. As a result, people with identical earnings histories will receive different levels of benefits depending on how long they live. Individuals who live to be 100 receive far more in benefits than individuals who die at 66. Therefore, those groups in our society with shorter life expectancies, such as the poor and African Americans, are put at a severe disadvantage.

Of course, Social Security does have a progressive benefit formula, whereby low-income individuals receive proportionally higher benefits per dollar paid into the system than do high-income workers.[33] The question, therefore, is to what degree shorter life expectancies offset this progressivity.

The findings of studies that use income as the sole criterion are mixed. Some studies, such as those by Eugene Steuerle and Jan Bakja of the Urban Institute and Dean Leimer of the Social Security Administration, conclude that shorter life expectancies diminish but do not completely offset Social Security's progressivity.[34] However, there is a growing body of literature—including studies by Daniel Garrett of Stanford University, the RAND Corporation, and others—that shows that the progressive benefit formula is completely offset, resulting in redistribution of wealth from poor people to the already wealthy.[35]

The question of Social Security's unfairness to ethnic minorities appears more straightforward, particularly in the case of African Americans. African Americans of all income levels have shorter life expectancies than do whites. As a result, a black man or woman, earning exactly the same lifetime wages and paying exactly the same lifetime Social Security taxes as his or her white counterpart, will likely receive far less in lifetime Social Security benefits. For example, assume that a 30-year-old black man and a 30-year-old white man both earn $30,000 per year over their working lifetimes. By the time they retire, they will each have paid $136,740 in Social Security taxes over their lifetimes[36] and will be entitled to monthly Social Security benefits of $1,162. However, the white man can expect to live until age 81.[37] If he does, he will receive $189,389 in total Social Security benefits. The black man, in contrast, can expect to live only to age 79.[38] He can expect to receive only $161,750, almost $27,000 less than his white counterpart. This may actually understate the unfairness of the current system, since it is based on life expectancies at age 65. However, if both men are age 30 today, the life expectancy for the white man is 78; for the black man it is only 69.[39] If those projections are accurate, the black man can expect to receive nearly $100,000 less in lifetime Social Security benefits than his white counterpart and, indeed, will receive less than half what he actually paid into the program.

It seems amazing that this disparate impact, which would not be tolerated in any other government program, is so easily accepted within the current Social Security system.[40]

The current program is also unfair to women who work outside the home. Under the current system, a woman is automatically entitled to 50 percent of her husband's benefits, whether or not she has worked outside the home or paid Social Security taxes.[41] However, if a woman is able to claim benefits both as a spouse and in her own right, she may receive only the larger of the two. Because many women work only part-time, take years off from work to raise children, or earn lower wages than their husbands, 50 percent of the husband's benefits is frequently larger than the benefits a woman would be entitled to as a result of her own earnings. She will, therefore, receive only the benefits based on her husband's earnings. She will receive no additional benefits even though she may have worked and paid thousands of dollars in payroll taxes. Indeed, she would receive exactly the same benefits as if she had never worked a day outside the home or paid a dime in Social Security taxes. The taxes she paid earn her exactly *nothing*.[42]

Anyone concerned with fairness and equity in government programs must acknowledge that our current Social Security system falls far short of meeting those goals.

Social Security and the Dignity of Older Americans

Finally, it should be noted that the current Social Security system makes American seniors dependent on government and the political process for their retirement income. In essence, it reduces American seniors to supplicants, robbing them of their dignity and control over their own lives.

Americans, of course, do not get back the money that they individually paid into Social Security. Under our pay-as-you-go Social Security system, the money that workers pay in Social Security taxes is not saved or invested for their own retirement; it is instead used to pay for benefits for current retirees. Any overpayment is used by the federal government to pay its general operating expenses or, under various lock-box proposals, to pay down the national debt.

In exchange, workers receive a promise that the government will tax future workers in order to provide benefits to today's workers when they retire. However, that promise is not any sort of legally enforceable contract. It has long been settled law that there is no legal right to Social Security. In two important cases, *Helvering v. Davis* and *Flemming v. Nestor,* the U.S. Supreme Court has ruled that Social Security taxes are simply taxes and convey no property or contractual rights to Social Security benefits.[43]

As a result, a worker's retirement security is entirely dependent on political decisions made by the president and Congress. Benefits may be reduced or even eliminated at any time and are not directly related to Social Security taxes paid into the system.

Therefore, retirees are left totally dependent on the whims of politicians for their retirement income. A person can work hard, play by the rules, and pay thousands of dollars in Social Security taxes but at retirement his benefits depend entirely on the decisions of the president and Congress. Despite their best intentions, seniors have been turned into little more than wards of the state.

Conclusion

If Social Security didn't exist today, would we invent it? The current Social Security system is a failure by almost every criterion. It fails to lift many seniors out of poverty or to improve prospects for future generations. Indeed, it may actually redistribute money from the poor to the wealthy. Because it forces the poor to annuitize their savings, it prevents the accumulation of real wealth and prevents the poor from passing that wealth on to future generations. Social Security also fails as a retirement program. It does not provide an adequate retirement income or yield the best possible return on an individual's money. Nor is the program fair. It includes numerous inequities that unfairly discriminate against minorities, the poor, and working women. And, finally, because people do not have any legal ownership of their benefits, it leaves seniors dependent on politicians and politics for their retirement benefits.

Surely this cannot be what we seek from Social Security, especially when there are alternatives available. Workers should be allowed to take the money they are currently paying in Social Security taxes and redirect it to individually owned, privately invested accounts, similar to individual retirement accounts or 401(k) plans. The funds that accumulated in those accounts would be invested in real assets such as stocks and bonds, with safeguards against highly risky or speculative investments. The funds would be the account holders' personal property. At retirement, workers could convert all or part of their accumulated funds into an annuity or take a series of programmed withdrawals from the principal. If they choose the latter option, any funds remaining at their death would become part of their estate, fully inheritable by their heirs.

A retirement program based on individually owned, privately invested accounts would provide higher retirement benefits and a better rate of return than does Social Security. It would lift more seniors out of poverty, and, because funds are inheritable, accumulated wealth could be passed on to future generations. It would not penalize groups with shorter life expectancies and would eliminate the penalty on working women. And workers would own their benefits and thus be free from political risk and dependence.[44]

When it comes to Social Security, policymakers should consider whether it is more important to save a system or to provide a better retirement for American seniors.

Notes

1. Board of Trustees, Federal Old-Age and Survivors Insurance and Disability Insurance Trust Funds, *2000 Annual Report* (Washington: Government Printing Office, 2000).

2. As President Clinton's own budget notes: "[Trust fund] balances are available to finance future benefit payments and other trust fund expenditures—but only in a bookkeeping sense. These funds are not set up to be pension funds like the funds of private pension plans. They do not consist of real economic assets that can be drawn down in the future to fund benefits. Instead, they are claims on the Treasury that, when redeemed, will have to be financed by raising taxes, borrowing from the public, or reducing benefits or other expenditures. The existence of large trust fund balances, therefore, does not, by itself, have any impact on the government's ability to pay benefits." Executive Office of the President of the United States, *Analytical Perspectives: Budget of the United States Government, Fiscal Year 2000* (Washington: Government Printing Office, 1999), p. 337.

3. W. Andrew Achenbaum, *Social Security: Visions and Revisions* (Cambridge: Cambridge University Press, 1986), pp. 54–55. See also Peter Ferrara, *Social Security: The Inherent Contradiction* (Washington: Cato Institute, 1980).

4. Bill Archer, Comments at Hearing on Social Security before the House Committee on Ways and Means, 106th Cong., 1st sess., June 9, 1999, transcript, p. 48, Federal News Service.

5. Daryl Jackson et al., "Understanding Social Security: The Issues and Alternatives," American Institute of Certified Public Accountants, Washington, November 1998, p. 17.

6. Bureau of the Census, Current Population Reports, Series P60, 1998.

7. Kathryn Porter, Kathy Larin, and Wendell Primus, "Social Security and Poverty among the Elderly: A National and State Perspective," Center on Budget and Policy Priorities, Washington, April 1999.

8. Ibid., p. 16.

9. Neil Gilbert and Neung-Hoo Park, "Privatization, Provision, and Targeting: Trends and Policy Implications for Social Security in the United States," *International Social Security Review* 49 (January 1996): 22.

10. Martin Feldstein and Anthony Pellechio, "Social Security and Household Wealth Accumulation: New Microeconomic Evidence," *Review of Economics and Statistics* 61 (August 1979): 361–68.

11. Dean Leimer and David Richardson, "Social Security, Uncertainty, Adjustments, and the Consumption Decision," *Economica* 59 (August 1992): 29.

12. Bureau of the Census, Current Population Reports, Series P60.

13. Steven Sandell, "Adequacy and Equity of Social Security," *Report of the 1994–1995 Advisory Council on Social Security* (Washington: Government Printing Office, 1997), vol. 2, pp. 321–27.

14. Bureau of the Census, Population Report P60-175, 1996, Table 6, p. 18.

15. Assumes investment in stocks earning actual returns and that the individual was born in 1935, earned the minimum wage his entire working life, and retires in 2000.

16. Survivors' benefits may be extended to age 21 if the child is enrolled in college.

17. Jagadeesh Gokhale et al., "Simulating the Transmission of Wealth Inequality via Bequests," *Journal of Public Economics* (forthcoming, 2000).

18. Jagadeesh Gokhale and Laurence Kotlikoff, "The Impact of Social Security and Other Factors on the Distribution of Wealth," National Bureau of Economic Research, Cambridge, Mass., October 1999.

19. Martin Feldstein, "Social Security and the Distribution of Wealth," *Journal of the American Statistical Association* 71 (December 1976): 800–807.

20. Quoted in Warren Shore, *Social Security: The Fraud in Your Future* (New York; Macmillan, 1975), p. 2.

21. Barbara Bovbjerg, "Social Security: Issues in Comparing Rates of Return with Market Investments," U.S. General Accounting Office Report HEHS-99-110, August 1999.

22. Dean Leimer, "Cohort-Specific Measures of Lifetime Net Social Security Transfers," Social Security Administration, Office of Research and Statistics, Working Paper no. 59, February 1994.

23. For example, in our 1998 book, *A New Deal for Social Security,* Peter Ferrara and I updated a study that Ferrara conducted for the National Chamber Foundation in 1986. Using economic and demographic assumptions taken from the Social Security trustees' intermediate assumptions, adjusting for survivors' and disability benefits, and assuming that, somehow, Social Security would pay all promised benefits, we found that most workers who entered the workforce after 1985 would receive rates of return of 1.0 to 1.5 percent or less. Peter J. Ferrara and Michael Tanner, *A New Deal for Social Security* (Washington: Cato Institute, 1998), p. 69. Those results closely matched the results of a study that Ferrara conducted in 1985 with Professor John Lott, then at the Wharton School and now at Yale Law School. The 1985 study, which looked at workers entering the workforce in 1983, also showed rates of return from Social Security for most workers in the range of 1.0 to 1.5 percent. Peter J. Ferrara and John Lott, "Social Security's Rates of Return for Young Workers," in *Social Security: Prospects for Real Reform,* ed. Peter Ferrara (Washington: Cato Institute, 1985), pp. 13–36. The Heritage Foundation concluded

in 1998 that the rate of return to an average two-earner family (both 30 years old) was just 1.23 percent, while the return to African American men was actually negative. William Beach and Gareth Davis, "Social Security's Rate of Return," Report no. 98-01 of the Heritage Center for Data Analysis, Washington, January 15, 1998. In a 1988 study for the National Bureau of Economic Research, John Geanakopolis, Olivia Mitchell, and Stephen Zeldes concluded that workers born after 1970 could expect a rate of return of less than 2 percent. John Geanakopolis, Olivia Mitchell, and Stephen Zeldes, "Social Security's Money Worth," National Bureau of Economic Research Working Paper no. 6722, Washington, September 1988. The U.S. General Accounting Office reports that a two-earner couple born in 1973 and making average wages would receive a rate of return from Social Security of approximately 2.1 percent. Bovbjerg, p. 13. The nonpartisan Tax Foundation suggests future rates of return as low as a negative 3 percent. Arthur Hall, "Forcing a Bad Investment on Retiring Americans," Tax Foundation Special Report no. 55, November 1995.

24. See, for example, Jagadeesh Gokhale and Laurence Kotlikoff, "Social Security's Treatment of Postwar Americans: How Bad Can It Get?" National Bureau of Economic Research Working Paper no. 7362, Cambridge, Mass., September 1999. See also Hall; Beach and Davis; and Geanakopolis, Mitchell, and Zeldes.

25. Gokhale and Kotlikoff, "Social Security's Treatment of Postwar Americans," p. 15.

26. Jeremy J. Siegel, *Stocks for the Long Run* (New York: McGraw-Hill, 1998), p. 26. Of course, critics of privatization point out, correctly, that the past is no guarantee of future performance. But the critics' contention that the future performance of private capital markets will be significantly lower than past averages is unpersuasive. See, for example, Peter Ferrara, "Social Security Is Still a Hopelessly Bad Deal for Today's Workers," Cato Institute Social Security Paper no. 18, November 29, 1999.

The critics generally argue that, using the Social Security trustees' projections for future economic growth, economic growth will be too slow to sustain continued stock market gains. Dean Baker and Mark Weisbrot, for example, suggest that future returns will be below 3.5 percent. Dean Baker and Mark Weisbrot, *Social Security: The Phony Crisis* (Chicago: University of Chicago Press, 1999), pp. 88–104. However, the critics fail to acknowledge that the issue is not simply the return to capital markets but the spread between the return to capital markets and the return to Social Security. As Gokhale and Kotlikoff point out, Social Security tax payments and benefit receipts are closely linked to overall labor productivity growth, which is highly correlated with economic performance, which, in turn, is correlated with stock market performance. It is entirely reasonable to compare the real rate of return from stocks with the return from Social Security. Gokhale and Kotlikoff, "Social Security's Treatment of Postwar Americans," p. 15. In other words, if economic growth is so slow as to reduce the returns from private capital investment, it will also reduce the taxes collected by the Social Security system, exacerbating its fiscal imbalance, leading to lower benefits or higher taxes and a reduced Social Security rate of return. Thus, both Social Security's return and the return on capital could go up or they could go down, but private capital markets will always outperform Social Security. It is even possible to envision a scenario in which capital returns increase while Social Security tax receipts do not, for example, if wage growth takes place largely above the cap, or if economic growth translates to nonwage compensation rather than increased real wages. However, it is difficult to foresee a scenario under which real wages (and therefore Social Security revenues) rise while private capital markets do not.

Critics of privatization also suggest that the return to private capital markets should be reduced to reflect administrative costs and the costs associated with the transition to a privatized system. Both arguments have been refuted extensively elsewhere. However, it is worth noting that the U.S. General Accounting Office suggests that administrative costs would range from a low of 10 basis points to a high of 300 basis points, with most estimates closer to the low end of the range. U.S. General Accounting Office, "Social Security Reform: Administrative Costs for Individual Accounts Depends on System Design," GAO/HEHS-99-131, June 1999. A study for the Cato Institute concluded that administrative costs would range between 30 and 65 basis points. Robert Genetski, "Administrative Costs and the Relative Efficiency of Public and Private Social Security Systems," Cato Institute Social Security Paper no. 15, March 9, 1999.

The question of transition costs is also highly misleading. First, it has been clearly demonstrated that it is possible to pay for the transition without additional taxes. See, for example, Ferrara and Tanner, pp. 175–204. Even more important, however, Milton Friedman and others have shown that, when Social Security's current unfunded liabilities are considered, there are no new costs associated with the transition. Milton Friedman, "Speaking the Truth about Social Security Reform," Cato Institute Briefing Paper no. 46, April 12, 1999. Indeed, as William Shipman has demonstrated, the cost of paying for the transition, regardless of the financing mechanism chosen, will always be less than the cost of preserving the current system. William Shipman, "Facts and Fantasies about Transition Costs," Cato Institute Social Security Paper no. 13, October 13, 1998.

27. Calculated from Moody's Investor Service, *Moody's Industrial Manual and Moody's Bond Survey,* 1920–96.

28. Assumes husband retires at age 67, husband collects full Social Security benefit, and wife collects spousal benefit until husband dies at age 75. Wife then collects widow's benefit until she dies at age 81.

29. Assuming historical rates of return.

30. A. Haeworth Robertson, *Social Security: What Every Taxpayer Should Know* (Washington: Retirement Policy Institute, 1992), p. 218.

31. David Koitz, "Social Security Reform: Assessing Changes to Future Retirement Benefits," Congressional Research Service Report for Congress RL-30380, December 14, 1999.

32. Daniel Shapiro, "The Moral Case for Social Security Privatization," Cato Institute Social Security Paper no. 14, October 29, 1998.

33. Social Security benefits are based on a formula that provides benefits equal to 90 percent of the first $495 of monthly income (adjusted according to a formula that takes into account the growth in wages), 32 percent of the next $2,286, and 15 percent of remaining income up to the wage cap.

34. See C. Eugene Steuerle and John Bakija, *Retooling Social Security for the 21st Century: Right and Wrong Approaches to Reform* (Washington: Urban Institute, 1994), pp. 91–132; and Dean Leimer, "Lifetime Redistribution under the Social Security Program: A Literature Synopsis," *Social Security Bulletin* 62 (1999): 43–51.

35. Daniel Garrett, "The Effects of Differential Mortality Rates on the Progressivity of Social Security," *Economic Inquiry* 33 (July 1995): 457–75; W. Constantijn, A. Panis, and Lee Lillard, "Socioeconomic Differentials in the Return to Social Security," RAND Corporation Working Paper no. 96-05. February 1996; and Beach and Davis.

36. Counting only the OASI portion of the payroll tax. This figure does not include the disability portion.

37. Bureau of the Census, *Statistical Abstract of the United States, 1995* (Washington: Government Printing Office, 1996), Table B-1.

38. Ibid.

39. Projected life expectancy at age 30. Centers for Disease Control, "United States Abridged Life Tables, 1996," *National Vital Statistics Report,* no 13 (December 24, 1998): Table 3.

40. Supporters of the current system maintain that, overall, African Americans benefit from the current Social Security system because they earn lower incomes than
whites and are more likely to have periods of unemployment. Therefore, they
are more likely to benefit from the program's progressive benefit formula. However, as we have seen, the lifetime progressivity of Social Security is questionable.
Supporters of the status quo also suggest that African Americans benefit disproportionately from the program's disability and survivors' benefits. However, there
are no empirical studies to support that contention. Indeed, the Social Security Administration rejected a request from the 1996–98 Social Security Advisory Council
to conduct such a study. Sylvester Schieber and John Shoven, *The Real Deal: The
History and Future of Social Security* (New Haven, Conn.: Yale University Press,
1999), p. 227.

41. The provision is gender neutral, applying to both men and women. However, because of earning patterns in the United States, it affects women almost exclusively.

42. For a full discussion of the impact of the current Social Security system on women
and the benefits of privatization for women, see Darcy Ann Olsen, "Greater Fi-
nancial Security for Women with Personal Retirement Accounts," Cato Institute
Briefing Paper no. 38, July 20, 1998; and Ekaterina Shirley and Peter Spiegler,
"The Benefits of Social Security Privatization for Women," Cato Institute Social
Security Paper no. 12, July 20, 1998.

43. For a thorough discussion of this issue, see Charles Rounds, "Property Rights: The
Hidden Issue of Social Security Reform," Cato Institute Social Security Paper no.
19 April 19, 2000.

44. For a full discussion of how a privatized Social Security system would work, see
Ferrara and Tanner.

NO ⮌

Catherine Hill

Privatizing Social Security Is Bad, Particularly for Women

You've probably heard the rumor that Social Security won't be there for you when you retire. And you've also probably heard that [President] George Bush promised to "save" Social Security by allowing individuals to divert 2% of their wages (or earnings) into individual accounts. Stocks generally have higher returns than government bonds, so setting up individual accounts that take advantage of these higher returns should mean more money when you retire. Right? Wrong. In fact, privatizing Social Security will mean less income in retirement for almost all American workers, and it will be particularly damaging for women.

Social Security—The Basics

Since 1935, Social Security has been America's most successful social program, currently providing income to 48 million retired and disabled Americans and their families. More than three fifths of retired households depend on Social Security for more than half of their income. For 25% of older women living alone, it is their only source of income. Without Social Security, half of elderly people in the United States would be poor (meaning that an elderly couple would have an income under $10,000 annually and an elderly individual would have less than $8,000 to live on).

A payroll tax supplies the revenue for Social Security. The tax is currently 12.4% on wages up to $72,600 and is split between employers and employees (6.2% each) with self-employed people paying the full tax themselves. (Workers also pay 1.45% of wages or earnings for Medicare.) Note that, because most of the payroll revenues are immediately used to pay benefits, diverting "only" 2% of wages means a one-sixth reduction in the money available to pay benefits.

Social Security benefits are available to all workers and their families regardless of income. For this reason, Social Security has historically enjoyed a stronger base of political support than programs that provide benefits only to those who can document poverty, such as Supplemental Security Income (SSI). The average monthly check for a retired worker is $825 with a maximum benefit of $1,373 for a worker with a consistently high salary over a full career (35 years). While no one gets rich from Social Security, it is an important source of income for almost all retired and disabled Americans.

Why There Isn't a Solvency Crisis

Every year the Social Security Trustees forecast the long-term revenues and expenditures for the program over the next 75 years, based on demographic and economic assumptions. In the early 1980s, the Trustees forecasted a financial shortfall (misreported in the press as a "crisis"). In response, Congress increased the payroll tax rate slightly and increased the retirement age (eligibility for full Social Security benefits) from 65 to 67. These changes generated billions of dollars in surpluses for Social Security, which were placed in the Social Security Trust Fund (currently valued at a little more than $896 billion). The Trust Fund earns interest, and both principal and interest can be used to supplement payroll tax revenue during the peak Baby Boom retirement years. In 1991, the Trustees decided to use more pessimistic assumptions about future economic growth, resulting in the prediction that Social Security would not be able to pay full benefits after 2034. Strong economic performance in the last few years has resulted in a lengthening of the projected solvency to 2037. If the economy does not slow down as much as predicted, and payroll tax revenues continue to grow at a healthy rate, Social Security has no long-term solvency problem. In any case, if the economy does slow down, the Social Security program is well-positioned to continue paying full benefits for at least another thirty-seven years. After 2037, Social Security can provide three-quarters of promised benefits, and with small policy changes, Social Security can continue to pay full benefits indefinitely.

Who Wants You to Believe There Is a Crisis and Why

Privatizing Social Security would be the largest undertaking in the history of the U.S. financial-services industry. It could also be the most profitable, and Wall Street knows it. For nearly two decades, Wall Street and its conservative think tanks have been cultivating the public's fear that Social Security is "going bankrupt." As Jesse Jackson and other progressive leaders have noted, financial firms such as Morgan Stanley, Quick & Reilly, Inc., and State Street Boston Corporation have given millions of dollars to conservative groups like the Cato Institute to push privatizing Social Security. However, with the facts so squarely mounted against them, the movement appeared to lose momentum, and for a while, it looked like the campaign to privatize Social Security had run its course. Activists breathed a sigh of relief and went about tackling other issues. However, this summer [2000], privatizers got a second wind when Presidential candidate George Bush pledged to "partially privatize" Social Security by diverting 2% of the payroll tax (a little less than a sixth of the program's revenue) into individual accounts. The fight is on and the privatizers have come out swinging.

Why Privatizating Social Security Is a Bad Idea

There are four major hidden flaws of privatizing Social Security: the enormous transition from a "pay as you go" to a pre-funded system, the costs associated with purchasing equivalent life and disability coverage (or maintaining the current disability and life insurance program in the context of a 16% cut in revenue), market risk, and higher administrative costs.

Transition costs   Privatizers face a costly transition period lasting 40–70 years. If pre-funded individual accounts were to be adopted, the generations living through the transition would have to pay for two systems at once, saving for their own retirement while paying for the Social Security benefits of their parents and grandparents.

Replacing disability and life insurance   A sleight of hand used by many privatizers is to compare "returns" from Social Security—a social insurance and retirement program—to returns from private savings that provide only retirement benefits. Social Security taxes pay for disability and life insurance as well as retirement benefits. The program provides life and disability insurance to American workers and their families at an estimated value of a $230,000 disability policy and a $354,000 life-insurance policy for a typical worker. Privatizers argue that individuals can purchase disability and life insurance from private insurance firms. However, evidence from other countries' experiments with privatization suggests that insurance similar to Social Security would be costly. For people with pre-existing conditions, private disability and life insurance may not be available at any price.

Overly optimistic returns on stocks   Another problem with privatization is the assumption that the stock market will perform as well in the coming decades as it has in the recent past—a risky assumption. In fact, many economists believe that the stock market may be at a peak, and many stocks may be overvalued. Privatizers can't have it both ways—either the economy will be strong and the solvency problem projected for the current system won't materialize, or the economy will slow and the rate of return on stocks will drop, lowering the balances of individual accounts. Even if the stock market does well on average, individual accounts mean that there would be winners and losers. People who have greater knowledge and more money to invest will get higher returns than others. For low earners, who have less to invest and are less able to take risks, attaining average rates of return is unlikely. People who are unlucky or unwise could end up losing most or all of their money, placing additional burdens on SSI and other government programs that provide some safety net to poor people.

Administrative costs   Another problem with the privatizers' arithmetic is the failure to account for administrative costs. It costs a lot more to administer 150 million individual accounts than a single centralized system like Social Security. Experts conservatively estimate that it would cost about $25–$50 per participant per year to administer on top of the current system, which costs about $16 per person. Even small increases in management costs that are assessed monthly or annually can result in a large loss of value over one's lifetime. For example, if the costs of operating a system of individual accounts were 1% of account balances each year (a conservative estimate of the administrative costs of a 401(k) plan), these costs would consume approximately 20% of funds in personal accounts over a 40-year career, in addition to (not instead of) the current costs for administering Social Security. For lower income workers who have smaller accounts, administrative costs would absorb a greater percentage of their total value.

Why Privatizing Social Security Is a Particularly Bad Idea for Women

Social Security is important for women because older women enter retirement with fewer economic resources than men. For example, in 1998, older women had a higher poverty rate (12.8%) than older men (7.2%). Women of color are particularly at risk for poverty in their old age. Overall, there is a substantial gender gap in all sources of retirement income including Social Security, pensions, savings, and post-retirement employment. The greatest disparity lies in accumulated pension wealth and savings, with Social Security credits partially compensating for this gap.

Furthermore, the Social Security system is progressive. Those with lower incomes have a higher proportion of their earnings replaced, which is valuable for women since they tend to earn less than men do. Income inequality would be further exacerbated in a privatized system because women investors, who have fewer resources, would get a lower yield on their investment as they would (appropriately) avoid risk.

Another important component of Social Security for women is the spousal benefit available to wives (or husbands) or widows (or widowers) who earned significantly less than their spouses. A married person is eligible for the larger of either 100% of his or her own retired worker benefit or 50% of his or her spouse's retired worker benefit. Women (or men) divorced after ten years of marriage can claim spousal benefits, even if their former partner remarries. Women make up the vast majority of recipients using the spousal benefit provision. In 1997, 13% of women beneficiaries claimed spousal benefits compared with 2% of men. While the spousal benefit is an imperfect acknowledgement of unpaid care-giving, it is preferable to a system of individual accounts" which allocates no monetary reward for child-rearing or elder care.

Social Security's "gender neutral" benefits mean that women don't have to pay more to compensate for their longer life expectancies—another advantage that would be lost in privatization.

The fact that Social Security provides an inflation-adjusted benefit guaranteed for life is particularly important to older women (who live on average three years longer than men).

Another aspect of Social Security that is especially valuable to women is the life and disability insurance, which includes benefits to spouses caring for children under 16 if the worker retires, becomes disabled, or dies. As women provide the bulk of care-giving in our society (for the elderly and disabled as well as for children), any shortcomings in disability and life insurance caused by privatization would have a special adverse impact on women.

Social Security Can Do Better

Having looked at the serious drawbacks of privatizing Social Security, we can return to the real issues facing Social Security. Certainly, it is true that people are living longer and that prudent financial planning dictates that the government should maintain adequate reserves. To the extent there are long-term solvency concerns, there are a number of ways to increase revenue into Social Security. For example, the cap on the earnings subject to the payroll tax could be lifted, meaning that everyone—even those who make six or seven figures—would pay the same payroll tax rate. Another (no doubt unpopular) approach would be to allow all Social Security benefits to be taxed as income and use these revenues for benefits. Investing a portion of the Trust Fund in higher-yield public or private securities is another option. This recommendation differs from proposals that privatize Social Security through individual accounts because investments would be made by a central, independent organization, sharing risk across the entire system and holding down administrative costs. Moreover, only a small portion of the Social Security fund reserves would be dedicated to this alternative investment strategy; thus limiting the system's overall exposure to risk.

It is also true that Americans, especially low- and moderate-income Americans, don't save enough for retirement. Even with generous tax deferment for pensions, it is increasingly clear that private pension plans will never cover the entire workforce. More than two decades after the Employee Retirement Income Security Act (ERISA), more than half of American workers are not covered by a pension plan. The economic situation for older women is particularly bleak. Among the elderly, women are only about half as likely as men to receive income from private pensions (including income from a spouse's pension), and those who do receive pension benefits that are only about half as large as men's benefits. For example, in 1996, pension income for women averaged $3,679, compared with $6,442 for men.

Differences in access to pensions represent a significant gap in federal resources. Because pension funds' earnings are not taxed, because employer contributions to pensions are considered tax-deductible business expenses, and because employees are not taxed until they retire (and begin drawing a pension), there is a significant tax advantage for pension holders. For example, in 1999, the Office of Management and Budget estimated that the federal government lost $84 billion in tax revenue. Thus, unequal access to pensions means that these tax favors are also unequally distributed.

There are a number of ways to give low- and moderate-income families access to the tax benefits associated with pensions (now disproportionately enjoyed by their wealthier counterparts). Vice President [Al] Gore's recent proposal for Retirement Savings Plus accounts would be a step in the right direction. This program would help middle-income and even low-income families save for retirement by matching private savings with government money. Lower income families would get the most help (families making less than $30,000 would receive $3 for every dollar they save), but middle- and upper-income families would also benefit (families making $100,000 would receive one dollar for every $3 saved). The accounts would be limited to $2,000 annually and savings would grow tax-free until withdrawal, like an individual retirement account or a 401(k) plan. But remember, these "individual accounts" should come on top of, rather than as a partial substitute for, guaranteed Social Security benefits.

Last, but not least, progressives should begin fighting to improve Social Security benefits. The safety net for the poorest elderly and disabled people is dropping lower and lower as means-tested programs, such as SSI, fail to keep pace with a growing economy. Under constant pressure to protect Social Security from Wall Street's wrecking ball, advocacy groups and politicians have shied away from increasing benefits for anyone. However, there is ample evidence that such improvements are needed—particularly for disabled people and older women not living with men, who are at high risk for poverty. Again, Gore's proposals to increase benefits for widows and people who took time out of the labor force (or worked part-time) to care for children are another step in the right direction. Now is a time of great prosperity, and we can afford to begin mending the safety net so frayed over the past two decades—perhaps, even raise it!

POSTSCRIPT

Should Social Security Be Privatized?

Tanner bases his support for a private retirement system to replace Social Security on four arguments. First, he states that Social Security has been a failure as an antipoverty program. Second, he contends that Social Security has been a failure as a retirement program. Third, Tanner asserts that Social Security is fundamentally unfair. Here he is concerned with both intergenerational and intragenerational transfers. Tanner's final argument is that Social Security reduces the dignity of older Americans. This is the case because seniors must depend on government and the political process for their retirement income. The solution to all these problems, according to Tanner, is to privatize Social Security; that is, by replacing the current system with individually owned, privately invested accounts.

Hill defends the current Social Security system and opposes privatization. She begins her argument by lauding the current system: it is the sole source of income for 25 percent of elderly women living alone, half of all elderly Americans would be poor without Social Security, and benefits are available to all workers and their families. Turning to privatization, Hill identifies general flaws and finds additional problems with regard to the impact of privatization on women. In rejecting privatization, Hill suggests some changes to the current system that would address the Social Security crisis. These suggestions range from the expansion of the base for Social Security payroll taxes to actions to stimulate private savings for retirement.

Additional readings on this issue include "How Not to Fix Social Security" by Mark Weisbrot, in *Dollars and Sense* (March/April 1997) and "The Great Social Security Scare," by Jerry L. Mashaw and Theodore R. Marmor, *The American Prospect* (November/December 1996). Also see three articles in *Economic Commentary:* "Should Social Security Be Privatized?" by Jagadeesh Gokhale (September 1995); "Social Security: Are We Getting Our Money's Worth?" by Jagadeesh Gokhale and Kevin J. Lansing (January 1, 1996); and "A Simple Proposal for Privatizing Social Security," by David Altig and Jagadeesh Gokhale (May 1, 1996). In addition, see the Institute for Women's Policy Research report *Why Privatizing Social Security Would Hurt Women: A Response to the Cato Institute's Proposal for Individual Accounts* by Catherine Hill, Lois Shaw, and Heidi Hartman (March 2000); "Strengthening Social Security for the Twenty-First Century" by Marilyn Watkins, an Economic Opportunity Institute Policy Brief; and "Assuring Retirement Income for All Workers" by Daniel I. Halperin and Alicia H. Munnell, Working Paper no. 2000-05, Center for Retirement Research, Boston College (March 2000).

ISSUE 9

Does the Consumer Price Index Overstate Inflation and Changes in the Cost of Living?

YES: Michael J. Boskin et al., from "Consumer Prices, the Consumer Price Index, and the Cost of Living," *Journal of Economic Perspectives* (Winter 1998)

NO: James Devine, from "The Cost of Living and Hidden Inflation," *Challenge* (March–April 2001)

ISSUE SUMMARY

YES: Economist Michael J. Boskin and his colleagues argue that the Consumer Price Index (CPI) suffers from quality and new product bias, which means that the CPI overstates inflation and increases in the cost of living.

NO: Professor of economics James Devine counters that the Consumer Price Index understates inflation and changes in the cost of living because it fails to account for all pertinent changes in the quality of life.

Each month the Bureau of Labor Statistics (BLS) releases a new estimate of the Consumer Price Index (CPI). This release usually merits front-page attention in U.S. newspapers because changes in the CPI are interpreted as changes in the cost of living of Americans. If nominal income does not increase to keep pace with increases in the cost of living, as determined by increases in the CPI, then real income falls.

Because of this connection between changes in the CPI and changes in the cost of living, a number of monetary arrangements in the economy are altered when the CPI changes; that is, they are indexed. For example, some private sector collective bargaining agreements tie wages to changes in the CPI. If the CPI increases, then wages automatically rise by the same percentage. But indexing is not limited to the private sector of the economy; the federal government has resorted to indexing in a variety of areas. In counting the number of poor persons, the poverty thresholds (the income levels that separate poor from nonpoor) are adjusted upward each year by the percentage increase in the CPI. With the individual income tax, the dollar value of the personal exemption is adjusted to reflect changes in the cost of living as determined by changes in the CPI. Social Security benefits are also adjusted each year to reflect changes in the cost of living and the CPI.

It is clearly important, then, to measure changes in the CPI and in the cost of living accurately. This issue addresses the question of the extent to which this accuracy is achieved. As a first step in understanding this debate, it is important to know how the CPI is calculated. The CPI, in technical terms, is a Laspeyres fixed-weight index. Accordingly, the first step in the calculation of the CPI is to determine the fixed weights—the goods and services that consumers purchase at a particular point in time known as the base period. This is known as the market basket and is accomplished by surveys of consumer purchasing behavior. The market basket can be considered the expenditure pattern of the typical consumer. The second step is to gather information regarding the prices of the goods and services in the market basket, and this is done every month. The price information is necessary to determine the cost of the market basket. The cost of the market basket changes as prices change, but the market basket itself does not (it is fixed). If the cost of the market basket increases, then it costs the typical consumer more to buy an unchanged bundle of goods and services; that is, the cost of living has increased. The ratio of the cost of the market basket in the current period to the cost of the market basket in the base period (multiplied by 100) provides the current numerical value of the CPI. The percentage change in the CPI between any two periods represents the rate of inflation in consumer prices between those two periods and, by extension, the percentage change in the cost of living between those two periods. But a number of conditions must be satisfied if the CPI is to be an accurate measure of price and cost of living changes.

One condition is that the market basket must either remain unchanged or be properly adjusted to account for new products or changes in the quality of old products. The Bureau of Labor Statistics recognizes this and attempts to make adjustments to rectify the problem. In the following selection, Michael J. Boskin et al. assert that the adjustments are insufficient. They conclude that the CPI suffers from quality and new product bias and, as a consequence, overstates price and cost of living changes.

A second condition that needs to be satisfied if the CPI is to be accurate is that the CPI must include all of the things that truly impact individual and societal well-being. In the second selection, James Devine contends that because the CPI ignores some important factors affecting the quality of life, such as environmental quality, amount of leisure time, and the distribution of income, it understates changes in the cost of living. It should be noted that Boskin et al. were members of the Advisory Commission to Study the Consumer Price Index (the Boskin commission), constituted by the Senate Finance Committee. The selection by Boskin et al. is based on the commission's final report, *Toward a More Accurate Measure of the Cost of Living*, which was submitted early in 1996.

Michael J. Boskin et al.  **YES**

Consumer Prices, the Consumer Price Index, and the Cost of Living

Accurately measuring prices and their rate of change, inflation, is central to almost every economic issue. There is virtually no other issue that is so endemic to every field of economics. Some examples include aggregate growth and productivity; industry prices and productivity; government taxes and spending programs that are indexed to inflation; budget deficits and debt; monetary policy; real financial returns; real wages, real median incomes and poverty rates; and the comparative performance of economies.

In mid-1995, the Senate Finance Committee, pursuant to a Senate Resolution, appointed an Advisory Committee to study the Consumer Price Index (CPI) with the five authors of this article as its members. The CPI Commission concluded that the change in the Consumer Price Index overstates the change in the cost of living by about 1.1 percentage points per year, with a range of plausible values of 0.8 to 1.6 percentage points (Boskin et al., 1996). That is, if inflation as measured by the percentage change in the CPI is running 3 percent, the true change in the cost of living is about 2 percent. This bias might seem small, but when compounded over time, the implications are enormous. Over a dozen years, the cumulative additional national debt from overindexing the budget would amount to more than $1 trillion. The implications of overstating inflation for understanding economic progress are equally dramatic. Over the last quarter-century, average real earnings have risen, not fallen, and real median income has grown, not stagnated. The poverty rate would be lower. Because the CPI component price indexes are inputs into the national income accounts, an overstated CPI implies that real GDP (gross domestic product] growth has been understated (Boskin and Jorgenson, 1997)....

Since the publication of our report, in a series of professional meetings, Congressional hearings, and other events, there has been much support for, and criticism of, the findings and recommendations of the CPI Commission. The purpose of this paper is to provide a readily accessible and self-contained discussion of the issues involved.

At this point in the debate, we see no reason to change our original estimate of a 1.1 percentage point per annum upward bias in the change in the

Consumer Price Index. We strongly endorse the proposed improvements the Bureau of Labor Statistics (BLS) is currently planning to make, research, or explore (Abraham et al., 1998), but believe it can and should, if given the appropriate resources, do far more to improve the CPI than it currently contemplates....

The Debate Over Quality Change and New Product Bias

Most of the criticism has focused on our extensive analysis of quality change and new product bias. On the question as to whether estimates of quality change bias are inevitably too "subjective" and "judgmental" to be taken seriously, it is, of course, at least as subjective to assume that every CPI category not subject to careful research has a zero bias as to extrapolate research-based estimates from one category to another. The notion that assuming zero bias is scientific, whereas attempting to generalize cautiously from related goods or practical reasoning is not precise enough, strikes us as unreasonable. Even though we will never precisely measure the value of the invention of, say, the jet airplane, as economists we *know* the consumer surplus triangles are positive, not zero. Likewise, we have known for years that PC's with Pentium processors are objectively higher quality (faster) than the 386 and 486 machines they replaced.

Hence, the Commission examined 27 subcomponents of the CPI, and most of our estimates of quality change are based on the collection of price data from independent sources and the careful quality adjustment of those independent data. Independent sources of price data are employed in our bias estimates for shelter, appliances, radio-TV, personal computers, apparel, public transportation, prescription drugs, and medical care. Estimates derived from these categories are extrapolated, sometimes partially rather than fully, to other house furnishings, nonprescription drugs, entertainment, commodities, and personal care. This leaves only a few remaining categories where we added a bias estimate to the CPI category in which there are already quality adjustments, rather than computing the bias estimate indirectly by subtracting an independent estimate from the CPI estimate for the same category. These categories are food and beverages, other utilities, new and used cars, and motor fuel, and personal expenses. The BLS does not object to our "down in the trenches" approach to the problem. Indeed, Moulton and Moses (1997) state, "This is the first time that a systematic analysis of quality bias has been done category by category, which we consider to be a noteworthy accomplishment of the Commission.... [the] overall approach seems to us to be a sensible and useful way to approach the problem of coming up with an overall assessment of bias, and we expect this type of structure will prove to be useful in the future."

Some outside critics of the Commission have argued that the BLS already does a great deal of quality adjustment, and that the Commission report is flawed for ignoring the extent of the BLS adjustments. However, for most categories, the extent of current BLS quality adjustments is irrelevant to an assessment of the Commission report's treatment of quality change. We were comparing our own evidence to the corresponding CPI indexes—however they are quality-adjusted, in a major or minor way—and thus our estimates of quality change bias are a residual that remains after the BLS has completed its efforts.

However, it is still instructive to discuss what the BLS calls quality adjustment, since it illustrates the substantive and communication difficulties in this field. There is presently very little explicit adjustment for quality change (Nordhaus, 1998). Most of the reported "quality adjustment" by the BLS comes from "linking" procedures, where a missing item is replaced by another.[1] *No* judgment at all is made about the quality differential between the new and old item. The price change during the link period is imputed, by using either the inflation rate in the overall CPI or of other commodities in the particular class. Roughly one out of three items disappear sometime during the year and have to be replaced by a different item in the same general class, such as a larger versus a smaller package of yogurt, a blue raincoat versus black, a 12-cubic-foot refrigerator with its freezer at the bottom rather than at the top. But this churning is not what we had in mind by "quality change," which rather involves the appearance of new and improved goods, greater speed, durability, variety, convenience, safety, energy efficiency, and so on. Some examples include the increased variety and freshness of vegetables and fish due to improving transport facilities and the globalization of trade, the substitution of laparoscopic procedures for gallstone operations, and many more.

Yes, the BLS does lots of "price adjustments." It is forced to by its sampling framework and the product turmoil in the markets. However, the BLS is not looking for the "quality change" that we were worried about. And it does not adjust explicitly for quality *change,* as we were defining it, except in the case of automobiles, apparel, and possibly rental apartment units and the occasional truly new goods caught by their substitution procedures.[2] While some of the Commission's estimates can be questioned—in both directions—there is very little overlap between them and the recent numbers produced by the BLS.

The helpful Moulton and Moses (1997) discussion of several categories would probably lead us to reduce our overall quality change bias estimate by perhaps 0.1 of the total 0.6 percentage points, if that were the only new information since the report, but other new research information and criticism goes in the opposite direction. Eventually, even though it may turn out that some of our estimates of quality change may be too high, others are likely to be too low.[3] Remember that except for a few cases, with low overall weight in the index, we did not explicitly estimate the additional welfare gain of the numerous new commodities in the economy. In the Commission's report, we indicate this is, in our view, a major source of the improvement in living standards. We also indicate that major problems occurred with the very late introduction of VCRs, microwave ovens, personal computers, and the soon to be introduced cellular telephone service. We indicated that the appropriate way to deal with new products is to value the consumer surplus from their introduction, as first demonstrated by Hicks (1940), and recently nicely elaborated and applied by Hausman (1996). However, we were *cautious* in this regard because, while we conjecture that the rate of introduction of new products is likely to be no different in the foreseeable future than it has been in the past (and some would even argue that the pace of introduction of new products is accelerating), it is difficult to predict which new products will become important that will not be picked up with the current BLS procedures. Perhaps many Internet-related activities are candidates. In any event, we chose to deal with this by being deliberately cautious, but indicating that there was an asymmetrical bias with more potential bias on the upside than the downside because of the likely future new product introductions which were unlikely to be captured in the CPI program.

Nor did we try to quantify all of the intangible aspects of quality change, such as the improved safety of home power tools or the improved quality of stereo sound and TV pictures. But we did try to do so in some cases; for example, the increased freshness and timeliness of fruits and vegetables.

Our report considered that new goods may drive out older goods which are still valued by a subgroup of the population, or the loss of economies of scale may drive up their price. Existing goods and services may deteriorate in quality, although only a few examples can be found, as on balance, the improvement in quality is overwhelming. For example, despite the recent complaints about how health maintenance organizations have tightened up the rules of access to medical care, few would argue that unrestricted access to the technologies of yesteryear is preferable to more restricted access to the recent improvements in bypass operations, ulcer treatments, or cataract surgeries....

Conclusion

While the CPI is the best measure currently available, it is not a cost-of-living index and it suffers from a variety of conceptual and practical problems. Despite important BLS updates and improvements over time, the change in the CPI has substantially overstated the actual rate of inflation, and is likely to continue to overstate the change in the cost of living for the foreseeable future. This overstatement will have important unintended consequences, including overindexing government outlays and tax brackets and increasing the federal deficit and debt. Moreover, such revisions as have occurred have not been carried out in a way that can provide an internally consistent series on the cost of living over an extended span of time.

The CPI Commission's report and findings have, in our opinion, held up to criticism and scrutiny quite well. Our overall estimate of about 1.1 percentage point of upward bias per year in the growth of the CPI still seems right to us, especially because we were so cautious in the treatment of the bias from new products. The purposes of our Commission's report included: disseminating information about the complexity of constructing a cost-of-living index; generating additional intellectual capital from academe and the private sector; and suggesting potential improvements. But these improvements must be considered, as we said in the report, with more appreciation of the efforts of our colleagues in the BLS and other government statistical agencies and an understanding of the constraints under which they are working. The BLS and other government statistical agencies have a remarkably complex task in a dynamic flexible market economy.

The analytical and econometric research done over recent decades has dramatically improved economists' understanding of the issues surrounding a cost-of-living index. We believe that improvements in geometric means, superlative indexes, more rapid introduction of new goods and new outlets, speedier updating of consumption weights, making use of hedonics and of related statistical tools, the use of scanner data, and other recommendations made here can substantially reduce the bias in the CPI going forward. Now, the time has come for governments in the United States and elsewhere to recognize these problems and to commit the resources to dealing with them. Virtually every major private firm in the world is spending heavily on information technology, and we should not expect better statistics from our government agencies without a corresponding investment.

We had hoped to provide an opportunity for the BLS (and the related statistical community) to implement an agenda for the most fundamental improvements in the nation's price statistics in many decades and to obtain financing (as necessary) for it. While we strongly support the modest improvements BLS is hoping to make (BLS, 1997; Abraham et al., 1998), we would hope that over time the size and scope of the reform agenda will expand.[4]

Ultimately, the president and Congress must decide whether they wish to continue the widespread overindexing of government programs. If the purpose of the indexing is to compensate recipients of the indexed programs or taxpayers from changes in the cost of living, no more and no less, they should move to wholly or partly adjust the indexing formulas, taking due account of the partial improvements BLS will make along the way. Such changes will have profound ramifications for our fiscal futures, but these changes should be made even if the budget was in surplus and there was no long-run entitlement cost problem. They should be made first and foremost in the interest of accuracy not only for the budget and the programs, but for the economic information upon which citizens depend.

Notes

1. In Moulton and Moses (1997), 1.65 out of the 1.76 percentage points in BLS quality adjustments come from linking procedures. If one excludes outliers, defined as commodity pairs where the implicit price-quality differential exceeds 100 percent, the quality adjustment number shrinks to 0.3 percentage points.

2. In Moulton and Moses (1997), such explicit quality adjustments account for only about 6 percent of the total "treatment of substitutions" effect, and amount to only 0.08 percent per year in the "outlier-cleaned" recomputations.

3. Recent evidence that we may have underestimated the biases in some of the areas we did examine comes from an alternative measure of consumer prices, the PCE (personal consumption expenditures) deflator, which has been rising by about one-third percent less per year (since 1992) than the CPI. An unpublished examination of this difference by the BLS indicates that most of it arises from the use by the BEA of alternative price indexes for hospital expenditures and airfares. These indexes do not adjust for any of the quality changes mentioned by us.

4. We have been told by leaders in government statistics agencies around the world that they were surprised that the BLS initially reacted defensively to the Commission Report, and failed to capitalize fully on the opportunity it presented.

References

Abraham, Katherine G., John S. Greenlees, and Brent R. Moulton, "Working to Improve the Consumer Price Index," *Journal of Economic Perspectives,* Winter 1998, *12*:1.

Boskin, Michael J., and Dale W. Jorgenson, "Implications of Overstating Inflation for Indexing Government Programs and Understanding Economic Progress," 1997 Papers and Proceedings, *American Economic Review,* May 1997, *87*: 2, 89–93.

Boskin, Michael J., E. Dulberger, R. Gordon, Z. Griliches, and D. Jorgenson, "Toward a More Accurate Measure of the Cost of Living," Final Report to the Senate Finance Committee, December 4, 1996.

Hausman, Jerry, "Valuation of New Goods Under Perfect and Imperfect Competition." In Bresnahan, T. and Robert J. Gordon, eds. *The Economics of New Goods.* Chicago: University of Chicago Press, 1996.

Hicks, John R., "The Valuation of the Social Income," *Economica,* May 1940, *7*:26, 105–24.

Moulton, Brent R., and Karin E. Moses, "Addressing the Quality Change Issue in the Consumer Price Index," forthcoming in *Brookings Papers on Economic Activity,* 1997.

Nordhaus, William D., "Quality Changes in Price Indexes," *Journal of Economic Perspectives,* Winter 1998, *12*:1.

U.S. Bureau of Labor Statistics, "Measurement Issues in the Consumer Price Index." Response to the U.S. Congress, Joint Economic Committee, June 1997.

James Devine

NO

The Cost of Living and Hidden Inflation

Economists generally argue that inflation is overstated by the federal
government because it does not sufficiently account for the improved
quality of products. This economist believes that if we account for all
pertinent changes in the quality of life, inflation is understated.

Despite low reported inflation rates in recent years and official recalculations
of the inflation rate that reduce it even further, these measures underestimate
the true increases in the cost of living. Official measures of inflation, such as
the Consumer Price Index (CPI) and the Personal Consumption Expenditure
(PCE) deflator, are market-oriented, measuring only the decrease in our money's
power to purchase products currently available for sale. This article presents a
preliminary alternative measure of inflation, the cost-of-living (COL) inflation
rate, which brings in nonmarket elements of people's existence, such as the
costs arising from pollution. Compared to the government's official measures
of consumer prices, these elements raise the amount of money income needed
to keep real standards of living from falling.

The COL measure suggests that in terms of the issues that working people
care about, inflation continues above the officially measured rate, even using
the most conservative measure of the COL: For the period 1951–1998, the annual COL inflation rate averaged 4.1 percent, about 0.4 of a percentage point
higher than the inflation rate implied by the PCE deflator and about 0.1 percent higher than the inflation rate implied by the CPI. (Since the PCE deflator's
method of calculation is similar to that of the COL, the former comparison
is more meaningful.) Worse, the gaps between the COL and official inflation
have widened: Between 1980 and 1998, on average the COL rose about 0.7 of a
percentage point per year more than the PCE price and 0.3 more than the CPI.

These numbers imply that the gap between officially measured real wages
and the real benefit received from wages has widened (at an increasing rate). To
understand this assertion, however, we must reexamine the basics.

From James Devine, "The Cost of Living and Hidden Inflation," *Challenge*, vol. 44, no. 2 (March–
April 2001). Copyright © 2001 by M. E. Sharpe, Inc., Armonk, NY 10504. Reprinted by permission.
References omitted.

Measuring Inflation and "Real" Wages

In addition to measuring the inflation rate (the percentage rise in prices), indices such as the CPI are commonly used to find the "real value" of nominal magnitudes. Real wages, for example, are measured as follows:

Constant-price wage = (money wage)/CPI

Thus, for example, because the CPI rose so quickly between 1970 and 1979, real average private-sector weekly earnings fell by 2 percent—even though money (nominal) wages rose by almost 90 percent.

During the late 1990s, controversy raged over technical issues concerning the method of calculation of the CPI.[1] Appointed by Congress to suggest recalculation of the CPI, Stanford professor Michael Boskin and his colleagues argued that the CPI should be reformulated to make it a more accurate measure of the "cost of living." For example, the CPI should be adjusted for the quality improvements that they assumed occurred for many products in the consumption basket used to measure the index, the availability of new products, and the rise of low-cost retail outlets like Wal-Mart.

The Bureau of Labor Statistics (BLS) has accepted many or most of the Boskin recommendations, adjusting their estimates of CPI inflation downward. According to *Business Week,* "a significant chunk of the reported downturn in inflation since 1995—perhaps three-quarters of a percentage point—reflects changes in the behavior of statisticians rather than changes in the underlying pace of price hikes" (Koretz 1999). This estimation trend has gone further, with the Federal Reserve recently shifting its emphasis to the PCE deflator for calculating the inflation rate (Cooper and Madigan 2000). This measure generally rises more slowly than even the revamped CPI, because it reflects the rise in prices of the products that consumers actually buy, while ignoring the costs of the way that inflation pushes people to substitute one product for another (chicken for steak, for example).[2]

Other economists argued that the traditional formulation of the CPI was relatively accurate and did not need Boskin-type revisions.[3] They hoped to protect social security beneficiaries and government workers with escalator clauses in their contracts from getting automatic raises below that of the actual inflation rate, which they saw as being better measured by the old version of the CPI. These revisions may not be all bad, however, since they delayed or moderated the Federal Reserve's use of economic slowdown or recession as a preemptive strike against inflation.

Often forgotten is that the official CPI is not truly a measure of the "cost of living" that people face, with or without Boskin revisions. As one BLS official notes, "A more complete cost-of-living index would go beyond [the CPI] to take into account the changes in other governmental or environmental factors that affect consumers' well-being" (Gibson 1998, p. 3). Robert Kuttner (1996) argues this point more strenuously: Official price indices leave out even more aspects of the true cost that people face in order to live, such as the cost of crime, lawsuits, pollution, and family breakdown. For example, the cutback in hours at the public library raises the cost of living by pushing people to buy books instead or lowers their quality of life by preventing them from reading. However, this cutback does not raise the measured CPI or PCE.[4] This is why I use the term "hidden inflation."

A calculation in light of Kuttner's criticism implies a gigantic and expensive research project, one that only the government could afford—and seems unlikely to engage in. Rather, I follow another hint from Kuttner: He points to the "Genuine Progress Indictor" (the GPI) calculated by the Redefining Progress think tank as an example of efforts to measure our economic welfare or "true living standards"—an alternative to real gross domestic product (GDP) as an indicator of society's progress. The GPI adjusts the official national income and product account measures for real benefits missed, such as contributions from housework, and costs that should be subtracted, such as that of using up non-reproducible natural resources. This article applies this research to calculate estimates of the "cost of living" and the "COL inflation rates" that are implied.

It is beyond this short article's scope to criticize official measures of inflation. However, even if Boskin-type adjustments are needed, if my estimates are anywhere close to being accurate, the costs of increases in pollution, commuting time, labor time, and the like more than cancel out Boskin-type adjustments.[5] As a first guess for calculating inflation rates, we might split the difference, clinging to the official price level as calculated before Boskin-type adjustments. Better, we should use different inflation rates for different purposes (Mitchell 1998). The CPI and the PCE attempt to measure purchasing power of a dollar in the market, while the COL gauges the actual cost of the benefits of everyday life.

The COL is measured by the amount of money spending needed to buy a constant quality of consumption as measured by the GPI calculations. Thus, a new version of the "real wage" can be calculated:

Constant-COL wage = (money wage)/COL

. . .

Calculating the COL

The basic idea for calculating the COL index is similar to that behind the PCE deflator. The latter is the average price level implied by calculations of real consumption spending. As a first approximation,

PCE deflator = (money spent on consumer goods)/(inflation-corrected sum of those goods)

The denominator is often interpreted as the "real" benefit to consumers of consumer spending.

Based on the Redefining Progress critique of real gross domestic product as a measure of social welfare, my most conservative COL estimate replaces real consumption with a measure of benefit received:

COL = (money spent on consumer goods)/(benefit received from current consumption)

where the denominator is a measure of those parts of the GPI that contribute to an individual's current enjoyment. Like those of the denominator of the PCE deflator, the components of this number are corrected for inflation. But it changes the official estimates of real consumer purchases by including the impact of extra current benefits and costs usually missed by the National Income and Product Accounts.[6]

Two types of examples explain the idea of COL inflation. Assume that consumption spending in both money and inflation-corrected terms is constant, so that the PCE price is constant and the official inflation rate using this measure equals zero. Suppose that the current benefits to consumers missed by the official accounts (extra current benefits) decrease. If the amount of unpaid housework, volunteer labor done, leisure time, or the services provided by publicly supplied streets and highways decreases, this means that fewer real benefits are received. Since money spending is constant, there has been a rise in dollars paid on the market per real benefit actually received. As with the public library example, there has been a decline in the benefit received from money spent.

Second, if the current costs missed by the official accounts (extra current costs) rise, that is, if people are suffering from increased pollution while spending the same amount of money buying consumer goods, it represents a decline in their living standard and a decrease in the value of the money spent. Similarly, if individuals suffer from increased costs of commuting (which are necessary to earn income), increased costs of auto accidents and crime, or decreased leisure time or family stability, the money that they spend is providing them with fewer benefits than it used to. Third, spending more money on necessary defensive goods (such as car locks or insurance) does not raise the real benefits received. Rather, it implies that the real benefits one does receive are more expensive to preserve.

Alternative COL Estimates

My "most conservative" COL estimates are consistent with common-sense notions of inflation and thus do not go as far away from the GDP calculations as the GPI does. First, the COL discussed above ignores distributional issues. As with the CPI, the PCE price, and most conceptions of "inflation," the concept of the cost of living used above is individualistic, referring to an average individual. While widening gaps in the distribution of income encourage the fraying of the social fabric and go against official societal goals, it is hard to assert that changes in distribution directly imply a higher cost of living for any individual. Those results of rising inequality that raise the cost of living, such as increases in street crime, are already measured as part of extra current costs and thus as part of the COL.

Next, forward-looking costs and benefits, which play a major role in the GPI, play no role in the calculation of the COL discussed above. When calculating the CPI or PCE price, aspects of living that refer to future impacts are omitted, since the concern is with current consumption, not with all benefits and costs received by future generations. In other words, the ecologically crucial cost of the destruction of wetlands or the ozone layer has little or no impact on our current cost of living or on the inflation rate as most conceive it. This attitude is very shortsighted, but exactly the same attitude is implicit in official calculations.

Less conservative estimates of COL inflation not only are higher but show an upward trend relative to official measures of the inflation rate. Though these more radical estimates of COL inflation do not fit with the common-sense meaning of the word "inflation" discussed above, these trends are important.

Table 1

Average Annual Additions to Inflation Rates (Percentage Points)

Dates	Conservative COL	With distributional adjustment	With forward-looking adjustment	With both adjustments
Additions to "conservative" COL				
1951–98	n.a.	0.2	0.8	1.4
1980–98	n.a.	0.6	1.0	2.6
Additions to PCE deflator inflation				
1951–98	0.4	0.6	1.2	1.8
1980–98	0.7	1.3	1.7	3.4
Additions to CPI inflation				
1951–98	0.1	0.2	0.9	1.8
1980–98	0.3	0.9	1.0	2.6

n.a.: not applicable.

If we drop the individualistic perspective of both the conservative COL and official numbers to include the effects of distributional shifts, my measures of COL inflation rise more in relation to official inflation rates. On average between 1951 and 1998, bringing in distributional issues added 0.2 of a percentage point to the conservative COL inflation rate and 0.6 of a percentage point to the PCE price inflation rate each year (see Table 1). For the period 1980–1998, these additions are 0.6 of a percentage point and 1.3 percentage point, respectively.

This results from the well-known widening of the gap between the rich and poor, as indicated by the falling share of total income accruing to the poorest fifth of the population. Alternatively, this says that COL inflation has hit the poorest fifth the hardest.

Another interpretation is that our ability to maintain low COL and CPI inflation rates simply means that the costs of societal problems are being shoved onto the backs of the poor. In terms of the distributional-conflict theory (cf. Rowthorn 1977), inflation can be reduced if one participant in the conflict—here, the poor—is pushed out. In other words, if the widening distributional gap could have been avoided, there would have been higher official inflation rates (or higher unemployment to restrain such inflation). Improving programs such as the minimum wage, unemployment insurance benefits, or "welfare" that help the poorest earn higher wages in order to allow constancy of the income distribution encourages businesses hiring such labor to raise prices. Recent slowing of official inflation rates despite falling unemployment rates is thus linked not only to measurement changes but to the widening distributional gap.

Both the conservative COL and the PCE-based inflation rates are also falling behind COL rates that include future-oriented costs and benefits, such as the cost of global warming and the loss of old-growth forests and the benefits of net investment. For 1951–1998, including such issues added 0.8 of a percentage point to the conservative COL estimate and 1.2 percentage points to the official inflation rate. These additions rise to 1.3 percentage points and 0.9 of a point for the 1980–1998 period. This result indicates that the paying of more and more of the costs of living on earth is being postponed to the future. We are currently enjoying relatively low inflation, as measured by both the conservative COL estimate and the CPI. However, the long-term costs in terms of the environment or slow growth of potential output (due to inadequate investment) will likely have to be paid in the future, in the form of environmental disaster, slow productivity growth, and the like. My measures suggest that if the nation were paying more of the environmental costs now or investing more in the future, both the official and COL inflation rates would be higher (or unemployment would be higher to restrain such inflation).

Policy Issues

Should the Federal Reserve make COL inflation its central concern? Under a literal interpretation of the current Fed goal of attaining zero inflation, it would spark slowdowns more than it has done already. But this is a wrong interpretation, since monetary policy cannot raise the extra current benefits or lower extra current costs as defined here. Since the Fed's main constituency (bondholders and bankers) does not care about negative future effects, distributional changes, current external costs, or uncompensated labor, its policy experts understand this point. The job of fixing the extra costs and promoting the extra benefits belongs to other branches of the government. The problems, of course, arise because these other branches are doing inadequate jobs at dealing with these problems.

Where the COL measure is relevant is in indexing. That is, retirees, workers, and taxpayers should have their income protected (via indexing) from rises in the cost of living, not just those reflected by the official measures. Imposing Boskin-type adjustments on the CPI and thus on indexed incomes implies real cutbacks in benefits received not only because these modifications may be technically wrong, but also because they ignore the real meaning of the cost of living and thus overlook hidden inflation. Even though the idea of indexing incomes to prevent loss of real purchasing power seems politically utopian at this point, the Boskin "reforms" are nonetheless attacks on people's standards of living.

Notes

1. See the discussions in *Challenge* 40, no. 2 (March/April 1997), *Journal of Economic Perspectives* 12, no. 1 (winter 1998), and Baker (1998a, 1998b).

2. These costs are relevant only when inflation occurs relative to nominal incomes, but it is the race between prices and money incomes that evokes interest in measuring inflation in the first place.

3. See Madrick (1997a, 1997b) and the response by Gordon and Griliches (1997).

4. This example assumes that we do not benefit from tax cuts that match the decrease in public services. Throughout this paper, I assume that decreases in the tax burden do not cancel out increases in the COL. Given the relative constancy of tax obligations as a percentage of GDP, this is reasonable. But given the increasing regressivity of the tax system over recent decades, it suggests that the COL has risen faster for the bottom half of the income distribution than is indicated by the most conservative COL numbers.

5. This is in comparison to the similarly calculated CPE deflator, which, like the CPI, reflects Boskin-type revisions.

6. This makes the main assumption of the GPI calculation to calculate the benefits received from consumption, i.e., that pleasures received by people can be quantified and added up.

POSTSCRIPT

Does the Consumer Price Index Overstate Inflation and Changes in the Cost of Living?

Boskin et al. defend their estimate of the magnitude of quality change and new product bias with two fundamental arguments. First, they dismiss as unreasonable the criticism that estimates of such bias are too subjective. Second, they contend that the procedures used by the BLS are irrelevant because the Boskin et al. estimates are "a residual that remains after the BLS has completed its efforts." Boskin et al. note that most of the quality adjustments made by the BLS involve linking procedures when a new item replaces an old item. They contend that in these linking procedures there is no effort to judge the quality difference between the new and old items. This procedure thereby misses real quality differences associated with the "greater speed, durability, variety, convenience, safety, [and] energy efficiency" accompanying the introduction of new and improved goods.

Devine argues that price indexes that are used to calculate inflation and measure changes in the cost of living, such as the CPI and the Personal Consumption Expenditure (PCE) deflator, only reflect changes in money's ability to purchase products that are currently available for sale. A true measure of inflation and the cost of living, he maintains, should also include nonmarket elements that affect individual and societal well-being. Devine therefore proposes a more comprehensive measure of inflation and cost of living changes: the cost of living (COL) inflation rate. Devine finds that the conservative COL adds 0.3 percent to the average annual CPI inflation rate over the 1980–1998 period, while the COL with distribution and forward-looking adjustments adds 2.6 percent. Devine concludes that imposing the types of adjustments recommended by Boskin et al. on the CPI and on indexed incomes "implies real cutbacks in benefits received not only because these modifications may be technically wrong, but also because they ignore the real meaning of the cost of living and thus overlook hidden inflation."

Additional readings on this issue include "The Downside of Bad Data," by Everett Ehrlich, *Challenge* (March/April 1997); "How Right Is the Boskin Commission? Interview With Janet Norwood," *Challenge* (March/April 1997); "Quality Changes in the CPI: Some Missing Links," by Charles Hulten, *Challenge* (March/April 1997); "The Boskin Commission's Trillion-Dollar Fantasy," by Wynne Godley and George McCarthy, *Challenge* (May/June 1997); and "Bias in the Consumer Price Index: What Is the Evidence?" by Brent R. Moulton, *Journal of Economic Perspectives* (Fall 1996).

ISSUE 10

Is President George W. Bush's Tax Cut Plan Good Economic Policy?

YES: Peter J. Ferrara, from "Time for a Tax Cut," *Americans for Tax Reform Policy Brief* (March 2001)

NO: Isaac Shapiro and Robert Greenstein, from "Overview Assessment of President Bush's Tax Proposal," Paper of the Center on Budget and Policy Priorities (February 8, 2001)

ISSUE SUMMARY

YES: Associate professor of law Peter J. Ferrara argues that President George W. Bush's tax cut plan will stimulate longer-term economic growth and provide a needed antidote to the current economic slowdown. Moreover, the tax plan is fair because it is tilted toward lower- and moderate-income taxpayers.

NO: Isaac Shapiro and Robert Greenstein, staff members at the Center on Budget and Policy Priorities, oppose President Bush's tax cut plan because "it would be likely to absorb the entire non–Social Security surplus that is realistically available" and because it would benefit the rich more than low- and middle-income groups.

In 1789 Benjamin Franklin wrote, "In this world nothing is certain but death and taxes." Surveying the economic landscape in modern America, there is nothing to prove old Ben wrong in his assessment of either death or taxes. Americans face a tax system that is impressive both in the variety of taxes and the amounts of revenues generated by those taxes. In fiscal year 1999 the federal government had receipts of more than $1.8 trillion, including almost $800 billion in individual income taxes, $185 billion in corporation income taxes, $612 billion in social insurance and retirement receipts (primarily taxes to finance Social Security and Medicare), $70 billion in excise taxes, $28 billion in estate and gift taxes, and $18 billion in custom duties and fees (primarily tariffs, or taxes on imports). At the state and local level, the numbers are less recent but almost as formidable. In the fiscal year extending over 1996-1997 state and local governments combined to collect $219 billion in property taxes, $262 billion in sales and gross receipts taxes, $159 billion in individual income taxes, and $34 billion in corporate income taxes. And this excludes state and local revenues from other taxes, such as hospitality taxes and taxes on alcohol and tobacco products.

After reviewing this list of taxes and the dollar amounts collected, one might be tempted to add one item to Benjamin Franklin's short list of certainties: no one likes to pay taxes. People's displeasure with taxes, however, can be tempered if the tax system meets certain criteria. The first general criterion is that the tax be equitable or fair. Fairness—from an economic perspective—involves both horizontal and vertical equity. The former suggests that people in identical economic circumstances pay identical amounts in taxes, while the latter holds that people in more favorable economic circumstances pay more in taxes than those in less favorable economic circumstances. But what does it mean to "pay more"? Does it mean more in dollar terms or more in percentage terms?

Besides being equitable, a tax system needs to satisfy a second general criterion: It should not interfere with the efficient operation of the economy. Consider, for example, a tax that takes all of a person's income. Such a tax would not be efficient, for it would destroy all work incentives. Why work if the government takes all of your pay? Or consider the case where the government imposes a lower tax rate on property income than on labor income. This preferential treatment of property income could cause a distortion in economic behavior. People would be less willing to invest in human capital—for example, to spend money on their education—and more willing to invest in such things as commercial real estate.

A third general criterion, one that perhaps touches on both equity and efficiency considerations, is that taxes should be no higher than is necessary to finance the agreed-upon government activities. It is in this context that the current issue is framed. Since fiscal year 1998 the federal government has been running a budget surplus—collecting more in revenues than it is spending. These surpluses are expected to continue for at least another decade.

During the 2000 presidential campaign both candidates promised some reduction in taxes, with George W. Bush advocating larger tax cuts than Al Gore. One of Bush's first acts upon assuming the presidency was to submit his tax cut plan to Congress. This served to rekindle the arguments raised during the campaign. In the following selections, Peter J. Ferrara defends the plan, arguing that the proposed tax cuts are fair and economically beneficial. Isaac Shapiro and Robert Greenstein object to the plan on the grounds that the size of the cuts are problematic and unfair to low- and moderate-income families.

Peter J. Ferrara

 **YES**

Time for a Tax Cut

Introduction

President Bush's tax cut proposal is well-crafted to increase economic growth, whether in good economic times or bad. Because the economy is now at a crucial juncture, and a tax cut could make the difference between a slowdown and a recession, President Bush's proposal is especially well-timed.

Consider the following:

- Economic growth slowed dramatically to 1.4% in the last quarter of 2000.
- Unemployment has begun to rise.
- Bankruptcies have begun to rise.
- The manufacturing sector has declined for 6 straight months.
- Layoffs are sweeping the economy.
- Consumer confidence has declined for 4 straight months.

Moreover, Federal Reserve Chairman Alan Greenspan suggests that the economy may have stopped growing altogether this quarter. In fact, the Fed's recent sudden and sharp interest rate reductions indicate that Greenspan and the Fed think the economy is already slipping into a recession.

President Bush's tax cut package will reverse this economic decline and restore robust economic growth. Indeed, the Kennedy tax cuts of the early 1960s and the Reagan tax cuts of the early 1980s stimulated roaring economic booms through at least their respective decades. Bush's tax cut plan would do the same for our stumbling economy.

We will explain below why this is so, first on supply side grounds, then on traditional Keynesian grounds. We will then discuss the fairness question. But first we will describe the major components of the Bush tax cut plan.

President Bush's Tax Cut Package

The major components of the Bush tax cut package are as follows:

- The Bush plan would reduce income tax rates across the board, replacing the current rate structure of 15%, 28%, 31%, 36% and 39.6% with rates of 10%, 15%, 25% and 33%. The new lower 10% rate would apply to the first $6,000 of taxable income for singles, the first $10,000 for single parents and the first $12,000 for married couples. The 28% and 31% rates of the current system would be reduced to 25%. The 36% and 39.6% rates of the current system would be reduced to 33%.
- The Bush plan would double the child tax credit to $1,000. It would also raise the annual income threshold for phasing out the credit from $110,000 to $200,000 for married couples and from $75,000 to $200,000 for singles.
- The Bush plan would reduce the marriage penalty by restoring a deduction for the lower income-earning spouse equal to 10% of the first $30,000 in wages.
- The Bush plan would phase out the death tax.
- The Bush plan would expand the tax deduction for charitable donations to non-itemizers.
- The Bush plan would make the Research and Development tax credit permanent.

Marginal Tax Rate Reductions

The most powerful economic effect of the Bush proposal would result from the marginal rate reductions. Economic decisions are heavily influenced by how taxes change at the margin, for that determines the reward the actor will receive for economic activity. Higher marginal tax rates reduce the reward for extra work, saving, investment, entrepreneurship and risk-taking. Consequently, such taxes discourage all these activities, reducing economic growth.

Lower marginal tax rates, by contrast, increase the reward and encourage such activities, increasing economic growth. It is important to recognize that this economic effect occurs not because the tax cut allows people to keep more of their own money to spend, or even to save. It occurs because the incentives change, so people will change what they do with their current money and time, as well as the money they keep as a result of the tax cut.

The great power of these economic effects was shown by the Kennedy tax rate cuts of the early 1960s. Kennedy's across the board rate reductions led to an economic boom for the rest of the decade.

Ronald Reagan followed the same policy in the early 1980s, with his 25% across the board tax rate reductions. And Reagan enjoyed the same result. After the Reagan tax cuts were fully implemented at the beginning of 1983, the economy experienced one of the most remarkable turnarounds in U.S. economic history with an historic boom over the following 7 years. Just about every important economic trend turned around that year in a positive direction, after over 10 years of increasing stagnation and deterioration.

This history of Kennedy and Reagan tax cuts establishes a bipartisan tax policy to enhance economic growth. That bipartisan history should be followed by both parties today in enacting the Bush tax cut plan.

The Bush tax rate reductions also address one of the most important economic problems resulting from our current tax systems. Lower income workers with children face effective marginal tax rates that are among the highest in the country. They start to face the marginal tax rates of the income tax as their income grows. They also must pay the Social Security payroll tax and any state income taxes.

But, in addition, they start to lose the Earned Income Tax Credit as their income grows as well. This operates effectively as a marginal tax, since they face an income penalty as their earnings grow. When all these marginal tax burdens are added together, a single mother with 2 children earning $25,000 faces the same total marginal tax rate as a lawyer earning $250,000.

This is a highly damaging economic policy. For it excessively burdens low income workers trying to get off welfare and break out of the underclass. Instead of imposing a heavy marginal tax burden on them, we should be doing all we can to encourage them.

The Bush tax plan is designed precisely to solve this problem. The tax rate reduction to 10% for the first several thousand dollars of taxable income plus the child tax credit reduces the marginal tax rate by over 40% for low income families with children, bringing those rates out of the stratosphere intended for the highest income workers.

This will encourage increased work by lower income workers and further reduce welfare dependency.

Elimination of the Death Tax

Another beneficial economic effect will result from elimination of the death tax. This addresses the other major economic problem in our tax code besides high marginal tax rates—the multiple taxation of capital.

The return on savings and investment is taxed multiple times in our tax system. The same dollar of return on investment is taxed not only by the individual income tax, but also by the corporate income tax.

The capital gains tax is a third layer of taxation on such income. The capital value of an asset is merely the present discounted value of the expected future income to that asset. When the capital value of the asset rises, that is because the expected future income from the asset has risen as well. That future income, of course, will be taxed when it is earned. To tax the increase in capital value today as well is effectively taxing that future income again.

The death tax is still another layer of taxation on savings and investment. It taxes the savings and capital earnings that the deceased has saved over a lifetime to leave to children or other heirs. But that entire savings was taxed as well when it was first saved as income.

The death tax consequently discourages saving and investment. The Joint Economic Committee estimated in 1998 that the tax reduces national savings and capital by about $500 billion. Less savings and capital means fewer jobs and lower wages and income. Another study from the Institute for Research on the Economics of Taxation estimates that the death tax causes a loss of close to $50 billion per year in GDP [gross domestic product] and about a quarter of a million jobs.

Eliminating the death tax would remove one layer of the multiple over-taxation of capital. That would improve incentives for savings, investment, entrepreneurship and risk-taking. As a result, savings and investment would increase, new businesses would be established, more jobs would be created, and wages and other income would increase, adding up overall to increased economic growth.

Where Have All the Keynesians Gone?

For decades, the standard analysis for national economic policy offered by the liberal left and the Democratic Party was Keynesian economics. Indeed, it was cause for great celebration in those precincts when President Nixon stated in explaining his economic policy that "We are all Keynesians now." Keynesian economics is still taught in colleges and universities across the country as the basis for macroeconomics.

Under Keynesian analysis, deficits stimulate economic growth and budget surpluses reduce growth. The enormous projected surpluses of $5.3 trillion over the next decade would produce an enormous drag on the economy based on Keynesian analysis, likely producing a very serious recession and long term stagnation. Indeed, Keynesian analysis suggests that recent large surpluses may be the chief cause of the current economic slowdown.

It is not clear if or when Democrats and liberals have abandoned Keynesian economics. Leading Democrat economists, such as Professor Alan Blinder of Princeton who was the top economic advisor to the Gore campaign, still profess to adhere to it. If so, then standard Keynesian analysis should be a major, overwhelming reason for Democrats and liberals to support the proposed tax cut.

The Bush Tax Cut Is Fair

Opponents of the Bush tax plan complain that it is unfair because it is tilted too heavily towards the rich. But the Bush tax proposal is fair, for three major reasons.

First, it is not tilted toward the rich. In fact, it is tilted towards lower and moderate-income taxpayers. Marginal income tax rates for those workers would be cut by a higher percentage in the Bush plan than the rate cuts for higher income workers. Opponents object to the absolute dollar amount of reductions higher income workers would receive due to the marginal rate cuts, which they see as too large. But those reductions are smaller than they would be if rates were cut by an equal percentage across the board, as they were in the Reagan and Kennedy tax cuts.

Moreover, moderate-income workers would be helped more by the doubling of the child tax credit, the reduction in the marriage penalty and the expansion of the charitable deduction to non-itemizers.

High-income workers already pay an astounding portion of the total income tax burden. According to the Internal Revenue Service, the top 1% of taxpayers pay 34.8% of all income taxes. The top 5% pay 54%. Because the Bush tax plan in truth is proportionally tilted towards lower income workers, higher income workers will, in fact, pay a higher proportion of total income taxes after the Bush plan is adopted. Our income tax code does not have a problem of favoring the rich today and will not after the Bush tax cut goes into effect.

Secondly, the Bush tax cut is fair because taxes are currently way too high, and that is what is unfair. The total Federal tax burden is now 20.7% of GDP, just about the highest ever in peacetime. The average family today spends more on taxes than on food, clothing, and shelter combined. With huge projected surpluses, there is no reason not to let hardworking families keep more of their own money.

Finally, the Bush tax cut is fair because economic opportunity is the greatest fairness. What struggling, lower-income families want and need is greater opportunity for more personal prosperity. They are not benefited by curtailing the prosperity of higher-income workers, and they are not interested in that. That sentiment is the preserve of left-wing ideologues and politicians grasping for more power and money to feed political machines.

The Bush tax cut will deliver greater economic opportunity and prosperity for lower and moderate-income workers. They will not only benefit directly from the sweeping tax cuts for them in the package. They will benefit as well from all the beneficial economic effects from the package described above. Those beneficial effects mean new jobs, higher wages and more rapid advancement overall for low and moderate-income workers. That is what the American Dream, and American concept of fairness, is all about.

Conclusion

The Bush tax cut plan will substantially enhance savings, capital investment, job creation, wage growth and overall economic growth. The most important factors in this outcome are the marginal income tax rate reductions and the elimination of the death tax. These tax policies have a bipartisan history and both parties should join in supporting them today, particularly with the weakening economy.

NO ☜ Isaac Shapiro and Robert Greenstein

Overview Assessment of President Bush's Tax Proposal

In assessing the tax cut package proposed... by President Bush, two questions loom large. Are the benefits of the tax cuts distributed in a desirable fashion? Is the size of the tax cut appropriate and prudent? This analysis assumes, as appears to be the case, that the Bush administration has made no significant changes to its proposal, and thus reflects the Bush campaign proposal as recently introduced by Senators [Phil] Gramm and [Zell] Miller.

No matter how the benefits of the tax cut are measured, those at the top of the income spectrum benefit the most. Not only would the highest-income individuals receive by far the largest average tax benefit in actual dollars, the degree to which their taxes are cut in percentage terms would be larger than among any other group. The top one percent of the population would receive about 40 percent of the tax cuts from the proposal, which is double the share of federal taxes that they pay. In addition, the share of the tax cuts that would be received by the top one percent of the population significantly exceeds the share that would be received by the bottom 80 percent of the population combined.

When properly measured, the Bush tax cut costs at least $2.1 trillion over ten years, rather than the often-cited $1.6 trillion figure. The primary reason for the larger estimate is that it accounts for the extra federal interest costs automatically generated by the tax cut. If the full effect of the rate cuts were accelerated forward to this year and not offset by reductions in the remainder of the tax package, the costs would increase an additional several million dollars over 10 years. A tax cut of more than $2 trillion would exceed the surplus that is likely to be available outside Social Security and Medicare when realistic budget assumptions are used.

The issues of the distribution of the Bush tax cut plan and its size are explored below....

How Are the Benefits of the Bush Tax Plan Distributed?

The package of tax cuts President Bush has proposed are heavily skewed toward those at the top of the income spectrum. The broad middle class would receive substantially less relief.

- The one percent of the population with the highest incomes would receive between 36 percent and 43 percent of the tax cut, depending on the calculation used. The bottom 80 percent of the population would receive 29 percent of the tax cut.
- The Bush plan would deliver an average tax reduction of at least $39,000 to the top one percent of the population (in 1999 dollars). The Administration claims the typical family of four would receive $1,600 when the plan is fully in effect. The Administration's family is hardly typical. When the income tax cuts take full effect in 2006, Citizens for Tax Justice has found that 85 percent of households would receive a tax cut of less than $1,600 in that year.[1]
- The Treasury Department has reported that the top one percent of the population pays 20 percent of all federal taxes under current law. Under the Bush plan, the share of the tax cut that would go to the top one percent—36 percent to 43 percent—is about double the share of the federal taxes they pay.
- The proposal would repeal the estate tax, even though IRS data show that the estate tax is levied only on two percent of all estates and that in 1997 half of all estate taxes were paid by the 2,400 largest taxable estates. If the estate tax had been repealed in 1997, these 2,400 estates would have received an average tax cut of about $3.5 million apiece. In addition, of those estates that are subject to tax, very few include family-owned farms or businesses.

  Of the approximately 2.3 million people who died in 1998, only 47,482 (or two percent) left estates subject to any estate tax. Only 1,418 of the estates that were taxable—or three percent of them—were estates in which family-owned businesses or farms formed the majority of the estate. This means that only six of every 10,000 people who died in 1998 left an estate that was taxable and consisted primarily of a family-owned farm or business. A Treasury analysis found that these estates paid *less than one percent* of all estate taxes. Estate tax relief can be directed at these estates at a small fraction of the cost of repealing the estate tax.

- White House officials have claimed that lower-income families would receive the largest percentage tax reductions. Such claims focus only on *income* taxes. Low- and moderate-income families pay more in other federal taxes—principally payroll taxes—than in income taxes. It is possible to eliminate a large percentage of the small income tax liability that many moderate-income families incur and register only a small impact on the total federal taxes that such families pay.

For example, a two-parent family of four with income of $26,000 would indeed have its income taxes eliminated under the Bush plan, which is being portrayed as a 100 percent reduction in taxes. The family, however, owes only $20 in income taxes under current law. As a percentage of all taxes paid (considering only the effects of income and payroll taxes and counting the benefits the family would receive from the Earned Income Tax Credit), the family would have its taxes reduced by less than one percent. Its net tax bill would still exceed $2,680.[2]

Figures that the Bush campaign issued, which showed the top one percent receiving a *smaller* share of the tax cut than the share of taxes this group pays, reflected only federal *income* taxes. Those figures omitted payroll, estate, and other taxes. As a result, the figures provided an incomplete picture. Leaving payroll taxes out of the analysis makes the share of taxes that the top one percent pays look larger, while leaving out the estate tax makes the share of the tax cut they will receive appear smaller.

Relief to Low-income Families?

Over the past week President Bush and his Administration have repeatedly emphasized that his plan will provide tax relief to low-income families and help them enter the middle class. The proposal, however, would provide no assistance to working poor families or to many families modestly above the poverty line. (As described below, these families can pay substantial amounts in other taxes, such as payroll and excise taxes, even after the Earned Income Tax Credit is taken into account.) To estimate the number of families with children who would not benefit from the Bush proposal, we tabulated the latest data from the Census Bureau. These data are for 1999. This analysis considers the effects of the plan on families with children under age 18 as if it were in full effect that year. We found:

- An estimated 12.2 million low- and moderate-income families with children—31.5 percent of all families with children—would not receive any tax cut from the Bush proposal. Some 80 percent of these families have workers.
- Approximately 24.1 million children—33.5 percent of all children—live in the excluded families.
- Among African-Americans and Hispanics, the figures are especially striking. While one-third of all children would not benefit from the Bush tax plan, *more than half* of black and Hispanic children would not receive any assistance. An estimated 55 percent of African-American children and 56 percent of Hispanic children live in families that would receive nothing from the tax cut.

Even the Bush proposal to double the child tax credit—the feature of his tax plan that one might expect to provide the most assistance to children in low- and moderate-income families—would provide the largest tax reductions to families with incomes in the $110,000 to $250,000 range, and confer a much larger share of its benefits on upper-income families than on low- and middle-income families. Under the plan, the maximum child credit would be raised from $500 per child to $1,000. Also, the proposal raises the income level above which the child credit begins to phase out from $110,000 to $200,000, extending the credit for the first time to those in this income category. For many of these relatively affluent taxpayers, the child credit would rise from zero to $1,000 per child. By contrast, millions of children in low- and moderate-income working families would continue to receive no child credit, or their credit would remain at its current level of $500 per child or rise to less than $1,000 per child.

Since the reason 12 million families and their children would not benefit from the Bush plan is that they do not owe federal income taxes, some have argued that it is appropriate they not benefit. "Tax relief should go to those who pay taxes" is the short-hand version of this argument. This line of reasoning is not persuasive for several reasons.

1. *Many of these families owe taxes other than federal income taxes, often paying significant amounts.* For most families, their biggest federal tax burden by far is the payroll tax, not the income tax. Data from the Congressional Budget Office indicate that in 1999, three-quarters of all U.S. households paid more in federal payroll taxes than in federal income taxes. (This comparison includes both the employee and employer share of the payroll tax; most economists concur that the employer's share of the payroll tax is passed along to workers in the form of lower wages.) While the Earned Income Tax Credit offsets these taxes for most working families with incomes below the poverty line, many families with incomes modestly above the poverty line who would not benefit from the Bush plan are net taxpayers. . . .

2. *While many workers would see their marginal tax rates reduced, the Bush plan fails to reduce marginal rates at all for the working families that face the highest marginal rates of any families*—working families with children that have incomes between about $13,000 and $20,000. For each additional dollar these families earn, they lose up to 21 cents in the EITC [Earned Income Tax Credit], 15.3 cents in payroll taxes, 24 cents to 36 cents in food stamp benefits, and additional amounts if they receive housing assistance or a child care subsidy or pay state income tax. Ways to reduce marginal rates on these families are well known. The Bush plan does not include them.

3. *Low-income working families face some of the most severe marriage tax penalties.* The Administration's plan, however, departs from a bipartisan consensus formed in Congress over the past two years to reduce marriage tax penalties for low-wage working families, not just for middle- and upper-income families. Analysts generally concur that some of the most serious marriage penalties in the tax code are those that can face

low-income working individuals as a result of the way the phase-out of the EITC is designed. Every major tax bill from both parties in the last year and a half—including major tax bills that Congress passed and President Clinton vetoed in 1999 and 2000—has contained EITC reforms to provide marriage penalty relief for low-income working families. (Clinton vetoed the bills for other reasons; his budget, too, proposed EITC marriage penalty relief.)

4. *Children in low-income working families would benefit from the added income that tax benefits could provide.* A major new study issued by the well-respected Manpower Demonstration Research Corporation (MDRC) finds that increases in employment among former welfare recipients need to be accompanied by increases in family incomes if the lives of the poor children in these families are to register significant improvement. MDRC examined five studies covering 11 welfare reform programs and found that increased employment among parents did not by itself significantly improve their children's lives. Only in programs where the parents experienced increased employment *and* increased income were there positive effects, such as better school achievement, for elementary-school-age children. This suggests that tax measures that increase the disposable income of these families could have significant positive effects on children.

The Size of the Tax Cut

The Bush tax cut is often described as costing $1.6 trillion over the ten-year period from 2002–2011. This figure, however, fails to account for the nearly $400 billion in additional interest payments on the debt that would ensue. This is because CBO's [Congressional Budget Office's] budget projections assume that no tax cuts or spending increases will be enacted over the next decade and therefore that the debt will fall rapidly. As a result, the costs of interest on the debt—a sizable component of federal spending—also will fall rapidly. If a ten-year, $1.6 trillion tax cut is enacted, however, surpluses will be smaller and the debt larger than CBO projects, and interest costs will be almost $400 billion higher than CBO assumed when developing its estimate of the surplus.

Once the additional debt costs of nearly $400 billion as well as the additional amounts necessary to ensure that the value of the new tax cuts are not diluted by the Alternative Minimum Tax [AMT] are accounted for,[3] the cost of the Bush tax package rises to $2.1 trillion over 10 years. The price tag could rise even further if the plan were accelerated forward. When President Bush announced his tax package on February 8 [2001], he expressed support for accelerating a portion of his tax cuts to the beginning of 2001. He did not specify which aspects of the plan should be accelerated, but offered to work with Congress to achieve this goal. If the rate cuts in his plan, which are not scheduled to become fully effective until 2006, are made fully effective retroactive to January 1, 2001, and these added costs are not offset by scaling back other parts of the plan, the ten-year cost of the plan increases another $400 billion, to $2.5 trillion.

Some would argue that even a tax cut in excess of $2 trillion over 10 years is affordable given the expected size of the expected surplus, and would refer to the recent surplus projections of the Congressional Budget Office. A closer look at the CBO estimates, however, suggests the opposite.

Under the new CBO forecast, the projected surplus excluding Social Security is $3.1 trillion over 10 years. However, as earlier analyses by the Center on Budget and Policy Priorities, the Brookings Institution, and the Concord Coalition all have explained, there is a difference between CBO's estimate of the size of the non-Social Security surplus and the amount that actually is available for tax cuts.

In making its surplus estimates, CBO follows certain rules under which it assumes that various tax increases and program reductions that neither party favors—and that are very unlikely to take place—will go into effect. For example, about 20 popular tax credits and other tax preferences—such as the research and experimentation tax credit—are typically renewed for only a few years at a time. There is no question that the tax credits will be extended. The CBO projections, however, assume that these tax credits all will expire and the beneficiaries of the credits will thus be subject to tax increases. Furthermore, CBO includes the temporary surpluses building in the Medicare Hospital Insurance trust fund in its estimate of the non-Social Security surplus. Both chambers of Congress voted last year by large bipartisan margins to set these Medicare surpluses to the side and not use them to finance tax cuts or program increases.

Setting the Medicare surpluses to the side—and using the more prudent and more realistic assumption that the tax increases and program reductions reflected in the CBO projections will not occur—produces an estimate of the available surplus that is about $1.1 trillion lower. This leaves an available surplus of $2.0 trillion over the next 10 years.

The Bush tax cut would consume all, or more than all, of this available $2.0 trillion. This is problematic for four reasons.

First, the $2.0 trillion estimate of the available surplus is only a projection. Any number of events—such as slower-than-forecast economic growth or faster-than-expected growth in health care costs—could cause these projections to be too high. Based on its own track record, CBO concludes that "the estimated surpluses could be off in one direction or the other, on average, by about $52 billion in 2001, $120 billion in 2002, and $412 billion in 2006." Committing all or more than all of the available projected surplus to a tax cut is not prudent in the face of such uncertainty.

A second reason that it would be unwise to consume all of the $2.0 trillion available surplus is that even if the surplus forecast proved correct, acting now to commit all of the available surpluses for the next 10 years would leave no funds available for subsequent Congresses to use to address needs that cannot be foreseen but inevitably will arise. Such needs could be military, international, or domestic. While we cannot know today what these needs will be, we can count on some new problems emerging that will have to be addressed. A third reason that passing a tax cut that consumed all, or more than all, of the projected $2.0 trillion would be imprudent relates to Social Security and Medicare. If legislation to restore long-term Social Security solvency is to be enacted, a transfer of non-Social Security, general revenues from the Treasury to the Social Security Trust Fund (or to private, individual retirement accounts) almost certainly will be required. Without such a transfer, the magnitude of the reductions in retirement benefits that would be required—regardless of whether a solvency plan includes individual accounts—would almost surely make the plan impossible to pass. As a result, policymakers ought to set aside, or reserve, a portion of the projected non-Social Security surplus funds for this purpose. Earlier Center analyses estimated that to be prudent, a minimum of $500 billion over 10 years should be reserved for this purpose.[4]

Finally, dissipating all of the projected available surplus in the form of a tax cut is not prudent because it fails to achieve a balance between tax cuts and other critical needs. Spending all of the available surplus on a tax cut precludes our ability to make critical investments in spending programs. It would also make it impossible to enact new initiatives that have already drawn bipartisan support, such as a new prescription drug benefit or efforts to reduce the ranks of the uninsured. More of these potential tradeoffs will become clear once the President's budget is introduced and a better sense of how the tax cut influences other aspects of the budget will be obtainable. Even at this stage, however, it is clear that devoting the entire available surplus to a tax cut fails to achieve a reasonable balance between tax cuts and other critical needs.

Conclusion

Income disparities in the United States are at their widest point in at least a quarter century and probably since the end of World War II. Congressional Budget Office data, currently available for the years from 1977 to 1995, show that the average after-tax income of the bottom fifth of the population fell 14 percent during this period, after adjusting for inflation, and the average after-tax income of the middle fifth of households was stagnant. But the average after-tax income of the top fifth of households rose 27 percent, while the average after-tax income of the top one percent soared, climbing 87 percent. (Official Census data are not helpful here because they do not examine after-tax income and do not break out measurements for incomes for the top one percent.)

In addition, the Internal Revenue service has issued data on changes in adjusted gross incomes and federal income taxes from 1995 to 1997, indicating that the average after-tax income for the top one percent of tax filers climbed a remarkable 31 percent in this two-year period. By contrast, this measure of income rose an average of only three percent for the bottom 90 percent of filers. The average *increase* in the after-tax income of the top one percent of filers from 1995 to 1997 was $121,000, itself substantially larger than the incomes of the vast majority of American families and several times larger than the income of the typical family.

Especially in light of these trends, the Bush tax proposal is of dubious design. It would be likely to absorb the entire non-Social Security surplus that is realistically available, restricting if not preventing the nation from addressing other, more pressing priorities. At the same time that after-tax income gains have been dramatic for the richest among us and that income disparities are likely wider than at any point since the end of World War II, the tax plan would devote about 40 percent of its benefits to the top one percent of the population, which is considerably more than the broad middle class of the population would receive. This is not the best use of the available surplus.

Notes

1. The income tax cuts are phased in over five years. In 2002, the maximum tax cut for most middle-income families would be $320. In addition, due to inflation, a "1,600 tax cut" in 2006 is worth less than $1,600 in today's dollars. Citizens for Tax Justice finds that even when the package is fully in effect, 90 percent of families would receive a tax cut of less than $1,600 in today's dollars.

2. This family's current tax bill consists of income taxes of $20, payroll taxes of $3,978, offset by an Earned Income tax Credit of $1,289. Its current net federal tax bill, not considering excise taxes, is $2,709. Under the Bush plan, its tax bill would be $2,689.

3. The AMT was established to prevent wealthy taxpayers from engaging in so much tax shelter activity that they owe little or no income tax. Some 1.3 million taxpayers were subject to the AMT last year. Due to a flaw in the AMT's design, however, it will encroach heavily upon the middle class in the coming years if Congress does not act to prevent that from occurring, causing 15 million taxpayers to be subject to the AMT by 2010. Virtually all observers agree policymakers will act to prevent that from taking place. This anticipated action to remedy the flaw in the AMT will increase the cost of the Bush tax plan by $200 billion over 10 years.

4. Any claim that this problem can be addressed without a transfer of funds because the projected Social Security surpluses can be used to shore up the Social Security system would be spurious; the Social Security surpluses already are taken into account in the Social Security trustees' estimate that the program will become insolvent in the late 2030s. Addressing the solvency problem entails reducing Social Security benefits or increasing revenues to the Social Security system.

POSTSCRIPT

Is President George W. Bush's Tax Cut Plan Good Economic Policy?

$\mathbf{F}$errara begins his case for the Bush tax cut plan by asserting that its timing is especially good: the economy is slowing, and the tax cut could prevent the economy from slipping into a recession. Like the tax cuts enacted during the Kennedy and Reagan administrations, he asserts, the Bush tax cuts should propel the economy to greater prosperity. Ferrara concludes his case by offering three reasons why the Bush tax cut plan is fair. First, marginal income tax rates for low- and moderate-income taxpayers are cut by a larger percentage than those of higher-income workers. Second, taxes are currently "way too high," and the average family consequently "spends more on taxes than on food, clothing, and shelter combined." Third, the plan will "deliver greater economic opportunity and prosperity for lower and moderate-income workers."

Shapiro and Greenstein begin their assessment of Bush's tax cut plan by raising what they consider to be the most important questions about the proposal: Are the benefits distributed in a desirable fashion? Is the size of the proposed cuts appropriate and prudent? In attempting to answer the first question, Shapiro and Greenstein make a number of points, including (1) the top 1 percent of the population with regard to income would receive between 36 percent and 43 percent of the tax cut; (2) the estate tax is levied on only 2 percent of all estates; and (3) approximately 12.2 million low- and moderate-income families with children would not receive a tax cut. In trying to answer the second question, Shapiro and Greenstein contend that the true cost of Bush's tax cut plan is $2 trillion, not the claimed $1.6 trillion. The higher figure is more accurate, they maintain, because it includes the nearly $400 billion in additional interest payments on federal government debt that would occur if the plan were enacted. On the basis of their analysis, Shapiro and Greenstein conclude that the benefits of Bush's tax cut plan are not distributed in a desirable fashion and that the proposed cuts are too large.

For additional readings on this issue, start with various studies completed for the Center of Budget and Policy Priorities, including "Those $1,600 Tax Cut Checks," by Isaac Shapiro and Robert Greenstein (February 14, 2001) and "Cost of the Bush Tax Cuts," by Robert Greenstein (February 13, 2001). Also see "The President's Agenda for Tax Relief," a statement issued by the Bush White House (March 13, 2001); "The Economic and Budgetary Effects of President Bush's Tax Relief Plan," by D. Mark Wilson and William W. Beach, Report of the Heritage Center for Data Analysis (March 13, 2001); and "Debt and Taxes," by Barbara R. Bergman, *The American Prospect* (March 12–16, 2001).

ISSUE 11

Is the New Economy Really New?

YES: William A. Sahlman, from "The New Economy Is Stronger Than You Think," *Harvard Business Review* (November–December 1999)

NO: Dean Baker, from "The New Economy: A Millennial Myth," *Dollars and Sense* (March/April 2000)

ISSUE SUMMARY

YES: Professor of business administration William A. Sahlman contends that the development and rapid spread of a new business model, increasing admiration of entrepreneurs, increasing tolerance of failure, easy access to capital, and globalization have combined to create a new economy that is strong and resilient.

NO: Economist Dean Baker argues that until the economy proves it can continue to generate rapid output and productivity growth in the face of a stock market crash, it cannot really be considered new.

It is not hard to document economic change. Consider the following comparisons of the U.S. economy in 1990 with the economy in 2000. In 1990 total output, as measured by gross domestic product (measured in chained 1996 dollars), stood at $6,684 billion, but 10 years later it was 28 percent higher, or $9,318 billion. In 1990 the civilian labor force consisted of close to 126 million people, with an unemployment rate of 5.6 percent; by 2000 the civilian labor force had grown to over 140 million people, and the unemployment rate had fallen to 4 percent. In 1990 the inflation rate, as measured by the percentage change in the Consumer Price Index, was 6.1 percent, while in 2000 the inflation rate was 3.4 percent. There was even a significant change in the federal government's budget position: in fiscal year 1990 the federal government's expenditures exceeded its revenues by $221 billion, but in fiscal year 2000 the situation was reversed, with revenues exceeding expenditures by an estimated $236 billion. The change even extended to the stock market: in 1990 the Dow Jones Industrial Average stood at 2,679, rising over the decade to 10,666 by November 2000, while the NASDAQ composite index rose from 409 in 1990 to 3,055 in November 2000.

Certainly, then, there has been change in the U.S. economy. But the issue addressed here is whether or not the change is so fundamental, so basic, that it has created a new economy. There are several different ways to address this question. First, some focus on the dominant kind of activity in the economy. In its beginnings the American economy was centered on agriculture. Over time agriculture was replaced by manufacturing. The economy has since entered its third wave, and manufacturing has been displaced by the new dominant industry, the production of information. Those who take this long-run interpretation would argue that the economy is indeed new.

A second way to determine whether or not change has been fundamental is to concentrate on the nature of the economic system. This argument says that change is basic only if there is a change from one type of economic system (say socialism), to another type of economic system (say capitalism). In the capitalist American economy of the 1800s, decision making was concentrated in the private sector, the private sector owned most of the means of production, and prices and markets were the primary coordinating mechanism. In twenty-first-century America, decision making is still concentrated in the private sector, the private sector still owns most of the means of production, and prices and markets remain the primary coordinating mechanism. So according to this approach to the evaluation of economic change, the economy is not really new.

A third way to decide whether or not change has been fundamental is to examine a group of important economic regularities. For example, through the early part of the twentieth century, consumers purchased approximately two-thirds of total output. During the middle part of the twentieth century there appeared to be an inverse relationship between the unemployment rate and the inflation rate—the so-called Phillips tradeoff. Also during the middle of the twentieth century, international trade was relatively unimportant to the U.S. economy, at least quantitatively. So according to this analysis technique, after isolating a series of similar relationships for the early period, one must determine whether or not all or most of these relationships continue to hold. If they do, then the economy has not changed—it is not new.

A fourth way of assessing whether or not change is fundamental is to examine economic behavior in more detail. For example, business firms still produce goods and services in the pursuit of profits. But have there been changes in the ways in which business firms conduct their activities? Consumers still purchase goods and services in pursuit of satisfaction. But have there been changes in the ways in which consumers manage their affairs?

In the following selections, William A. Sahlman and Dean Baker employ a combination of the last two ways of determining whether or not change in the U.S. economy is fundamental. Sahlman argues that the old inflation-unemployment tradeoff is no longer a concern and that business firms are using a new business model. Baker, on the other hand, maintains that there has never been an inflation-unemployment tradeoff and that the recent growth in output and productivity is not that different from growth that was experienced earlier.

William A. Sahlman  **YES**

The New Economy Is Stronger Than You Think

Chicken Little told us that the sky was falling. Alan Greenspan and his cohorts at the Fed would have us believe it just might—what with the "irrational exuberance" of the capital markets and their increasing fear that inflation may soon rear its ugly head. I'm here to assure you that Chicken Little and Alan Greenspan have a lot in common; they fret for no good reason. The sky—that is, the U.S. economy—is just fine, thank you. In fact, it's never been better—sturdy, resilient, and raring to grow. And it will remain that way for years and years to come if the government just manages to stay out of its way.

The new economy is strong because it is based on a business system that works. It makes sense—simple as that. Any business system that relentlessly drives out inefficiency, forces intelligent business process reengineering, and gives customers more of what they want will be sustainable. On top of that, the new economy is strong because it is built on several important factors to which traditional economists don't usually lend much credence: America's admiration for entrepreneurs and its tolerance of failure, not to mention its easy access to capital. The new economy is strong, too, because it is attracting the best and brightest minds in the country. There was a time when all the smart MBAs went into consulting and investment banking. Now they're becoming entrepreneurs or zipping off to Silicon Valley to join an existing team, where they turn the cranks and pull the levers that make the new economy thrive. And finally, the new economy is strong because it's spreading. It may be primarily an American phenomenon now, but in a few short years, it will start to show its effects everywhere, making the whole world more productive.

I am not claiming that the road ahead is without potholes and sharp curves. Some of the fastest, shiniest companies in today's economy may very well crash—and big—even Yahoo! or Microsoft. Some of the most promising new technologies fueling the economy's growth, such as Internet telephony and gene mapping, may never fully pan out, or more likely, they may change abruptly, making huge investments obsolete. But that is what the new economy is all about—companies attacking the status quo and entrenched players, and experimenting to find new technologies that improve or replace earlier ones. Such activity presents no cause for alarm. The economic, social, and cultural

From William A. Sahlman, "The New Economy Is Stronger Than You Think," *Harvard Business Review*, vol. 77, no. 6 (November–December 1999). Copyright © 1999 by *Harvard Business Review*. Reprinted by permission by Harvard Business School Publishing.

factors undergirding the new economy are rock solid. All we have to do is leave them alone.

The New Business Model

In the old days—until about 25 years ago—the U.S. economy was characterized by relatively inefficient, bloated companies that were protected by carefully constructed entry barriers. Due to limited financing, start-ups were few and far between. In 1975, for instance, there was virtually no venture capital money floating around the economy and no money for initial public offerings. That is not to say the U.S. economy was terrible; it just wasn't particularly competitive. Companies could keep their costs high, and their prices came along for the ride.

We all know what happened next. Foreign competition poured cold water on the party. The oil supply dried up, and prices rose precipitously. The Federal Reserve raised interest rates to counteract inflation, making it harder and more expensive to raise funds to finance investment. Large numbers of people were laid off, but few could start their own businesses because there was still no venture capital available. Things got ugly very quickly. And boy, are we lucky.

The tough times of the early 1970s planted the seeds for the entrepreneurship of the late 1970s and early 1980s. That's when little companies such as People Express, Staples, Dell, and Home Depot started popping up, with founders who said, "We went to work for the 'safe' big company and it wasn't safe at all! The current system stinks. Prices and costs are too high. Customers aren't getting what they want. We're going to do things differently. If we fail, at least it won't be because some bureaucrats made stupid decisions." These companies began to seek a new Holy Grail—a business model so efficient that costs would radically shrink, prices would drop commensurately, and volume would soar. And if that model meant reengineering the company's business processes from end to end, they said, so be it.

The quest for a new business model was perfectly timed; indeed, it coincided with critical changes in the American competitive scene. The first—deregulation in several large markets, including transportation and financial services—occurred in the mid- to late 1970s. That made it possible for newcomers like People Express to enter the field. Even though some of the companies born of deregulation ultimately failed, they forced significant restructuring in the industries they entered.

At roughly the same time as deregulation, the microprocessor and the tools of genetic engineering were developed. These new technologies were not embraced by the leading companies of the day, but they were quickly seized by new entrants like Apple Computer, Microsoft, Amgen, and Genzyme to attack the status quo....

Enter the Internet, circa 1994. This advance continued to fuel the trend toward a more entrepreneurial economy. If new companies were working assiduously to cut out inefficiencies before, the Internet made the cuts deeper and faster. It also lowered or eliminated entry barriers in dozens of industries....

The combination of entrepreneurship and the Internet has allowed new economy companies to achieve those very efficient business models they were after. Costs came down and are being pushed lower every day. Needless to say, prices are sinking, too. In fact, the new economy has created such downward pressure on prices that it is safe to say inflation is dead—dead as a doornail. That is, unless the Fed gums things up by raising interest rates or unless other government agencies interfere with the competitive process. The business model of the new economy, you see, works perfectly on its own. It creates a system in which both businesses and their customers win.

Take the case of FreeMarkets Online, a company based in Pittsburgh. FreeMarkets has developed software that enables large industrial buyers to organize on-line auctions for qualified suppliers of semistandard parts like fabricated electronic components. In the 48 auctions that FreeMarkets has conducted to date, most participants have saved more than 15%, some as high as 50%. FreeMarkets is growing at 40% per quarter. The company believes that its auction technology is applicable to over $300 billion worth of industrial purchases in the United States alone.

You may wonder why suppliers would want to get involved in these auctions if they drive down prices. After all, in the old days, high-cost (and high-price) suppliers could still sneak by because buyers were not aware of lower-cost options or because of personal relationships between purchasing agents and salespeople. But now that auctions exist, suppliers have no choice but to participate; some even want to. Auctions allow suppliers to lower their own costs; paying a national sales force, with all its travel and other overhead, is expensive. Auctions also allow suppliers to reach previously inaccessible customers. Who wouldn't want that? Also, it's not always the low-price bidder who wins —companies can still charge a price premium for high quality. The big difference now is that companies without such differentiating capabilities can't justify higher prices....

Inefficiency is also being driven out of the economy by the new on-line megamerchants like Amazon.com and eToys, with their ability to offer greater selection at lower prices, all while using dramatically lower amounts of capital. Amazon, to illustrate, requires essentially no capital to operate its on-line store: when you buy a book at Amazon, you pay immediately. Amazon pays its suppliers in 50 to 60 days. Amazon invests little in plant and equipment because it has modest inventories—it has outsourced many logistics and inventory functions to suppliers like Ingram. Yes, recent investments by Amazon in warehouses will require more investment, but not to worry. The cost of the warehouses, estimated at several hundred million dollars, will not materially affect the company's business model relative to traditional book retailers. In fact, the new warehouses will bring Amazon closer to the customer by making much faster delivery possible—a change that will likely increase revenues by more than enough to offset the new costs....

The Amazon model is being rolled out across the economy in sectors ranging from pet supplies to pharmaceuticals to furniture. Without question, this new wave of competition is still in its infancy. As it gains momentum, pressure on existing industries will be intense. Within five years, no corner of the economy will be untouched by downward cost and price pressure. Companies will be forced to increase productivity, reengineer business processes, and basically delight customers in ever better ways. If that's not an inexorable force for positive economic transformation, nothing is.

You might ask, "What will keep companies like Amazon from raising prices—especially once they control the market?" The answer is that there are other, even newer competitors like Buy.com, On-Sale.com, and ValueAmerica.com that sell products at or near cost. Buy.com's unit, Buy-books.com, states that it will sell books for 10% below Amazon's prices. Its strategy is to make money on advertising. And its model is being replicated on computers, videos, music, and numerous other categories.

Prices will also be kept down by the Internet's ability to let people comparison shop. Services such as compare.net or MySimon.com search the Web for the lowest price for any given item. Talk about shopping around! Now consumers can make buying decisions as if they had an army of intelligent helpers running to all the stores around the world to pinpoint the lowest price. That could never happen in the physical world, yet on the Internet, it is relatively easy and instantaneous. And it almost always results in consumers getting a price near cost.

Is "at cost" too high for you? Still not a problem. Companies are now starting to provide items for free. Recently, for example, FreePC.com gave away a computer to the first 10,000 customers who signed up at its site. Over 1 million people registered. The company's business model is based on selling advertising on the "free computers"—not unlike ads on your "free" television programs. It also sells the information on its customers to other interested companies. This same basic model is currently being replicated in services like e-mail and Internet access. It probably won't be long before companies offer free phone service, perhaps over the Internet. We've come a long way very fast.

In all probability, it will not be long before companies go one step beyond free and start paying people to use products or services. Indeed, there is an early example of just such an approach at All-Advantage.com. The company passes through payments from advertisers to consumers who keep a banner open while browsing the Web. The company claims it will pay users up to $20 per month for keeping the advertising window open all the time.

How Far Will It Go?

The drive for efficiency propelling the new economy is all well and good, some people say, but it has its limits. That is, some sectors of the economy simply can't be transformed into lean, mean business machines. Take lawn mowing, for instance—an "industry" that is destined to be forever fragmented. And what about corner coffee shops? I can assure you they will never be replaced or made orders of magnitude more efficient by Internet alternatives, nor will the cottage industries that support fly-fishing tours and dude ranches. But even these industries will benefit by providing more information to more customers using the tools of the World Wide Web. Moreover, there probably is some enterprising entrepreneur out there who believes there are scale economies in "rolling up" the lawn-mowing industry to provide better service to customers. Indeed, that's what is happening right now in the notoriously fragmented dry-cleaning industry. A new company called Zoots is reengineering the process of picking up and cleaning laundry by allowing customers to track orders and change dry-cleaning preferences 24 hours a day on the Web.

Other sectors that once seemed impervious to systematic improvement are also under assault—for the better. Take education. There are literally hundreds of new competitors in the field, from electronic extension schools to on-line, degree-granting universities. Many of these new entrants offer high-quality programs that are priced well below their traditional counterparts. Perhaps you can't replicate a Harvard, Stanford, or Wellesley education on-line, but you can get quite a good education on your terms and at much lower cost.

How about health care? I will not attempt to address all the complex effects of entrepreneurial activity on health care costs. It is worth noting, however, that the biotechnology industry is dedicated to attacking the pharmaceutical industry by reengineering the drug discovery process. Companies like Millennium Pharmaceuticals are using computers to dramatically decrease the time required to find and evaluate new drug candidates, shrinking it from years to weeks. As this technology advances, pressure on drug prices will intensify—even though strong intellectual property protection remains in place. And the new drugs created by the biotech industry have the potential to increase the quality of life and decrease medical costs when compared with nondrug treatment alternatives such as surgery.

The Internet, meanwhile, can also push down health care costs by making more information available to both patients and doctors. Patients with minor ailments such as bone spurs or baldness can use the Web to educate themselves about treatment alternatives without traipsing from doctor to doctor and paying each along the way. They will be aided by companies like Silicon Valley-based Healtheon, whose stated mission is "to leverage advanced Internet technology to connect all participants in health care, and enable them to communicate, exchange information, and perform transactions that cut across the health care maze. This will simplify health care, reduce costs, enhance service, and result in more available and higher-quality health care." For their part, doctors will be helped by Internet-based programs that keep track of whether their patients have purchased their medicines—no small matter since a major reason people land in hospitals and doctors' offices in this country is a failure to buy and take their medications.

Inelastic Industries

Whenever I extol the strength of the new economy to a group of economists, one of them always tries to trump me with an argument about inelastic markets, like energy, lumber, and perhaps most important, labor. How, the economist asks, will the new economy drive down prices in sectors where supply cannot be budged? That's a good question—but not a case-busting one.

Take the situation in Silicon Valley. It's said that the area actually suffers from negative unemployment: everybody has a job and two job offers! Obviously, that means the cost of labor is increasing there, although some of the demand for higher salaries is being met with stock options rather than with increased base compensation. And once again, the entrepreneurial sector is attacking inefficiencies as they arise: one former Microsoft executive has started a company, Aditi, that has hired and trained several hundred talented programmers in Bangalore, India, to provide outsourced programming support for U.S. companies.

Or take the shrimp market. The supply of shrimp decreased tremendously as the oceans grew polluted and over-fished. By 1980, the supply was so tight, in fact, that a pound of the frozen critters cost $15 (in 1999 dollars). Enter a group of entrepreneurs in Ecuador and Thailand who came up with a way to "grow" shrimp in ponds. Today they sell it for $6.99 a pound, and at that price, it's no wonder that consumers are gobbling it up. Now over 60% of the U.S. shrimp supply comes from ponds rather than from oceans.

Labor and shrimp are one thing, you may say, but what about the tough stuff, like fuel? Again, not a problem; entrepreneurs are on the case. Consider, for example, a little company in Woburn, Massachusetts, named Quantum Energy Technologies. It has figured out a way to reengineer diesel fuel in order to increase efficiency and lower emissions, and thus the costs associated with them. A company called Trexel, also based in Woburn, Massachusetts, has invented a revolutionary process for creating durable foamed plastic using 25% to 50% less plastic than traditional methods (the key is inserting more air in the plastic without sacrificing strength).

Entrepreneurs have even found a way to cut inefficiencies out of the new economy's leanest and meanest operation, Microsoft. When its operating systems flaunted high prices and profits, programmers responded by developing new operating systems, the best example being Linux. This operating system is now being used on more than 12 million systems and has the ultimate low price—free. One company in the Linux software market, Red Hat, recently went public and quickly attained a multibillion dollar market capitalization. Red Hat sells free software packaged with a very good manual and strong customer support, which people are willing to pay for. In the new economy, one company's monopoly profits represent an overwhelmingly attractive business opportunity to another company.

The Changing Role of Distribution

When it comes to doubting the new economy, the final argument is usually that distributors will eventually bite back. They will block the new economy's forward march to total efficiency. Now, it is true that manufacturers around the world have long relied on distributors to perform valuable services, ranging from holding inventories to servicing products. And it is also true that many distributors are unhappy with the way the Internet is squeezing them out of the value chain equation. After all, if everyone starts buying their wardrobes online, that doesn't bode well for the trucking companies that ship the clothing from factory to warehouse to retail outlets.

But distribution is expensive, and businesses have always tried to bypass it or to reduce its costs. The new economy is doing that, just faster and better than ever before. It is making distribution more efficient—better, cheaper, and more responsive to the consumer. And therein lies its power and its sustainability. Indeed, efficient distribution capabilities will be vital in the new economy and will be justly rewarded....

The American Way

The unrelenting drive for efficiency in the new economy is a marvelous thing and will certainly hold down prices and stave off inflation. But the new economy is strong and sustainable for other interrelated reasons. Let's take a look at them.

The first is straightforward enough. But it has important implications. Americans love entrepreneurs. They are heroes in our society—examples range from Sam Walton at WalMart to Sandra Kurtzig at ASK Computer Systems to Jeff Bezos at Amazon. They make news wherever they go. Entrepreneurs write best-selling books, and books are written about them. Recent best-selling entrepreneur-authors include Howard Schultz at Starbucks, Michael Dell, and Bill Gates.

The American love affair with entrepreneurs couldn't happen if we didn't have such a high tolerance for failure. Americans admire people just for trying —the harder, the better. We find something honorable—gutsy, even—in a businessperson starting company after company until he or she gets it right. Many of our entrepreneurial heroes came perilously close to failing—like Fred Smith at Federal Express—or actually did fail—like Jerry Kaplan, former CEO of Go (which "went") and current CEO of the Internet company OnSale. Indeed, failure has so little stigma in Silicon Valley that it is simply synonymous with experience (as long as it is not caused by unethical behavior).

Because entrepreneurs are such heroes in America, two things are happening—now more than ever, in fact. The first is that entrepreneurship is attracting the best and brightest minds in America. Consider some statistics from my backyard, Harvard Business School. In the academic year that ended in June 1999, an astonishing 35% of the graduates went to work in new economy companies and the venture capital firms that support them. During the school year, there were at least 100 teams of students working on business plans, most focused on the Internet, and one very likely to succeed plan aimed at building nail salons in airports around the world. During the year, well over 30 teams actually started businesses, raising capital in amounts from a few hundred thousand to tens of millions. Students used to take more conservative paths upon graduation—to consulting firms and investment banks—but they no longer perceive great risk in jumping on the entrepreneurial bandwagon early in their careers. Indeed, they view the real risk as missing the greatest wave of opportunity in history. As a result, these young, ambitious entrepreneurs are running the new economy.

The second impact of America's love affair with entrepreneurs is that money is flowing to them with enormous ease. In fact, the United States has the most entrepreneur-friendly capital markets in the world. Last year, a remarkable $26 billion was invested by professional venture capitalists, one quarter of which went into new e-commerce companies. The public capital markets, too, have been very receptive to new issues. A company like Amazon has been able to raise well over $1 billion in the capital markets despite reporting large losses. At the peak, the market assigned a value to Amazon of over $30 billion, significantly higher than the market capitalization of a traditional retailer like Sears. FedEx, too, was able to attract millions of dollars in funding in its initial public offering, despite asking for it with perhaps the scariest prospectus I have ever read. It cataloged the company's operating challenges, its near bankruptcy episodes, and certain highly unusual company-saving financing tactics that stretched the rules more than a little. Investors apparently found this never-say-die story charming—and thank goodness.

Money in this country flows toward big dreams. Louis Borders, a man with absolutely no experience in the food industry—he started the bookstore chain—recently came up with the idea that he could create a same-day grocery delivery service. Within months, investors had given him $600 million to launch Webvan. (He needs $400 million more to get going, he says.) Or take Bill McGowan of MCI fame. Between 1972 and 1982—prior to the Justice Department consent decree with AT&T—he was able to raise almost $500 million to free consumers from the tyranny of AT&T. Nantucket Nectars used to be a tiny company run by two friends who sold their wares off the back of a boat. An entrepreneur fell in love with their business plan and gave them several million to expand the business before it was purchased by Ocean Spray for almost $100 million. And three young Harvard Business School Classmates, David Thompson, Bruce Ferguson, and Scott Webster, were able to raise millions to launch a commercial satellite into space. Their company, Orbital Sciences, is now listed on the New York Stock Exchange with hundreds of millions in revenues. Americans believe in the dreams of entrepreneurs, it seems, because they so often come true.

The World Economy

The new economy is largely an American phenomenon at the moment, but part of its strength is that it is spreading. What makes me say so? The first answer is entirely anecdotal. In the past, my foreign students received their MBAs and stayed right here, joining U.S. companies with great enthusiasm. Today, the majority grab their MBAs and run home to start their own local versions of our successful new-economy ventures. A great example is AsiaMail, a company that intends to provide free e-mail and other e-commerce services to users throughout Asia. The team, led by two recent JD-MBAs from Harvard Business School, has raised well over $20 million to finance its plan. Yet another team of foreign-born MBAs is starting a company to reengineer the drug delivery system in Europe, along the same model as the one used by Drugstore.com and PlanetRx.

To be sure, new economy business models are also sprouting up abroad without the help of U.S.-educated MBAs—and with great fervor and promise. Two 26-year-old entrepreneurs have launched OfficeNet in Argentina—a Latin American version of Staples that appears to be doing very well. Another example is Patagon.com, a company based in Buenos Aires that is trying to offer electronic trading for financial securities in Latin America. Again, the founders are two young native-born entrepreneurs who have been able to attract significant amounts of venture capital.

These examples are not meant to demonstrate a tidal wave of change. The globalization of the new economy is still a ripple. But the world today is so connected by the mass media, e-mail, and the Internet that it is only a matter of time. When something works as well as the new economy, everyone wants a piece of it. Indeed, entrepreneurship will continue to flourish as inefficiencies—and thus, opportunities—across world markets attract more human and financial capital.

The Golden Age

The naysayers of the new economy argue that the stock market has run amok and that doom looms ahead. Yet from a different perspective, the "irrational exuberance" of the stock market has actually played an important role in increasing productivity and decreasing inflation. Why? The more money that flows into the disruptive companies of the new economy, the better the new economy's inefficiency-busting, inflation-crushing model works. As new economy companies grow stronger, they put more competitive pressure on existing players, pushing prices and costs down, down, down. The real threat to the economy right now is not growth but the government putting an artificial stop to it by raising interest rates.

The new economy is strong and resilient. At the same time we are experiencing dramatic growth, we are experiencing deflationary pressures. Granted, the road ahead won't be easy for business executives. That's a given. After all, companies new and old will be under constant attack, having to reinvent themselves or get out of the way. Today's media heroes may well be tomorrow's goats. And labor, too, will pay a price. Many workers will be required to learn new skills or find new jobs altogether. As in every revolution, not all will benefit equally nor will the pain be spread evenly. But years hence, we will look back at this time as a golden age. That is, if the policy makers don't turn it to lead.

NO ↵

Dean Baker

The New Economy: A Millennial Myth

As the stock market soars to ever greater heights, the voices proclaiming a "New Economy" are becoming louder and more numerous. According to this chorus, computer technology and the Internet have created a qualitatively different economy. This New Economy is not bound by the same physical constraints as the old industrial economy. New ways of doing business and organizing the workplace are creating possibilities that were unimaginable just a decade ago as companies cut costs and become more flexible using new computer technology. As a result, companies and their workers are becoming more productive and the output of the economy overall is growing faster than would have been possible in earlier decades.

The New Economy also supposedly makes possible lower rates of unemployment without inflation than had previously been the case. In short, the New Economy is rapidly propelling the nation and the world into a new, possibly endless, era of prosperity.

The New Economy in the Eyes of Its Prophet

Management consultant Peter Drucker is one of the nation's leading New Economy gurus. Now 90 years old, he is the scholar who invented the phrase "knowledge work" and became a consultant to corporations after publishing a groundbreaking study of General Motors from the inside. In a January [2000] interview with *The Wall Street Journal*, he recently paraded some typical comments about how the Internet economy is transforming the old industrial and service economy. To Drucker, hi-tech means companies can more easily keep up-to-the-minute information on sales and production and so need not maintain large, expensive inventories. And hi-tech makes global commerce easier than ever—with astonishing results.

For example, Drucker says,

> Global markets, which are growing at more than twice the rate of domestic markets, intensify the pressure to cut costs, thereby creating wealth for society at large.... In a transparent marketplace, when everyone knows everyone's price, the price of everything trends downward. Consider the

magnitude of all this: Instead of causing prices to rise, economic growth is actually propelling them lower.

Yet it is far from clear that competition is more intense in an era where megamergers are the order of the day; ever-bigger companies can influence even a marketplace that spans the globe. A major piece of evidence suggesting otherwise is that corporations have managed to improve their profit margins in the last decade even while increasing their activities in the global marketplace.

At another point in the interview, Drucker comments that: "Inventories, which once triggered or prolonged recessions, are not just declining but in many places evaporating.... Long-term, wealth can only increase in a demate-rializing economy." But whatever the future may hold, the economy has not "dematerialized" just yet. According to the most recent data, the value of the nation's inventories is close to $1.4 trillion. Even in a $9 trillion economy like ours, this still makes a difference. In fact, in some ways the economy seems to be re-materializing. Amazon.com, the flagship internet retailer, made its biggest investment of 1999 in building a series of huge warehouses across the country.

Finally, Drucker celebrates the fact that in the New Economy, decisionmaking is no longer controlled by monolithic corporations; rather it is done by an "untold number of small firms and individuals." Microsoft, AOL-Time-Warner, and Dell—computer giants pursuing monopolistic control of their markets—are betting otherwise.

How Does the New Economy Measure Up?

Much of the argument for the New Economy rests on largely subjective assertions about the wonders of the new technology. Clearly computer technology and the Internet allow us to do many things that were not previously possible. But this is not the first time that technology has changed our lives or the economy. The real question is the quantitative impact of the latest set of technological innovations compared with prior breakthroughs. If Drucker's off-the-cuff insights on the New Economy seem a bit frayed, a closer look at the big measures economists like to cite as proof of a "New Economy" doesn't support their case either. The standard measures they look to are the rate of growth of the overall economy, or gross domestic product (GDP); the rate of growth of productivity—the amount of GDP produced in each hour of work; and the rate of growth in people's real wages.

However, before directly discussing this evidence, it is worth dispelling one myth about the old economy. One of the undeniably positive developments of the last few years has been the decline in the unemployment rate to levels not seen since the late 1960s. The overall unemployment rate has fallen to just over 4%. Just five years ago, there was near unanimity among the nation's leading economists that the unemployment rate could not fall below 6% without setting off an inflationary spiral. When the unemployment rate falls, workers are in a better position to get wage increases. When wages start to rise more rapidly this can cause prices to rise more rapidly. Higher prices will in turn lead workers to demand higher wages. The conventional wisdom among

Figure 1

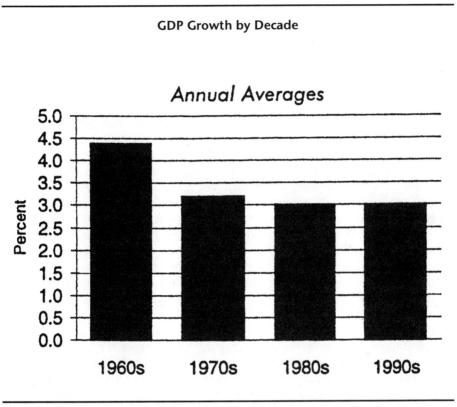

GDP Growth by Decade

Annual Averages

Note: The hi-tech economy in the 1990s does not look so rosy when its growth rate is compared to the 1960s. Gross Domestic Product (GDP) measures the overall output of the economy, and it grew slower in the '90s than in the '60s.

Source: National Income and Products Accounts, U.S. Commerce Dept.

economists was that this spiral kicked off when the unemployment rate fell below 6%.

The unemployment rate has been below 6% since the middle of 1994. It has been below 5% for two and a half years. During this time the inflation rate has actually fallen slightly. The New Economy advocates see this as compelling evidence of a new era where the economy can sustain low rates of unemployment without inflation.

There is a simpler explanation: the nation's leading economists were wrong about unemployment's effect on inflation. While lower rates of unemployment always imply more inflationary pressure than higher rates of unemployment (holding everything else equal), there never was much reason to believe that an inflationary spiral would be triggered if the unemployment rate fell below 6%, or any other level. There was no widely accepted theoretical reason why the economy should have a particular trigger point rate of unemployment, or "non-accelerating inflation rate of unemployment (NAIRU)," where inflation endlessly accelerates out of control if the unemployment rate falls lower.

The evidence for this view was very limited, relying on the few postwar expansions where the unemployment rate at least temporarily fell to relatively low levels. In each of these cases there were compelling alternative explanations for the increases in inflation. For example, the huge commitment of resources to the Vietnam War surely added to inflationary pressures in the 1960s independently of the rate of unemployment. Similarly, the 30% fall in the value of the dollar in the late 1980s created substantial inflationary pressures, quite apart from the impact of a brief period of relatively low unemployment.

There have been structural changes in the last two decades that have reduced workers' bargaining power. This reduces their ability to get higher wages, which companies supposedly pay for by charging higher prices, thus pushing up inflation. Weaker unions, deregulation of major industries like trucking and telecommunications, the increased use of nonstandard work arrangements like temporary and contract workers, and the growing importance of international competition all have had the effect of putting downward pressure on wages. Largely as a result of these changes there has been a significant redistribution from wages to profits over the course of this business cycle. But it does not follow that in the absence of these changes there would have been spiraling inflation in the 1990s. In any case, if the main innovation of the New Economy is a restructured labor market that depresses wage growth, it does not have much to offer most of the population.

But the final score on the New Economy must rest on its ability to produce more rapid increases in growth and productivity than the old economy. By this measure, the evidence is mixed at best. The rate of GDP growth over this business cycle has averaged 3% a year, exactly the same as the cycle from 1979 to 1989. This rate falls below the 3.2% growth rate from 1969 to 1979, and well below the 4.4% growth rate from 1959 to 1969. There is no evidence of a New Economy in this data.

The economy's performance over the business cycle looks somewhat better when focusing on productivity growth. The 1.9% average growth rate over this cycle is up significantly from the 1.4% rate of the 1980s. Still, this only brings productivity growth back to its average rate during the 1970s, and leaves it well below the 2.9% rate of the 1960s. Furthermore, changes in methods of measurement have added about 0.2 percentage points annually to the rate of productivity growth. This leaves productivity growth in the 1990s behind the 1970s and far behind the 1960s when a consistent measurement technique is used.

The Bubble Years

New Economy advocates can point to a considerably brighter picture in the last four years. Since 1995 GDP growth has averaged 4%, while productivity growth has averaged 2.5%. While this doesn't quite match the performance of the 1960s, it is in the same ballpark. But it is dangerous to draw broad conclusions based on the economy's performance over a relatively short period. This warning is especially appropriate at present, since the economy's growth during this period has been based on two unsustainable trends, an exploding trade deficit and a soaring stock market.

The trade deficit is the amount by which the value of the goods and services the United States buys from other nations exceeds the total value of goods and services that we sell to other nations. Most industrialized nations do not run trade deficits, since they sell more to the rest of the world than they buy. However, the United States has consistently run a trade deficit for the last quarter century.

Usually this deficit has been relatively small, but in the last four years it has grown from 0.8% of GDP to more than 3% of GDP, a gap of more than $300 billion a year. This means that the United States economy has not been producing enough to meet its demand. Instead it is relying on foreign economies and borrowing to fill the gap. In effect, over the last four years consumption in the United States has been allowed to grow by 2.2% more than would have otherwise have been the case if the trade deficit had remained constant.

If the trade deficit continues to grow at this rate it will hit an almost unimaginable 6% of GDP by 2005. Even if the trade deficit stabilizes at this level, the nation's foreign debt will reach 60% of GDP by 2010, a level of indebtedness completely without precedent for a major industrial nation. Few, if any, economists would dare make such a prediction.

Eventually, the rise in the trade deficit will have to be reversed. This means that consumption in the United States will have to grow less rapidly than the overall economy. As a practical matter this will be accomplished through a large fall in the value of the dollar, which will decrease the nation's ability to purchase imports and will increase domestic inflation. It is not clear how the economy will respond to this sort of shock.

The second unsustainable trend is the run-up in the stock market. Over the last decade, stock prices have risen by 350% while corporate profits have increased by just 150%. As a result, the ratio of stock prices to earnings per share vastly exceeds past records. At current price-to-earnings ratios and projected rates of earnings growth from agencies like the Congressional Budget Office (CBO), the return on stocks will not even be able to match the return from government bonds, unless the price to earnings ratio rises still further.

CBO projects that corporate earnings will grow only about one percentage point more rapidly than the inflation rate over the next decade. While some fast growing companies will clearly do much better than this, many others will perform much worse. When examining the market as a whole, it is only necessary to examine the aggregate growth of profits, and almost no economists project profit growth very different from that expected by the CBO.

If profits are barely growing, then the only way stock returns can continue to be good is if stock prices continue to rise more rapidly than corporate earnings. No one has yet produced a coherent argument explaining how the ratio of share prices to corporate earnings can rise indefinitely. A further rise in the price-to-earnings ratio would simply set the stage for an even larger collapse when the inevitable adjustment eventually occurs.

In short, the stock market is a classic bubble. It is every bit as "new" as the tulip bulb mania in Holland in the 17th century. While the bubble inflates, the economy looks good, since the surge in stock prices creates massive amounts of wealth, which leads to growth in consumer demand. In addition, the fact that many workers, especially higher paid workers, can be paid in stock options that may ultimately prove worthless helps relieve supply constraints on the economy.

The current situation can be compared to one in which $10 trillion of counterfeit money ($35,000 for every person in the country) entered into the economy. As long as people are willing to accept this money for payment for goods and services, it would provide considerable stimulus to the economy. Once it is recognized that the money is counterfeit, the situation would be very different.

Figure 2

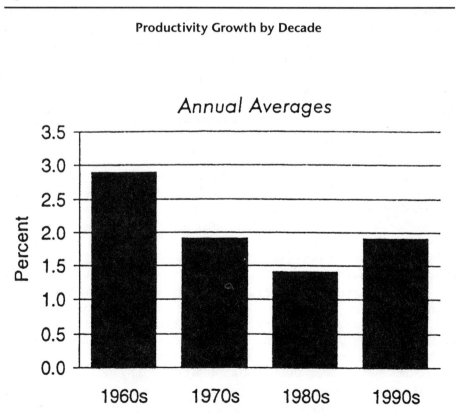

Productivity Growth by Decade

Note: Productivity—which measures economic output per hour of labor—grew faster in the hi-tech '90s compared to the last two decades, but was not as impressive when compared to the 1960s.

Source: U.S. Bureau of Labor Statistics

How or when the stock market collapses remains to be seen. It is likely that the crash will coincide with a sharp decline in the value of the dollar, further complicating the economic picture. It is virtually certain that the crash will produce a wave of bankruptcies and lawsuits, as investors attempt to reclaim some of their losses from the people who gave them bad advice or misleading information. It may take a considerable period of time to get the economy back in order. If the nation can continue to experience rapid economic and productivity growth in the wake of this collapse, then we will have evidence of a New Economy. Until then, the evidence suggests that the New Economy is nothing more than an old-fashioned bubble.

POSTSCRIPT

Is the New Economy Really New?

S ahlman begins his analysis by describing what he considers to be the major characteristics of the new economy. Probably the most important element, he maintains, is the development and rapid deployment of a new business model. Spurred by a combination of forces, including deregulation and the development of new technologies, entrepreneurs have created a new business model that drives out inefficiencies, forces "intelligent business reengineering," and gives customers what they want. Sahlman offers Amazon.com, Buy.com, and MySimon.com as examples of companies that are embracing the new business model. What is also important is that the new business model can be extended into still more areas of the economy, ranging from dry cleaning to health care. Sahlman then considers the argument that inelastic markets impose limits to the spread of the new business model (he offers the labor, shrimp, and energy markets as examples). Sahlman dismisses this argument for two reasons: the possibility of going international (labor supply may be inelastic from a local perspective, but it is elastic in an international context) and the possibility of technological breakthroughs (creating new competitive products or new sources of supply). Turning to distribution in the new economy, he finds that the Internet is making distribution better, cheaper, and more responsive to the consumer. As for the strengths of the new economy, Sahlman emphasizes the love affair that Americans have with entrepreneurs, making heroes of people like Sam Walton, Bill Gates, Jeff Bezos, and others. This love affair has drawn the best and brightest minds to entrepreneurship. The love affair also allows the new entrepreneurs to obtain financing for their business ventures with "enormous ease." Sahlman concludes that the "new economy is strong and resilient."

Baker begins his attack on the notion of a new economy by describing what he thinks the proponents of the new economy mean by that term. The essential element is that the computer and the Internet have created new ways of doing business that make firms and workers more productive. This, in turn, has created an environment that has lowered unemployment without inflation; that is, it has created a "new, possibly endless, era of prosperity." Baker attacks the concept of a new economy by developing several arguments. First, although he admits that there has been a decline in unemployment without inflation, he argues this is not because of a new economy. Instead, Baker asserts that economists were just plain wrong in specifying an unemployment-inflation tradeoff. Second, the empirical evidence on the growth of output and productivity does not support the notion of a new economy. As for output growth, the percentage of change in gross domestic product over the current business cycle is not much different from that of previous business cycles: 3 percent for the current business cycle, 3 percent for the 1979–1989 period, 3.2 percent for the 1969–1979 period, and 4.4 percent for 1959–1969 period. The same argument can be made for productivity growth: 1.9 percent for the current expansion, 1.4 percent for the 1980s, 1.9 percent for the 1970s, and 2.9 percent for the 1960s. Third, Baker sees two critical problems that may impede continued prosperity. He shows that the U.S. international trade deficit is large and growing. If a turnaround does not occur soon, the United States will reach previously unseen levels of international indebtedness. The other critical problem is the run-up in the stock market (Baker's article was published before the decline in stock prices that began in summer 2000). Baker argues that over the preceding decade, stock prices increased by 350 percent, while corporate profits increased only by 150 percent. Thus, the run-up in stock prices appears to be a classic "bubble." Baker concludes that he will be more willing to accept the idea of a new economy if the stock market collapses (and he believes that it eventually must) and the economy continues to experience growth in output and productivity.

There is an extensive literature exploring this issue. Interesting analyses can be found in "The New Economy as a Decent Society," by Robert Reich, *The American Prospect* (February 12, 2001); "Is the New Economy Family Friendly?" by Alyssa Rayman-Read, *The American Prospect* (January 1, 2001); "What New Economy?" *Technology Review* (January/February 2001); "Crash or Boom? On the Future of the New Economy," by Irwin A. Stelze, *Commentary* (October 2000); "The Information Society, the New Economy, and the Hype," by James B. Rule, *Dissent* (Fall 2000); "Does the 'New Economy' Measure Up to the Great Inventions of the Past?" by Robert J. Gordon, *Journal of Economic Perspectives* (Fall 2000); "Economics and the New Economy: The Invisible Hand Meets Creative Destruction," by Leonard I. Nakamura, *Federal Reserve Bank of Philadelphia Business Review* (July 2000); "Is There a New Economy?" by Kevin Stiroh, *Challenge* (July–August 1999); "State of the Union: The New Economy Does Not Lurk in the Statistical Discrepancy," by Dean Baker, *Challenge* (July–August 1998); "A Business Model for the New Economy," by Richard E. S. Boulton, Barry D. Libert, and Steve M. Samek, *Journal of Business Strategy* (July 2000); "The New Economy: Fact or Fiction?" by Ignazio Visco, *OECD Observer* (Summer 2000); "The New Economy: Fact or Fantasy?" by John S. McCallum, *Ivey Business Journal* (November 1999); "Old Economic Logic in the New Economy," by Laura D'Andrea Tyson, *California Management Review* (Summer 1999); and "The Ups and Downs of the New Economy," by Gail Robinson, *New Statesman* (July 10, 2000).

ISSUE 12

Is It Time to Abolish the Minimum Wage?

YES: Thomas Rustici, from "A Public Choice View of the Minimum Wage," *Cato Journal* (Spring/Summer 1985)

NO: Charles Craypo, from "In Defense of Minimum Wages," An Original Essay Written for This Volume (2002)

ISSUE SUMMARY

YES: Orthodox neoclassical economist Thomas Rustici asserts that the effects of the minimum wage are clear: it creates unemployment among the least-skilled workers.

NO: Labor economist Charles Craypo argues that a high minimum wage is good for workers, employers, and consumers alike and that it is therefore good for the economy as a whole.

In the midst of the Great Depression, Congress passed the Fair Labor Standards Act (FLSA) of 1938. In one bold stroke, it established a minimum wage rate of $.25 an hour, placed controls on the use of child labor, designated 44 hours as the normal workweek, and mandated that time and a half be paid to anyone working longer than the normal workweek. Fifty years later the debates concerning child labor, length of the workweek, and overtime pay have long subsided, but the debate over the minimum wage rages on.

The immediate and continued concern over the minimum wage component of the FLSA should surprise few people. Although $.25 an hour is a paltry sum compared to today's wage rates, in 1938 it was a princely reward for work. It must be remembered that jobs were hard to come by and unemployment rates at times reached as high as 25 percent of the workforce. When work was found, any wage seemed acceptable to those who roamed the streets with no "safety net" to protect their families. Indeed, consider the fact that $.25 an hour was 40.3 percent of the average manufacturing wage rate for 1938.

Little wonder, then, that the business community in the 1930s was up in arms. Business leaders argued that if wages went up, prices would rise. This would choke off the little demand for goods and services that existed in the marketplace, and the demand for workers would be sure to fall. The end result would be a return to the depths of the depression, where there was little or no hope of employment for the very people who were supposed to benefit from the Fair Labor Standards Act.

This dire forecast was demonstrated by simple supply-and-demand analysis. First, as modern-day introductory textbooks in economics invariably show, unemployment occurs when a minimum wage greater than the equilibrium wage is mandated by law. This simplistic analysis, which assumes competitive conditions in both the product and factor markets, is predicated upon the assumptions that as wages are pushed above the equilibrium level, the quantity of labor demanded will fall and this quantity of labor supplied will increase. The result is that this wage rigidity prevents the market from clearing. The end result is an excess in the quantity of labor supplied relative to the quantity of labor demanded.

The question that should be addressed in this debate is whether or not a simple supply-and-demand analysis is capable of adequately predicting what happens in real-world labor markets when a minimum wage is introduced or an existing minimum wage is raised. The significance of this is not based on idle curiosity. The minimum wage has been increased numerous times since its introduction in 1938. Most recently, effective September 1, 1997, legislation establishing the current minimum wage of $5.15 was signed into law by President Bill Clinton.

Did this minimum wage increase, and other increases before it, do irreparable harm to those who are least able to defend themselves in the labor market, the marginal worker? That is, if a minimum wage of $5.15 is imposed, what happens to all those marginal workers whose value to the firm is something less than $5.15? Are these workers fired? Do firms simply absorb this cost increase in the form of reduced corporate profits? What happens to productivity?

This is the crux of the following debate between Thomas Rustici and Charles Craypo. Rustici argues that the answer is obvious: there will be an excess in the quantity of labor supplied relative to the quantity demanded. In lay terms, there will be unemployment. Craypo rejects this neoclassical view. He recommends judging the minimum wage on the intent of the original legislation: increased aggregate demand and elimination of predatory labor market practices.

Thomas Rustici

A Public Choice View of
the Minimum Wage

Why, when the economist gives advice to his society, is he so often cooly ignored? He never ceases to preach free trade... and protectionism is growing in the United States. He deplores the perverse effects of minimum wage laws, and the legal minimum is regularly raised each 3 to 5 years. He brands usury laws as a medieval superstition, but no state hurries to repeal its laws.

— George Stigler

Introduction

Much of public policy is allegedly based on the implications of economic theory. However, economic analysis of government policy is often disregarded for political reasons. The minimum wage law is one such example. Every politician openly deplores the spectacle of double-digit teenage unemployment pervading modern society. But, when economists claim that scientific proof, a priori and empirical, dictates that minimum wage laws cause such a regretful outcome, their statements generally fall on deaf congressional ears. Economists too often assume that policymakers are interested in obtaining all the existing economic knowledge before deciding on a specific policy course. This view of the policy-formation process, however, is naive. In framing economic policy politicians will pay some attention to economists' advice, but such advice always will be rejected when it conflicts with the political reality of winning votes....

Economic Effects of the Minimum Wage

Economic analysis has demonstrated few things as clearly as the effects of the minimum wage law. It is well known that the minimum wage creates unemployment among the least skilled workers by raising wage rates above free market levels. Eight major effects of the minimum wage can be discussed: unemployment effects, employment effects in uncovered sectors of the economy, reduction in nonwage benefits, labor substitution effects, capital substitution effects, racial discrimination in hiring practices, human capital development, and distortion of the market process with respect to comparative advantage. Although the minimum wage has other effects, such as a reduction in hours of employment, these eight effects are the most significant ones for this paper.

Unemployment Effects

The first federal minimum wage laws were established under the provisions of the National Recovery Administration (NRA). The National Industrial Recovery Act, which became law on 16 June 1933, established industrial minimum wages for 515 classes of labor. Over 90 percent of the minimum wages were set at between 30 and 40 cents per hour.[1] Early empirical evidence attests to the unemployment effects of the minimum wage. Using the estimates of C. F. Roos, who was the director of research at the NRA, Benjamin Anderson states: "Roos estimates that, by reason of the minimum wage provisions of the codes, about 500,000 Negro workers were on relief in 1934. Roos adds that a minimum wage definitely causes the displacement of the young, inexperienced worker and the old worker."[2]

On 27 May 1935 the Supreme Court declared the NRA unconstitutional, burying the minimum wage codes with it. The minimum wage law reappeared at a later date, however, with the support of the Supreme Court. In what became the precedent for the constitutionality of future minimum wage legislation, the Court upheld the Washington State minimum wage law on 29 March 1937 in *West Coast Hotel v. Parrish*.[3] This declaration gave the Roosevelt administration and Labor Secretary Frances Perkins the green light to reestablish the federal minimum wage, which was achieved on 25 June 1938 when President Roosevelt signed into law the Fair Labor Standards Act (FLSA).

The FSLA included legislation affecting work-age requirements, the length of the workweek, pay rates for overtime work, as well as the national minimum wage provision. The law established minimum wage rates of 25 cents per hour the first year, 30 cents per hour for the next six years, and 40 cents per hour after seven years. The penalty for noncompliance was severe: violators faced a $10,000 fine, six months imprisonment, or both. In addition, an aggrieved employee could sue his employer for twice the difference between the statutory wage rate and his actual pay.[4]

With the passage of the FLSA, it became inevitable that major dislocations would result in labor markets, primarily those for low-skilled and low-wage workers. Although the act affected occupations covering only one-fifth of the labor force,[5] leaving a large uncovered sector to minimize the disemployment effects, the minimum wage was still extremely counterproductive. The Labor Department admitted that the new minimum wage had a disemployment effect, and one historian sympathetic to the minimum wage was forced to concede that "[t]he Department of Labor estimated that the 25-cents-an-hour minimum wage caused about 30,000 to 50,000 to lose their job. About 90% of these were in southern industries such as bagging, pecan shelling, and tobacco stemming."[6]

These estimates seriously understate the actual magnitude of the damage. Since only 300,000 workers received an increase as a result of the minimum wage,[7] estimates of 30,000–50,000 lost jobs reveal that 10–13 percent of those covered by the law lost their jobs. But it is highly dubious that only 30,000–50,000 low-wage earners lost their jobs in the entire country; that many unemployed could have been found in the state of Texas alone, where labor authorities saw devastation wrought via the minimum wage on the pecan trade. The *New York Times* reported the following on 24 October 1938:

> Information received today by State labor authorities indicated that more than 40,000 employees of the pecan nut shelling plants in Texas would be thrown out of work tomorrow by the closing down of that industry, due to the new Wages and Hours Law. In San Antonio, sixty plants, employing ten thousand men and women, mostly Mexicans, will close.... Plant owners assert that they cannot remain in business and pay the minimum wage of 25 cents an hour with a maximum working week of forty-four hours. Many garment factories in Texas will also close.[8]

It can reasonably be deduced that even if the Texas estimates had been wildly inaccurate, the national unemployment effect would still have exceeded the Department of Labor's estimates.

The greatest damage, however, did not come in Texas or in any other southern state, but in Puerto Rico. Since a minimum wage law has its greatest unemployment effect on low-wage earners, and since larger proportions of workers in poor regions such as Puerto Rico tend to be at the lower end of the wage scale, Puerto Rico was disproportionately hard-hit. Subject to the same national 25-cents-per-hour rate as workers on the mainland, Puerto Rican workers suffered much more hardship from the minimum wage law. According to Anderson:

> It was thought by many that, in the first year, the provision would not affect many industries outside the South, though the framers of the law apparently forgot about Puerto Rico, and very grave disturbances came in that island.... Immense unemployment resulted there through sheer inability of important industries to pay the 25 cents an hour.[9]

Simon Rottenberg likewise points out the tragic position in which Puerto Rico was placed by the enactment of the minimum wage:

> When the Congress established a minimum wage of 25 cents per hour in 1938, the average hourly wage in the U.S. was 62.7 cents.... It resulted in a mandatory increase for only some 300,000 workers out of a labor force of more than 54 million. In Puerto Rico, in contrast... the new Federal minimum far exceeded the prevailing average hourly wage of the major portion of Puerto Rican workers. If a continuing serious attempt at enforcement... had been made, it would have meant literal economic chaos for the island's economy.[10]...

After two years of economic disruption in Puerto Rico, Congress amended the minimum wage provisions.[11] The minimum wage was reduced to 12.5 cents per hour, but it was too late for many industries and for thousands of low-wage earners employed by them, who suddenly found unemployment the price they had to pay for the minimum wage.

In sum, the tragedy of the minimum wage laws during the NRA and the FLSA was not just textbook-theorizing by academic economists, but real-world disaster for the thousands who became the victims of the law. But these destructive effects have not caused the law to be repealed; to the contrary, it has been expanded in coverage and increased in amount.

... Evidence for the unemployment effects of the minimum wage continues to mount. Many empirical studies since the early 1950s—from early research by Marshall Colberg and Yale Brozen to more recent work by Jacob Mincer and James Ragan—have validated the predictions of economic theory regarding the unemployment effects of the minimum wage law. In virtually every case it was found that the net employment effects and labor-force participation rates were negatively related to changes in the minimum wage. In the face of 50 years of evidence, the question is no longer *if* the minimum wage law creates unemployment, but *how much* current or future increases in the minimum wage will adversely affect the labor market.

Employment in Uncovered Sectors

The labor market can be divided into two sectors: that covered by the minimum wage law, and that not covered. In a partially covered market, the effects of the minimum wage are somewhat disguised. Increasing it disemploys workers in the covered sector, prompting them to search for work in the uncovered sector if they are trainable and mobile. This then drives down the wage rate in the uncovered sector, making it lower than it otherwise would have been. Since perfect knowledge and flexibility is not observed in real-world labor markets, substantial unemployment can occur during the transition period.

Employees in the covered sector who do not lose their jobs get a wage-rate increase through the higher minimum wage. But this comes only at the expense of (1) the disemployed workers who lose their jobs and suffer unemployment during the transition to employment in the uncovered sector, and (2) everyone in the uncovered sector, as their wage rate falls due to the influx of unemployed workers from the covered sector. While increasing the incomes of some low-wage earners, increasing the minimum wage tends to make the lowest wage earners in the uncovered sector even poorer than they otherwise would have been.

Yale Brozen has found that the uncovered household sector served to absorb the minimum wage-induced disemployed in the past.[12] But the "safety valve" of the uncovered portion of the economy is rapidly vanishing with the continual elimination of various exemptions.[13] Because of this trend we can expect to see the level of structural unemployment increase with escalation of the minimum wage.[14]

Nonwage Benefits

Wage rates are not the only costs associated with the employment of workers by firms. The effective labor cost a firm incurs is usually a package of pecuniary and nonpecuniary benefits. As such, contends Richard McKenzie,

> employers can be expected to respond to a minimum wage law by cutting back or eliminating altogether those fringe benefits and conditions of work, like the company parties, that increase the supply of labor but which do not affect the productivity of labor. By reducing such non-money benefits of employment, the employer reduces his labor costs from what they otherwise would have been and loses nothing in the way of reduced labor productivity."[15]

If one takes the view that employees desire both pecuniary and nonpecuniary income, then anything forcing them to accept another mix of benefits would clearly make them worse off. For example, suppose worker A desires his income in the form of $3.00 per hour in wages, an air-conditioned workplace, carpeted floors, safety precautions, and stereo music. If he is *forced* by the minimum wage law to accept $3.25 per hour and fewer nonpecuniary benefits, he is worse off than at the preminimum wage and the *higher* level of nonpecuniary income. A priori, the enactment of minimum wage laws must place the worker and employer in a less-than-optimal state. Thus it may not be the case that only unemployed workers suffer from the minimum wage; even workers who receive a higher wage and retain employment may be net losers if their nonpecuniary benefits are reduced.

Labor Substitution Effects

The economic world is characterized by a plethora of substitutes. In the labor market low-skill, low-wage earners are substitutes for high-skill, high-wage earners. As Walter Williams points out:

> Suppose a fence can be produced by using either one high skilled worker or by using three low skilled workers. If the wage of high skilled workers is $38 per day, and that of a low skilled worker is $13 per day, the firm employs the high skilled worker because costs would be less and profits higher ($38 versus $39). The high skilled worker would soon recognize that one of the ways to increase his wealth would be to advocate a minimum wage of, say, $20 per day in the fencing industry.... After enactment of the minimum wage laws, the high skilled worker can now demand any wage up to $60 per day ... and retain employment. Prior to the enactment of the minimum wage of $20 per day, a demand of $60 per day would have cost the high skilled worker his job. Thus the effect of the minimum wage is to price the high skilled worker's competition out of the market.[16]

Labor competes against labor, not against management. Since low-skill labor competes with high-skill labor, the minimum wage works against the lower-skill, lower-paid worker in favor of higher-paid workers. Hence, the consequences of the law are exactly opposite its alleged purpose.

Table 1

Value of the Minimum Wage, 1955–1995

Year	Value of the Minimum Wage, Nominal Dollars	Value of the Minimum Wage, 1995 Dollars†	Minimum Wage as a Percent of the Average Private Nonsupervisory Wage
1955	$0.75	$3.94	43.9%
1956	1.00	5.16	55.6
1957	1.00	5.01	52.9
1958	1.00	4.87	51.3
1959	1.00	4.84	49.5
1960	1.00	4.75	47.8
1961	1.15	5.41	53.7
1962	1.15	5.36	51.8
1963	1.25	5.74	54.8
1964	1.25	5.67	53.0
1965	1.25	5.59	50.8
1966	1.25	5.43	48.8
1967	1.40	5.90	52.2
1968	1.60	6.49	56.1
1969	1.60	6.21	52.6
1970	1.60	5.92	49.5
1971	1.60	5.67	46.4
1972	1.60	5.51	43.2
1973	1.60	5.18	40.6
1974	2.00	5.89	47.2
1975	2.10	5.71	46.4
1976	2.30	5.92	47.3
1977	2.30	5.56	43.8
1978	2.65	6.00	46.6
1979	2.90	5.99	47.1
1980	3.10	5.76	46.5
1981	3.35	5.68	46.2
1982	3.35	5.36	43.6
1983	3.35	5.14	41.8
1984	3.35	4.93	40.3
1985	3.35	4.76	39.1
1986	3.35	4.67	38.2
1987	3.35	4.51	37.3
1988	3.35	4.33	36.1
1989	3.35	4.13	34.7
1990	3.80	4.44	37.9
1991	4.25	4.77	41.1
1992	4.25	4.63	40.2
1993	4.25	4.50	39.2
1994	4.25	4.38	n/a
1995	4.25	4.25	n/a

† Adjusted for inflation using the CPI-U-X1.

Source: Center on Budget and Policy Priorities

Capital Substitution Effects

To produce a given quantity of goods, some bundle of inputs is required. The ratio of inputs used to produce the desired output is not fixed by natural law but by the relative prices of inputs, which change continuously with new demand and supply conditions. Based on relative input prices, producers attempt to minimize costs for a given output. Since many inputs are substitutes for one another in the production process, a given output can be achieved by increasing the use of one and diminishing the use of another. The optimal mix will depend on the relative supply and demand for competing substitute inputs.

As a production input, low-skill labor is often in direct competition with highly technical machinery. A Whirlpool dishwasher can be substituted for low-skill manual dishwashers in the dishwashing process, and an automatic elevator can take the place of a nonautomatic elevator and a manual operator. This [is] not to imply that automation "destroys jobs," a common Luddite myth. As Frederic Bastiat explained over a century ago, jobs are obstacles to be overcome.[17] Automation shifts the *kinds* of jobs to be done in society but does not reduce their total number. Low-skill jobs are done away with, but higher-skill jobs are created simultaneously. When the minimum wage raises the cost of employing low-skill workers, it makes the substitute of automated machinery an attractive option.

Racial Discrimination in Hiring Practices

At first glance the connection between the level of racial discrimination in hiring practices and the minimum wage may not seem evident. On closer examination, however, it is apparent that the minimum wage law gives employers strong incentives to exercise their existing racial preferences.[18] The minimum wage burdens minority groups in general and minority teenagers most specifically. Although outright racism has often been blamed as the sole cause of heavy minority teenage unemployment, it is clearly not the only factor. William Keyes informs us that

> In the late 1940's and early 1950's, young blacks had a lower unemployment rate than did whites of the same age group. But after the minimum wage increased significantly, especially in 1961, the black youth unemployment rate has increased to the extent that it is now a multiple of the white youth unemployment rate.[19]

To make the case that racism itself is the cause of the employment and unemployment disparity among blacks and whites, one would have to claim that America was more racially harmonious in the past than it is now. In fact, during the racially hostile times of the early 1900s 71 percent of blacks over nine years of age were employed, as compared with 51 percent for whites.[20] The minimum wage means that employers are not free to decide among low-wage workers on the basis of price differentials; hence, they face fewer disincentives to deciding according to some other (possibly racial) criteria.

To see the racial implications of minimum wage legislation, it is helpful to look at proponents of the law in a country where racial hostility is very strong, South Africa. Since minimum wage laws share characteristics in common with equal pay laws, white racist unions in South Africa continually support both minimum wage and equal-pay-for-equal-work laws for blacks. According to Williams:

> Right-wing white unions in the building trades have complained to the South African government that laws reserving skilled jobs for whites have been broken and should be abandoned in favor of equal pay for equal work laws.... The conservative building trades made it clear that they are not motivated by concern for black workers but had come to feel that legal job reservation had been so eroded by government exemptions that it no longer protected the white worker.[21]

The reason white trade unions are restless in South Africa is a $1.52-per-hour wage differential between black and white construction workers.[22] Although the owners of the construction firms are white, they cannot afford to restrict employment to whites when blacks are willing to work for $1.52 per hour less. As minimum wages eliminate the wage differential, the cost to employers of hiring workers with the skin color they prefer is reduced. As the cost of discrimination falls, and with all else remaining the same, the law of demand would dictate that more discrimination in employment practices will occur.

Markets frequently respond where they can, even to the obstacles the minimum wage presents minority groups. In fact, during the NRA blacks would frequently be advanced to the higher rank of "executives" in order to receive exemptions from the minimum wage.[23] The free market demands that firms remain color-blind in the conduct of business: profit, not racial preference, is the primary concern of the profit-maximizing firm. Those firms who fail the profit test get driven out of business by those who put prejudice aside to maximize profits. When markets are restricted by such laws as the minimum wage, the prospects for eliminating racial discrimination in hiring practices and the shocking 40–50 percent rate of black teenage unemployment in our cities are bleak.

Human Capital Development

Minimum wage laws restrict the employment of low-skill workers when the wage rate exceeds the workers' marginal productivity. By doing so, the law prevents workers with the least skills from acquiring the marketable skills necessary for increasing their future productivity, that is, it keeps them from receiving on-the-job training.

It is an observable fact, true across ethnic groups, that income rises with age.[24] As human capital accumulates over time, it makes teenagers more valuable to employers than workers with no labor-market experience. But when teenagers are priced out of the labor market by the minimum wage, they lose their first and most crucial opportunity to accumulate the human capital that would make them more valuable to future employers. This stunting reduces their lifetime potential earnings. As Martin Feldstein has commented:

> [F]or the disadvantaged young worker, with few skills and below average education, producing enough to earn the minimum wage is incompatible with the opportunity for adequate on-the-job learning. For this group, the minimum wage implies high short-run unemployment and the chronic poverty of a life of low wage jobs.[25]

Feldstein also finds a significant irony in the minimum wage: "It is unfortunate and ironic that we encourage and subsidize expenditure on formal education while blocking the opportunity for individuals to 'buy' on-the-job training."[26] This is especially hard on teenagers from the poorest minority groups, such as blacks and hispanics—a truly sad state of affairs, since the law is instituted in the name of the poor.

Distortion of the Market Process

Relative prices provide the transmission mechanism by which information is delivered to participants in the market about the underlying relative scarcities of competing factor inputs. They serve as signals for people to substitute relatively less scarce resources for relatively more scarce resources, in many cases without their even being aware of it.[27]

Table 2

Dates and Amounts of Minimum Wage Changes

Date	Amount	As a Percent of the Average Wage in Manufacturing (Old Minimum/New Minimum)
February 1967	$1.40	44.8%/50.2%
February 1968	$1.60	47.6%/54.4%
May 1974	$2.00	37.8%/47.3%
January 1975	$2.10	42.7%/44.9%
January 1976	$2.30	41.7%/45.6%
January 1978	$2.65	38.5%/44.4%
January 1979	$2.90	40.8%/44.6%
January 1980	$3.20	41.7%/44.5%
January 1981	$3.35	40.1%/43.3%
April 1990	$3.80	31.4%/35.6%
April 1991	$4.25	33.6%/37.6%

Whenever relative price differentials exist for input substitutes in the production process, entrepreneurs will switch from higher-priced inputs to lower-priced inputs. In a dynamically changing economy, this switching occurs continually. But when prices are not allowed to transmit market information accurately, as in the case of prices artificially controlled by government, then distorted information skews the market and guides it to something clearly less than optimal.[28]

Minimum wages, being such a distortion of the price system, lead to the wrong factor input mix between labor and all other inputs. As a result, industry migrates to locations of greater labor supply more slowly, and labor-intensive industries tend to remain fixed in non-optimal areas, areas with greater labor scarcity. Large labor pools of labor-abundant geographical areas are not tapped because the controlled price of labor conveys the wrong information to all the parties involved. Thus, the existence of price differentials, as knowledge to be transmitted through relative prices, is hidden.[29] The slowdown of industrial migration keeps labor-abundant regions poorer than they otherwise would be because economic growth there is stifled. As Simon Rottenberg explains for the case of Puerto Rico:

> The aggregate effect of all these distortions was that Puerto Rico could be expected to produce fewer goods and services than would have otherwise been produced and that the rate at which insular per capita income rose toward mainland United States income standards could be expected to be dampened. In sum, the minimum wage law could be expected to reduce the rate of improvement in the standard of life of the Puerto Rican people and to intensify poverty in the island.[30]

In summary, the evidence is in on the minimum wage. All eight major effects of the minimum wage examined here make the poor, disadvantaged, or young in society worse off—the alleged beneficiaries turn out to be the law's major victims....

Conclusion

George Stigler may have startled some economists in 1946 when he claimed that minimum wage laws create unemployment and make people who had been receiving less than the minimum poorer.[31] Fifty years of experience with the law has proven Stigler correct, leaving very few defenders in the economics profession.[32]

But economists have had little success in criticizing this very destructive law. Simon Rottenberg demonstrated the government's disregard for what most economists have to say about this issue in his investigation of the Minimum Wage Study Commission created by Congress in 1977. He noted the numerous studies presented to the commission that without exception found that the law had a negative impact on employment and intensified the poverty of low-income earners. The commission spent over $17 million to conduct the investigation and on the basis of the evidence should have eliminated the law.

What was the outcome? The commission voted to *increase the minimum wage by indexing and expanding coverage.* As dissenting commissioner S. Warne Robinson commented about the investigation:

> The evidence is now in, and the findings of dozens of major economic studies show that the damage done by the minimum wage has been far more severe than even the critics of forty years ago predicted. Indeed, the evidence against the minimum wage is so overwhelming that the only way the Commission's majority was able to recommend it be retained was to ask us not to base any decisions on the facts.[33]

It cannot be that our elected representatives in Congress are just misinformed with respect to the minimum wage law. To the contrary, the *Congressional Record* demonstrates that they fully understand the law's effects and how the utilization of those effects can ensure reelection. Economists would do well to realize that governments have little interest in the truth when its implementation would contradict self-serving government policies. Rather than attempting to bring government the "facts," economists should educate the public. This is the only solution to the malaise created when people uncritically accept such governmental edicts as the minimum wage.

Notes

1. Leverett Lyon et al. *The National Recovery Administration: An Analysis and Appraisal* (New York: Da Capo Press, 1972), pp. 318–19.
2. Benjamin M. Anderson, *Economics and the Public Welfare: A Financial and Economic History of the United States, 1914–1946* (Indianapolis: Liberty Press, 1979), p. 336.
3. Jonathan Grossman, "Fair Labor Standards Act of 1938: Maximum Struggle for a Minimum Wage," *Monthly Labor Review* 101 (June 1978): 23.
4. "Wage and Hours Law," *New York Times,* 24 October 1938, p. 2.
5. Grossman, "Fair Labor Standards Act," p. 29.
6. Ibid., p. 28.
7. Ibid., p. 29.
8. "Report 40,000 Jobs Lost," *New York Times,* 24 October 1938, p. 2.
9. Anderson, *Economics and the Public Welfare,* p. 458.
10. Simon Rottenberg, "Minimum Wages in Puerto Rico," in *Economics of Legal Minimum Wages,* edited by Simon Rottenberg (Washington, D.C.: American Enterprise Institute, 1981), p. 330.
11. Rottenberg, "Minimum Wages in Puerto Rico," p. 333.
12. Yale Brozen, "Minimum Wage Rates and Household Workers," *Journal of Law and Economics* 5 (October 1962): 103–10.
13. Finis Welch, "Minimum Wage Legislation in the United States," *Economic Inquiry* 12 (September 1974): 286.
14. Brozen, "Minimum Wage Rates and Household Workers," pp. 107–08.
15. Richard McKenzie, "The Labor Market Effects of Minimum Wage Laws: A New Perspective," *Journal of Labor Research* 1 (Fall 1980): 258–59.
16. Walter Williams, *The State Against Blacks* (New York: McGraw-Hill, 1982), pp. 44–45.

17. Frederic Bastiat, *Economic Sophisms* (Irvington-on-Hudson, N.Y.: Foundation for Economic Education, 1946), pp. 16–19.

18. Walter Williams, "Government Sanctioned Restraints That Reduce the Economic Opportunities for Minorities," *Policy Review* 22 (Fall 1977): 15.

19. William Keyes,"The Minimum Wage and the Davis Bacon Act: Employment Effects on Minorities and Youth," *Journal of Labor Research* 3 (Fall 1982): 402.

20. Williams, *State Against Blacks,* p. 41.

21. Ibid., p. 43.

22. Ibid., pp. 43–44.

23. Lyon, *National Recovery Administration,* p. 339.

24. U.S. Department of Commerce, Bureau of the Census, *Statistical Abstract of the United States 1982-83,* p. 431.

25. Martin Feldstein, "The Economics of the New Unemployment," *The Public Interest,* no. 33 (Fall 1973): 14–15.

26. Ibid., p. 15.

27. Thomas Sowell, *Knowledge and Decisions* (New York: Basic Books, 1980), p. 79.

28. Ibid.

29. Ibid., pp. 167–68.

30. Rottenberg, "Minimum Wages in Puerto Rico," p. 329.

31. George Stigler, "The Economies of Minimum Wage Legislation," *American Economic Review* 36 (June 1946): 358–65.

32. Although there are a few supporters left such as John K. Galbraith, many "liberal" economists such as Paul Samuelson and James Tobin have recently come out against the minimum wage. See Emerson Schmidt, *Union Power and the Public Interest* (Los Angeles: Nash, 1973).

33. Simon Rottenberg, "National Commissions: Preaching in the Garb of Analysis," *Policy Review* no. 23 (Winter 1983): 139.

In Defense of Minimum Wages

This article refutes the dominant view held by orthodox neoclassical economists such as Thomas Rustici. These economists assert that minimum wage laws should be abolished because they misallocate resources and cause production inefficiencies. I reject Rustici's conclusion and instead take the position that in most instances high minimum wages are good for workers, employers and consumers alike and hence are good for the economy as a whole.

Three things are wrong with Rustici's neoclassical view of things. It depends on an idealized world that by assumption favors more rather than less market competition as the solution to economic problems. Second, it ignores the reasons why governments enact minimum wage laws in the first place and instead interprets and judges them on inappropriate grounds. Third, the neoclassical argument against minimum wages is supported by contradictory empirical evidence that casts doubt on its theoretical validity and practical significance.

Critics of the orthodox neoclassical interpretation of minimum wages include both neoclassical and institutional applied labor economists. In fact, most of the contradictory empirical studies in recent years have [been] produced by neoclassical economists whose findings prompt them to question the dominant view. In addition to the research of mainstream economists, research critical of the orthodox position has come from the various institutional schools of thought which emphasize evolutionary change and systemic rather than deductive reasoning from an idealized model.

Most of the debate surrounds the federal minimum wage law contained in the Fair Labor Standards Act (FLSA) of 1938, which represented an essential part of President Roosevelt's agenda to get the nation out of the Great Depression. Labor law reformers had long advocated federal wage and hour laws in response to an historic pattern of low earnings among working families and intense wage competition among employers. The courts, however, struck down early attempts to establish federal standards on grounds the separate states had constitutional primacy in such matters. Individual states were reluctant to pass regulatory laws, however, because they feared industry would avoid locating there. The enormities of the depression nevertheless drove working people to strike employers and protest politically. Soon the Supreme Court changed directions and ruled that the constitution does in fact allow Congress to regulate interstate commerce; Congress responded with numerous regulatory laws including the FLSA.

The inherent bias in neoclassical analysis. When polled, a large majority of American economists support Rustici in his opposition to minimum wage increases. This reflects their prior training in the neoclassical wage model, which generally rejects labor standards legislation on grounds that market outcomes are superior to anything government can achieve through regulation. Employers and others lobbying to abolish or weaken minimum wage laws therefore can count on the support of orthodox economists, despite widespread public approval of these laws. Indeed, in 1993, three-fourths of economists polled said that an increase in the minimum wage would increase unemployment, while a similar poll in 1996 found that 84% of the public favored an increase.

This vastly different view of the world underscores the first problem with Rustici's neoclassical analysis. The competitive market model it uses simply does not depict real labor markets accurately. It imagines all sorts of things that do not exist and ignores a great many other things that do. When this analysis is applied to particular labor market problems, such as declining real wages, it is likely to misdiagnose the ailment and to prescribe inappropriate public policy.

The problem is that in explaining how the interaction between worker skill and output determines wages the neoclassical model uses circular reasoning. It presumes that if we know the wage we also know the worth of the worker because market competition ensures that each worker is paid the value of his or her worth, as measured by the value of what each produces. It further presumes that the worker's productive value is determined by his or her level of skill and education, that is, by their accumulated "human capital." Therefore, if one worker is paid more than another worker, then the first worker must be worth more (that is, must have more skill and education) than the second; because the wage is, by definition, equal to output value, which in turn is determined by skill and education. Consequently, every worker must be worth what he or she is being paid, no more and no less. Workers who think they are not being paid enough must be wrong, because if they possessed more human capital they would be worth more therefore paid more.

This is tautological reasoning. It explains everything and nothing because it uses the thing it is trying to explain as the evidence with which to explain it. It does, however, allow neoclassical economists to reject any attempt to regulate wages on the grounds that the worker currently is being paid what he or she is worth. In the world of the neoclassical economist, forcing employers to pay a higher wage will simply place the individual employer at a competitive disadvantage and at the same time discriminate against workers who did not benefit from the regulated wage increase. As a result, neoclassical investigations of minimum wage effects usually ask a single question. How many workers will become unemployable following an increase in the minimum wage. The question derives from the competitive wage model, not from observed experiences or policy objectives.

With this mind-set, it is understandable that Rustici and other orthodox neoclassical economists see the solution to labor market problems, such as low earnings and unemployment, as more rather than less market determination and the elimination of existing regulations. If labor markets deliver less than ideal results it is because they are not free enough. Public policy must be to remove the imperfections. Unions and minimum wages are logical targets in this regard.

The problem with such deductive reasoning is that employers and employees seldom meet as equals in the labor market, although the model assumes that they do. In blue-collar settings, for example, the employment relationship favors employers, who typically offer jobs on a take-it-or-leave-it basis. Individual workers find there are far more workers than there are good jobs and they take what they can get on the terms that are offered. Employers simply have more options in the hiring process than do workers—except perhaps when unemployment is low and workers scarce in the lowest paying, least desirable occupations and industries, at which point employers turn to immigrant labor to fill job vacancies at the going wage levels. Additionally, employers know far more than hourly workers do about supply and demand conditions in local labor markets and are more mobile in terms of where and when to hire. They also can hold out much longer financially than can workers in the event of differences over wages and working conditions. Finally, and importantly, because they own the plant and equipment upon which the worker's livelihood depends, they can threaten to relocate the workplace or to replace the workers with machines or other workers.

In the absence of institutional protections such as union contracts and minimum wages, workers are in constant danger of having to compete with one another to see which of them will work for less pay and under the worst conditions. If one or a few employers are able to reduce labor standards by taking advantage of labor's inherent bargaining weakness, and in the process they expand markets and increase their profits, then the race is on among all employers to take down labor standards. The labor market degenerates into what institutional labor economists call destructive competition. As two institutional labor economists observed decades ago, "When an employer can hire workers for practically his own price, he can be slack and inefficient in his methods, and yet, by reducing wages, reduce his cost of production to the level of his more able competitor" (Commons and Andrews 1936:48).

The irrelevancy of the neoclassical analysis. This demonstrates the second thing wrong with Rustici's neoclassical interpretation. It examines and evaluates minimum wage laws only on the basis of what would result in a competitive market model. In doing so, it ignores the reasons why such laws are enacted in the first place and whether or not they solve the problems they were intended to solve. The problem with this approach is that it focuses on only one of the three forms of economic efficiency that are essential for a nation to sustain high-levels of production and consumption: a nation's need to provide high standards of living for its citizens.

Robert Kuttner (1997) argues that neoclassical preoccupation with allocative efficiency prevents an examination of macroefficiency and technical efficiency. Macroefficiency concerns a nation's ability to sustain or enhance total
production, employment, and family living standards; whereas technical efficiency refers to the ability to generate new products and production methods
through industrial invention and innovation. Allocative efficiency, on the other
hand, is limited to looking after the immediate interests of the consumer by
minimizing production costs and product prices. If only allocative efficiency is
taken into account, the long-term interests of both producers and consumers
is ignored as the nation neglects its overall economic growth, job and earnings
performance, and progress in research/development.

It must be remembered that neither macro- nor technical efficiency necessarily results in optimal allocation efficiency in the short run, that is, in the
lowest possible costs of production and consumer prices. Nor does optimal
allocative efficiency necessarily help to maximize either macro- or technical
efficiency. The postwar success of certain West European and Asian economies,
led by Germany and Japan, testifies to the need to distinguish between alternative forms of economic efficiency and between short- and long-run goals and
performance. Japanese industrial strategists made these distinctions for example when they targeted the global auto market in the late 1950s. They gave up
short-run cost efficiency in return for long-term product and workforce quality
on their way to world supremacy in autos by the 1980s (Halberstam 1986).

Because neoclassical economists largely ignore macro- and technical efficiency in their analysis of competitive labor markets, their competitive model
cannot estimate the macroeffects of incremental changes in prices and quantities in particular markets. The 1930s, for example, were characterized by the
kind of intense wage and price competition that neoclassical economists associate with allocative efficiency. Consequently, the economy should have been
performing at its best. But we still refer to what happened instead as the Great
Depression.

Remember that the question deriving from the neoclassical market model
is "How many workers are made unemployable because the new wage prices
them out of competitive labor markets?" That is not, however, the question
that advocates of the FLSA were concerned with in 1938, nor what people are
concerned with today in view of the long-term decline in median real wages and
the increase in unstable jobs. The problem then and now is not the ability to
produce enough goods and services, but rather it is creating jobs at wages high
enough to buy back what is produced and in the process sustain high living
standards for everyone.

This was the task of the 1938 federal minimum wage. It was designed to
do two things: (i) increase employment and purchasing power in order to stimulate the slumping economy; and (ii) drive out of the market employers who
competed on the basis of cheap labor instead of through better products and
state-of-the-art production methods. The country had been in economic crisis
for the better part of a decade. It had become increasingly clear that much of the
problem was due to low pay, long workweeks, and growing use of child rather
than adult labor. Advocates of minimum wages were not the least dissuaded by

neoclassical forecasts that some jobs would be lost and some employers driven out of business. That is precisely what they wanted to do, on grounds that a job that does not pay enough to support a family should not exist and an employer who cannot pay a living wage, even though other employers in that industry can and do pay the mandated living wage, should be driven from the marketplace.

In brief, if a job pays less than enough to sustain workers and their dependents at the customary standard of living, then that job is not paying its way in a productive economy because it is being subsidized by some household, charitable organization, or government transfer payment. The beneficiary of this subsidy is either the employer paying the low wage and making a profit by doing so, or the customer paying a low price for the good or service. Fast-food restaurant fare, for example, is cheap in part because fast-food workers earn poverty level wages. Home owners in wealthy suburbs can get their houses cleaned cheaply because the women who clean them live in low-income areas, need the money, and have few job options. A subsidy is a subsidy, whether the worker is part of a poor household or an affluent household and whether the employer is a large or a small business.

If you work for a fast-food restaurant why should your family subsidize the owners of that restaurant? In a like manner, why should taxpayers subsidize manufacturers that employ fathers and mothers who cannot support their families without receiving food stamps or a tax rebate from the government? Why should the large employer have to compete with a smaller rival that is being subsidized by low-income households and taxpayers?

This subsidization does not have to occur. In Australia, for example, restaurant workers, "bag boys" in grocery stores, bartenders in taverns, and other workers who are generally low paid in the United States are paid in excess of $12 an hour. Nevertheless, McDonalds hamburgers and Pizza Hut pizzas still abound in Australia. In the United States unionized waitresses in Las Vegas also earn $12 an hour, before tips, and Las Vegas is one of the fastest growing economic regions in America. Waitresses in other parts of the country commonly receive about half the level of the minimum wage, before tips, which forces them to show a certain amount of servitude in order to earn enough tips to make the job worthwhile (a subsidy to the employer from the customer) and leaves the worker unsure of her or his earnings from day-to-day and week-to-week. Such market outcomes reflect the low-status, devalued nature of these workers and occupations more than it does their value to both customers and employers.

Contradictory evidence for the neoclassical view.   Rustici's neoclassical approach necessarily ignores the economic and social problems associated with low-wage jobs because it concentrates on workers rather than jobs. Such focus also shifts responsibility for low-wage incomes from jobs to workers by focusing on worker behavior rather than industrial strategies and government policies. Recall that the theory assumes the individual worker's wage is determined by his or her worth on the job; it further presumes that this worth is determined in large part by the amount of human capital the worker possesses in terms of formal education (college degrees) and occupational training (vocational and on-the-job training). Thus the job and its requirements are excluded from the analysis and low-wages are linked to the worker's efforts to acquire skill and education. When neoclassical researchers like Thomas Rustici want to verify their theory they study the earnings and employment experiences of groups of workers having low educational and vocational skills on grounds such workers are most likely to lose jobs as a result of minimum wage raises. Most neoclassical studies do indeed find greater unemployment among such groups following minimum wage increases.

But the findings of empirical studies themselves pose the third problem with Rustici's analysis. The results of far too many empirical studies—those conducted by neoclassical as well as institutional labor economists—have contradicted the neoclassical model for it to remain very convincing. During the Progressive Era prior to World War I, for example, government economists surveyed jobs before and after passage of state minimum wage laws covering women workers (Obenauer and von der Nienburg 1915). This and a later study conducted by Commons and Andrews (1936), found that mandated wages alleviated the degenerative effects of low wages and actually enhanced productivity by increasing worker desire and ability to produce. Only "parasitic" employers were threatened by minimum wages and relatively small numbers of jobs were eliminated.

Some years later, Princeton labor economist Richard Lester surveyed southern manufacturing employers after World War II and found they had not laid-off marginal workers in response to minimum wage increases, but instead had maintained their workforces and tried to offset the higher labor cost by increasing output and sales. This allowed them to take advantage of the economies of scale (lower per-unit costs of production) that accompany higher levels of plant and equipment utilization. Lester went on to note that workers doing the same jobs in different plants received different wages over long periods of time—another finding at odds with neoclassical reasoning— therefore, it was not possible to predict the employment effects of a minimum wage raise. His and other studies thus refuted the neoclassical notion of a single competitive wage. Workers with comparable skills often make quite different wages over long periods of time and those with different skills often earn the same wages. "Such matters are elementary and commonplace to a student of labor, but they seem to be largely overlooked by theorists of the [neoclassical] marginalist faith," he concluded (1947:148).

In the 1990s, another group of neoclassical revisionists using much the same investigative methods as Lester, but with more sophisticated equipment and techniques at their disposal, produced similar findings and came to much the same conclusion. Princeton economists David Card and Alan Krueger demonstrated that modest increases in minimum wage rates have little if any negative impact on the most exposed workers—teenagers. Instead of analyzing what happens to workers following minimum wage increases, they, like Lester before them, asked what happened to the jobs themselves. And like Lester, they discovered that employers did not respond as anticipated. Jobs in fast-food restaurants and other low-wage establishments did not decline, and in fact they even increased slightly in New Jersey when that state increased its minimum wage above the federal level. More surprising perhaps, in adjacent Pennsylvania, where no increase in the state minimum wage had occurred, fast-food employment actually fell slightly! Card and Krueger substantiated these findings in similar studies involving fast-food restaurant jobs in Texas and teenage workers in all industries in California (Card and Krueger 1995: Chapters 2 and 3).

These results, clearly at odds with the neoclassical literature, prompted one somewhat shaken but faithful neoclassical reviewer of Card and Krueger's work to conclude in 1995, just as the debate was getting underway on a proposal to raise the federal minimum wage to $5.15, that "we just don't know how many jobs would be lost if the minimum wage were increased to $5.15." Orthodox certainty was beginning to be eroded by the contradictory findings, but the basic model was not questioned. Many neoclassical economists hold doggedly to the view that jobs *must be* lost if minimum wages are increased. Consider, for example, a standard neoclassical labor economics text now in its sixth edition. The authors dismiss the Card-Krueger findings and insist instead that: "While the impact of the minimum wage on employment, especially that of young workers will undoubtedly continue to receive a great deal of research and public policy discussion, the best evidence remains that the overall impact of the law is to lower employment of unskilled workers while increasing the earnings of those who are able to get jobs" (Filer, Hamermesh, and Rees 1996:175).

In sum, neoclassical economists like Rustici find fault with the minimum wage because they contrast it with a theoretical system that is said to provide optimal results; but it is a system that ultimately is nonfalsifiable because of its tautological nature. They purport to refute the minimum wage on grounds it destroys low-wage jobs despite the fact that this is precisely what it is supposed to do. Finally, by limiting the inquiry to the dictates of a model that is inherently hostile to government regulation, they preclude serious debate on regulation as a policy tool.

Alternative analyses of minimum wage laws.   The shortcomings of traditional neoclassical analysis become apparent when considered in terms of macro- and technical efficiency. Wage-based competition during the 1930s reduced already depressed earnings and worker purchasing power, which in turn decreased product demand and caused additional workers to be unemployed. The effect was to cut output, incomes, and profits. With no recovery in sight, large firms could not be expected to make more cars, radios, and appliances than they could sell, nor could they be expected to design and manufacture new products when consumers could afford neither old nor new models.

Economic recovery did not occur until total war production during 1940–45, when all the neoclassical rules of allocative efficiency were repealed: industry was cartelized, wages and prices were controlled, and productive decision making was centralized. Yet, despite the total violation of market rules, the defense plants were running day and night, workers were acquiring formal and informal education and training, incomes and profits were high. Then, from the late 1940s until the mid-1970s, industrial oligopolies and labor unions replaced government in administering the productive system, again in violation of allocative efficiency. But we look back fondly on those decades as the golden age of increased living standards and job security.

Since then, however, the economy has been deregulated in keeping with neoclassical doctrine and both product and labor markets made more competitive by domestic and global changes in industrial structure and behavior. Labor productivity has been increasing, albeit modestly, and labor resources probably have been allocated more efficiently than in the postwar decades, but real earnings are falling, job security declining, and living standards stagnating (Mishel, et al. 1997).

As a society we have three broad policy responses. One, we can remove a certain portion of the population from the productive system by offering social insurance and welfare benefits to able-bodied individuals including laid-off or displaced males and single mothers. This should raise wages by reducing the supply of workers. Two, we can "reform welfare," so to speak, and force welfare recipients to take jobs work under the terms offered by cutting off their welfare support and giving them no alternative. This should lower wages by putting the new low-wage workers in competition with existing ones. Finally, we can raise minimum wages enough to ensure that the lowest paid workers and households are self-sufficient. This would raise wages directly rather than indirectly, eliminate wage and price subsidies to employers and consumers and raise prices, that is, to the extent that higher labor costs are not offset by productivity gains or profit reductions.

Although liberal economists might consider the first remedy better than none, they, like economists generally, resist policies that allow and presumably encourage able-bodied persons to be consumers but not producers in a market-based economy. Other liberal social scientists, however, are more likely to prefer the welfare alternative on ethical and humanitarian grounds. Wealthy societies like the U.S. should, they argue, be willing to provide sustenance for their disadvantaged individuals and families, regardless of any economic inefficiencies that might result. Moreover, they say, all of society benefits when public assistance makes these families more stable and functioning than otherwise.

Surprisingly perhaps, some conservative economists have supported direct welfare payments. They did so, however, as a second best solution. Milton Friedman, for example, once argued that if the political majority is determined to assist the disadvantaged—as it was in the 1960s—then the least interventionist method is to send them government checks and be done with it, rather than pursue minimum wage or other interventionist labor market policies.

It is the second alternative, abolishing financial support, that conservative economists find most consistent with conventional theory. Others agree mainly for moral and ethical reasons. This has been true since industrial poverty first appeared in 1830s Britain (Persky 1997). Free market advocates urged the abolition of welfare support and wage supplements on grounds their elimination would increase the number of laborers and worker productivity while also lowering taxes and birth rates. As a secondary benefit, they and others claimed, it would enhance family stability and values by making parents responsible for their children and both children and wives dependent on and therefore respectful of and obedient to male wage earners. Conservatives are still moved by such thinking.

The third alternative is preferred by liberal economists and policy makers. It seeks to assure low-wage workers self-sufficiency by supplementing their inadequate earnings through the Earned Income Tax Credit, a tax rebate of up to several thousand dollars a year to the employee based on his or her Social Security payments. Advocates favor this approach because it effectively increases the employee's real wage rate and at the same time offsets the undesirable market outcomes of low wages without distorting wage and employment structures and obstructing allocative efficiency. They also believe that the long-run solution is worker training and education to enhance human capital.

Conservative and liberal economists tend to agree on the latter point, although they differ on whether such efforts should be publicly financed and broadly available or individuals should be primarily responsible for their own human capital enhancement.

In view of the bipartisan support for more education—which can accompany any of the three alternative policy responses—a word of caution is in order. More education is always laudable, but by itself cannot solve the problem of low wages. This is because employers use formal educational credentials, especially college degrees, to screen applicants for good jobs. Therefore, as the overall educational level of the work force rises, the amount of education needed to get a given job also increases. This jeopardizes the effectiveness of education as the justification for high pay. For if a college degree were to be conferred magically upon the entire working population tomorrow, who would bus and wait tables the day after? Most likely, employers would find and apply other screening criteria, perhaps relative college rankings or graduate degrees, in order to determine which college grads became managers and which servers.

Moreover, the supply of educated workers does not automatically create the demand for them. American engineering students, for instance, may wonder exactly what it is they are going to engineer when they read about U.S. companies hiring pools of low-wage but college trained information technologists in developing countries to work on computer software projects using high-speed satellite information links, or when they hear about domestic aerospace companies transferring technology overseas in exchange for sales contracts, or of NASA purchasing rocketry equipment from other industrialized countries in order to get the lowest possible price (Barlett and Steele 1996: 49–52, 93–9).

The third alternative is the best. It goes directly to the problem of low-wage jobs by increasing pre-tax earnings and incomes rather than depend on welfare and other transfer payments, let alone on market forces to do so. It is reasonable to presume that with rare exceptions people want the dignity and independence that comes with gainful employment. Society should expect and enable them to work. Doing so makes them participating stakeholders in the productive system, affords them the purchasing power to be effective consumers and fosters the stability and purpose to be involved citizens. But such outcomes depend on the availability of jobs paying enough to afford a decent living.

In addition, the high wage economy is most consistent over time with the three economic efficiencies. High minimum wages are to be preferred because they contribute to sustained economic growth (macroefficiency) and industrial capitalization and innovation (technical efficiency). It is true that minimum wage are inconsistent with neoclassical allocative efficiency in the short-run; but it is the long-run that we should be concerned. High-paid workers stay with their employers, which encourages the latter to invest in worker human capital, which in turn encourages the employers to adopt state-of-the-art production methods and sophisticated product design and performance. High-paid workers also have the purchasing power to buy the goods and services that they and other high-paid workers produce.

A high wage policy is the best hope for a bright future for the American economy. It ensures a proficient labor force in a stable macroeconomy and encourages steady technological advancement. The larger society is only as prosperous as its individual parts. When labor standards are high the larger society prospers.

References

Barlett, Donald L., and James B. Steele. 1996. *America: Who Stole the Dream?* Kansas City: Andrews & McMeel.

Card, David Edward, and Alan B. Krueger. 1995. *Myth and Measurement: The New Economics of the Minimum Wage.* Princeton, NJ: Princeton University Press.

Commons, John R., and John B. Andrews. 1936. *Principles of Labor Legislation* (fourth edition). New York: Augustus M. Kelley (1967 Reprint).

Filer, Randall K., Daniel S. Hamermesh, and Albert Rees. 1996. *The Economics of Work and Pay*, sixth edition. New York: Harper Collins.

Halberstam, David. 1986. *The Reckoning.* New York: Morrow.

Kuttner, Robert. 1997. *Everything For Sale: The Virtues and Limits of Markets.* New York: Alfred A. Knopf.

Lester, Richard A. 1947. "Marginalism, Minimum Wages, and Labor Markets." *American Economic Review* 37 (March) pp. 135–48.

Mishel, Lawrence, Jared Bernstein, and John Schmitt. 1997. *The State of Working America, 1996–97.* Armonk, NY: M. E. Sharpe.

Obenauer, Marie L., and Bertha von der Nienburg. 1915. *Effect of Minimum Wage Determinations in Oregon.* Bureau of Labor Statistics, Bulletin No. 176. Washington: GPO.

Persky, Joseph. 1997. "Classical Family Values: Ending the Poor Laws as They Knew Them." *Journal of Economic Perspectives* 11 (Winter) pp. 179–89.

POSTSCRIPT

Is It Time to Abolish the Minimum Wage?

The impact of the minimum wage can be expressed in many ways. Two particularly rewarding ways of looking at such legislative initiatives are to examine minimum wages over time in real dollars and as a percentage of manufacturing wages.

A clear pattern should emerge from an examination of this data. The 1965–1970 period saw the highest level of the minimum wage in real terms. In constant 1982–1984 dollars, the minimum wage for these years was approximately $4.00 an hour and reached nearly 50 percent of the prevailing manufacturing wage. For the next 20 years, however, the value of the minimum wage in real terms and as a percentage of the manufacturing wage fell. It is only in recent years that it has begun to recover.

The renewed interest in the minimum wage can be traced in part to the research findings of David Card and Alan Krueger. These economists, as Craypo points out, have shaken the economics profession with their empirical research findings that moderate increases in the minimum wage have few negative consequences on employment patterns and in some cases are associated with increases in employment. Their work has been published widely in professional journals: *Industrial and Labor Relations Review* (October 1992 and April 1994) and the *American Economic Review* (1994 and 1995). They have also detailed their findings in a book entitled *Myth and Measurement: The New Economics of the Minimum Wage* (Princeton University Press, 1995).

Two vocal critics of Card and Krueger's research are David Newmark and William Wascher. Their empirical studies are supportive of the traditional neoclassical findings that the minimum wage causes unemployment, particularly among teenagers and young adults. See their work published in *Industrial and Labor Relations Review* (September 1992 and April 1994); *NBER Working Paper No. 4617* (1994); *Journal of Business and Economic Statistics* (1995); and *American Economic Review Papers and Proceedings* (May 1995). Still often considered the best anti–minimum wage statement, however, is George J. Stigler's 1946 essay "The Economics of Minimum Wage Legislation," *American Economic Review*.

On the Internet ...

DUSHKIN ONLINE

The European Union in the United States

This site of the European Union in the United States has everything from history to current status, as well as Web links and a search capability.

http://www.eurunion.org

OECD Online

The Organization for Economic Cooperation and Development (OECD) resulted from the need to rebuild Europe after World War II, but it expanded to become truly international, with policies designed to expand world trade on a multilateral, nondiscriminatory basis.

http://www.oecd.org

International Monetary Fund (IMF)

The home page of the International Monetary Fund links to information about its purpose and activities, news releases, and its publications, among other things.

http://www.imf.org

International Trade Administration

The U.S. Department of Commerce's International Trade Administration is dedicated to helping U.S. businesses compete in the global marketplace. At this site it offers assistance through many Web links under such headings as Trade Statistics, Tariffs and Taxes, Market Research, and Export Documentation.

http://www.ita.doc.gov

Social Science Information Gateway (SOSIG)

This project of the Economic and Social Research Council (ESRC) catalogs 16 subjects and lists more URL addresses from European and developing countries than many U.S. sources do.

http://sosig.esrc.bris.ac.uk

World Bank

At this home page of the World Bank you can click on News, Development Topics, Regions and Countries, Partnerships, and more, as well as use its search feature.

http://www.worldbank.org

PART 3

The World Around Us

*F*or many years America held a position of dominance in international trade. That position has been changed by time, events, and the emergence of other economic powers in the world. Decisions that are made in the international arena will, with increasing frequency, influence our lives. In the global marketplace, trade relations are influenced by swings in the economies of trading partners. The environment is also a major concern for economists and other analysts today.

- Is Free Trade a Viable Option for the New Millennium?

- Should We Sweat About Sweatshops?

- Does Global Warming Require Immediate Government Action?

- Should Pollution Be Put to the Market Test?

- Has the North American Free Trade Agreement Been a Success?

ISSUE 13

Is Free Trade a Viable Option for the New Millennium?

YES: Robert J. Samuelson, from "Trade Free or Die," *The New Republic* (June 22, 1998)

NO: Patrick J. Buchanan, from "Toward One Nation, Indivisible: A Course of Action," *Chronicles* (July 1998)

ISSUE SUMMARY

YES: Columnist Robert J. Samuelson charges that critics of free trade ignore economics, which he feels is the one thing that "trade has going for it."

NO: Social critic and three-time presidential hopeful Patrick J. Buchanan argues that the purpose of international trade is to benefit American workers, farmers, businessmen, and manufacturers, not mankind in general.

The economic logic that supports international trade has changed little in the nearly 200 years since English economist David Ricardo (1772–1823) provided us with his basic insight that the patterns and gains of trade depend on relative factor prices. He argued that if there are differences in the "opportunity costs" of producing goods and services, trade will occur between countries; more important, all of the countries that engage in trade will benefit.

Although a large majority of economists accept the logic and policy conclusions of Ricardo's theory, the timeless debate rages on between "free traders" and those who ask for protection. The basic logic of international trade is indistinguishable from the basic logic of purely domestic trade. That is, both domestic and international trade must answer these fundamental economic questions, What to produce? How to produce it? and, For whom to produce? The distinction is that the international trade questions are posed in an international arena, one filled with producers and consumers who speak different languages, use different currencies, and are often suspicious of the actions and reactions of foreigners.

If markets work the way they are expected to work, free trade simply increases the size or the extent of a purely domestic market and therefore increases the advantages of specialization. Market participants should be able to buy and consume a greater variety of inexpensive goods and services after the establishment of free trade than they could before free trade. Why, then, do some people wish to close U.S. borders and deny Americans the benefits of free trade? The answer to this question is that these benefits do not come without cost.

There are winners and losers in the game of free trade. The most obvious winners are the consumers of the less-expensive imported goods. These consumers are able to buy the low-priced color television sets, automobiles, and steel that is made abroad. Other winners are the producers of the exported goods. All the factors in the export industry, as well as those in industries that supply the export industry, experience an increase in their market demand, which increases their income. In the United States, agriculture is one such export industry. As new foreign markets are opened, farmers' incomes increase, as do the incomes of those who supply the farmers with fertilizer, farm equipment, gasoline, and other basic inputs.

On the other side in the free-trade game are the losers. The obvious losers are those who own the factors of production that are employed in the import-competing industries. These factors include the land, labor, and capital that are devoted to the production of such items as U.S.-made television sets, automobiles, and steel. The less-expensive foreign imports displace the demand for these products. The domestic consumers of goods that are also exported to other countries lose as well. For example, as U.S. farmers sell more of their products abroad, less of this output is available domestically. As a result, the domestic prices of these farm products and other export goods and services rise.

The bottom line is that there is nothing "free" in a market system. Competition—whether it is domestic or foreign—creates winners and losers. Historically, Americans have sympathized with the losers when they suffer at the hands of foreign competitors. However, such sympathies have not seriously curtailed free trade.

In the following selections, Robert J. Samuelson counters the protectionist arguments of Patrick J. Buchanan in the face of America's booming economy and trade deficits. Buchanan argues that the United States can no longer afford a free-trade policy in the new millennium. He maintains that America comes first and the rest of the world second: "What is good for the global economy is not automatically good for America."

Robert J. Samuelson

Trade Free or Die

I.

In many ways, the timing of Pat Buchanan's plea for more protectionism could not be worse. The American economy is humming along, with unemployment around 5 percent since late 1996. If more than two decades of trade deficits have crippled us, the consequences are not immediately obvious. Not only is the economy of the United States now the strongest among advanced societies, but American companies still remain formidable, if not always dominant, competitors in many critical industries: computers and software; aerospace; biotechnology; communications and entertainment; banking and finance; business consulting; and medicine. The auto and steel industries—once given up for dead—have recovered from fierce foreign competition.

The coexistence of extraordinary prosperity and constant trade deficits is a paradox to be explained, but Buchanan ignores it. Reading him, you would not know that the United States is in a mighty boom. The temptation, then, is to dismiss his book as irrelevant. That is not a good idea. An all-but-announced Republican presidential candidate in 2000, Buchanan is a born-again protectionist, who sees his conversion as a harbinger of a broader shift among the public. "The Young Turks of the New Conservatism who would capture the Republican Party for Barry Goldwater in 1964 and Ronald Reagan in 1980 [were] free traders," he writes. "I know, because I was one of them." His hopes of a protectionist revival are not preposterous, regardless of the fate of his own candidacy. In a weakening economy, the message could play. Fears of an overseas job drain can be exploited; and working class Democrats (Reagan Democrats) can be wooed with promises of greater job security. A populist majority might one day rally to economic nationalism.

Until now, of course, protectionism has been a political flop. Every politician who has tried to ride it to the White House has failed: John Connally in 1980, Richard Gephardt in 1988, Ross Perot in 1992, Pat Buchanan in 1996. It's worth trying to understand why. A common theory is that protectionism does not have much of a constituency. It is good rhetoric, but in the end it does not attract many voters, because not many Americans would benefit from import restrictions, especially if they resulted in retaliation against American exports. The raw numbers seem to confirm this. In 1997, for example, imports equaled only 13 percent of the economy's output, or Gross Domestic Product, and this was nearly offset by exports, 12 percent of GDP. Such figures suggest that protectionism has only a tiny constituency.

Buchanan, by contrast, argues quite plausibly that trade politics must be seen in a broader context, and that the free-trade consensus that arose after World War II has been crumbling for decades. It rested on three pillars, he says, each of them now weakened. The first pillar was a general sense that American industry was invincible; but that confidence shattered in the late 1970s and early 1980s, when many venerable American companies (Ford, Caterpillar, U.S. Steel, Xerox, Intel) came under siege from foreign competition. The second pillar of the postwar period was the cold war: greater trade with our allies promoted their prosperity (it was said), and this inoculated them against communism. The end of the cold war obviously dispensed with this argument. And the third pillar was the once-common belief that protectionism (and the Smoot-Hawley tariff) had been a major cause of the Great Depression. But memories fade, and much modern scholarship discounts protectionism as a major cause of the Depression.

The correct implication is that protectionism could again find a large following. The present optimism of Americans masks a deep uneasiness about the global economy that, once today's boom ends (as it will), could reemerge. We face a collision between an instinctive nationalism and the relentless expansion of global markets. Just because protectionism is not a desirable response does not mean that every protectionist grievance is bogus. Many of its complaints are clearly true: burgeoning global trade and investment do erode national sovereignty and self-sufficiency; and they do threaten some industries and workers; and they do create divided loyalties for American companies between enhancing profits and preserving American jobs.

It would be unnatural if Americans did not worry about these developments. Moreover, the economy's exposure to global competition is greater than the raw trade statistics indicate. In 1997, for example, imports accounted for only about 13 percent of American car and truck sales. But the entire auto industry faces global competition, because imports could capture almost any individual sale; and foreign car firms now produce here. The same is true of many industries. Global competition doesn't yet affect a majority of workers, but its impact—real and psychological—extends beyond an isolated minority....

II.

One thing is certain: the case for free trade cannot honestly be made on the basis of heritage. The greatest virtue of Buchanan's book is to remind us that America has mostly been a protectionist nation.

The political culture is certainly receptive. The godfather of protectionism was Alexander Hamilton, whose "Report on Manufactures," written in 1791, urged a protective tariff to nurture industry. To Hamilton, American "wealth... independence and security" depended on "the prosperity" of manufacturing. "Every nation," he argued, "ought to endeavor to possess within itself all the essentials of national supply." The Tariff Act of 1789, which imposed duties of 5 percent on many imports, was the second law passed by Congress. Later tariffs went higher, and they stayed high for most of the nineteenth century. With the exception of slavery, they were the largest source of conflict between North and South.

The Tariff Act of 1828—the Tariff of Abominations—almost triggered secession. It imposed an average duty of 62 percent on 92 percent of the country's imports. The South Carolina legislature subsequently declared it and a revised tariff "null, void." A secessionist crisis was avoided in 1833 only because Congress agreed to reduce the tariff to 20 percent over ten years. In general, the South, a big exporter of cotton and a big importer of manufactured products, detested high tariffs. The North, with a larger manufacturing base, adored them.

❦

One reason that tariffs stayed high was their role as the federal government's main source of revenue for most of the century. (The Civil War was the major exception.) But they were also kept high to protect industry. In the 1830s and 1840s, the Whig Party—headed by Henry Clay—urged national economic development through internal improvements (roads, harbors, bridges) and high tariffs. Lincoln, an early Whig, generally supported high tariffs.

Protectionism was often equated with patriotism. Listen to Justin Morrill, a Republican senator from Vermont who entered Congress as a Whig in 1855, and was among the most steadfast guardians of high tariffs until his death in 1898: "Free trade abjures patriotism and boasts of cosmopolitism. It regards the labor of our own people with no more favor than that of the barbarian on the Danube or the cooly on the Ganges." Buchanan enthuses over such flag-waving. He argues that high tariffs enabled America to become the world's great industrial power in the nineteenth century.

During the last half of the century, many individual tariff rates hovered around 50 percent, and the average tariff (on dutiable and non-dutiable items alike) was about 30 percent. They stayed high partly to repay the huge national debt run up during the Civil War. (The federal debt rose from $65 million in 1860 to $2.8 billion in 1866.) But there were other reasons for the persistence of the tariffs. They were blatant protectionism and fervent nationalism.

A historic reversal was accomplished by Cordell Hull, Roosevelt's secretary of state, who shepherded the Reciprocal Trade Agreements Act of 1934 through Congress. This law transferred much of Congress's power to set tariffs to the president, who could negotiate mutual tariff cuts with other countries. A former senator from Tennessee, Hull had long believed that trade fostered goodwill among nations. And the Depression produced a backlash against protectionism. The backlash continued after World War II. In the 1940s, the United States helped to create new global institutions to prevent the return of '30s protectionism and deflation. These included the International Monetary Fund, which would make short-term loans of foreign exchange, generally dollars, to countries with big trade deficits (the idea was to preempt competitive currency devaluations or protectionism); and the General Agreement on Tariffs and Trade, which would negotiate and police tariff cuts and international trade rules.

Trade also quickly emerged as a central weapon against communism. The Japanese needed to trade to buy basic raw materials (food, fuel, minerals). "Japan cannot remain in the free world unless something is done to allow her to make a living," President Eisenhower said. Otherwise, "it is going to the Communists." For Europe, trade succeeded the Marshall Plan as a recovery strategy from war. In trade negotiations, American officials often made more concessions than they received. In 1954, the State Department proposed unilateral concessions on roughly half of all Japanese imports, from glassware to optical goods to cars. Hardly anyone—the textile, apparel, and shoe industries were major exceptions—felt threatened, because American industry and technology were so dominant.

⋅⟨◉⟩⋅

In 1962, Congress passed John F. Kennedy's Trade Expansion Act, authorizing new trade talks, by huge margins (78–8 in the Senate and 299–125 in the House). As a 23-year-old editorial writer for the *St. Louis Globe-Democrat,* Buchanan was caught up in the fervor. Passage of the Trade Expansion Act, he wrote, was a "thumping administration triumph" that could "become the most potent cold war weapon in the free Western arsenal. . . ." Although he thinks expanded trade was then justified, he says that Americans went overboard. Free trade is not just an idea, Buchanan argues; it is a false religion that "holds out the promise that if we follow the gospel of free trade, paradise can be created on earth." Buchanan contemptuously quotes the nineteenth-century French economist Frederic Bastiat: "Free trade means harmony of interests and peace between nations. . . . We place this indirect and social effect a thousand times above the direct or purely economic effect."

On this, Buchanan is more clear-eyed than many free-trade enthusiasts. It is true that trade cemented America's cold war alliances, but this does not mean that trade can take us the next step—to universal peace and goodwill. What held the cold war alliance together was the cold war. It is dangerous to generalize from this experience; and a lot of history warns against viewing trade as a shield against war. Before World War I, Germany and Britain were major trading partners. Germany also traded heavily with Russia, Holland, and Belgium—and attacked them all.

Trade does not just bind countries together; it also arouses suspicions. In the 1980s, many Americans wrongly feared that the country would be taken over by the Japanese. Canadians feel constantly assaulted by American trade and culture, and so (to a lesser extent) do Europeans. Nationalism endures and endures; and although the tensions and conflicts rarely end in war, trade is not an automatic pacifier.

III.

[handwritten marginal note: B he arguing no is against free trade no making a personal attack on Buchanan? The latter!]

What trade has going for it, of course, is economics. The most astonishing thing about Buchanan's book is that, although it is ostensibly about economics, it almost never engages in genuinely economic thinking. For Buchanan, the decision to expand or to restrict trade is mainly a political choice. Thus he ignores lower communications and transportation costs (container ships, transoceanic telephone cables, jets, satellites, and, now, the Internet) as driving forces; and as the cost of doing business across borders goes down, the demand to do business —including political pressures to permit it—goes up.

Neither Buchanan nor anyone else can repeal this relationship. Certainly countries can prevent trade by shutting themselves off from the world (as China did until the late 1970s), but it is harder and harder to do with surgical precision. With trade comes travel, and modern communications, and global finance. Controlling the process has proven arduous even for the countries (such as Japan) most determined to do so.

This is one reason why more and more countries have embraced the global economy across a broad range of industries and activities. The other reason is that the potential economic gains of doing so have become self-evident. Buchanan treats the process mainly as a zero-sum game: one country's gain is another country's loss. If this were true, there would not be much global trade and investment. When losers recognized their losses, they would withdraw. Trade would occur mainly as a consequence of sheer economic necessity —countries importing essential raw materials (fuel, food, minerals) or goods produced only in a few countries (commercial jets, for example); or as a consequence of coercion—the strong compelling the weak to trade on disadvantageous terms, an informal neocolonialism. Otherwise trade would wither.

What is true, of course, is that individual companies or individual workers can lose in trade. General Motors can lose to Toyota; Hitachi can lose to IBM. But what is bad for a company or an industry is not necessarily bad for a country. Moreover, domestic competition causes more job losses than trade. Consider, for example, the job losses counted by the consulting firm Challenger, Gray & Christmas. Between 1993 and 1997, it found almost 2.5 million job cuts by American companies. The top five industries were: aerospace and defense, 270,166; retailing, 256,834; telecommunications, 213,675; computers, 212,033; financial services (banking, brokerage houses), 166,672; and transportation (airlines, trucking companies), 136,008. None of these cuts involved global trade. The causes ranged from defense cutbacks (aerospace) to new technology (computers). But Buchanan wishes to leave the false impression that, but for trade, the economy would be far less turbulent and harsh.

Given Buchanan's ignorance of economics, it is no surprise that his history, too, is badly warped. To suggest that the vast industrialization of the late nineteenth century, and America's rise as the world's most powerful economy, owes a great deal to protectionism is absurd. In the last half of the nineteenth century, the American economy benefited from a virtuous circle. Railroads expanded dramatically. Between 1860 and 1900, the miles of track rose from roughly 30,000 to more than 200,000. Lower transportation costs expanded markets. In turn, this encouraged investment in new manufacturing technologies that lowered costs through economies of scale. Industrial output soared for all manner of consumer goods (clothes, shoes, furniture), for farm implements, for machinery. Larger markets and lower costs fostered new methods of retailing and wholesaling: the mail-order house Sears, Roebuck was founded in 1891.

None of this depended on protectionism. Some basic technologies (steelmaking, railroads) originated in Europe. And the United States also imported another vital ingredient of growth: people. In each of the century's last four decades, immigration averaged more than 5 percent of the nation's population. As for trade, it grew as the American economy grew. Between 1870 and 1890, both imports and exports almost doubled. The decisive limit on imports was the ability to export (as it is for most countries), not high tariffs.

Tariffs may have protected some American industries, but any effect on the overall economy is exaggerated. Suppose there were no tariffs; some companies might then have faced cheaper imports. To survive, American companies would have had to cut prices; and they could have done so by reducing wages. In this era, wages were what economists call "flexible": employers cut them when they thought that they must or they could. Between 1866 and 1880, annual wages for nonfarm workers actually declined 21 percent. But this did not mean lower living standards, because prices dropped even more. Over the same period, purchasing power for average workers rose 23 percent.

⋯❀⋯

The point is that a country's capacity to achieve economic growth lies mainly in its own people, values, resources, and institutions. Trade supplements this in many ways. The simplest is comparative advantage, as it was classically conceived by David Ricardo. Countries specialize in what they do best, even if one country could produce everything more efficiently than another. Suppose the United States makes both shoes and supercomputers more efficiently than Spain. We need 100 workers to produce either one supercomputer or 1,000 pairs of shoes annually; and Spain needs 1,000 workers to make a supercomputer and 200 workers to make 1,000 pairs of shoes. Total production of computers and shoes will still be greatest if each country concentrates on its strength (shoes for Spain, computers for us) and trades with the other to satisfy its needs: America will have more supercomputers and shoes, and so will Spain.

Much trade of this type occurs. The United States imports shoes, toys, and sporting goods; it exports bulldozers, computers, and corn. Trade's greatest benefits, though, may transcend comparative advantage. Not everyone has to reinvent the wheel or the computer chip. Technologies, products, and management practices that have been developed abroad can be deployed at home. In theory, these gains can occur without a country opening itself to trade. Information can be stolen; products and processes can be imitated. In practice, however, it is much easier if a country is open.

For commercial or technological insight does not derive from a single dazzling flash. It consists in thousands upon thousands of small details. It encompasses how things are made, distributed, sold, financed, repaired, and replaced. The more isolated a country, the harder it is to come by all the details. Whatever its tariff rates, the United States in the nineteenth century was open in this critical sense. Its people traveled freely abroad; immigration was large; merchants were eager traders; and industrialists borrowed ideas from wherever they could.

These same processes also operated after World War II. All countries could (in theory) tap the same international reservoir of technologies, products, and management systems. Yet some countries did better than others, which was a reflection of their practices and policies. Despite mercantilist tendencies, Japan enthusiastically embraced trade; it systematically imported (via licensing agreements) foreign technology; and it routinely studied American management. The combination of high saving and proven investment opportunities propelled great economic growth, averaging about 10 percent a year in the 1960s. Countries that were more shut off (China, the former Soviet bloc, India) fared less well. And only when other Asian societies began imitating Japan did their economic growth accelerate.

※◇※

This explains why poorer countries should now like trade. It has helped lift millions of people in Europe and Asia from abject poverty. But what's in it for us? Trade can help to erode a country's relative economic superiority, and for the United States it has contributed to such an erosion. As other countries advanced rapidly, our dominance of the early postwar decades was lost. But this history cannot be undone. To preserve our position, we would have needed to be ruthlessly protectionist in the 1950s and 1960s: a policy that deliberately aimed to restrain the economic progress of Europe and Japan. But this would have been unwise, and even Buchanan does not contend otherwise. To long for our superiority of the 1940s is an exercise in nostalgia. Still, what is not true, then or now, is that trade impoverishes us. It is not depressing our living standards. It is elevating them. Trade may enable poorer nations to catch up, or to grow faster than we do; but this does not cause us to slow down. It is not a zero-sum game. We gain, too.

Competition is one way. Many countries now make and trade the same things, so comparative advantage doesn't really apply. Japan makes and trades cars, computer chips, and telephone switching centers; and so do the United States and Germany. The result is bigger markets that enable efficient producers to achieve greater economies of scale by spreading costs across more buyers. Prices to consumers drop. Boeing, Microsoft, and Caterpillar all have lower unit costs because they are selling to a world market. Domestic competition also intensifies. Imports compel domestic rivals to improve. Chevrolets and Chryslers are now better and more efficiently made because Americans can buy Toyotas and Hondas. In many industries—cars, copying machines, and machine tools, to name a few—American firms and workers have had to adapt to the best foreign practices and technologies.

⋘◉⋙

What haunts free trade is the specter that all production will flow to low wage countries. Yet this does not happen, for two reasons. First, low-wage workers in poor countries are usually less productive than well-paid workers in rich countries. In 1995, Malaysian wages were almost 10 percent of American wages; but the productivity of Malaysian workers (output per hour worked) was also about 10 percent of American levels, according to Stephen Golub of Swarthmore College. Companies shift production abroad, Golub maintains, only when relative productivity exceeds relative wages. If Malaysians earn and produce 90 percent less, there is no advantage in moving to Malaysia.

Table 1

Trade With Advanced Countries 1995 Percent of GDP

	Exports	Imports	Balance
Brazil	1.7	3.1	-1.4
China	8.8	7.7	+1.1
India	3.8	3.3	+0.5
Indonesia	6.4	8.7	-2.2
Korea	12.3	13.9	-1.6
Mexico	19.3	16.8	+2.5

Second, when developing countries export, they earn foreign exchange (mostly dollars) to import—and do so. The global market for pharmaceuticals and software could not exist without the global market for shoes and shirts. In practice, developing countries' trade with advanced countries is fairly balanced, whether in deficit or surplus, as [Table 1] shows. It gives developing countries' manufacturing trade with advanced countries as a share of their GDP. (The data is from Golub.) On economic grounds, then, the case against trade is puny. Gains dwarf losses. Still, the puzzle remains: If trade is good for us, why do we run massive trade deficits? We must (it seems) be doing something wrong if we regularly import more than we export. Well, we aren't. The explanation is that our trade accounts are incomplete. They omit a major American export which —if it were included in the reckoning—would bring our trade flows closer to balance. That American export is money.

The dollar serves as the world's major money: a means of exchange, a store of value. It is used to conduct trade and to make investments. In 1996, countries kept 59 percent of their official foreign exchange reserve in dollars;

the next largest reserve currency was the German mark at 14 percent. Multinational companies keep accounts in dollars. So do wealthy individuals. In some countries, where people distrust the local money, dollars circulate as a parallel currency to conduct everyday business. Indeed, the Federal Reserve estimates that more paper dollars (the folding stuff) exist outside the United States than inside.

The United States provides the world a service, in the form of a fairly stable currency. To pay for this service, the world sends us imports. It is a good deal for us: every year Americans buy 1 or 2 percent more than we produce. This is the size of our current account deficit, a measure of trade and other current overseas flows (such as tourism and freight).

The concept here is the old idea of seigniorage: the profit that a government earns when it can produce money at a cost less than its face value. If a government can print a dollar for 5 cents, it reaps a 95 cent windfall when it spends that dollar. Similarly, the United States reaps a windfall when the world uses our money. The transfer occurs through the exchange rate; the world's demand for dollars holds the dollar's exchange rate high enough so that we do not balance our visible trade. (A high exchange rate makes imports cheaper and exports more expensive.) But for many reasons—intellectual laziness, theoretical messiness—most economists have not applied seigniorage to the world economy.

That is too bad. If they did, we would see that the trade debate's main symbol—the nagging trade deficit—does not symbolize what it is supposed to symbolize. It does not show that we are becoming "uncompetitive," or that we are "deindustrializing," or that we are "losing jobs" abroad. In any single year, shifts in the trade balance may reflect temporary factors. Stronger or weaker growth abroad will affect demand for our exports; stronger or weaker growth here will affect our demand for imports. Changes in technology or exchange rates may alter trade flows in particular industries and products. Yet the continuous trade deficits of the United States do not reflect any of these things. They reflect the world's demand for dollars. Perhaps that demand will someday abate (Europe's single currency, the euro, may provide an alternative global money); and if it does, the American trade account will swing closer to balance. For now, though, it is virtually condemned to deficit.

If we acknowledged this, much of the present trade debate would disappear, because the presumed goal of a "good" trade policy—a trade balance or a trade surplus—would be seen as unrealistic and probably undesirable. Instead, the debate over the economics of trade is simplistic and distorted. The supporters of free trade claim that it creates jobs; the opponents of free trade claim that it destroys jobs. Although both are true for individual workers and industries, they are usually not true for the economy as a whole. We could have "full employment" if we didn't trade at all; and in a workforce of nearly 140 million people, the number of net jobs affected by trade (jobs created by exports minus jobs lost to imports) is tiny. Trade's true advantage is that it raises living standards.

IV.

The trouble is that the trade debate should concern more than wages or jobs. Buchanan's political appeal lies in his unabashed nationalism, and he is correct that we do not trade for the benefit of the British or the Brazilians or the Chinese. Trade needs to be connected to larger national purposes, and free-traders have grown lax about making such a connection. They are too eager to reduce the debate to a technical dispute over economic gain and loss. Although Buchanan engages in the same exercise—and reaches the wrong conclusion—he is much more willing to cast trade in terms of advancing broader American interests, preserving our national identity, and maintaining our moral values. A lot of this patriotic chest-thumping is nothing more than rhetorical flourish. And yet Buchanan is actually onto something.

Since World War II, American trade policy has made two central assumptions. The first, inherited from the Depression, is that protectionism destabilizes the world economy and that free trade stabilizes it. The second is that free trade enhances American security interests. Both notions were once right, but times have changed. Matters are now more ambiguous. A big outbreak of protectionism would still harm the world economy. Too much economic activity depends on trade for it to be cut painlessly. Yet deepening economic ties among countries—"globalization"—may also create instability. As for trade and security, they were fused by the cold war. Our main trading partners were military allies, and they generally embraced democratic values. Now trade has spread to some countries that do not share our values and to some countries that one day might be adversaries (China and Russia, most obviously).

What has gradually disintegrated is the postwar convergence among economic, strategic, and moral interests. Global economics has raced well ahead of global politics, creating potentially dangerous instabilities that are only barely perceived and may not be easily subdued. Commercial interests may increasingly conflict with security interests or moral values. If we decide, for whatever reason, not to trade with India or China, other countries will probably fill the void. The possibility is hardly theoretical. After India's recent nuclear tests, the United States immediately imposed sanctions; but most other countries—Japan was an exception—did not. There are other examples, involving Iran, Libya, and Cuba. Commercial rivalries can undermine security alliances: If our "allies" aid our "adversaries," are they truly our allies? The very expansion of global commerce has also raised economic interdependence to a new level. Until now, the "world economy" has been viewed less as an organic whole than as the sum of its parts. It is the collective consequence of individual economies whose performance (though affected by trade) mainly reflects their own strengths and weaknesses. This may still be true, but it is less so. The growing connections among nations—through trade, financial markets, computer systems, people flows—may be creating an independent beast whose behavior affects everyone and is not easily controlled by anyone. Asia's economic crisis is surely testing the notion that growing "globalization" can boomerang. South Korea, Thailand, and Indonesia all borrowed too much abroad; Japanese, European, and

American banks lent too much. Excesses went unchecked by either local or international governmental supervision. Economic growth in all these countries has now plunged. There are spillover effects, and this could portend future crises.

⋅◦⟨◉⟩◦⋅

Protectionism's best case is that it might insulate us against potential global instability. We would sacrifice somewhat higher living standards for somewhat greater tranquility. But this is not what protectionists have in mind; and if it were, it would be hard—maybe impossible—to achieve.

Consider Buchanan's program. He would impose sliding tariffs on countries reflecting his likes and dislikes. Europe would be hit with a 15 percent tariff; Canada would be spared if it adopted our tariffs (otherwise foreign goods would pour into the United States via Canada). Aside from a 15 percent tariff, Japan would have to end its trade surplus or face tariffs that would do so. Poorer countries would face an "equalization" tariff to offset their lower wages (such tariffs could go to 90 or 95 percent).

The result, Buchanan says, would be "millions of high-paying manufacturing jobs for all our workers—immigrant and native-born, black and white, Hispanic and Asian—... and trade and budget surpluses as American workers find higher-paying jobs and contribute more to Social Security and Medicare, deficit reduction and tax reduction." Well, not exactly. If the program worked as planned, it would repatriate low-wage jobs making toys and textiles and eliminate high-wage jobs making planes and bulldozers. Overseas markets for American exports would shrink, because countries that could not sell to us could not buy from us. And it is extremely doubtful that Buchanan's program would work as planned. He ignores floating exchange rates: if we raise tariffs by 15 percent, other countries' currencies may fall by 15 percent, leaving import prices unchanged.

Moreover, anything like Buchanan's plan might also create so much uncertainty that it would depress global economic growth. Companies might not invest in the United States—to make toys or textiles—because they could not be sure that high tariffs would not be repealed or neutralized by exchange rates. Yet companies might not invest elsewhere, because they could not know whether the tariffs might work or, if they did not work, whether they might inspire higher tariffs. All countries would suffer from lower investment and growth.

⋅◦⟨◉⟩◦⋅

The point is that global commerce has become so widespread that it cannot be wrenched apart, short of some calamity. It is increasingly hard to find major American companies (trucking firms, railroads, or electric utilities, perhaps) that do not have major overseas stakes, either through trade or investment. Coca-Cola sells 70 percent of its beverages outside North America; McDonald's has almost half its 23,000 outlets in foreign countries; Intel derives 56 percent of its revenues abroad. The quest for global markets is one of the economic hallmarks of our times. The recent announcement of the Chrysler/Daimler-Benz merger emphasizes the point. To the extent that people like Buchanan try to frustrate it, they will simply inspire more ingenious—and probably more inefficient—ways for companies and investors to try to evade new barriers.

... Here is the nub of the matter. The ultimate promise of ever-greater global commerce is a universal contentment based on a spreading addiction to material well-being. Prosperity has a tranquilizing effect. It dulls the dangers of undiluted nationalism. People increasingly lead the same lifestyles: drinking Coke, driving Toyotas, conversing on the Internet. All this numbs national differences and permits a growing overlay of international agencies and authorities needed to regulate the global economy. Countries see that they have a common stake in cooperation. There are disagreements and conflicts, to be sure, but they are smalltime, and they substitute for larger human tragedies of war and poverty.

This is the underlying moral logic that justifies the commercialization of the world, though hardly anyone puts it quite so forthrightly. It is a seductive vision that can draw much inspiration from the experience of the last half century. Over this period, the world economy has been a spectacular success. It has helped power an enormous advance in human well-being. Free trade has triumphed to an extent that hardly anyone could have foreseen at the end of World War II.

In the end, however, the vision is almost certainly false. Just because people watch the same movies and eat at the same fast-food outlets does not mean that they have been homogenized. National identities are not so easily retired. For good and ill, ethnic and religious differences show a remarkable ability to survive the march of material progress. National affections and animosities endure; and combined with the terrible and unpredictable potential of modern technology, they preserve humankind's capacity for ordinary trouble and unimaginable tragedy.

The world is fusing economically more than it is fusing (or will ever fuse) politically. We have created a system that requires ever-greater amounts of global cooperation, because it generates new and unfamiliar forms of international conflicts. One day, perhaps, the irresistible force of world markets may meet the immovable object of nationalism. Protectionism and isolationism are not so much agendas as moods, and countries—including the United States— might react to domestic disruption and international disorder by blaming foreigners and trying to withdraw from a global system on which most nations now increasingly depend. Buchanan has inadvertently identified the dilemma, but he has done exactly nothing to resolve it.

Patrick J. Buchanan  **NO**

Toward One Nation, Indivisible:
A Course of Action

It is time we looked at the world from a new perspective, one of enlightened nationalism. Clichés about a "new" global economy aside, there has always been an international economy—ever since Columbus stumbled onto the Western Hemisphere while seeking new trade routes to the East, in the hire of a nation-state, Spain. The Dutch East India Company was founded in 1602 to displace the Portuguese in the lucrative Far Eastern trade; and the Dutch West India Company, in 1621, to capture the American trade.

The American, economy, however, is more than simply a part of the international economy, and its purpose is not to benefit mankind but to benefit Americans first: our workers, farmers, businessmen, and manufacturers. What is good for the global economy is not automatically good for America, any more than what is good for our transnational elite is necessarily good for the United States.

A Revenue Tariff

America should declare to the world that the present global regime *must* be revised, that we no longer intend to make the world prosperous at the expense of our own country. A 15 percent revenue tariff on all imported manufactures and goods in competition with American-made goods would be a fitting way to declare our economic independence.

As part of the "Nixon Shock" of August 15, 1971—to jolt the world into understanding that the United States could no longer continue under the Bretton Woods agreement—a 10 percent tariff was imposed on Japan. Thus, we need not go back to the Tariff of 1816 to find a precedent for unilateral American action in defense of our economic security. Unlike Clinton's threat of a 100 percent tariff on Lexus cars, a 15 percent tariff would not destroy American businesses set up in good faith. The tariff could be imposed in stages: five percent immediately, five percent in six months, and the final five percent a year later, giving merchants 18 months to adjust. If Ronald Reagan could impose a 50 percent tariff to save Harley Davidson, surely we can impose a 15 percent tariff to inaugurate a new industrial age in the United States.

From Patrick J. Buchanan, "Toward One Nation, Indivisible: A Course of Action," *Chronicles*, vol. 22, no. 7 (July 1998). Adapted from Patrick J. Buchanan, *The Great Betrayal* (Little, Brown, 1998). Copyright © 1998 by PJB Enterprises, Inc. Reprinted by permission of Little, Brown & Company.

The revenue tariff should be high enough to generate a powerful stream of revenue, but low enough not to destroy trade. With American merchandise imports now exceeding $700 billion a year, this 15 percent tariff would yield a cornucopia of revenue while giving American products a marginal new advantage in their home market. Every dollar in tariff revenue, in fact, could be used to cut taxes on income, savings, and investment.

Bismarck built the German nation by shifting taxation away from incomes and onto foreign goods. In a December 15, 1878, letter to the Reichstag, the chancellor spoke of a crisis in the German middle class, similar to our own, and proposed to emulate the Americans: "Reform of the taxation... must begin with the revision of the tariff on as broad a basis as possible so as to benefit this class of the community. *The more money that is raised from tariffs the greater can —and must—be the relief in direct taxes.*" (Emphasis added.) High tariffs, argued Bismarck, would also give Germany leverage in "fresh negotiations with foreign countries concerning new commercial treaties."

Bismarck was an apt pupil of the economic nationalists who made America the world's greatest industrial power. Under Bismarck's policy, Germany increased its share of world production from 8.5 percent in 1880 to 14.8 percent by 1913; in 1880, Germany and the United States together had less than a fourth of world output, but by 1913 the two countries had nearly half, while free-trade Britain's share was sliced from one-fourth to one-seventh. The great unacknowledged truth of the second half of the 19th century—and of the second half of the 20th—is that the nations that followed the free trade dogma of the classical liberals lost ground to the nations that pursued the Hamiltonian policy of economic nationalism.

Reciprocity With the European Union [EU]

Europe would howl, but even under the old GATT [General Agreement on Tariffs and Trade] rules a nation running a chronic trade deficit may use tariffs to end the hemorrhaging. And our response should satisfy Europe. Believing in fairness, we accept full reciprocity: a 15 percent EU tariff on all manufactured goods made in the United States.

Lincoln called the cost of ocean transport "useless labor." Much of this useless labor can be done away with if European companies that wish to sell in America produce in America, and vice versa. Ford and GM have always built cars in Europe; Europeans forced them to. When American companies feared a protectionist Common Market, they created European subsidiaries to avoid being frozen out. Turnabout is fair play. Let BMW and Mercedes make their parts and assemble their cars here in the United States if they wish to sell here on equal terms. As for those who prefer the cachet of European-made goods, they ought not be denied the freedom to buy. But a 15 percent tariff does not amount to persecution of elites who call 55 percent inheritance taxes "progressive." That new BMW can be built in South Carolina as easily as in Bavaria.

Americans may face a social crisis, a racial crisis, a crime crisis. We do not face a crisis of consumer goods. There is nothing made anywhere that we cannot make here. America-Canada and the EU are huge and self-sufficient markets, with similar laws and regulations. Their standards of living and wage rates are comparable. A reciprocal trade agreement could strengthen and solidify both blocs.

But would reduced imports cost us our technological edge? History proves otherwise. The telegraph, electric light bulb, telephone, "horseless carriage," and airplane affected society as dramatically as the computer. Yet Americans invented and exploited them as no other nation, behind a tariff wall built by Justin Morrill, Bill McKinley, and "Pig Iron" Kelley.

With the American market alone almost as large as the European Union, we can support and sustain a diversity and level of production no other country can match. The small and medium-sized nations of Europe and Asia have no alternative but to create interdependencies. Germany is, after all, smaller than Oregon and Washington; the United Kingdom is smaller than Mississippi and Alabama; and Japan is smaller than Montana and less endowed with natural resources.

Canada and Japan

Should any country be exempt from the 15 percent tariff? Yes, Canada—if Canada adopts the same external tariffs. In NAFTA [North American Free Trade Agreement] Canada married her economy to ours, to the economic benefit of Ottawa. The United States today takes 80 percent of Canadian exports, and Canada's merchandise trade surplus with the United States in 1996 was $23 billion.

However, Canada would have to remain inside the U.S.-Canada free trade zone and accept American tariffs, or go outside. If Canada chose to depart, the 15 percent tariff on all manufactured goods would be applied to Canadian goods as well. With the United States far and away Canada's biggest customer, and with that surplus on the line, Canada would surely choose to remain inside an American free trade zone. But Canada would have to choose.

As the United States strengthens ties to Canada, we should put an early end to our huge, chronic trade deficits with Japan. The Japanese are a proud people. It is unseemly and destructive to be hectoring them endlessly to open their markets, buy our rice, remove non-tariff barriers, adopt free trade. Japan does not practice free trade for a simple reason: Japan does not believe in free trade. Japan puts its national interest in manufacturing and technology ahead of a free trade ideology that has America in its grip. Japan is different because it prefers to be different We should respect that. But while Japan's economic structure is no business of the United States, our trade deficits are our business. We should notify Japan that if an end to these trade deficits cannot be achieved through negotiation, it will be attained through unilateral U.S. action.

An horrendous imbalance in autos and auto parts is central to the American trade deficit with Japan. The United States should follow the Harley formula and impose a special tariff on imported Japanese autos and auto parts on top of the 15 percent revenue tariff. The Japan Tariff would enable the United States to recapture much of Japan's 30-percent share of the American auto market.

To avoid the tariffs, Japan could shift production of parts and the assembly of autos to the United States. These Japanese cars would be treated exactly like Fords or Chevrolets made in Michigan. Toyota, Nissan, BMW, and all foreign car makers would be welcome here, but to avoid tariffs they would have to produce here. The same would hold for GM, Chrysler, and Ford. Fords made overseas would face the same tariff as Mazdas made overseas. America would have the most competitive auto market on earth, but every company, foreign-owned or domestic, would play by the same rules, pay the same taxes, abide by the same laws, employ the same high-wage, high-quality North American labor. Jobs in the American auto industry would explode.

Japan is a great nation, and its people have wrought a great miracle. But the present unequal relationship cannot continue. Our sales to Japan in 1995, $65 billion, were one percent of our GDP; Japan's sales to us, $125 billion, were four percent of its GDP. With an economy twice as large as Japan's, we still spend six times as much on defense. We remit annually to Tokyo tens of billions of dollars in interest payments on the hundreds of billions of dollars of Treasury debt that Tokyo now holds as a result of having run up decades of trade surpluses at the expense of American workers. Historians will marvel that America let this happen.

Even the American Chamber of Commerce in Japan (ACCJ) is showing signs of despair. According to the ACCJ, only 13 of 45 U.S.-Japan trade agreements since 1980 were successful in helping American businesses penetrate Japan's market. Ten were total failures. Said ACCJ President Bill Beagles:

> For many years, the American view was that a trade agreement with Japan spoke for itself.... However, the U.S. Government and American industry came to realize that this is not the case. An apparently successful negotiation may not necessarily produce the expected market result.

This is unhealthy. As a First World nation, Japan has much in common with the United States. Our strategic interests are in harmony, and the possibility remains for a close relationship.

But it is not 1950 anymore. Reciprocity is required. If Japan can begin to harmonize her trade policies with ours, open her markets to our manufactures and agricultural products as we do for Japan's, there is no reason we cannot establish with Tokyo the same defense and trade relationship we have with Europe. There is no reason we cannot grow closer rather than drift farther apart.

Our China Problem

China is fast becoming America's number one trade problem. In its drive for dominance in Asia, Beijing has exploited slave labor, consumed all the Western credit it could extort, stolen intellectual property, and strong-armed American companies like Boeing and McDonnell Douglas to manufacture in China as the price of a deal. "Forced technology transfers" are a routine demand in dealing with China. "When you invest in China," says one auto company executive, "China assumes it owns all of your intellectual property." The Manufacturing Policy Project puts the piracy rate of U.S. intellectual property in China at

98 percent: "Three days after Microsoft introduced Windows 95 in the United States for $89.95, copies were available throughout Asia for $4 or less."

Following the path to power laid out by Friedrich List, China treats the United States, the world's most advanced nation, like a colony, a source of raw materials and a dumping ground for manufactures. China sends us up to 40 percent of its exports—much of it high-tech manufactured goods—but buys less than two percent of our exports. While China runs a trade surplus in manufactures with the United States of more than $35 billion yearly, prominent among American exports to China are fertilizers, food residue and waste, ore slag and ash, wood pulp, animal and vegetable fats, meats, live animals, and cereals. The one high-tech export for which America runs a large trade surplus is aircraft; but once China masters the American technology it has extorted, Beijing will begin building its own planes. That is the way of economic nationalists.

From 1991 through 1996, China piled up $157 billion in surpluses trading with the United States. Its 1996 surplus of $40 billion was almost as large as the Pentagon procurement budget. In October 1996, China invested $11.8 billion of its surplus in U.S. bonds, making China the third-largest buyer of U.S. debt, after Japan and Britain. By September 1997, China had amassed more than $130 billion in foreign currency reserves, the world's largest hoard after Japan.

For a century Americans have been transfixed by the great "China market"; it was one of the reasons business groups urged McKinley to annex the Philippines. But the China market proved a mirage then, and it is a mirage now, a corporate illusion. If China vanished, the American economy would not feel a breeze. Our sales to China in 1996 ($11.9 billion) were one-fifth of one percent of our GDP. We sold more to Singapore. But China's sales to the United States— $52 billion worth of toys, textiles, shoes, bikes, computers, etc., in 1996—were a crucial share of its entire economy and were the primary source of China's hard currency reserves.

The United States has the whip hand in this relationship, and it is time we used it. China is not only a trade problem, it is a national security problem. China is using the hard currency from its trade surpluses and international bank loans to buy submarines, destroyers, anti-ship missiles, and fighter aircraft from Russia, and to build long-range missiles to reach the West Coast of the United States. Yet we permit China to launch American satellites on Long March rockets, thus subsidizing the development of the Chinese strategic missile force.

America is taking a terrible risk feeding a regime whose character may be seen in its treatment of dissidents, Tibetans, Christians, and women pregnant in violation of China's barbaric one-child policy. While America should seek no confrontation with China, we should treat Beijing as the great power it has become.

We cannot practice true free trade with a nation that has no independent judiciary, where labor is conscripted, corruption is endemic, American goods face a 17 percent value-added tax and a 23 percent tariff, and many of whose corporations are government fronts. The United States should cancel China's Most Favored Nation status and negotiate a reciprocal trade agreement that recognizes our different societies and conflicting interests.

What About Mexico?

Mexico is another special case. We share a 2,000-mile border, ten million Americans trace their ancestry to Mexico, and our destinies are not separable. But NAFTA is not sustainable. NAFTA puts blue-collar workers from America into competition with Mexican workers who earn ten percent as much. American farm labor, paid a minimum wage near five dollars an hour, competes with Mexican farm labor paid 50 cents an hour. American employers now hang over the heads of their workers this constant threat: accept reduced pay, or we go to Mexico!

What makes the threat credible is that hundreds of companies have already done so. Under the *maquiladora program,* tax concessions are offered to American companies that place factories in Mexico to ship products back to the United States. New plants are opening at the rate of two a day. From San Diego to Brownsville, the Mexican side of the border is littered with signs of Fortune 500 corporations. Xerox, Zenith, Chrysler, GM, Ford, IBM, Rockwell, Samsonite, and GE have all opened plants south of the Rio Grande. By moving to Mexico, they evade American laws on child labor, worker safety, minimum wages, and health and pollution standards, as well as U.S. taxes; their products come back to undercut those made in factories that stayed in America and obeyed the laws of the United States.

The Japanese are also exploiting NAFTA. Matsushita, Hitachi, Sony, and Sanyo have assembly plants in Tijuana. Toshiba's plant is in Ciudad Juárez. Japanese and Korean companies are building auto plants. This Japanese investment in Mexico represents a shift of capital away from the United States. The CEO of the Japanese Chamber of Commerce in Mexico describes how it works: "Japanese investments reaching Mexico do not come directly from Japan. It is the United States [subsidiaries], the son, who is investing in Mexico, the grandson, of the main office."

President Clinton points with pride to the growth of American exports to Mexico. But prominent among those exports are parts for assembly into products for shipment back to the United States and capital equipment for factories being built in Mexico. Such "exports" destroy American jobs.

NAFTA must be renegotiated, or America's new Sun Belt will be south of the Rio Grande, and the consequences will be social and political as well as economic. Export the future of our working young, and those whose dreams have been destroyed will be heard from. America's merchandise trade deficit, an all-time record of $191 billion in 1996, is a cancer. Either we cut it out, or it will kill America. History teaches that when a nation's manufacturing sector has entered a period of relative decline, that nation will decline.

Our forefathers broke all ties with the mother country and risked their lives to achieve the economic independence we are piddling away. We need less of the gauzy spirit of globalism and more of the patriotic spirit of old George Meany:

> Practically every country in the world . . . has some type of restriction, some type of barrier, some type of subsidization for their own people, that gives their own manufacturers and workers an unfair advantage over the American

worker.... When have we ever retaliated against the unfair barriers put up by these other countries which go back many, many years? And if we are to have a trade war, if that's the only answer, I imagine if we had an all-out trade war we would do quite well for one simple fact: We have the market. We have the greatest market in the world right in this country.

Amen. Let us emulate our greatest leaders and use our control of that national market to achieve our national aims. After the Revolution, the War of 1812, the Civil War, and World War I, tariff revenue helped erase America's deficits and pay off America's debt. The alternative is more years of receding wages and rising tempers among American workers until the social fabric is torn irreparably, the bonds of patriotism no longer hold, our vitality vanishes, and our economic divisions manifest themselves in class conflict between Industrial America and Third Wave America. We have nothing to lose by trying, except those policies that have put us on the slippery slope to national decline.

What About the WTO?

The World Trade Organization [WTO] was erected on ideas American patriots must reject. It subordinates everything to the demands of trade. It exercises a supranational authority in conflict with our forefathers' vision of an America forever sovereign and independent. Its dispute-resolution procedures shift to Geneva decisions that ought to be made in Washington: And if we refuse to abide by the WTO's edicts, America can be chastised and fined.

Run by nameless, faceless, foreign bureaucrats, the WTO is the embryonic trade ministry of a world government. There is no place for such an institution in a world where free nations negotiate their trade agreements in good faith and oversee the execution of those agreements themselves. The WTO is a monument to the one-world vision of Wilson and FDR. Our withdrawal—after the required six months' notice—would be an unmistakable signal that America is back and that this nation is again the independent self-reliant republic which the Founding Fathers intended it to be.

Keeping Capital at Home

In a 1952 address to the University Club of Milwaukee, Ludwig von Mises declared that the "essence of Keynesianism is its complete failure to conceive the role that saving and capital accumulation play in the improvement of economic conditions." He admonished Americans to appreciate the role that capital had played in creating their unrivaled prosperity:

> The average standard of living is in this country higher than in any other country of the world, not because the American statesmen and politicians are superior to the foreign statesmen and politicians, but because the per-head quota of capital invested is in America higher than in other countries ...
>
> Do the American voters know that the unprecedented improvements in their standard of living that the last hundred years brought was the result of the steady rise in the per-head quota of capital invested? Do they

realize that every measure leading to capital decumulation jeopardizes their prosperity?

Mises, a free trade libertarian, is toasting a century in which the United States was the most protectionist nation on earth. Hamilton was right: protectionism went hand-in-hand with record capital accumulation. A primary reason that America's growth rates have been anemic in recent decades, and our recoveries not as robust as they once were, is the $2 trillion in trade deficits this generation has run up. Too much of the seed corn of the American economy is now being exported all over the world. As Sir James Goldsmith warned:

> Today, capital is being transferred to the developing world in massively increasing amounts. In the period 1989–1992, the average capital transferred per year to emerging countries was 116 billion dollars. In 1993, the figure was 213 billion dollars and in 1994 it was an estimated 227 billion dollars. East Asia leads the field, with a rise in the annual rate of direct investment between 1984 and 1994 of 1100 percent.

How can the United States halt the hemorrhaging of capital? First, consider how America's capital goes abroad. There are several primary vehicles for the "decumulation" of American capital: imports ($2 trillion in trade deficits in 20 years); U.S. private bank loans; foreign investments by corporations, pension funds, etc.; foreign aid (perhaps $1 trillion in the Cold War) and IMF [International Monetary Fund], World Bank, and international bank loans; U.S. overseas defense expenditures; illicit trade (drugs); illicit wealth transfers to evade taxes. Each of these problems can be dealt with by strong action.

Imports. A 15 percent tariff on all products that compete with American-produced goods and a wage-equalization tariff on manufactures from low-wage countries would rapidly erase American merchandise trade deficits. Instead of capital going abroad to build plants for the assembly of goods to be sent back to the United States, capital would come home to expand our domestic industries and create American jobs. The deep tax cuts on investment and savings that the new customs revenue would finance would make America the most attractive investment site of all the industrial democracies.

Private bank loans. Although America cannot and ought not impose controls on the foreign loans or investment of America's big banks, all investment banks, mutual funds, and pension funds should be put on notice: the next time there is another default, another Mexico, another meltdown in Asia, those who made the profit take the loss. This is neither harsh nor punitive. Private banks and overseas investors must begin to realize that there is no global bankruptcy court to bail them out. Once they know their investments are no longer risk-free, the market will solve this problem.

Foreign investment and foreign lending. Again, the tariffs, which would wipe out the admission-free access that foreign countries now have to the American market, would have a chilling effect on the plans of transnational corporations to invest abroad or to move factories abroad. Comparative advantage would come home.

Foreign aid.   Annual wealth transfers to foreign regimes like Egypt ($18 billion in cash reserves), Israel (a median income above $16,000), Greece, Turkey, Russia, and Pakistan make little sense. The Cold War is over; it is time for relics like foreign aid to be entombed. We cannot bribe nations to embrace free enterprise, and we ought not to pay nations not to fight one another. Far more serious is backdoor foreign aid, the tens of billions of dollars funneled yearly to foreign regimes through the IMF, World Bank, Asian Development Bank, etc. These relics of our "Marshall Plan mentality" have become global-socialist centers for the redistribution of American wealth. Why should American taxpayers guarantee loans to India or China, the leading beneficiaries of the World Bank? If these governments have worthwhile projects, let them finance the projects themselves, like we did when we were a developing nation. American-taxpayer guarantees for World Bank and IMF loans reward nations whose policies rarely merit such rewards.

Overseas defense expenditures.   John Foster Dulles once said that a day was coming when the United States would have to conduct an "agonizing reappraisal" of commitments to defend nations that refused to bear their fair share of the cost of their own defense. With the Cold War over, that reappraisal is long overdue. NATO should not be expanded; new nations should not be added to the roster of those we are already committed to defending. And Europe should begin to bear the full economic cost of its own defense. While the United States retains a vital interest in preventing a hostile regime—that of a Hitler or Stalin —from overrunning Europe, that threat has never been more remote: England and France have nuclear deterrents; Germany is united and democratic; Russia is smaller than it was in the days of Peter the Great. No threat to any vital American interest remotely exists in Europe. It is time to bring American troops home and revise NATO so that America is no longer committed to go to war because some ancient border has been breached or because a forgotten trip wire has been activated in some forsaken corner of the old continent. The proper role of America in Europe is not to be a front-line fighting state but to be the "strategic reserve" of the West. America must restore to itself full constitutional freedom to decide when, where, and whether to involve itself in Europe's 21st-century wars.

The new relationship of America with Europe should be modeled on our *military* relationship with Israel. Where the Israelis provide the troops to maintain their own defense, the United States provides access to advanced weapons. Israel gives us no veto over what it does in its own interests, and we give Israel no ironclad guarantee that any war that Israel decides to fight will be our war as well.

In Asia, the great threat to stability and security is almost certain to come from China. But Beijing is already contained by geography: Islam to the west; a nuclear-armed Russia to the north; India and Vietnam to the south; Korea, Japan, and the American fleet to the east. Any Chinese military move would trigger an arms race across East Asia. Here, again, the United States should play the role of the arsenal of democracy and sell to the nations of Asia the modern weapons they need to resist intimidation or defend against Beijing's encroachments—while those nations provide the troops themselves. No more Koreas, no more Vietnams.

When the nations of Europe and Asia understand that they, not we, are primarily responsible for their security, they will cease acting like dependencies and begin acting like independent nations. It is past time for prosperous allies to begin paying the cost of their own defense. Defense of the West can thus begin to enhance, rather than drain, America's vitality.

Illicit drugs. Seventy to eighty percent of the marijuana and cocaine entering the United States, to destroy the soul of America's young, passes through Mexico. To secure our southern border from this deadly traffic, we should cancel that provision of NAFTA which permits Mexican trucks on America's highways. Second, we should expand the U.S. Border Patrol. Third, we should lengthen the triple fence already built at San Diego, which has begun to cut back illegal immigration and complicate life for drug smugglers. Fourth, we should demand of Mexico greater cooperation in running down narcotics traffickers, and greater freedom and protection for American agents operating in Mexico. Finally, though the U.S. military does not belong in a policing role, American troops brought home from abroad should be moved to a southern border that is certain to be a crisis area in the 21st century.

Illicit wealth transfers to evade taxes. The scores of billions of dollars in tariff revenue should be used to eliminate taxes on savings, capital gains, and inheritances. With taxes on capital at zero in the United States, departed capital would come running home and new capital would come pouring in. Finally, the Republican Party should heed Mises' advice:

> No party platform is to be considered as satisfactory that does not contain the following point: As the prosperity of the nation and the height of wage rates depend on a continual increase in the capital invested in its plants, mines and farms, it is one of the foremost tasks of good government to remove all obstacles that hinder the accumulation and investment of new capital.

Strategic Independence

At the end of World War II, the United States had a nearly autarkic industrial base; we produced everything needed for our national defense. That day is gone. In 1982, we began to run manufacturing trade deficits; by 1986, deficits in the trade of high-technology goods. American dependence on foreign sources for items critical to our advanced weapons systems has created a vulnerability unknown since doughboys had to use French artillery and tanks, British machine guns, and Allied planes—even though our own Wright brothers had invented the airplane. A decade ago, Admiral James Lyons, commander of the U.S. Pacific forces, warned, "All of the critical components of our modern weapons systems, which involve our F-16s and F/A 18s, our M-1 tanks, our military computers—and I could go on and on—come from East Asian industries.... Some day, we might view that with concern and rightly so." Lyons was echoed five years later by a former chairman of the Joint Chiefs of Staff, Admiral William Crowe, Jr.:

> The Gulf War was unique because America enjoyed the unanimous support of all its allies. Even so, cooperation was difficult.... The U.S. defense industrial base is already in danger of becoming too dependent upon foreign sources for strategic supplies. What if the next time we are called upon to respond, our allies decide it is in their best interest to sit it out?

Former Commerce official Erik R. Pages writes of the difficulties to which Crowe alluded:

> The Bush Administration was forced to intervene with foreign governments on over thirty occasions to guarantee delivery of critical military parts. As one high-level administration official commented, "If the foreign governments were neutral or were not disposed to help us out, we could have run into some real problems. We were sweating bullets over it and the military was sweating bullets too."

Peacetime America may ignore such concerns; but it is a dangerous vulnerability when technology is vital to national power, crucial to military victory, and essential to saving the lives of Americans sent into combat. (We got a glimpse of what might happen during Vietnam, when Japan withheld the transfer of Sony TV cameras for missile guidance.) Foreigners today control the American companies responsible for the heat shield of the D-5 Trident missile and the flight controls of the B-2 bomber, the F-117 Stealth, and the F-22—the backbone of the 21st-century Air Force.

Overseas factories are far more vulnerable to espionage, labor problems, sabotage, political dictation, and attack by enemy or terrorist forces. There is no guarantee that American secrets are safe abroad. A clear and present danger exists when corporations with allegiance to no country gain virtual monopolies over items critical to American security. During World War II, Stalin's spies and our own homegrown traitors looted vital defense secrets, including those related to the atom bomb. Given this experience, for us to allow technology indispensable to our security to be kept outside the United States, vulnerable to theft or denial, is foolhardy. The time to end foreign military dependence is when new weapons systems are in the design stage. America should guarantee that no foreign dependency is built into any future generations of weapons. When it comes to technology vital to national defense, "Buy American" and "Made in the USA" are the rules that should apply.

The world is a dynamic place. No nation can ground its security in existing technological superiority. Superpowers that rest on their laurels invite the fate of the first global powers of the modern era: Holland and Spain. When former Treasury Secretary Richard Darman blurted, "Why do we want a semiconductor industry? We don't want some kind of industrial policy in this country. If our guys can't hack it, let 'em go," his was the smug voice of the elites of numerous nations that are no longer counted as great.

Unfortunately, President Clinton subscribes to the Darman view. His administration is outsourcing to foreign producers more components of American weapons systems than ever before. This penny-wise, pound-foolish policy strikes at the heart of American security and independence and ignores a truth taught by Adam Smith: "The great object of the political economy of every country is to increase the wealth and the power of that country."

POSTSCRIPT

Is Free Trade a Viable Option for the New Millennium?

Survey after survey confirms that the desirability of free trade is an issue on which a large majority of professional economists agree. Although economists are ardent supporters of free trade, they must grapple with the reality that the world David Ricardo modeled in 1807 is starkly different from the world we know as we enter the new millennium.

The concern that Ricardo could not predict is the present ability of capital and technology to cross national boundaries almost at will. This mobility of capital and technology suggests that a country's comparative advantages can radically change in a short period of time. Not so in Ricardo's world, where comparative advantages were stable and predictable. To illustrate comparative advantage, Ricardo spoke of the trade between England and Portugal in cloth and wine. In the nineteenth century it was highly unlikely that agrarian Portugal would seriously challenge the manufacturing base of England and equally unlikely that dreary English weather would ever produce a wine to compete with the vineyards of sun-drenched Portugal.

This kind of trade stability is found rarely in the modern world. Examples abound of comparative advantages won and lost overnight, as dollars and technology chase one another around the globe. Japan provides an interesting case study. Consider how quickly this country moved from dominance among Pacific Rim countries to fighting for its economic life as Korea, Malaysia, and their other Asian neighbors stole market after market from it.

The bottom line is clear: comparative advantage does lead to economic efficiency. But as with any market adjustment, there are serious dislocations, as less-efficient producers must make way for more-efficient producers. In the modern world this occurs quickly and sometimes unexpectedly. This does not mean that there is a shortage of advocates for free trade. Look at any textbook in economics; the case for free trade will be laid out clearly, forcefully, and without apologies. Alternatively, look to the conservative press, and it too will provide ample support for Samuelson's position. See *The National Review* (April 20, 1998) for three articles critical of Buchanan: "The Great Betrayed," by Robert Bartley; "Pat Answers," by Ramesk Ponnure; and "Nationalist Anthem," by John O'Sullivan.

We suggest that you examine Buchanan's book *The Great Betrayal: How American Sovereignty and Social Justice Are Being Sacrificed to the Gods of the Global Economy* (Little, Brown, 1998). You might also read Michael Find's "Marx, Smith or List?" *The Nation* (October 5, 1998) and John Gray's book *False Dawn: The Delusions of Global Capitalism* (New Press, 1999).

ISSUE 14

Should We Sweat About Sweatshops?

YES: Richard Appelbaum and Peter Dreier, from "The Campus Anti-Sweatshop Movement," *The American Prospect* (September–October 1999)

NO: Nicholas D. Kristof and Sheryl WuDunn, from "Two Cheers for Sweatshops," *The New York Times Magazine* (September 24, 2000)

ISSUE SUMMARY

YES: Sociologist Richard Appelbaum and political scientist Peter Dreier chronicle the rise of student activism on American campuses over the issue of sweatshops abroad. Students demand that firms be held responsible for "sweatshop conditions" and warn that if conditions do not improve, American consumers will not "leave their consciences at home when they shop for clothes."

NO: News correspondents Nicholas D. Kristof and Sheryl WuDunn agree that the working conditions in many offshore plant sites "seem brutal from the vantage point of an American sitting in his living room." But they argue that these work opportunities are far superior to the alternatives that are currently available in many parts of the world and that what is needed are more sweatshops, not fewer sweatshops.

The sleeping giant of student activism awoke in the late 1990s. This giant slumbered for nearly three decades. It was last heard from in the late 1960s and the early 1970s, when students on college campuses across the United States caused so much disruption that public awareness of the war in Vietnam slowly but surely came into focus. Prior to the antiwar activism, students were on the forefront of the civil rights movement. As in the case of the antiwar activists, the civil rights activists rebelled. They confronted their parents and grandparents but with less violent, less confrontational means than the antiwar activists.

Many argue that in both of these cases public policy might have eventually changed, but if it did change it would have taken much longer for that change to occur. In essence, these social historians maintain that without the idealism of college-aged students, society has a tendency to become inflexible and rigid. It is slower to change and more likely to assume that what exists today should always exist. The lack of student activism and the resulting return to more traditional values was the pattern throughout the late 1970s, the 1980s, and most of the 1990s. That peaceful atmosphere was shattered in the late 1990s.

It all began rather quietly on a talk show cohosted by Kathie Lee Gifford. In 1996 Charles Kernaghan, who is executive director of the National Labor Committee for Worker and Human Rights, charged that the Walmart apparel that bears Gifford's name was produced in offshore sweatshops that employed child labor. On air she roundly denied that charge. Kernaghan persisted. The media eventually covered the charges and the countercharges, and the more the story was denied, the more the media investigated. Kernaghan's allegations turned out to be true. Because of Gifford's high profile and the extensive coverage that this story received, college students soon learned of the widespread use of sweatshops to produce a wide range of items that they habitually wore.

Students were outraged; they wanted action immediately. Just as many of their uncles, aunts, fathers, and mothers had done 30 years earlier, the students staged sit-ins. University presidents could not duck the issue by simply assigning the problem to a study committee. Student activism had returned to college campuses. If university administrators did not want the situation to erupt into the widespread disruption and possible violence that marked the antiwar period, they had to act.

But how could these colleges and universities respond? More important, *should* they respond? They do not purchase their T-shirts and football jerseys directly from factories in China or Brazil; rather, they license firms who request the use of that university's logo to be sewn onto football jerseys or printed on T-shirts. Should colleges and universities require their licensees to guarantee that neither they nor their subcontractors will produce any items bearing the university's logo under sweatshop conditions? Is this wise? College T-shirts and football jerseys are cheap because they are produced in low-wage countries. If the same items were produced in the United States or another high-wage country, their prices would be substantially higher. Should universities deny their students the chance to buy these items at a low cost? If the answer is yes, what happens to the workers in El Salvador and other poor countries who will lose their jobs if the sweatshops are closed down? Is that what student activists want?

These and other questions are raised in the following selections. Richard Appelbaum and Peter Dreier detail the horrors of working in the sweatshops that allow Americans to pay less for their apparel and the student activism that has brought this issue to the attention of the public. Nicholas D. Kristof and Sheryl WuDunn argue that workers in sweatshops do not want to see them closed because they offer the best jobs many workers in poor countries have ever had.

The Campus Anti-Sweatshop Movement

If University of Arizona activist Arne Ekstrom was aware of today's widely reported student apathy, he certainly was not deterred when he helped lead his campus anti-sweatshop sit-in. Nor, for that matter, were any of the other thousands of students across the United States who participated in anti-sweatshop activities during the past academic year, coordinating their activities on the United Students Against Sweatshops (USAS) listserv (a listserv is an online mailing list for the purpose of group discussion) and Web site.

Last year's student anti-sweatshop movement gained momentum as it swept westward, eventually encompassing more than 100 campuses across the country. Sparked by a sit-in at Duke University, students organized teach-ins, led demonstrations, and occupied buildings—first at Georgetown, then northeast to the Ivy League, then west to the Big Ten. After militant actions at Notre Dame, Wisconsin, and Michigan made the *New York Times, Business Week, Time,* National Public Radio, and almost every major daily newspaper, the growing student movement reached California, where schools from tiny Occidental College to the giant ten-campus University of California system agreed to limit the use of their names and logos to sweatshop-free apparel. Now the practical challenge is to devise a regime of monitoring and compliance.

꧁꧂

The anti-sweatshop movement is the largest wave of student activism to hit campuses since students rallied to free Nelson Mandela by calling for a halt to university investments in South Africa more than a decade ago. This time around, the movement is electronically connected. Student activists bring their laptops and cell phones with them when they occupy administration buildings, sharing ideas and strategies with fellow activists from Boston to Berkeley. On the USAS listserv, victorious students from Wisconsin counsel neophytes from Arizona and Kentucky, and professors at Berkeley and Harvard explain how to calculate a living wage and guarantee independent monitoring in Honduras.

The target of this renewed activism is the $2.5 billion collegiate licensing industry—led by major companies like Nike, Gear, Champion, and Fruit of the Loom—which pays colleges and universities sizable royalties in exchange for

From Richard Appelbaum and Peter Dreier, "The Campus Anti-Sweatshop Movement," *The American Prospect*, vol. 10, no. 46 (September–October 1999). Copyright © 1999 by *The American Prospect*. Reprinted by permission.

the right to use the campus logo on caps, sweatshirts, jackets, and other items. Students are demanding that the workers who make these goods be paid a living wage, no matter where in the world industry operates. Students are also calling for an end to discrimination against women workers, public disclosure of the names and addresses of all factories involved in production, and independent monitoring in order to verify compliance.

These demands are opposed by the apparel industry, the White House, and most universities. Yet so far students have made significant progress in putting the industry on the defensive. A growing number of colleges and clothing companies have adopted "codes of conduct"—something unthinkable a decade ago —although student activists consider many of these standards inadequate.

In a world economy increasingly dominated by giant retailers and manufacturers who control global networks of independently owned factories, organizing consumers may prove to be a precondition for organizing production workers. And students are a potent group of consumers. If students next year succeed in building on this year's momentum, the collegiate licensing industry will be forced to change the way it does business. These changes, in turn, could affect the organization of the world's most globalized and exploitative industry—apparel manufacturing—along with the growing number of industries that, like apparel, outsource production in order to lower labor costs and blunt worker organizing.

The Global Sweatshop

In the apparel industry, so-called manufacturers—in reality, design and marketing firms—outsource the fabrication of clothing to independent contractors around the world. In this labor-intensive industry where capital requirements are minimal, it is relatively easy to open a clothing factory. This has contributed to a global race to the bottom, in which there is always someplace, somewhere, where clothing can be made still more cheaply. Low wages reflect not low productivity, but low bargaining power. A recent analysis in *Business Week* found that although Mexican apparel workers are 70 percent as productive as U.S. workers, they earn only 11 percent as much as their U.S. counterparts; Indonesian workers, who are 50 percent as productive, earn less than 2 percent as much.

The explosion of imports has proven devastating to once well-paid, unionized U.S. garment workers. The number of American garment workers has declined from peak levels of 1.4 million in the early 1970s to 800,000 today. The one exception to these trends is the expansion of garment employment, largely among immigrant and undocumented workers, in Los Angeles, which has more than 160,000 sweatshop workers. Recent U.S. Department of Labor surveys found that more than nine out of ten such firms violate legal health and safety standards, with more than half troubled by serious violations that could lead to severe injuries or death. Working conditions in New York City, the other major domestic garment center, are similar.

The very word "sweatshop" comes from the apparel industry, where profits were "sweated" out of workers by forcing them to work longer and faster at their sewing machines. Although significant advances have been made in such aspects of production as computer-assisted design, computerized marking, and computerized cutting, the industry still remains low-tech in its core production process, the sewing of garments. The basic unit of production continues to be a worker, usually a woman, sitting or standing at a sewing machine and sewing together pieces of limp cloth.

The structure of the garment industry fosters sweatshop production. During the past decade, retailing in the United States has become increasingly concentrated. Today, the four largest U.S. retailers—Wal-Mart, Kmart, Sears, and Dayton Hudson (owner of Target and Mervyns)—account for nearly two-thirds of U.S. retail sales. Retailers squeeze manufacturers, who in turn squeeze the contractors who actually make their products. Retailers and manufacturers preserve the fiction of being completely separate from contractors because they do not want to be held legally responsible for workplace violations of labor, health, and safety laws. Retailers and manufacturers alike insist that what happens in contractor factories is not their responsibility—even though their production managers and quality control officers are constantly checking up on the sewing shops that make their clothing.

The contracting system also allows retailers and manufacturers to eliminate much uncertainty and risk. When business is slow, the contract is simply not renewed; manufacturers need not worry about paying unemployment benefits or dealing with idle workers who might go on strike or otherwise make trouble. If a particular contractor becomes a problem, there are countless others to be found who will be only too happy to get their business. Workers, however, experience the flip side of the enormous flexibility enjoyed by retailers and manufacturers. They become contingent labor, employed and paid only when their work is needed.

Since profits are taken out at each level of the supply chain, labor costs are reduced to a tiny fraction of the retail price. Consider the economics of a dress that is sewn in Los Angeles and retails for $100. Half goes to the department store and half to the manufacturer, who keeps $12.50 to cover expenses and profit, spends $22.50 on textiles, and pays $15 to the contractor. The contractor keeps $9 to cover expenses and profits. That leaves just $6 of the $100 retail price for the workers who actually make the dress. Even if the cost of direct production labor were to increase by half, the dress would still only cost $103 —a small increment that would make a world of difference to the seamstress in Los Angeles, whose $7,000 to $8,000 in annual wages are roughly two-thirds of the poverty level. A garment worker in Mexico would be lucky to earn $1,000 during a year of 48 to 60 hour workweeks; in China, $500.

At the other end of the apparel production chain, the heads of the 60 publicly traded U.S. apparel retailers earn an average $1.5 million a year. The heads of the 35 publicly traded apparel manufacturers average $2 million. In 1997, according to the *Los Angeles Business Journal,* five of the six highest-paid apparel executives in Los Angeles all came from a single firm: Guess?, Inc. They took home nearly $12.6 million—enough to double the yearly wages of 1,700 L.A. apparel workers.

❦

Organizing workers at the point of production, the century-old strategy that built the power of labor in Europe and North America, is best suited to production processes where most of the work goes on in-house. In industries whose production can easily be shifted almost anywhere on the planet, organizing is extremely difficult. Someday, perhaps, a truly international labor movement will confront global manufacturers. But in the meantime, organized consumers may well be labor's best ally. Consumers, after all, are not as readily moved as factories. And among American consumers, college students represent an especially potent force.

Kathie Lee and Robert Reich

During the early 1990s, American human rights and labor groups protested the proliferation of sweatshops at home and abroad—with major campaigns focusing on Nike and Gap. These efforts largely fizzled. But then two exposés of sweatshop conditions captured public attention. In August 1995, state and federal officials raided a garment factory in El Monte, California—a Los Angeles suburb—where 71 Thai immigrants had been held for several years in virtual slavery in an apartment complex ringed with barbed wire and spiked fences. They worked an average of 84 hours a week for $1.60 an hour, living eight to ten persons in a room. The garments they sewed ended up in major retail chains, including Macy's, Filene's and Robinsons-May, and for brand-name labels like B.U.M., Tomato, and High Sierra. Major daily papers and TV networks picked up on the story, leading to a flood of outraged editorials and columns calling for a clamp-down on domestic sweatshops. Then in April 1996, TV celebrity Kathie Lee Gifford tearfully acknowledged on national television that the Wal-Mart line of clothing that bore her name was made by children in Honduran sweatshops, even though tags on the garments promised that part of the profits would go to help children. Embarrassed by the publicity, Gifford soon became a crusader against sweatshop abuses.

For several years, then–Labor Secretary Robert Reich (now the *Prospect's* senior editor) had been trying to inject the sweatshop issue onto the nation's agenda. The mounting publicity surrounding the El Monte and Kathie Lee scandals gave Reich new leverage. After all, what the apparel industry primarily sells is image, and the image of some of its major labels was getting a drubbing. He began pressing apparel executives, threatening to issue a report card on firms' behavior unless they agreed to help establish industry-wide standards.

In August 1996, the Clinton administration brought together representatives from the garment industry, labor unions, and consumer and human rights groups to grapple with sweatshops. The members of what they called the White House Apparel Industry Partnership (AIP) included apparel firms (Liz Claiborne, Reebok, L.L. Bean, Nike, Patagonia, Phillips-Van Heusen, Wal-Mart's Kathie Lee Gifford brand, and Nicole Miller), several nonprofit organizations (including the National Consumers League, Interfaith Center on Corporate Responsibility, International Labor Rights Fund, Lawyers Committee for Human Rights, Robert

F. Kennedy Memorial Center for Human Rights, and Business for Social Responsibility), as well as the Union of Needletrades, Industrial and Textile Employees (UNITE), the Retail, Wholesale, and Department Store Union, and the AFL-CIO.

After intense negotiations, the Department of Labor issued an interim AIP report in April 1997 and the White House released the final 40-page report in November 1998, which included a proposed workplace code of conduct and a set of monitoring guidelines. By then, Reich had left the Clinton administration, replaced by Alexis Herman. The two labor representatives on the AIP, as well as the Interfaith Center on Corporate Responsibility, quit the group to protest the feeble recommendations, which had been crafted primarily by the garment industry delegates and which called, essentially, for the industry to police itself. This maneuvering would not have generated much attention except that a new factor—college activism—had been added to the equation.

A "Sweat-Free" Campus

The campus movement began in the fall of 1997 at Duke when a group called Students Against Sweatshops persuaded the university to require manufacturers of items with the Duke label to sign a pledge that they would not use sweatshop labor. Duke has 700 licensees (including Nike and other major labels) that make apparel at hundreds of plants in the U.S. and in more than 10 other countries, generating almost $25 million annually in sales. Following months of negotiations, in March 1998 Duke President Nannerl Keohane and the student activists jointly announced a detailed "code of conduct" that bars Duke licensees from using child labor, requires them to maintain safe workplaces, to pay the minimum wage, to recognize the right of workers to unionize, to disclose the locations of all factories making products with Duke's name, and to allow visits by independent monitors to inspect the factories.

The Duke victory quickly inspired students on other campuses. The level of activity on campuses accelerated, with students finding creative ways to dramatize the issue. At Yale, student activists staged a "knit-in" to draw attention to sweatshop abuses. At Holy Cross and the University of California at Santa Barbara, students sponsored mock fashion shows where they discussed the working conditions under which the garments were manufactured. Duke students published a coloring book explaining how (and where) the campus mascot, the Blue Devil, is stitched onto clothing by workers in sweatshops. Activists at the University of Wisconsin infiltrated a homecoming parade and, dressed like sweatshop workers in Indonesia, carried a giant Reebok shoe. They also held a press conference in front of the chancellor's office and presented him with an oversized check for 16 cents—the hourly wage paid to workers in China making Nike athletic shoes. At Georgetown, Wisconsin, Michigan, Arizona, and Duke, students occupied administration buildings to pressure their institutions to adopt (or, in Duke's case, strengthen) anti-sweatshop codes.

In the summer of 1998, disparate campus groups formed United Students Against Sweatshops (USAS). The USAS has weekly conference calls to discuss their negotiations with Nike, the Department of Labor, and others. It has sponsored training sessions for student leaders and conferences at several campuses where the sweatshop issue is only part of an agenda that also includes helping to build the labor movement, NAFTA, the World Trade Organization, women's rights, and other issues.

Last year, anti-sweatshop activists employed the USAS listserv to exchange ideas on negotiating tactics, discuss media strategies, swap songs to sing during rallies, and debate the technicalities of defining a "living wage" to incorporate in their campus codes of conduct. In May, the USAS listserv heated up after the popular Fox television series *Party of Five* included a scene in which one of the show's characters, Sarah (played by Jennifer Love Hewitt), helps organize a Students Against Sweatshops sit-in on her campus. A few real-life activists worried that the mainstream media was trivializing the movement by skirting the key issues ("the importance of unionized labor, the globalization of the economy, etc.") as well as focusing most of that episode on the characters' love life. University of Michigan student Rachel Paster responded:

> Let's not forget that we ARE a student movement, and students do complain about boyfriends and fashion problems. One of the biggest reasons why USAS and local student groups opposing sweatshops have been as successful as we have been is that opposition to sweatshops ISN'T that radical. Although I'm sure lots of us are all for overthrowing the corporate power structure, the human rights issues involved are what make a lot of people get involved and put their energies into rallies, sit-ins, et cetera. If we were a 'radical' group, university administrations would have brushed us off.... The fact that they don't is testament to the fact that we have support, not just from students on the far left, but from students in the middle ground who don't consider themselves radicals. Without those people we would NEVER have gotten as far as we have.

Indeed, the anti-sweatshop movement has been able to mobilize wide support because it strikes several nerves among today's college students, including women's rights (most sweatshop workers are women and some factories have required women to use birth control pills as a condition of employment), immigrant rights, environmental concerns, and human rights. After University of Wisconsin administrators brushed aside anti-sweatshop protestors, claiming they didn't represent student opinion, the activists ran a slate of candidates for student government. Eric Brakken, a sociology major and anti-sweatshop leader, was elected student body president and last year used the organization's substantial resources to promote the activists' agenda. And Duke's student government unanimously passed a resolution supporting the anti-sweatshop group, calling for full public disclosure of the locations of companies that manufacture Duke clothing.

The Labor Connection

At the core of the movement is a strong bond with organized labor. The movement is an important by-product of the labor movement's recent efforts, under President John Sweeney, to repair the rift between students and unions that dates to the Vietnam War. Since 1996, the AFL-CIO's Union Summer has placed almost 2,000 college students in internships with local unions around the country, most of whom work on grassroots organizing campaigns with low-wage workers in hotels, agriculture, food processing, janitorial service, and other industries. The program has its own staff, mostly young organizers only a few years out of college themselves, who actively recruit on campuses, looking for the next generation of union organizers and researchers, particularly minorities, immigrants, and women. Union Summer graduates are among the key leadership of the campus anti-sweatshop movement.

UNITE has one full-time staff person assigned to work on sweatshop issues, which includes helping student groups. A number of small human rights watchdog organizations that operate on shoestring budgets—Global Exchange, Sweatshop Watch, and the National Labor Committee [NLC]—give student activists technical advice. (It was NLC's Charles Kernaghan, an energetic researcher and publicist, who exposed the Kathie Lee Gifford connection to sweatshops in testimony before Congress.) These groups have helped bring sweatshop workers on speaking tours of American campuses, and have organized delegations of student activists to investigate firsthand the conditions in Honduras, Guatemala, El Salvador, Mexico, and elsewhere under which workers produce their college's clothing.

Unions and several liberal foundations have provided modest funding for student anti-sweatshop groups. Until this summer USAS had no staff, nor did any of its local campus affiliates. In contrast, corporate-sponsored conservative foundations have, over the past two decades, funded dozens of conservative student publications, subsidized student organizations and conferences, and recruited conservative students for internships and jobs in right-wing think tanks and publications as well as positions in the Reagan and Bush administrations and Congress, seeking to groom the next generation of conservative activists. The Intercollegiate Studies Institute, the leading right-wing campus umbrella group, has an annual budget over $5 million. In comparison, the Center for Campus Organizing, a Boston-based group that works closely with anti-sweatshop groups and other progressive campus organizations, operates on a budget under $200,000.

This student movement even has some sympathizers among university administrators. "Thank God students are getting passionate about something other than basketball and bonfires," John Burness, a Duke administrator who helped negotiate the end of the 31-hour sit-in, told the *Boston Globe.* "But the tone is definitely different. In the old days, we used to have to scramble to cut off phone lines when they took over the president's office, but we didn't have to worry about that here. They just bring their laptops and they do work."

At every university where students organized a sit-in (Duke, Georgetown, Arizona, Michigan, and Wisconsin) they have wrested agreements to require licensees to disclose the specific location of their factory sites, which is necessary for independent monitoring. Students elsewhere (including Harvard, Illinois, Brown, the University of California, Princeton, Middlebury, and Occidental) won a public disclosure requirement without resorting to civil disobedience. A few institutions have agreed to require manufacturers to pay their employees a "living wage." Wisconsin agreed to organize an academic conference this fall to discuss how to calculate living-wage formulas for countries with widely disparate costs of living, and then to implement its own policy recommendations. [See Richard Rothstein, "The Global Hiring Hall: Why We Need Worldwide Labor Standards," *TAP,* Spring 1994.]

The Industry's New Clothes

Last November, the White House-initiated Apparel Industry Partnership created a monitoring arm, the Fair Labor Association (FLA), and a few months later invited universities to join. Colleges, however, have just one seat on FLA's 14-member board. Under the group's bylaws the garment firms control the board's decisionmaking. The bylaws require a "supermajority" to approve all key questions, thus any three companies can veto a proposal they don't like.

At this writing, FLA member companies agree to ban child and prison labor, to prohibit physical abuse by supervisors, and to allow workers the freedom to organize unions in their foreign factories, though independent enforcement has not yet been specified. FLA wants to assign this monitoring task to corporate accounting firms like PricewaterhouseCoopers and Ernst & Young, to allow companies to select which facilities will be inspected, and to keep factory locations and the monitoring reports secret. Student activists want human rights and labor groups to do the monitoring.

This is only a bare beginning, but it establishes the crucial moral precedent of companies taking responsibility for labor conditions beyond their shores. Seeing this foot in the door, several companies have bowed out because they consider these standards too tough. The FLA expects that by 2001, after its monitoring program has been in place for a year, participating firms will be able to use the FLA logo on their labels and advertising as evidence of their ethical corporate practices. [See Richard Rothstein, "The Starbucks Solution: Can Voluntary Codes Raise Global Living Standards?" *TAP*, July-August 1996.]

The original list of 17 FLA-affiliated universities grew to more than 100 by mid-summer of this year. And yet, some campus groups have dissuaded college administrations (including the Universities of Michigan, Minnesota, Oregon, Toronto, and California, as well as Oberlin, Bucknell, and Earlham Colleges) from joining FLA, while others have persuaded their institutions (including Brown, Wisconsin, North Carolina, and Georgetown) to join only if the FLA adopts stronger standards. While FLA members are supposed to abide by each country's minimum-wage standards, these are typically far below the poverty level. In fact, no company has made a commitment to pay a living wage.

The campus movement has succeeded in raising awareness (both on campus and among the general public) about sweatshops as well as the global economy. It has contributed to industry acceptance of extraterritorial labor standards, something hitherto considered utopian. It has also given thousands of students experience in the nuts and bolts of social activism, many of whom are likely to carry their idealism and organizing experiences with them into jobs with unions, community and environmental groups, and other public interest crusades.

So far, however, the movement has had only minimal impact on the daily lives of sweatshop workers at home and abroad. Nike and Reebok, largely because of student protests, have raised wages and benefits in their Indonesian footwear factories—which employ more than 100,000 workers—to 43 percent above the minimum wage. But this translates to only 20 cents an hour in U.S. dollars, far below a "living wage" to raise a family and even below the 27 cents Nike paid before Indonesia's currency devaluation. Last spring Nike announced its willingness to disclose the location of its overseas plants that produce clothing for universities. This created an important split in industry ranks, since industry leaders have argued that disclosure would undermine each firm's competitive position. But Nike has opened itself up to the charge of having a double standard, since it still refuses to disclose the location of its non-university production sites.

Within a year, when FLA's monitoring system is fully operational, students at several large schools with major licensing contracts—including Duke, Wisconsin, Michigan, North Carolina, and Georgetown—will have lists of factories in the U.S. and overseas that produce university clothing and equipment. This information will be very useful to civic and labor organizations at home and abroad, providing more opportunities to expose working conditions. Student activists at each university will be able to visit these sites—bringing media and public officials with them—to expose working conditions (and, if necessary, challenge the findings of the FLA's own monitors) and support organizing efforts by local unions and women's groups.

If the student activists can help force a small but visible "ethical" niche of the apparel industry to adopt higher standards, it will divide the industry and give unions and consumer groups more leverage to challenge the sweatshop practices of the rest of the industry. The campus anti-sweatshop crusade is part of what might be called a "conscience constituency" among consumers who are willing to incorporate ethical principles into their buying habits, even if it means slightly higher prices. Environmentalists have done the same thing with the "buy green" campaign, as have various "socially responsible" investment firms.

Beyond Consumer Awareness

In a global production system characterized by powerful retailers and invisible contractors, consumer action has an important role to play. But ultimately it must be combined with worker organizing and legislative and regulatory remedies. Unionizing the global apparel industry is an organizer's nightmare. With globalization and the contracting system, any apparel factory with a union risks losing its business.

Domestically, UNITE represents fewer than 300,000 textile and garment industry workers, down from the 800,000 represented by its two predecessor unions in the late 1960s. In the low-income countries where most U.S. apparel is now made, the prospects for unionization are dimmer still. In Mexico, labor unions are controlled by the government. China outlaws independent unions, punishing organizers with prison terms. Building the capacity for unfettered union organizing must necessarily be a long-term strategy for union organizers throughout the world. Here, the student anti-sweatshop movement can help. The independent verification of anti-sweatshop standards that students want can also serve the goal of union organizing.

Public policy could also help. As part of our trade policy, Congress could require public disclosure of manufacturing sites and independent monitoring of firms that sell goods in the American market. It could enact legislation that requires U.S. companies to follow U.S. health and safety standards globally and to bar the import of clothing made in sweatshops or made by workers who are denied the basic right to organize unions. In addition, legislation sponsored by Representative William Clay could make retailers and manufacturers legally liable for the working conditions behind the goods they design and sell, thereby ending the fiction that contractors are completely independent of the manufacturers and retailers that hire them. Last spring the California Assembly passed a state version of this legislation. Student and union activists hope that the Democrat-controlled state senate and Democratic Governor Gray Davis—whose lopsided victory last November was largely attributed to organized labor's get-out-the-vote effort—will support the bill.

※◆ॐ•

Thanks to the student movement, public opinion may be changing. And last spring, speaking both to the International Labor Organization in Geneva and at the commencement ceremonies at the University of Chicago (an institution founded by John D. Rockefeller and a stronghold of free market economics, but also a center of student anti-sweatshop activism), President Clinton called for an international campaign against child labor, including restrictions on government purchases of goods made by children.

A shift of much apparel production to developing countries may well be inevitable in a global economy. But when companies do move their production abroad, student activists are warning "you can run but you can't hide," demanding that they be held responsible for conditions in contractor factories no matter where they are. Students can't accomplish this on their own, but in a very short period of time they have made many Americans aware that they don't have to leave their consciences at home when they shop for clothes.

**Nicholas D. Kristof and
Sheryl WuDunn**

 **NO**

Two Cheers for Sweatshops

It was breakfast time, and the food stand in the village in northeastern Thailand was crowded. Maesubin Sisoipha, the middle-aged woman cooking the food, was friendly, her portions large and the price right. For the equivalent of about 5 cents, she offered a huge green mango leaf filled with rice, fish paste and fried beetles. It was a hearty breakfast, if one didn't mind the odd antenna left sticking in one's teeth.

One of the half-dozen men and women sitting on a bench eating was a sinewy, bare-chested laborer in his late 30's named Mongkol Latlakorn. It was a hot, lazy day, and so we started chatting idly about the food and, eventually, our families. Mongkol mentioned that his daughter, Darin, was 15, and his voice softened as he spoke of her. She was beautiful and smart, and her father's hopes rested on her.

"Is she in school?" we asked.

"Oh, no," Mongkol said, his eyes sparkling with amusement. "She's working in a factory in Bangkok. She's making clothing for export to America." He explained that she was paid $2 a day for a nine-hour shift, six days a week.

"It's dangerous work," Mongkol added. "Twice the needles went right through her hands. But the managers bandaged up her hands, and both times she got better again and went back to work."

"How terrible," we murmured sympathetically.

Mongkol looked up, puzzled. "It's good pay," he said. "I hope she can keep that job. There's all this talk about factories closing now, and she said there are rumors that her factory might close. I hope that doesn't happen. I don't know what she would do then."

He was not, of course, indifferent to his daughter's suffering; he simply had a different perspective from ours—not only when it came to food but also when it came to what constituted desirable work.

Nothing captures the difference in mind-set between East and West more than attitudes toward sweatshops. Nike and other American companies have been hammered in the Western press over the last decade for producing shoes, toys and other products in grim little factories with dismal conditions. Protests against sweatshops and the dark forces of globalization that they seem to represent have become common at meetings of the World Bank and the World

Trade Organization and, this month, at a World Economic Forum in Australia, livening up the scene for Olympic athletes arriving for the competition. Yet sweatshops that seem brutal from the vantage point of an American sitting in his living room can appear tantalizing to a Thai laborer getting by on beetles.

Fourteen years ago, we moved to Asia and began reporting there. Like most Westerners, we arrived in the region outraged at sweatshops. In time, though, we came to accept the view supported by most Asians: that the campaign against sweatshops risks harming the very people it is intended to help. For beneath their grime, sweatshops are a clear sign of the industrial revolution that is beginning to reshape Asia.

This is not to praise sweatshops. Some managers are brutal in the way they house workers in firetraps, expose children to dangerous chemicals, deny bathroom breaks, demand sexual favors, force people to work double shifts or dismiss anyone who tries to organize a union. Agitation for improved safety conditions can be helpful, just as it was in 19th-century Europe. But Asian workers would be aghast at the idea of American consumers boycotting certain toys or clothing in protest. The simplest way to help the poorest Asians would be to buy more from sweatshops, not less.

⋘◉⋙

On our first extended trip to China, in 1987, we traveled to the Pearl River delta in the south of the country. There we visited several factories, including one in the boomtown of Dongguan, where about 100 female workers sat at workbenches stitching together bits of leather to make purses for a Hong Kong company. We chatted with several women as their fingers flew over their work and asked about their hours.

"I start at about 6:30, after breakfast, and go until about 7 p.m.," explained one shy teenage girl. "We break for lunch, and I take half an hour off then."

"You do this six days a week?"

"Oh, no. Every day."

"Seven days a week?"

"Yes." She laughed at our surprise. "But then I take a week or two off at Chinese New Year to go back to my village."

The others we talked to all seemed to regard it as a plus that the factory allowed them to work long hours. Indeed, some had sought out this factory precisely because it offered them the chance to earn more.

"It's actually pretty annoying how hard they want to work," said the factory manager, a Hong Kong man. "It means we have to worry about security and have a supervisor around almost constantly."

It sounded pretty dreadful, and it was. We and other journalists wrote about the problems of child labor and oppressive conditions in both China and South Korea. But, looking back, our worries were excessive. Those sweatshops tended to generate the wealth to solve the problems they created. If Americans had reacted to the horror stories in the 1980's by curbing imports of those sweatshop products, then neither southern China nor South Korea would have registered as much progress as they have today.

The truth is, those grim factories in Dongguan and the rest of southern China contributed to a remarkable explosion of wealth. In the years since our first conversations there, we've returned many times to Dongguan and the surrounding towns and seen the transformation. Wages have risen from about $50 a month to $250 a month or more today. Factory conditions have improved as businesses have scrambled to attract and keep the best laborers. A private housing market has emerged, and video arcades and computer schools have opened to cater to workers with rising incomes. A hint of a middle class has appeared—as has China's closest thing to a Western-style independent newspaper, Southern Weekend.

Partly because of these tens of thousands of sweatshops, China's economy has become one of the hottest in the world. Indeed, if China's 30 provinces were counted as individual countries, then the 20 fastest-growing countries in the world between 1978 and 1995 would all have been Chinese. When Britain launched the Industrial Revolution in the late 18th century, it took 58 years for per capita output to double. In China, per capita output has been doubling every 10 years.

In fact, the most vibrant parts of Asia are nearly all in what might be called the Sweatshop Belt, from China and South Korea to Malaysia, Indonesia and even Bangladesh and India. Today these sweatshop countries control about one-quarter of the global economy. As the industrial revolution spreads through China and India, there are good reasons to think that Asia will continue to pick up speed. Some World Bank forecasts show Asia's share of global gross domestic product rising to 55 to 60 percent by about 2025—roughly the West's share at its peak half a century ago. The sweatshops have helped lay the groundwork for a historic economic realignment that is putting Asia back on its feet. Countries are rebounding from the economic crisis of 1997–98 and the sweatshops—seen by Westerners as evidence of moribund economies—actually reflect an industrial revolution that is raising living standards in the East.

~◈~

Of course, it may sound silly to say that sweatshops offer a route to prosperity, when wages in the poorest countries are sometimes less than $1 a day. Still, for an impoverished Indonesian or Bangladeshi woman with a handful of kids who would otherwise drop out of school and risk dying of mundane diseases like diarrhea, $1 or $2 a day can be a life-transforming wage.

This was made abundantly clear in Cambodia, when we met a 40-year-old woman named Nhem Yen, who told us why she moved to an area with particularly lethal malaria. "We needed to eat," she said. "And here there is wood, so we thought we could cut it and sell it."

But then Nhem Yen's daughter and son-in-law both died of malaria, leaving her with two grandchildren and five children of her own. With just one mosquito net, she had to choose which children would sleep protected and which would sleep exposed.

In Cambodia, a large mosquito net costs $5. If there had been a sweatshop in the area, however harsh or dangerous, Nhem Yen would have leapt at the chance to work in it, to earn enough to buy a net big enough to cover all her children.

For all the misery they can engender, sweatshops at least offer a precarious escape from the poverty that is the developing world's greatest problem. Over the past 50 years, countries like India resisted foreign exploitation, while countries that started at a similar economic level—like Taiwan and South Korea—accepted sweatshops as the price of development. Today there can be no doubt about which approach worked better. Taiwan and South Korea are modern countries with low rates of infant mortality and high levels of education; in contrast, every year 3.1 million Indian children die before the age of 5, mostly from diseases of poverty like diarrhea.

The effect of American pressure on sweatshops is complicated. While it clearly improves conditions at factories that produce branded merchandise for companies like Nike, it also raises labor costs across the board. That encourages less well established companies to mechanize and to reduce the number of employees needed. The upshot is to help people who currently have jobs in Nike plants but to risk jobs for others. The only thing a country like Cambodia has to offer is terribly cheap wages; if companies are scolded for paying those wages, they will shift their manufacturing to marginally richer areas like Malaysia or Mexico.

Sweatshop monitors do have a useful role. They can compel factories to improve safety. They can also call attention to the impact of sweatshops on the environment. The greatest downside of industrialization is not exploitation of workers but toxic air and water. In Asia each year, three million people die from the effects of pollution. The factories springing up throughout the region are far more likely to kill people through the chemicals they expel than through terrible working conditions.

By focusing on these issues, by working closely with organizations and news media in foreign countries, sweatshops can be improved. But refusing to buy sweatshop products risks making Americans feel good while harming those we are trying to help. As a Chinese proverb goes, "First comes the bitterness, then there is sweetness and wealth and honor for 10,000 years."

POSTSCRIPT

Should We Sweat About Sweatshops?

Economists have not remained mute as this debate has raged across college campuses. In a letter circulated across American campuses in September 2000, 90 academics, mostly economists, urged college and university presidents not to yield to student pressure demanding the adoption of strict codes of conduct for the manufacturers of university apparel that is produced in poor countries. There were many distinguished signers, including Nobel Laureate Robert Lucas, several former presidents of the American Economic Association, several former presidents of the Econometric Society, and Paul McCracken, former chairman of the President's Council of Economic Advisers. These market-oriented economists warned against codes of conduct that required offshore plants to pay wages that are above the prevailing wage rates. They asserted that these higher wages might result "in shifts in employment that will worsen the collective welfare of the very workers in poor countries who are supposed to be helped." This group is supported by the Academic Consortium on International Trade (ACIT), an organization of economists and lawyers dedicated to the establishment of free trade on a worldwide basis. Their Web site is at http://www.spp.umich.edu/rsie/acit/.

In "White Hats or Don Quixotes? Human Rights Vigilantes in the Global Economy," NBER Working Paper No. W8102 (January 2001), published by the National Bureau of Economic Research, Kimberly Ann Elliott and Richard Freeman examine the pros and cons of codes of conduct for multinationals working in poor countries. They analyze the incentives for corporations to respond to the demand for more equitable treatment of the workforce in these offshore facilities. They conclude that the pressure applied by student activist groups and others who are concerned about sweatshop conditions may be one of those cases "when 'doing good' actually does good." Elliott and Freeman also suggest that a counterpetition to the Academic Consortium on International Trade is being prepared by Robert Pollin of the University of Massachusetts at Amherst and James K. Galbraith of the University of Texas at Austin. As of April 2001 that petition had not appeared.

There is a wealth of antisweatshop literature to examine, much of which is produced by organized labor. The National Labor Committee, for example, provides a wellspring of data on this topic. They can be contacted at nlc@nlcnet.org. In addition, there is an article on sweatshop abuses in nearly every issue of *Working USA*, a journal sponsored by organized labor. In addition to various organized labor groups, you might also check out the Global Alliance for Workers and Communities. This is an initiative of the International Youth Foundation in partnership with the John D. and Catherine T. MacArthur Foundation. Their Web site is http://www.theglobalalliance.org, and their e-mail address is gawc@iyfnet.org. Other pro-worker rights organizations are the Campaign for Labor Rights, the Clean Clothes Campaign, the Collegiate Living Wage Association, the Ethical Trading Initiative, the Global Exchange, the International Labour Organisation, the International Labor Rights Fund, the Investor Responsibility Research Center, Sweatshop Watch, and the UNITE! Stop Sweatshops Campaign.

On the other side you will have no difficulty finding material to support globalization. Start with the National Retail Federation (NRF), which is the largest retail trade organization in the world. It represents 1.4 million U.S. retail establishments, which employ nearly 1 in every 5 American workers—about 20 million workers in all. In October 1999 the NRF issued a document entitled "Myths and Truths: America's Retailers and Sweatshops" and published a statement entitled "A Commitment to Fairness," which details the steps that industry is taking to ensure fair working conditions (see http://www.nrf. com/content/press/swprinciples.htm). The ACIT also provides an up-to-date list of articles that support globalization, which often entails acceptance of sweatshop use. Some of these articles are Daniel W. Drezner, "Bottom Feeders," *Foreign Policy* (November/December 2000); Michael B. Barkey, "Globalization, Social Justice and the Plight of the Poor," Acton Commentary, http:// www.acton.org/research/comment/2000aug/28.html (August 2000); Philip Knight, "A Forum for Improving Globalisation," *Financial Times* (August 1, 2000); Thomas Friedman, "Knight Is Right," *The New York Times* (June 20, 2000); "Assessing Globalization," World Bank Briefing Papers (April 2000); "Globalization: Threat or Opportunity?" IMF Issues Brief (April 12, 2000); and "Trade and Poverty: Is There a Connection?" WTO Special Study No. 5 (March 2000).

Does Global Warming Require Immediate Government Action?

YES: Cynthia Pollock Shea, from "Protecting Life on Earth: Steps to Save the Ozone Layer," *Worldwatch Paper 87* (1988)

NO: Lester B. Lave, from "The Greenhouse Effect: What Government Actions Are Needed?" *Journal of Policy Analysis and Management* (vol. 7, no. 3, 1988)

ISSUE SUMMARY

YES: Cynthia Pollock Shea, a senior researcher with the Worldwatch Institute, argues that governments and industries should initiate a "crash program" designed to halt emissions of chemicals such as chlorofluorocarbons, which deplete the ozone, before irreparable damage is done to world agriculture, marine life, and human health.

NO: Professor of economics Lester B. Lave warns against drastic solutions that could themselves be harmful or, at a minimum, "costly if the greenhouse consequences are more benign than predicted."

The heat wave of the summer of 1988 was a memorable event. Electric bills skyrocketed as air conditioners ran day and night. Bright green lawns turned yellow-brown. Lakes, streams, and reservoirs fell to critically low levels; car washing was discouraged, lawn sprinkling was banned, and toilets were bricked. Citizens and policymakers alike were concerned that the world was entering the long-predicted and much-feared period of global warming associated with the greenhouse effect.

As summer turned to fall, then–presidential candidate George Bush promised voters that if he were elected, he would become the "environmental president." He would protect the environment from the advancing global warming—at least he would attempt to slow its progress. Once elected he joined other heads of state in a Paris environmental summit. This, in turn, led to the policy prescriptions that he introduced in a speech delivered at Georgetown

University in early February 1990. Four broad policies were detailed in this speech:

1. *Increase the information base.* He proposed a sharp increase in U.S. expenditures on studies focused on "global climate change."
2. *Redirect and increase expenditures on basic energy research and development from $16.4 billion to $17.5 billion.* This represented a modest 6.4 percent increase in the Department of Energy's budget and some redistribution of funds from civilian applied research and development programs to grants for basic research.
3. *A phaseout of most chlorofluorocarbons.* In line with a 1987 international agreement, the Montreal Protocol, President Bush proposed a 50 percent cut in the production of these powerful greenhouse gases that attack the ozone layer.
4. *A "plant-a-tree" program.* The Bush administration proposed planting a billion trees each year at a cost of $170 million annually.

The question is whether or not these presidential initiatives are appropriate in light of the costs and benefits of public action to slow or reverse the progress of global warming. Marginal analysis will help to determine how aggressive public policy should be in slowing the progress of global warming. Alternative policies will likely have increasing marginal costs and decreasing marginal benefits as more ambitious programs are employed. Two views of these costs and benefits are provided in the following essays. Cynthia Pollock Shea warns that if decisive action is not taken immediately to protect the ozone layer, we will face serious health hazards, reduced crop yields, decreased fish populations, and industrial damage. Lester B. Lave, on the other hand, argues that there is too much uncertainty to justify rushing forward with sweeping policy action. He preaches moderation.

Since the consequences of these policy decisions may be irreversible and not fully felt for many decades in the future, extreme care must be taken. Older generations may be totally immune from the consequences. It is the younger generations that will pay for any mistakes that are made now.

Cynthia Pollock Shea

 **YES**

Protecting Life on Earth:
Steps to Save the Ozone Layer

W hen British scientists reported in 1985 that a hole in the ozone layer had been occurring over Antarctica each spring since 1979, the news came as a complete surprise. Although the theory that a group of widely used chemicals called chlorofluorocarbons (CFCs) would someday erode upper atmospheric ozone had been advanced in the mid-1970s, none of the models had predicted that the thinning would first be evident over the South Pole—or that it would be so severe.

Ozone, the three-atom form of oxygen, is the only gas in the atmosphere that limits the amount of harmful solar ultraviolet radiation reaching the earth. Most of it is found at altitudes of between 12 and 25 kilometers. Chemical reactions triggered by sunlight constantly replenish ozone above the tropics, and global air circulation transports some of it to the poles.

By the Antarctic spring of 1987, the average ozone concentration over the South Pole was down 50 percent. Although the depletion was alarming, many thought that the thinning was seasonal and unique to Antarctica. But an international group of more than 100 experts reported in March 1988 that the ozone layer around the globe was eroding much faster than models had predicted. Between 1969 and 1986, the average concentration of ozone in the stratosphere had fallen by approximately 2 percent.

As ozone diminishes, the earth receives more ultraviolet radiation, which promotes skin cancers and cataracts and depresses the human immune system. As more ultraviolet radiation penetrates the atmosphere, it will worsen these health effects, reduce crop yields and fish populations, damage some materials such as plastics, and increase smog. Compounds containing chlorine and bromine, which are released from industrial processes and products, are now widely accepted as the primary culprits in ozone depletion. Most of the chlorine comes from CFCs; the bromine originates from halons used in fire extinguishers.

Spurred to action by the ozone hole, 35 countries have signed an international agreement—the Montreal Protocol—aimed at halving most CFC emissions by 1998 and freezing halon emissions by 1992. But the agreement is so riddled with loopholes that its objectives will not be met. Furthermore, scientific findings subsequent to the negotiations reveal that even if the treaty's goals were met, significant further deterioration of the ozone layer would still occur.

New evidence that a global warming may be under way strengthens the need to further control and phase out CFC and halon emissions. With their strong heat-absorbing properties, CFCs and halons are an important contributor to the greenhouse effect. Currently available control technologies and stricter standards governing equipment operation and maintenance could reduce CFC and halon emissions by some 90 percent. But effective government policies and industry practices to limit and ultimately phase out chlorine and bromine emissions have yet to be formulated. Just as the effects of ozone depletion and climate change will be felt worldwide, a lasting remedy to these problems must also be global.

The Ozone Depletion Puzzle

As a result of the efforts of many scientists, the pieces of the ozone depletion puzzle have gradually been falling into place. During the long, sunless Antarctic winter—from about March to August—air over the continent becomes isolated in a swirling polar vortex that causes temperatures to drop below -90 degrees Celsius. This is cold enough for the scarce water vapor in the dry upper atmosphere to freeze and form polar stratospheric clouds. Chemical reactions on the surface of the ice crystals convert chlorine from nonreactive forms such as hydrogen chloride and chlorine nitrate into molecules that are very sensitive to sunlight. Gaseous nitrogen oxides, ordinarily able to inactivate chlorine, are transformed into frozen, and therefore nonreactive, nitric acid.

Spring sunlight releases the chlorine, starting a virulent ozone-destroying chain reaction that proceeds unimpeded for five or six weeks. Molecules of ozone are transformed into molecules of ordinary, two-atom oxygen. The chlorine emerges unscathed, ready to attack more ozone. Diminished ozone in the vortex means the atmosphere there absorbs less incoming solar radiation, thereby perpetuating lower temperatures and the vortex itself.

Paradoxically, the phenomenon of global warming encourages the process. Higher concentrations of greenhouse gases are thought to be responsible for an increase in the earth's surface temperature and a decrease in the temperature of the stratosphere. In addition, methane, one of the primary greenhouse gases, is a significant source of stratospheric water vapor. Colder temperatures and increased moisture both facilitate the formation of stratospheric clouds.

While many of the meteorological and chemical conditions conducive to ozone depletion are unique to Antarctica, ground-based research in Greenland in the winter of 1988 found elevated chlorine concentrations and depressed ozone levels over the Arctic as well. Although a strong vortex does not develop there and temperatures are not as low, polar stratospheric clouds do form.

The theories on how chlorine interacts on the surface of particles in polar stratospheric clouds are leading to worries that similar ozone-depleting reactions may occur around the globe. If chemicals such as sulfate aerosols from volcanoes and human-made sulfurs are capable of hosting the same catalytic reactions, global ozone depletion may accelerate even more rapidly than anticipated.

Consensus about the extent of ozone depletion and its causes strengthened with the release of the NASA Ozone Trends Panel report on March 15, 1988. Ozone losses were documented around the globe, not just at the poles. The blame was firmly placed on chlorofluorocarbons. The panel reported that between 30 and 64 degrees north latitude, where most of the world's people live, the total amount of ozone above any particular point had decreased by between 1.7 and 3 percent in the period from 1969 to 1986 (Table 1). The report further stated that while the problem was worst over Antarctica during the spring, "ozone appears to have decreased since 1979 by 5 percent or more at all latitudes south of 60 degrees south throughout the year." The hole alone covers approximately 10 percent of the Southern Hemisphere.

Within a matter of weeks the report's conclusions were widely accepted, and public debate on the issue began to build. Ozone depletion is occurring far more rapidly and in a different pattern than had been forecast. Projections of the amount and location of future ozone depletion are still highly uncertain. Although the fundamental mechanisms of ozone depletion are generally understood, the effect of cloud surface chemistry, the rate of various chemical reactions, and the specific chemical pathways are still in doubt. According to Sherwood Rowland, one of the first to sound a warning, policy decisions now and for at least another decade must be made without good quantitative guidelines of what the future holds.

Effects of Ultraviolet Radiation

At present, ozone absorbs much of the ultraviolet light that the sun emits in wavelengths harmful to humans, animals, and plants. The most biologically damaging wavelengths are within the 290- to 320-nanometer band, referred to as UV-B. But according to uncertain projections from computer models, erosion of the ozone shield could result in 5 to 20 percent more ultraviolet radiation reaching populated areas within the next 40 years—most of it in the UV-B band.

In light of the findings of the NASA Ozone Trends Panel, the U.S. Environmental Protection Agency (EPA) damage projections cited in this section are conservative. Although the EPA ranges are based on current control strategies, they assume ozone depletion levels of 1.2 to 6.2 percent. Yet all areas of the globe have already suffered depletion beyond this lower bound.

Globally, skin cancer incidence among Caucasians is already on the rise, and it is expected to increase alarmingly in the presence of more UV-B. Some 600,000 new cases of squamous and basal cell carcinoma—the two most common but rarely fatal skin cancer types—are reported each year in the United States alone. Worldwide, the number of cases is at least three times as high. Each 1 percent drop in ozone is projected to result in 4 to 6 percent more cases of these types of skin cancer. The EPA estimates that ozone depletion will lead to an additional 31,000 to 126,000 cases of melanoma—a more deadly form of

Table 1

Global Decline in Atmospheric Ozone, 1969–1986*

Latitude	Year-round decrease (percent)	Winter decrease (percent)
53–64° N	-2.3	-6.2
40–53° N	-3.0	-4.7
30–40° N	-1.7	-2.3
19–30° N	-3.1	n.a.
0–19° N	-1.6	n.a.
0–19° S	-2.1	n.a.
19–29° S	-2.6	n.a.
29–39° S	-2.7	n.a.
39–53° S	-4.9	n.a.
53–60° S	-10.6	n.a.
60–90° S	-5.0 or more	n.a.

---

*Data for the area 30 to 64 degrees north of the equator are based on information gathered from satellites and ground stations from 1969 to 1986. Data for the area from 60 degrees south to the South Pole are based on information gathered from satellites and ground stations since 1979. All other information was compiled after November 1978 from satellite data alone.

Sources: U.S. National Aeronautics and Space Administration, Ozone Trends Panel; Cass Peterson, "Evidence of Ozone Depletion Found Over Big Urban Areas," *The Washington Post,* March 16, 1988.

skin cancer—among U.S. whites born before 2075, resulting in an additional 7,000 to 30,000 fatalities.

Under the same EPA scenarios, from 555,000 to 2.8 million Americans born before 2075 will suffer from cataracts of the eyes who would not have otherwise. Victims will also be stricken earlier in life, making treatment more difficult.

Medical researchers also fear that UV-B depresses the human immune system, lowering the body's resistance to attacking micro-organisms, making it less able to fight the development of tumors, and rendering it more prone to infectious diseases. In developing countries, particularly those near the equator that are exposed to higher UV-B levels, parasitic infections could become more common. The response may even decrease the effectiveness of some inoculation programs, such as those for diphtheria and tuberculosis.

Terrestrial and aquatic ecosystems are also affected. Screenings of more than 200 plant species, most of them crops, found that 70 percent were sensitive to UV-B. Increased exposure to radiation may decrease photosynthesis, water-use efficiency, yield, and leaf area. Soybeans, a versatile and protein-rich crop, are particularly susceptible. One researcher at the University of Maryland discovered that a simulated ozone loss of 25 percent reduced the yield of one important soybean species by as much as 25 percent. He also found that plant sensitivity to UV-B increased as the phosphorus level in the soil increased, indicating that heavily fertilized agricultural areas may be the most vulnerable.

Aquatic ecosystems may be the most threatened of all. Phytoplankton, the one-celled microscopic organisms that engage in photosynthesis while drifting on the ocean's surface, are the backbone of the marine food web. Because they require sunlight, they cannot escape incoming ultraviolet radiation and continue to thrive. Yet if they remain at the water's surface, studies show that a 25 percent reduction in ozone would decrease their productivity by about 35 percent. A significant destruction of phytoplankton and its subsequent decomposition could even raise carbon dioxide levels, speeding the warming of the atmosphere.

Zooplankton and the larvae of several important fish species will be doubly strained: Their sole food supply, phytoplankton, will be scarcer. For some shellfish species, a 10 percent decrease in ozone could result in up to an 18 percent increase in the number of abnormal larvae. Commercial fish populations already threatened by overharvesting may have more difficulty rebuilding due to effects of increased UV-B. Some species will undoubtedly be more vulnerable to increased ultraviolet radiation than others, and the changes are likely to be dramatic. Ultimately, entire ecosystems may become more unstable and less flexible.

Increased UV-B levels also affect synthetic materials, especially plastics, which become brittle. Studies conducted for the EPA estimated that without added chemical stabilizers, the cumulative damage to just one polymer, polyvinyl chloride, could reach $4,700 million by 2075 in the United States alone.

Ironically, as more ultraviolet radiation reaches the ground, the photochemical process that creates smog will accelerate, increasing ground-level ozone. Studies show that ground-level ozone retards crop and tree growth, limits visibility, and impairs lung functions. Urban air quality, already poor in most areas of the world, will worsen. In addition, stratospheric ozone decline is predicted to increase tropospheric amounts of hydrogen peroxide, an acid rain precursor.

Despite the many uncertainties regarding the amount of future ozone depletion, rising UV-B levels, and their biological effects, it is clear that the risks to aquatic and terrestrial ecosystems and to human health are enormous. The central conclusion of the EPA studies is that "the benefits of limiting future CFC/halon use far outweigh the increased costs these regulations would impose on the economy."

Chemical Wonders, Atmospheric Villains

Chlorofluorocarbons are remarkable chemicals. They are neither toxic nor flammable at ground levels, as demonstrated by their discoverer, Thomas Midgley, Jr., in 1930, when he inhaled vapors from a beaker of clear liquid and then exhaled to extinguish a candle. A safe coolant that was inexpensive to produce was exactly what the refrigeration industry needed. E.I. du Pont de Nemours

& Company marketed the compound under the trademark Freon. (In chemical shorthand, it is referred to as CFC-12). International production soared, rising from 545 tons in 1931 to 20,000 tons in 1945. Another use for the chemical, as a blowing agent in rigid insulation foams, was discovered in the late 1940s.

Over time, the versatility of the various CFCs seemed almost endless. CFC-11 and CFC-12 were first used as aerosol propellants during World War II in the fight against malaria. In the postwar economy, they were employed in aerosol products ranging from hairspray and deodorant to furniture polish. By the late 1950s, a combination of blowing agents CFC-11 and carbon dioxide was used to make softer furniture cushions, carpet padding, and automobile seats.

Many social and technological developments in recent decades were assisted by the availability of CFCs. Air conditioners made it possible to build and cool shopping malls, sports arenas, high-rise office buildings, and even automobiles. Artificial cooling brought comfort, business, and new residents to regions with warm climates. And healthier, more interesting diets are now available because food can be refrigerated in the production and distribution chain.

Even the computer revolution was aided by CFCs. As microchips and other components of electronic equipment became smaller and more sophisticated, the need to remove the smallest contaminants became critical. CFC-113 is used as a solvent to remove glue, grease, and soldering residues, leaving a clean, dry surface. CFC-113 is now the fastest growing member of the CFC family; worldwide production exceeds 160,000 tons per year.

An industry-sponsored group, the Alliance for Responsible CFC Policy, pegs the market value of CFCs produced in the United States at $750 million annually, the value of goods and services directly dependent on the chemicals at $28,000 million, and the end-use value of installed equipment and products at $135,000 million. Around the world, aerosols are still the largest user of CFCs, accounting for 25 percent of the total (Table 2). Rigid-foam and solvent applications, the fastest growing uses for CFCs, are tied for second place.

In 1987, global CFC production (excluding the People's Republic of China, the Soviet Union, and Eastern Europe) came close to 1 million tons. Combined production of CFC-11 and CFC-12 accounts for at least three-fourths of this total. Total per capita use of the three most common CFCs is highest in the United States—at 1.22 kilograms—but Europe and Japan are not far behind (Table 3).

From 1931 through 1986, virtually all the CFC-11 and CFC-12 produced was sold to customers in the Northern Hemisphere. Since raw chemicals and products made with and containing CFCs were then exported, in part to developing countries, final usage was not quite as lopsided. Indeed, the Third World accounted for 16 percent of global CFC consumption in 1986 (Table 4). As populations, incomes, and the manufacturing base grow in developing countries, CFC use there is projected to rise.

Halons, which are used in fighting fires in both hand extinguishers and total-flooding systems for large enclosed areas, contain bromine, a more effective ozone destroyer than chlorine. Demand for halons, which were developed in the 1940s, quadrupled between 1973 and 1984 and is still growing at a rate of 15 percent annually.

Table 2

Global CFC Use, by Category, 1985

Use	Share of total (percent)
Aerosols	25
Rigid-foam insulation	19
Solvents	19
Air conditioning	12
Refrigerants	8
Flexible foam	7
Other	10

Source: Daniel F. Kohler and others, *Projections of Consumption of Products Using Chlorofluorocarbons in Developing Countries,* Rand N-2458-EPA, 1987.

Alarming though the latest ozone measurements are, they reflect only the responses to gases released through the early 1980s. Gases now rising through the lower atmosphere will take up to eight years to reach the stratosphere. And an additional 2 million tons of substances containing chlorine and bromine are still on the ground, trapped in insulation foams, appliances, and fire-fighting equipment.

Chlorine concentrations in the upper atmosphere have grown from 0.6 to 2.7 parts per thousand million in the past 25 years. Under even the most optimistic regulatory scenarios, they are expected to triple by 2075. Bromine concentrations are projected to grow considerably faster. Without a complete and rapid phaseout of CFC and halon production, the real losers will be future generations who inherit an impoverished environment.

Table 3

Per Capita Use of CFC-11, CFC-12, and CFC-113, 1986 (Kilograms Per Capita)

	CFC-11	CFC-12	CFC-113	Total*
United States	.34	.58	.31	1.22
Europe	.47	.34	.12	.93
Japan	.23	.29	.43	.91

---

*Rows not completely additive due to trade.

Source: U.S. Environmental Protection Agency, *Regulatory Impact Analysis: Protection of Stratospheric Ozone,* 1987.

Table 4

CFC Consumption by Region, 1986

Region	Share of total (percent)
United States	29
Other industrial countries*	41
Soviet Union, Eastern Europe	14
Other developing countries	14
People's Republic of China, India	2

---

*The European Community accounts for more than half, followed by Japan, Canada, Australia, and others.
Source: "The Ozone Treaty: A Triumph for All," *Update from State,* May/June 1988.

Reducing Emissions

On September 16, 1987, after years of arduous and heated negotiation, the Montreal Protocol on Substances That Deplete the Ozone Layer was signed by 24 countries. Provisions of the agreement include a freeze on CFC production (at 1986 levels) by 1989, a 20 percent decrease in production by 1993, and another 30 percent cut by 1998. Halon production is subject to a freeze based on 1986 levels starting in 1992....

The means to achieve these reductions are left to the discretion of individual nations. Most signatory countries are responding with production limits on chemical manufacturers. Although this approach complies with treaty guidelines, it effectively ensures that only those willing to pay high prices will be able to continue using CFCs. It also places the onus of curbing emissions on the myriad industrial users of the chemicals and on the consumers of products that incorporate them. Moving quickly to protect the ozone layer calls for a different approach—one that targets the largest sources of the most ozone-depleting chemicals.

When concern about the ozone layer first emerged in the 1970s, some industrial country governments responded. Since 56 percent of combined CFC-11 and CFC-12 production in 1974 was used in aerosols, spray cans were an obvious target. Under strong public pressure, Canada, Norway, Sweden, and the United States banned CFC propellants in at least 90 percent of their aerosol products. The change brought economic as well as environmental benefits. Hydrocarbons, the replacement propellant, are less expensive than CFCs and saved the U.S. economy $165 million in 1983 alone. The European Community adopted a different approach. In 1980, the member countries agreed not to increase their capacity to produce these two CFCs and called for a 30 percent reduction in their use in aerosol propellants by 1982 (based on 1976 consumption figures).

Despite rapid growth, CFC-113 emissions may be some of the easiest and most economical to control. The chemical is only used to clean the final product and is not incorporated in it. Thus emissions are virtually immediate; three-fourths result from vapor losses, the remainder from waste disposal. A U.S. ban on land disposal of chlorinated solvents that took effect in November 1986, consideration of similar regulations elsewhere, the high cost of incinerating CFC-113 (because it contains toxic fluorine), and accelerating concern about ozone depletion have all created strong incentives for solvent recovery and recycling.

Since CFC-113 costs about twice as much as other CFCs, investments in recovery and recycling pay off more quickly. Recycling of CFC-113 is now practiced on-site at many large computer companies. Smaller electronics firms, for which in-house recycling is not economical, can sell their used solvents to commercial recyclers or the distributors of some chemical manufacturers.

Capturing CFC emissions from flexible-foam manufacturing can also be accomplished fairly quickly but requires investment in new ventilation systems. New suction systems coupled with carbon adsorption technologies are able to recover from 40 to 90 percent of the CFCs released.

Another area that offers significant savings, at a low cost, is improved design, operating, and maintenance standards for refrigeration and air conditioning equipment. Codes of practice to govern equipment handling are being drawn up by many major trade associations. Key among the recommendations are to require worker training, to limit maintenance and repair work to authorized personnel, to install leak detection systems, and to use smaller refrigerant charges. Another recommendation, to prohibit venting of the refrigerant directly to the atmosphere, requires the use of recovery and recycling technologies.

Careful study of the automobile air conditioning market in the United States, the largest user of CFC-12 in the country, has found that 34 percent of emissions can be traced to leakage, 48 percent occur during recharge and repair servicing, and the remainder happen through accidents, disposal, and manufacturing, in that order. Equipment with better seals and hoses would reduce emissions and result in less need for system maintenance.

Over the longer term, phasing out the use and emissions of CFCs will require the development of chemical substitutes that do not harm the ozone layer. The challenge is to find alternatives that perform the same function for a reasonable cost, that do not require major equipment modifications, that are nontoxic to workers and consumers, and that are environmentally benign....

The time has come to ask if the functions performed by CFCs are really necessary and, if they are, whether they can be performed in new ways. If all known technical control measures were used, total CFC and halon emissions could be reduced by approximately 90 percent. Many of these control strategies are already cost-effective, and more will become so as regulations push up the price of ozone-depleting chemicals. The speed with which controls are introduced will determine the extent of ozone depletion in the years ahead and when healing of the ozone layer will begin.

Beyond Montreal

An international treaty to halve the production of a chemical feared responsible for destroying an invisible shield is unprecedented. But unfortunately, for several reasons, the Montreal Protocol will not save the ozone layer.

First, many inducements were offered to enhance the treaty's appeal to prospective signatories—extended deadlines for developing and centrally planned economies, allowances to accommodate industry restructuring, and loose definitions of the products that can legitimately be traded internationally. The cumulative effect of these loopholes means that, even with widespread participation, the protocol's goal of halving worldwide CFC use by 1998 will not be met.

Second, recent scientific findings show that more ozone depletion has already occurred than treaty negotiators assumed would happen in 100 years. A recent EPA report concluded that by 2075, even with 100 percent global participation in the protocol, chlorine concentrations in the atmosphere would triple. The agreement will not arrest depletion, merely slow its acceleration.

Third, several chemicals not regulated under the treaty are major threats to the ozone layer. Methyl chloroform and carbon tetrachloride together contributed 13 percent of total ozone-depleting chemical emissions in 1985. As the use of controlled chemicals diminishes, the contribution of these two uncontrolled compounds will grow.

The recognition that global warming may have already begun strengthens the case for further and more rapid reductions in CFC emissions. CFCs currently account for 15 to 20 percent of the greenhouse effect and absorb wavelengths of infrared radiation that other greenhouse gases allow to escape. Indeed, one molecule of the most widely used CFCs is as effective in trapping heat as 15,000 molecules of carbon dioxide, the most abundant greenhouse gas. In light of these findings, logic suggests a virtual phase out of CFC and halon emissions by all countries as soon as possible. Releases of other chlorine and bromine-containing compounds not currently covered under the treaty also need to be controlled and in some cases halted.

The timing of the phaseout is crucial. Analysts at EPA examined the effects of a 100 percent CFC phaseout by 1990 and a 95 percent phaseout by 1998. Peak chlorine concentrations would differ by 0.8 parts per thousand million, some one-third of current levels. And under the slower phasedown, atmospheric cleansing would be prolonged considerably: Chlorine levels would remain higher than the peak associated with the accelerated schedule for at least 50 years.

As noted, it is technically feasible to reduce CFC and halon emissions by at least 90 percent. Sweden is the first country to move beyond endorsing a theoretical phaseout. In June 1988 the parliament, after extensive discussions with industry, passed legislation that includes specific deadlines for banning the use of CFCs in new products. Consumption is to be halved by 1991 and virtually eliminated by 1995. Environmental agencies in Britain, the United States, and the Federal Republic of Germany have endorsed emissions reductions of at least

85 percent. Chemical producers in these three countries account for over half the global output of controlled substances.

Levying a tax on newly manufactured CFCs and other ozone-depleting substances is one way governments can cut emissions and accelerate the adoption of alternative chemicals and technologies. If the tax increased in step with mandatory production cutbacks, it would eliminate windfall profits for producers, encourage recovery and recycling processes, stimulate use of new chemicals, and provide a source of funding for new technologies and for needed research. Encouraging investments in recycling networks, incinerators for rigid foams, and collection systems for chemicals that would otherwise be discarded could substantially trim emissions from existing products, from servicing operations, and from new production runs. Research on new refrigeration, air conditioning, and insulation processes is worthy of government support. Unfortunately, international funding for developing such technologies totals less than $5 million.

As mentioned in the text of the Montreal Protocol, results of this research, as well as new technologies and processes, need to be shared with developing countries. Ozone depletion and climate warming are undeniably global in scope. Not sharing information on the most recent developments ensures that environmentally damaging and outdated equipment will continue to be used for years to come, further eroding the Third World technology base....

The scientific fundamentals of ozone depletion and climate change are known, and there is widespread agreement that both have already begun. Although current models of future change vary in their predictions, the evidence is clear enough to warrant an immediate response. Because valuable time was lost when governments and industries relaxed their regulatory and research efforts during the early 1980s, a crash program is now essential. Human health, food supplies, and the global climate all hinge on the support that can be garnered for putting an end to chlorine and bromine emissions.

NO ⤶

Lester B. Lave

The Greenhouse Effect: What Government Actions Are Needed?

Human beings are causing global-scale changes for the first time.... [A]rticles by Gordon MacDonald and Irving Mintzer document the "greenhouse" effect and give some indications of the environmental changes that will result. The possibility of such global changes rouses deep emotions in people: awe that humans have become so powerful, rage that we are tampering with the natural environment on a large scale, and fear that we might create an environment hostile to our progeny. Technologists tend to focus on the first emotion with the optimism that we can also find ways to head off or solve the problems. Environmentalists fix on the second, fearing that humans can only ruin nature. This article focuses on the third, asking what governmental or other social actions are possible and warranted. What should be done now and in the foreseeable future as a result of what is currently known about the atmospheric concentration of greenhouse gases, the resulting climate change, and the consequences for people?

Why Does the Greenhouse Effect Receive So Much Attention?

Scientists have been giving great attention to the greenhouse effect for more than a decade, despite the vast qualitative and quantitative uncertainties. The public joins scientists in the concern that current activities could create a much less hospitable planet in the future. Congress has also directed its concern to these issues. Congress generally regards programs whose impact is more than three to ten years in the future as hopelessly long term; it seems bizarre that greenhouse effects, which are a century or so into the future, have received major Congressional attention....

Greenhouse effects have the attributes of being (1) global (in the sense that all regions are affected), (2) long term (in the sense that near-term effects are undetectable and important effects on people and their well being are perhaps a century in the future), (3) ethical (in the sense that they involve the preferences and well being of people who have not been born yet, as well

From Lester B. Lave, "The Greenhouse Effect: What Government Actions Are Needed?" *Journal of Policy Analysis and Management,* vol. 7, no. 3 (1988). Copyright © 1988 by John Wiley & Sons, Inc. Reprinted by permission. Notes omitted.

339

as plants, animals, and the environment more generally), (4) potentially catastrophic (in the sense that large changes in the environment might result, as well as massive loss of human life and property), and (5) contentious (in the sense that coming to decisions, translating these into agreements, and enforcing agreements would be difficult due to important "spillover" or external effects, uncertainty, the incentives for individual nations to cheat, the difficulty of detecting cheating, and the difficulty of enforcing agreements even after cheating is detected). In addition, many of the likely public investments such as attempts to substitute for carbon dioxide producing activities would be expensive and disruptive. In other words, this set of issues exercises almost all of the tools of policy analysis and poses deep problems to decision analysts. Below, I point out some particularly attractive research areas, such as behavioral reactions, crucial to formulating policy regarding greenhouse gases.

Uncertainty. A dominant question in formulating greenhouse policy is: What is the uncertainty concerning current statements about emissions, atmospheric accumulation, resulting climate changes, and resulting effects on the managed and unmanaged biospheres? . . .

The Department of Energy has put major resources over the past decade into understanding the carbon cycle, the current sources and sinks of carbon in the environment and the mechanisms that handle increasing carbon emissions into the environment. It is safe to say that the carbon cycle is not understood well, with uncertainty regarding perhaps 20% of total sources and sinks of carbon entering the environment. Controversies surround the importance of deforestation, the amount of carbon retained in the atmosphere, the amount being absorbed by the oceans, and the amount being taken up in plants.

The dynamics can be even more difficult to understand, because the oceans hold less carbon as they warm. Thus, there could be a destabilizing feedback of a warmer atmosphere leading to ocean warming, which induces release of carbon to the atmosphere. With the oceans becoming a net source rather than a sink, atmospheric concentrations would increase more rapidly, leading to rapidly increasing atmospheric temperatures, which induce ocean warming and carbon release. Is this scenario one that leads to disaster—or one where the ocean warming takes so long that fossil fuels are fully used and the increased carbon taken up by plants before the oceans warm enough to release appreciable carbon dioxide to the atmosphere? To what extent, and how quickly, would increased plant growth, due to a warmer climate, more rain, and higher atmospheric concentrations of carbon dioxide, absorb much more of the atmospheric carbon and slow or stop atmospheric warming?

The speed with which natural ecosystems can adapt to climate change is also a matter of concern. A large-scale climate change, comparable to a carbon dioxide doubling, has occurred over the last 18,000 years since the end of the last great ice age. While the temperature changes are comparable, the previous change occurred over 18,000 years while the change due to the greenhouse effect would occur over a century or so, perhaps one-hundred times faster. This rate of change could exceed the abilities of natural ecosystems to adapt. The amount of change is small, however, compared to what is currently experienced for the changes from day to night or season to season.

The issues related to carbon dioxide are much different from the issues related to other greenhouse gases. Neither of the two feedback mechanisms sketched above apply to CFC (chlorofluorucarbons) or methane. The Environmental Protection Agency estimates that about half of the atmospheric warming, after a century, would be attributed to gases other than carbon dioxide—an estimate that is markedly different from those of ten years ago. Much needs to be done to understand feedback mechanisms for the other greenhouse gases and to investigate possible interactions among the gases. For example, atmospheric warming is likely to increase the demand for air conditioning, which would lead to greater electricity use (resulting in increased carbon dioxide emissions) and to greater emissions of CFC from compressor leaks. The warming would also increase the demand for insulation, some of which would be foam insulation made with CFC, releasing much more of this gas to the atmosphere.

The current global circulation models are magnificent examples of technical virtuosity. The physical movements and energy fluxes of the atmosphere are described by partial differential equations that are too complicated to be solved explicitly. Thus the models depend upon expert judgment to decide what aspects of the problem should be treated explicitly within the model and how much attention each aspect should get. The current predictions of the consequences of doubling atmospheric carbon dioxide come mainly from models that treat the oceans as if little mixing occurred and there were no currents. The models also ignore many chemical reactions in the atmosphere. Clearly, these models are "wrong" in the sense of being bad examples of reality. But the central question is whether failing to include these elements results in an error of 10% or whether the models could be wrong to the extent of predicting warming when these gases actually result in atmospheric cooling. . . .

As shown below, exploring the consequences of this warming requires detailed predictions or assumptions for each area about climate, storm patterns, and the length of the growing season. These predictions are little more than educated guesses. For the modelers, this uncertainty is a stimulus to do better. For the policy analyst, the uncertainty must be treated explicitly in deciding what actions are warranted now and in the future.

Even vast uncertainty need not preclude taking preventive action. Uncertainty should induce caution and prevent decision makers from rushing into actions and commitments, however. For example, precipitous action would have led to forbidding military and 747 flights in the stratosphere in the early 1970s. Then, in the late 1970s, precipitous action might have led to building aircraft to fly in the stratosphere as much as possible. Finally, today aircraft flights in the stratosphere are regarded as irrelevant to stratospheric ozone levels.

It is prudent to be concerned about potentially disastrous effects and to be willing to take some actions now, even given the uncertainty. For example, American regulators insisted on building strong containment vessels around civilian nuclear reactors, even though they regarded the chance of a mishap that would require the containment vessel as remote. The USSR regulators did not insist on such safeguards, with quite different results between the problems at Three Mile Island and the tragedy at Chernobyl.

While there is major uncertainty, the policy conclusions about CFC emissions are different today from those about carbon dioxide emissions, as I discuss below.

Accounting for the uncertainty. The long-term effects of an increase in greenhouse gases are unknown and almost certainly unknowable. The physical changes, such as the gross increase in temperature for each latitude might be predicted, but it is unlikely that the dates of last frost and first freeze and detailed patterns of precipitation will be known for each growing area. Still more difficult to forecast is the adaptive behavior of individuals and governments. The accumulation of greenhouse gases could be enormously beneficial or catastrophic for humans. Or more likely, it would be beneficial at some times and places and catastrophic at others.

Preventive actions are akin to purchasing an insurance policy against potentially catastrophic greenhouse effects. Most people voluntarily purchase life insurance, even though the likelihood of dying in a particular year is very small. I suspect that people would be willing to pay a premium for a policy that would protect against an inhospitable Earth a century or so hence. But, the question is what type of insurance policy is most attractive and how much of a premium are people willing to pay.

Preventing all greenhouse effects is virtually impossible. If the climate changes and resultant human consequences are to be headed off, then heroic actions would be required immediately to reduce emissions of all the greenhouse gases throughout the world. For example, nuclear plants could be built to phase out all coal-burning plants within several decades. The decision to do that would be enormously expensive and disruptive. Such a decision would have to be agreed to in every country and enormous resources would be required to implement it. I would not support such a decision for many reasons.

Short of such heroic measures, are there any actions that might be taken now, even though uncertainty dominates the predictions of effects? Prudence would dictate that we should take actions that might prove highly beneficial, even if they are unlikely to be needed, if their cost is small. Proscribing coal use is not an attractive insurance policy, but we should give serious consideration to limiting the growth rate of coal use. The world discovered after 1974 that there was not a one-to-one coupling of energy use and economic activity. Since then, the developed countries have experienced a considerable increase in economic activity while most countries use little or no more energy than in 1974. Reducing the emissions of other greenhouse gases would be less difficult and disruptive than large reductions in coal use. In particular, it is not difficult or expensive to switch to CFC substitutes that are less damaging and to stop using these chemicals as foaming agents for plastics and in consumer products.

Thus, one of the best ways to deal with uncertainty is to look for robust actions, actions that would be beneficial in the worst case, not harmful in other cases, and not very costly to take. Emphasizing energy conservation is perhaps the best example of a prudent policy. Conservation makes sense without any appeal to greenhouse effects, given the deaths and disease associated with mining, transport, and air pollution from coal. The greenhouse effects simply underline what is already an obvious conclusion, but not one that is being pursued vigorously. So much energy could be saved by adjusting fully to current market prices that sufficient conservation might be attained merely by encouraging this adjustment. In particular, large subsidies to energy use distort resource-allocation decisions significantly.

A second example of an inexpensive insurance policy is switching to less damaging CFCs and using less of them.

Another approach is to develop a strategy of reevaluation at fixed intervals or as new information becomes available. Instead of viewing the current decision as the only opportunity to worry about greenhouse issues, one can attempt to clarify which particular outcomes would cause greatest concern. Then one could revisit the issues periodically to see if uncertainty has been resolved or at least substantially diminished.

Social and Economic Consequences of Climate Change

Announcement of an invention, such as a new drug, is generally greeted with public approval. Certainly there is recognition that innovations may bring undesired consequences, such as occurred with Thalidomide, and so premarket testing and technology assessment have been established and emphasized in many regulatory areas. An innovation seems to be defined in terms of the intent of the inventor to produce something that will make society better or at least to make him richer. On net, it is fair to say that such innovations are viewed positively, with the untoward consequences to be dealt with if they arise.

In contrast, an environmental change such as the greenhouse effect is viewed with horror. Such changes are generally not desired by anyone, but rather emerge as the unintended consequences of society's actions. Those who are horrified might admit that there are some changes that are likely to be beneficial, but they would still regard the overall effect as catastrophic. People tend to be more alarmed by large-scale, rapid environmental changes because the consequences would be important and uncontrollable.

Why are Americans such determined optimists about new technology and such determined pessimists about environmental changes? I suspect that much of the difference is explained by the good intent of the inventor versus the unintended nature of the environmental change. If so, this suggests that people have unwarranted faith in the good intentions of inventors, compared to the unintended changes from taking resources or using the environment as a garbage pail.

Deriving the social and economic consequences of climate change is more difficult than might appear. To be sure, if an area becomes so hot or dry that habitation is impossible, or if an area is under water, the consequences are evident. Thus, if sea level rose, the low-lying parts of Louisiana, Florida, Bangladesh, and the Netherlands would be drastically affected. The vast number of short-term effects are difficult to predict and evaluate. Furthermore, the long-term changes are likely to be less drastic (adjustment occurs to mitigate the difficulties, although this might take a long term for an ecosystem), and so the consequences will be even more difficult to infer.

In particular, a change in climate presents a challenge to farmers. If summers are hotter and drier in the corn belt, then a farmer growing corn in Illinois is going to experience crop failure more frequently, due both to droughts and to heat damage. As the climate changes, rare crop damage will give rise to occasional and then frequent damage. Will the Illinois farmer keep planting corn, surviving with the aid of ever-larger government subsidies? Or will he plant new crops that flourish under the hotter, drier climate?

Climate change also presents an opportunity. Sylvan Wittwer, a noted agronomist, observed that " ... the present level of atmospheric carbon dioxide is suboptimal, and the oxygen level is supraoptimal, for photosynthesis and primary productivity in the great majority of plants." The increased atmospheric carbon dioxide concentrations would enhance growth and water-use efficiency, leading to more and faster growth. Charles Cooper remarks that a doubled atmospheric concentration of carbon dioxide " ... is about as likely to increase global food, at least in the long run, as to decrease it. It is certain though, that some nations, regions, and people will gain and others will lose." A new climate regime with more precipitation and a longer growing season bodes well for agriculture—if we figure out what crops to plant and figure out generally how to tailor agriculture to the new climate regime, and how to deal with new pests.

The midcontinental drying, if it occurs, could mean the end of current agricultural practices in the midwest. This climate change might induce more irrigation, dry farming practices such as have been demonstrated in Israel, new cultivars, different crops, or even ceasing to cultivate this land. The increased rains might mean there was sufficient winter precipitation to provide water for summer irrigation; it would certainly mean that there was sufficient water elsewhere in the country to be transported to the midwest for irrigation. Large dams and canals might be required, but the technology for this is available. Certainly this water would be more expensive than that currently available, but there is no reason to be concerned about starvation or even large increases in food prices for the U.S. On net, food and fibers might be slightly more expensive or less expensive in the U.S. under the new climate, but the change is almost certain to be small compared to other economic changes.

For the U.S., there is no difficulty with finding the appropriate technology for breeding new crops that fit the climate, developing a less water-intensive agriculture, or for moving water for irrigation. The difficulty would be whether agronomists are given the right tasks, whether farmers give up their old crops and farming methods, and whether society can solve the myriad social problems associated with damming newly enlarged rivers and moving the water to where it is needed.

The "less managed" areas, including forests, grasslands, and marsh, might experience large changes and a system far from long-term equilibrium. These effects would be scarcely discernable in measured gross national product, but would be viewed as extremely important by many environmentalists.

Water projects and resources more generally might pose a greater problem. Large-scale water projects, such as dams and canals, are built to last for long periods. Once built, they are not easily changed. Thus, major climate change could lead to massive dams fed by tiny streams or dams completely inadequate for the rivers they are designed to control. Similarly, treaty obligations for the Colorado are inflexible and could pose major problems if there is less water flowing down the river. Similarly, the climate change would induce migration, both across areas in the U.S. and from other countries. The legal and illegal migration could pose major problems. Finally, Americans treasure certain natural resources, such as waterfalls. Climate change that stopped the flow at popular falls would be regarded seriously.

Commenting on energy modeling, Hans Landsberg wrote: " ... all of us who have engaged in projecting into the more distant future take ourselves too seriously.... What is least considered is how many profound turns in the road one would have missed making 1980 projections in 1930! I am not contending that the emperor is naked, but we surely overdress him."

Reprise: Why So Much Concern for the Greenhouse Effect?

It is the symbolic nature of the issues that has drawn attention to the greenhouse effect. Anyone who thinks he can see 100 years into the future is mad. If humans have now acquired the power to influence the global environment, then it is likely that we will cause changes even larger than those discussed here within the next century or so. Both the greenhouse effect and other global changes could be predominantly beneficial or harmful to humans and various aspects of the environment, although they are likely to be beneficial in some times and places and detrimental in others. But a large element of the public debate is almost scandalized at the notion that the changes might be beneficial or made beneficial by individual actions and government policies.

The difficulty is public concern that global scale effects are now possible; we have had a "loss of innocence." In the past, if an individual ruined a plot of land, he could move on. If human actions caused major problems such as the erosion of the Dalmatian coast of Yugoslavia, there was always other inviting land. But, if the Earth is made inhospitable, there is no other inviting planet readily at hand.

I share this concern, but find it naive. Having acquired the power to influence the global environment, there is no way to relinquish it. No one intends to change the global environment by emitting greenhouse gases. Rather, the change is an inadvertent consequence of business as usual. The culprit is not a malevolent individual or rapacious company. Instead, it is the scope of human activities stemming from a large population, modern technology, and an unbelievable volume of economic activity. These culprits are not going to disappear, however much we might all wish that people did not have the ability to affect our basic environment. In this sense, the human race has lost its environmental innocence.

The symbolism is important because of the need to educate the public and government and gauge their reactions to this first global environmental issue. If people and governments show themselves to be concerned and willing to make sacrifices, the prospect for the future looks brighter. If instead, each individual and nation regards the effects as primarily due to others, and as someone else's problem, the increases in economic activity and advances in technology promise a future with major unintended changes in the Earth's environment.

Such changes could be dealt with by concerned global action to stop the stimulus and thus the response. Or they could be dealt with by individual and national actions to adapt to the consequences. However much I might wish for concerted action among countries, I do not believe this is likely to occur. There are too many disparate interests, too much to be gained by cheating, too much suspicion of the motives of others, and too little control over all the relevant actors. Thus, reluctantly, I conclude that mitigation through adaptation must be our focus.

For example, within the United States, federal environmental laws have been only a modest success in preventing environmental pollution. Ozone problems have worsened, ground water has become more polluted, and we seem no closer to dealing with radioactive and toxic wastes. When the scope of the problem becomes international, as with acid rain, there is little or no progress. Curtailing sulfur oxides emissions into the air necessarily involves promoting some interests while hurting others. Those who would be hurt are, not surprisingly, more skeptical about whether low levels of acid sulfate aerosols cause disease than those who believe that they would benefit. Getting agreement on action has proven essentially impossible for abating sulfur oxides. It is hard to imagine that a debate among 140 nations on the greenhouse effect would lead to an agreement to adopt binding programs to abate emissions.

A multinational agreement on controlling CFC has been negotiated in 1987. This is an extremely encouraging, and surprising development. There are many obstacles to effective implementation, however, from ratification by each country to best faith efforts to abide by the sense of the agreement.

Conclusion

The greenhouse effect is the first of what are likely to be many long-term, global problems. Analysis is difficult because of the vast uncertainty about causes and effects, as well as of the consequences of the resulting climate change. The current uncertainties together with the costs of precipitous action imply that heroic actions to curtail the emissions of all greenhouse gases are not justified. Nonetheless, the current facts support a program of energy conservation, abatement, research, and periodic reconsideration that is far more activist than the current policy of the U.S. government.

I would like to thank Stephen Schneider and Jesse Ausubel for comments. This work was supported in part by the National Science Foundation (Grant No. SES-8715564).

POSTSCRIPT

Does Global Warming Require Immediate Government Action?

The harsh reality is that the environment is deteriorating. Very few, if any, physical scientists dispute this fact. What is disputed is the rate of decline in the global environment and whether or not citizens acting at the beginning of the twenty-first century should try to alter this process. Do we have enough knowledge of the future to take dramatic steps today that will reshape the world of tomorrow? This is a hard question. If we answer incorrectly, our children and our children's children may curse us for our lack of resolve to solve environmental problems that were clear for all to see.

Shea and Lave agree that there is a clear and present danger associated with ozone-depleting chemicals, such as chlorofluorocarbons, which are also the gases that contribute to the greenhouse effect. What they disagree on is whether or not we know enough today to take immediate, decisive action. Do *you* know enough? If you do not, we suggest that you read further in this area. *It is your future that is being discussed here.*

A brief history of scientific concerns about the greenhouse effect, which stretches back to the late nineteenth century, is found in Jesse H. Ausubel, "Historical Note," in the National Research Council's *Changing Climate: Report of the Carbon Dioxide Assessment Committee* (National Academy Press, 1983). We should note that there are a number of other essays in *Changing Climate* that may be of interest to you. The Environmental Protection Agency (EPA) has published many studies you might want to examine. See, for example, the EPA's study entitled *The Potential Effects of Global Climate Change on the United States* (December 1989) and *Policy Options for Stabilizing Global Climate* (February 1989). An extensive analysis of the scientific, economic, and policy implications are also found in the *1990 Economic Report of the President.*

Should Pollution Be Put
to the Market Test?

YES: Alan S. Blinder, from *Hard Heads, Soft Hearts: Tough-Minded Economics for a Just Society* (Addison-Wesley, 1987)

NO: Frank Ackerman and Kevin Gallagher, from "Getting the Prices Wrong: The Limits of Market-Based Environmental Policy," *Global Development and Environment Institute Working Paper 00-05* (October 2000)

ISSUE SUMMARY

YES: Alan S. Blinder, a former member of the Board of Governors of the Federal Reserve System, urges policymakers to use the energy of the market to solve America's environmental problems.

NO: Economist Frank Ackerman and environmental policy analyst Kevin Gallagher contend that there is an important distinction between using market forces as a "tool" and using competitive markets as a "blueprint" to solve environmental problems. They argue that environmental goals should be set through the use of "public deliberation" and that at times those goals "may have no inherent relationship to the market."

Markets sometimes fail. That is, markets sometimes do not automatically yield optimum, economically efficient answers. This is because prices sometimes do not reflect the true social costs and benefits of consumption and production. The culprit here is the presence of externalities. Externalities are spillover effects that impact third parties who had no voice in the determination of an economic decision.

If, for example, my friend and coeditor Frank J. Bonello decided to "cut a few corners" to hold down the costs of his commercially produced banana cream pies, he might well create a *negative externality* for his neighbors. That is, if in the dark of night, Bonello slipped to the back of his property and dumped his banana skins, egg shells, and other waste products into the St. Joe River, which borders his property, part of the cost of producing banana cream pies would be borne by those who live downstream from the Bonello residence. Since the full costs of production are not borne by Bonello, he can set a competitively attractive price and sell many more pies than his competitors, whom we assume must pay to have their waste products carted away.

If Bonello is not forced to internalize the negative externality associated with his production process, the price attached to his pies gives an improper market signal with regard to the true scarcity of resources. In brief, because Bonello's pies are cheaper than his competitors', demanders will flock to his doorstep to demand more and more of his pies, unknowingly causing him to dump more and more negative externalities on his neighbors downstream.

In this case, as in other cases of firms casting off negative externalities, the public sector may have to intervene and mandate that these externalities be internalized. This is not always an easy task, however. Two difficult questions must be answered: (1) Who caused the external effect? Was it only Bonello's banana cream pie production? and (2) Who bore the costs of the negative externality, and what are their losses? These questions require detective work. We must not only identify the source of the pollution, but we must also identify the people who have been negatively affected by its presence and determine their "rights" in this situation. Once this has been achieved, the difficult task of evaluating and measuring the negative effects must be undertaken.

Even if this can be successfully negotiated, one last set of questions remains: What alternative methods can be used to force firms to internalize their externalities, and which of these methods are socially acceptable and economically efficient? This is the subject of the debate that follows.

Alan S. Blinder warns about the limitations inherent in a market solution to the pollution problem; however, he still strongly advocates using the market to rid the world of the harmful effects of pollution. Frank Ackerman and Kevin Gallagher, on the other hand, contend that there are clear limits to the effectiveness of private market solutions. They maintain that, many times, old-fashioned regulations can be even more effective.

 **YES**

Cleaning Up the Environment: Sometimes Cheaper Is Better

We cannot give anyone the option of polluting for a fee.

— Senator Edmund Muskie
(in Congress, 1971)

In the 1960s, satirist Tom Lehrer wrote a hilarious song warning visitors to American cities not to drink the water or breathe the air. Now, after the passage of more than two decades and the expenditure of hundreds of billions of dollars, such warnings are less appropriate—at least on most days! Although the data base on which their estimates rest is shaky, the Environmental Protection Agency (EPA) estimates that the volume of particulate matter suspended in the air (things like smoke and dust particles) fell by half between 1973 and 1983. During the same decade, the volume of sulfur dioxide emissions declined 27 percent and lead emissions declined a stunning 77 percent. Estimated concentrations of other air pollutants also declined. Though we still have some way to go, there is good reason to believe that our air is cleaner and more healthful than it was in the early 1970s. While the evidence for improved average water quality is less clear (pardon the pun), there have at least been spectacular successes in certain rivers and lakes.

All this progress would seem to be cause for celebration. But economists are frowning—and not because they do not prize cleaner air and water, but rather because our current policies make environmental protection far too costly. America can achieve its present levels of air and water quality at far lower cost, economists insist. The nation is, in effect, shopping for cleaner air and water in a high-priced store when a discount house is just around the corner. Being natural cheapskates, economists find this extravagance disconcerting. Besides, if we shopped in the discount store, we would probably buy a higher-quality environment than we do now. . . .

Is Pollution an Economic Problem?

. . . Nothing in this discussion . . . implies that the appropriate level of environmental quality is a matter for the free market to determine. On the contrary, the market mechanism is ill suited to the task; if left to its own devices, it will certainly produce excessive environmental degradation. Why? Because users of clean air and water, unlike users of oil and steel, are not normally made to pay for the product.

Consider a power plant that uses coal, labor, and other inputs to produce electricity. It buys all these items on markets, paying market prices. But the plant also spews soot, sulfur dioxide, and a variety of other undesirables into the air. In a real sense, it "uses up" clean air—one of those economic goods which people enjoy—without paying a penny. Naturally, such a plant will be sparing in its use of coal and labor, for which it pays, but extravagant in its use of clean air, which is offered for free.

That, in a nutshell, is why the market fails to safeguard the environment. When items of great value, like clean air and water, are offered free of charge it is unsurprising that they are overused, leaving society with a dirtier and less healthful environment than it should have.

The analysis of why the market fails suggests the remedy that economists have advocated for decades: charge polluters for the value of the clean air or water they now take for free. That will succeed where the market fails because an appropriate fee or tax per unit of emissions will, in effect, put the right price tag on clean air and water—just as the market now puts the right price tag on oil and steel. Once our precious air and water resources are priced correctly, polluters will husband them as carefully as they now husband coal, labor, cement, and steel. Pollution will decline. The environment will become cleaner and more healthful....

The Efficiency Argument

It is now time to explain why economists insist that emissions fees can clean up the environment at lower cost than mandatory quantitative controls. The secret is the market's unique ability to accommodate individual differences—in this case, differences among polluters.

Suppose society decides that emissions of sulfur dioxide must decline by 20 percent. One obvious approach is to mandate that every source of sulfur dioxide reduce its emissions by 20 percent. Another option is to levy a fee on discharges that is large enough to reduce emissions by 20 percent. The former is the way our current environmental regulations are often written. The latter is the economist's preferred approach. Both reduce pollution to the same level, but the fee system gets there more cheaply. Why? Because a system of fees assigns most of the job to firms that can reduce emissions easily and cheaply and little to firms that find it onerous and expensive to reduce their emissions.

Let me illustrate how this approach works with a real example. A study in St. Louis found that it cost only $4 for one paper-products factory to cut particulate emissions from its boiler by a ton, but it cost $600 to do the same job at a brewery. If the city fathers instructed both the paper plant and the brewery to cut emissions by the same amount, pollution abatement costs would be low at the paper factory but astronomical at the brewery. Imposing a uniform emissions tax is a more cost-conscious strategy. Suppose a $100/ton tax is announced. The paper company will see an opportunity to save $100 in taxes by spending $4 on cleanup, for a $96 net profit. Similarly, any other firm whose pollution-abatement costs are less than $100 per ton will find it profitable to cut emissions. But firms like the brewery, where pollution-abatement costs exceed $100 per ton, will prefer to continue polluting and paying the tax. Thus the profit motive will automatically assign the task of pollution abatement to the low-cost firms—something no regulators can do.

Mandatory proportional reductions have the seductive appearance of "fairness" and so are frequently adopted. But they provide no incentive to minimize the social costs of environmental clean-up. In fact, when the heavy political hand requires equal percentage reductions by every firm (or perhaps from every smokestack), it pretty much guarantees that the social clean-up will be far more costly than it need be. In the previous example, a one-ton reduction in annual emissions by both the paper factory and the brewery would cost $604 per year. But the same two-ton annual pollution abatement would cost only $8 if the paper factory did the whole job. Only by lucky accident will equiproportionate reductions in discharges be efficient.

Studies that I will cite later . . . suggest that market-oriented approaches to pollution control can reduce abatement costs by 90 percent in some cases. Why, economists ask, is it more virtuous to make pollution reduction hurt more? They have yet to hear a satisfactory answer and suspect there is none. On the contrary, virtue and efficiency are probably in harmony here. If cleaning up our air and water is made cheaper, it is reasonable to suppose that society will buy more clean-up. We can have a purer environment and pay less, too. The hard-headed economist's crass means may be the surest route to the soft-hearted environmentalist's lofty ends.

The Enforcement Argument

Some critics of emissions fees argue that a system of fees would be hard to enforce. In some cases, they are correct. We obviously cannot use effluent charges to reduce concentrations of the unsightly pollutant glop if engineers have yet to devise an effective and dependable devise for measuring how much glop firms are spewing out. If we think glop is harmful, but are unable to monitor it, our only alternative may be to require firms to switch to "cleaner" technologies. Similarly, emissions charges cannot be levied on pollutants that seep unseen— and unmeasured—into groundwater rather than spill out of a pipe.

In many cases, however, those who argue that emissions fees are harder to enforce than direct controls are deceiving themselves. If you cannot measure emissions, you cannot charge a fee, to be sure. But neither can you enforce mandatory standards; you can only delude yourself into thinking you are enforcing them. To a significant extent, that is precisely what the EPA does now. Federal antipollution regulations are poorly policed; the EPA often declares firms in compliance based on nothing more than the firms' self-reporting of their own behavior. When checks are made, noncompliance is frequently uncovered. If emissions can be measured accurately enough to enforce a system of quantitative controls, we need only take more frequent measurements to run a system of pollution fees.

Besides, either permits or taxes are much easier to administer than detailed regulations. Under a system of marketable permits, the government need only conduct periodic auctions. Under a system of emissions taxes, the enforcement mechanism is the relentless and anonymous tax collector who basically reads your meter like a gas or electric company. No fuss, no muss, no bother—and no need for a big bureaucracy. Just a bill. The only way to escape the pollution tax is to exploit the glaring loophole that the government deliberately provides: reduce your emissions.

Contrast this situation with the difficulties of enforcing the cumbersome command-and-control system we now operate. First, complicated statutes must be passed; and polluting industries will use their considerable political muscle in state legislatures and in Congress to fight for weaker laws. Next, the regulatory agencies must write detailed regulations defining precise standards and often prescribing the "best available technology" to use in reducing emissions. Here again industry will do battle, arguing for looser interpretations of the statutes and often turning the regulations to their own advantage. They are helped in this effort by the sheer magnitude of the information-processing task that the law foists upon the EPA and state agencies, a task that quickly outstrips the capacities of their small staffs.

Once detailed regulations are promulgated, the real problems begin. State and federal agencies with limited budgets must enforce these regulations on thousands, if not millions, of sources of pollution. The task is overwhelming. As one critic of the system put it, each polluter argues:

> (1) he is in compliance with the regulation; (2) if not, it is because the regulation is unreasonable as a general rule; (3) if not, then the regulation is unreasonable in this specific case; (4) if not, then it is up to the regulatory agency to tell him how to comply; (5) if forced to take the steps recommended by the agency, he cannot be held responsible for the results; and (6) he needs more time....

Other Reasons to Favor Emissions Fees

Yet other factors argue for market-based approaches to pollution reduction.

One obvious point is that a system of mandatory standards, or one in which a particular technology is prescribed by law, gives a firm that is in compliance with the law no incentive to curtail its emissions any further. If the law says that the firm can emit up to 500 tons of glop per year, it has no reason to spend a penny to reduce its discharges to 499 tons. By contrast, a firm that must pay $100 per ton per year to emit glop can save money by reducing its annual discharges as long as its pollution-abatement costs are less than $100 per ton. The financial incentive to reduce pollution remains.

A second, and possibly very important, virtue of pollution fees is that they create incentives for firms to devise or purchase innovative ways to reduce emissions. Under a system of effluent fees, businesses gain if they can find cheaper ways to control emissions because their savings depend on their pollution abatement, not on how they achieve it. Current regulations, by contrast, often dictate the technology. Firms are expected to obey the regulators, not to search for creative ways to reduce pollution at lower cost.

For this and other reasons, our current system of regulations is unnecessarily adversarial. Businesses feel the government is out to harass them—and they act accordingly. Environmental protection agencies lock horns with industry in the courts. The whole enterprise takes on the atmosphere of a bullfight rather than that of a joint venture. A market-based approach, which made clear that the government wanted to minimize the costs it imposed on business, would naturally create a more cooperative spirit. That cannot be bad.

Finally, the appearance of fairness when regulations take the form of uniform percentage reductions in emissions, as they frequently do, is illusory. Suppose Clean Jeans, Inc. has already spent a considerable sum to reduce the amount of muck it spews into the Stench River. Dirty Jeans, Inc., just downriver, has not spent a cent and emits twice as much. Now a law is passed requiring every firm along the Stench to reduce its emissions by 50 percent. That has the appearance of equity but not the substance. For Dirty Jeans, the regulation may be a minor nuisance. To comply, it need only do what Clean Jeans is already doing voluntarily. But the edict may prove onerous to Clean Jeans, which has already exploited all the cheap ways to cut emissions. In this instance, not only is virtue not its own reward—it actually brings a penalty! Such anomalies cannot arise under a system of marketable pollution permits. Clean Jeans would always have to buy fewer permits than Dirty Jeans. . . .

Objections to "Licenses to Pollute"

Despite the many powerful arguments in favor of effluent taxes or marketable emissions permits, many people have an instinctively negative reaction to the whole idea. Some environmentalists, in particular, rebel at economists' advocacy of market-based approaches to pollution control—which they label "licenses to pollute," a term not meant to sound complimentary. Former Senator Muskie's dictum, quoted at the beginning of this chapter, is an example. The question is: Are the objections to "licenses to pollute" based on coherent arguments that should sway policy, or are they knee-jerk reactions best suited to T-shirts?* My own view is that there is little of the former and much of the latter. Let me explain.

Some of the invective heaped upon the idea of selling the privilege to pollute stems from an ideologically based distrust of markets. Someone who does not think the market a particularly desirable way to organize the production of automobiles, shirts, and soybeans is unlikely to trust the market to protect the environment. As one congressional staff aide put it: "The philosophical assumption that proponents of [emissions] charges make is that there is a free-market

---

* [Earlier in his book, Blinder warns his readers about simplistic answers to complex questions. He concludes that "if it fits on a T-shirt, it is almost certainly wrong."—Eds.]

system that responds to ... relative costs.... I reject that assumption." This remarkably fatuous statement ignores mountains of evidence accumulated over centuries. Fortunately, it is a minority view in America. Were it the majority view, our economic problems would be too severe to leave much time for worry about pollution.

Some of the criticisms of pollution fees are based on ignorance of the arguments or elementary errors in logic. As mentioned earlier, few opponents of market-based approaches can even explain why economists insist that emissions fees will get the job done more cheaply.

One commonly heard objection is that a rich corporation confronted with a pollution tax will pay the tax rather than reduce its pollution. That belief shows an astonishing lack of respect for avarice. Sure, an obstinate but profitable company *could* pay the fees rather than reduce emissions. But it would do that only if the marginal costs of pollution abatement exceed the fee. Otherwise, its obduracy reduces its profits. Most corporate executives faced with a pollution tax will improve their bottom lines by cutting their emissions, not by flouting the government's intent. To be sure, it is self-interest, not the public interest, that motivates the companies to clean up their acts. But that's exactly the idea behind pollution fees....

One final point should lay the moral issue to rest. Mandatory quantitative standards for emissions are also licenses to pollute—just licenses of a strange sort. They give away, with neither financial charge nor moral condemnation, the right to spew a specified amount of pollution into the air or water. Then they absolutely prohibit any further emissions. Why is such a license morally superior to a uniform tax penalty on all pollution? Why is a business virtuous if it emits 500 tons of glop per year but sinful if it emits 501? Economists make no claim to be arbiters of public morality. But I doubt that these questions have satisfactory answers.

The choice between direct controls and effluent fees, then, is not a moral issue. It is an efficiency issue. About that, economists know a thing or two.

Having made my pitch, I must confess that there are circumstances under which market-based solutions are inappropriate and quantitative standards are better. One obvious instance is the case of a deadly poison. If the socially desirable level of a toxin is zero, there is no point in imposing an emission fee. An outright ban makes more sense.

Another case is a sudden health emergency. When, for example, a summertime air inversion raises air pollution in Los Angeles or New York to hazardous levels, it makes perfect sense for the mayors of those cities to place legal limits on driving, on industrial discharges, or on both. There is simply no time to install a system of pollution permits.

A final obvious case is when no adequate monitoring device exists, as in the case of runoff from soil pollution. Then a system of emissions fees is out of the question. But so also is a system of direct quantitative controls on emissions. The only viable way to control such pollution may be to mandate that cleaner technologies be used.

But each of these is a minor, and well recognized, exception to an overwhelming presumption in the opposite direction. No sane person has ever proposed selling permits to spill arsenic into water supplies. None has suggested that the mayor of New York set the effluent tax on carbon monoxide anew after hearing the weather forecast each morning. And no one has insisted that we must meter what cannot be measured. Each of these objections is a debater's point, not a serious challenge to the basic case for market-oriented approaches to environmental protection....

Rays of Hope: Emissions Trading and Bubbles

There are signs, however, that environmental policy may be changing for the better. The EPA seems to be drifting slowly, and not always surely, away from technology-driven direct controls toward more market-oriented approaches. But not because the agency has been convinced by the logic of economists' arguments. Rather, it was driven into a corner by the inexorable illogic of its own procedures. Necessity proved to be the midwife of common sense.

The story begins in the 1970s, when it became apparent that many regions of the country could not meet the air quality standards prescribed by the Clean Air Act. Under the law, the prospective penalty for violating of the standards was Draconian: no new sources of pollution would be permitted in these regions and existing sources would not be allowed to increase their emissions, implying a virtual halt to local economic growth. The EPA avoided the impending clash between the economy and the environment by creating its "emissions-offsets" program in 1976. Under the new rules, companies were allowed to create new sources of pollution in areas with substandard air quality as long as they reduced their pollution elsewhere by greater amounts. Thus was emissions trading born.

The next important step was invention of the "bubble" concept in 1979. Under this concept, all sources of pollution from a single plant or firm are imagined to be encased in a mythical bubble. The EPA then tells the company that it cares only about total emissions into the bubble. How these emissions are parceled out among the many sources of pollution under the bubble is no concern of the EPA. But it is vital to the firm, which can save money by cutting emissions in the least costly way. A striking example occurred in 1981 when a DuPont plant in New Jersey was ordered to reduce its emissions from 119 sources by 85 percent. Operating under a state bubble program, company engineers proposed instead that emissions from seven large stacks be reduced by 99 percent. The result? Pollution reduction exceeded the state's requirement by 2,300 tons per year and DuPont saved $12 million in capital costs and $3 million per year in operating costs.

Partly because it was hampered by the courts, the bubble concept was little used at first. But bubbles have been growing rapidly since a crucial 1984 judicial decision. By October 1984, about seventy-five bubbles had been approved by the EPA and state authorities and hundreds more were under review or in various stages of development. The EPA estimated the cost savings from all these bubbles to be about $800 million per year. That may seem a small sum compared to the more than $70 billion we now spend on environmental protection. But remember that the whole program was still in the experimental stage, and these bubbles covered only a tiny fraction of the thousands of industrial plants in the United States.

The bubble program was made permanent only when EPA pronounced the experiment a success and issued final guidelines in November 1986. Economists greeted this announcement with joy. Environmentalist David Doniger... complained that, "The bubble concept is one of the most destructive impediments to the cleanup of unhealthy air." By now, many more bubbles have been approved or are in the works. Time will tell who was right.

The final step in the logical progression toward the economist's approach would be to make these "licenses to pollute" fully marketable so that firms best able to reduce emissions could sell their excess abatement to firms for which pollution abatement is too expensive. Little trading has taken place to date, though the EPA's November 1986 guidelines may encourage it. But at least one innovative state program is worth mentioning.

The state of Wisconsin found itself unable to achieve EPA-mandated levels of water quality along the polluted Fox and Wisconsin Rivers, even when it employed the prescribed technology. A team of engineers and economists then devised a sophisticated system of transferable discharge permits. Firms were issued an initial allocation of pollution permits (at no charge), based on historical levels of discharges. In total, these permits allow no more pollution than is consistent with EPA standards for water quality. But firms are allowed to trade pollution permits freely in the open market. Thus, in stark contrast to the standard regulatory approach, the Wisconsin system lets the firms along the river —not the regulators—decide how to reduce discharges. Little emissions trading has taken place to date because the entire scheme has been tied up in litigation. But one study estimated that pollution-control costs might eventually fall by as much as 80 percent compared to the alternative of ordering all firms along the river to reduce their discharges by a uniform percentage.

The state of Wisconsin thus came to the conclusion that economists have maintained all along: that applying a little economic horse sense makes it possible to clean up polluted rivers and reduce costs at the same time—a good bargain. That same bargain is available to the nation for the asking. ...

A Hard-Headed, Soft-Hearted Environmental Policy

Economists who specialize in environmental policy must occasionally harbor self-doubts. They find themselves lined up almost unanimously in favor of market-based approaches to pollution control with seemingly everyone else lined up on the other side. Are economists crazy or is everyone else wrong?

... I have argued the seemingly implausible proposition that environmental economists are right and everyone else really is wrong. I have tried to convey a sense of the frustration economists feel when they see obviously superior policies routinely spurned. By replacing our current command-and-control system with either marketable pollution permits or taxes on emissions, our environment can be made cleaner while the burden on industry is reduced. That is about as close to a free lunch as we are likely to encounter.

And yet economists' recommendations are overwhelmed by an unholy alliance of ignorance, ideology, and self-interest.

This is a familiar story. The one novel aspect in the sphere of environmental policy is that the usual heavy hitter of this triumvirate—self-interest—is less powerful here than in many other contexts. To be sure, self-interested business lobbies oppose pollution fees. But, as I pointed out, they can be bought off by allowing some pollution free of charge. Doing so may outrage environmental purists, but it is precisely what we do now.

It is the possibility of finessing vested financial interests that holds out the hope that good environmental policy might one day drive out the bad. For we need only overcome ignorance and ideology, not avarice.

Ignorance is normally beaten by knowledge. Few Americans now realize that practical reforms of our environmental policies can reduce the national clean-up bill from more than $70 billion per year to less than $50 billion, and probably to much less. Even fewer understand the reasons why. If the case for market-based policies were better known, more and more people might ask the obvious question: Why is it better to pay more for something we can get for less? Environmental policy may be one area where William Blake's optimistic dictum—"Truth can never be told so as to be understood and not believed"—is germane.

Ideology is less easily rooted out, for it rarely succumbs to rational argument. Some environmentalists support the economist's case. Others understand it well and yet oppose it for what they perceive as moral reasons. I have argued at length that here, as elsewhere, thinking with the heart is less effective than thinking with the head; that the economist's case does not occupy the moral low ground; and that the environment is likely to be cleaner if we offer society clean-up at more reasonable cost. As more environmentalists come to realize that T-shirt slogans are retarding, not hastening, progress toward their goals, their objections may melt away.

The economist's approach to environmental protection is no panacea. It requires an investment in monitoring equipment that society has not yet made. It cannot work in cases where the sources of pollution are not readily identifiable, such as seepage into groundwater. And it will remain an imperfect antidote for environmental hazards until we know a great deal more than we do now about the diffusion of pollutants and the harm they cause.

But perfection is hardly the appropriate standard. As things stand now, our environmental policy may be a bigger mess than our environment. Market-based approaches that join the hard head of the accountant to the soft heart of the environmentalist offer the prospect of genuine improvement: more clean-up for less money. It is an offer society should not refuse.

NO ⬅

Frank Ackerman and
Kevin Gallagher

Getting the Prices Wrong

Introduction: The Transformation of the Debate

Public discussion and debate over environmental policy has been transformed, in recent years, to focus on the idea of market-based mechanisms. In the 1970s and 1980s, many newly recognized environmental problems were addressed with laws and regulations that told polluters to stop polluting—a straightforward, common-sense approach that is now frequently stigmatized as "command and control." During the 1990s, a near-consensus emerged in policymaking circles for a sharp turn away from past patterns of regulation toward the theoretically greater efficiency and lower cost of environmental taxes, tradeable emission permits, and other market incentives. Today, to cite just one example, the official U.S. position on climate change negotiations slights the obvious regulatory options such as increased vehicle fuel efficiency standards. Instead it relies above all on the hopes that an unprecedented international emissions trading system can be created, and will prove effective.

There are many voices in the chorus of market enthusiasts. Most economists have always called for reliance on the market; in recent years they have gained a much higher public profile, with widely discussed publications, and major conferences on market-based environmental policy at leading universities. The influential "Project 88" papers and conferences in 1988–91 first brought the economists' theories to the attention of a wide and receptive audience of policymakers (Stavins et al. 1988, 1991). Important activist groups and individuals within the environmental movement have become advocates of market-based policies, while researchers continue to elaborate the economic models and theories on which those policies rest.

For some of the participants in the debate, the environment is almost an afterthought. The most passionate free marketeers seek to roll back all government programs, laws, and regulations that affect business and property.

From Frank Ackerman and Kevin Gallagher, "Getting the Prices Wrong: The Limits of Market-Based Environmental Policy," *Global Development and Environment Institute Working Paper 00-05* (October 2000). Copyright © 2000 by The Global Development and Environment Institute, Tufts University. Reprinted by permission.

For the true believer, the market is the answer regardless of the question, and even irreversible climate change is just another opportunity for private profit:

... free market environmentalism suggests two avenues for dealing with global warming. The first takes changes in the Earth's temperatures as given and asks whether individuals have the incentive to respond with innovative solutions. The second focuses on the evolution of property rights to the atmosphere. (Anderson and Leal, 1991: 163).

On a more sensibly nuanced view, the market is the answer to some but not all questions. The challenge is to understand what the market can do, and what it cannot. In the current climate, there is little danger of overlooking the market's strengths. To restore a balanced perspective, more attention needs to be focused in the opposite direction, examining the cases in which market incentives are less effective or appropriate.

Uses of the Market: Tool or Blueprint?

Market-based policies have made an undeniable contribution to environmental protection. Innovations such as emissions trading have in some cases lowered the cost of pollution abatement by increasing flexibility, decreasing the burden of bureaucratic regulation, and using the market to pursue environmental goals in an efficient manner. But such success has not been, and will not be, achieved on every issue.

There is a fundamental distinction between using the market as a *tool* to achieve society's goals, and adopting it as a *blueprint* of those goals. These two similar-sounding positions turn out to have very different implications. Is the market, as tool, the most efficient means to reach the environmental objectives that society has chosen? Or is the competitive market itself the blueprint, the ultimate description of society's objectives, with some environmental concerns pencilled in?

Under the tool perspective, environmental goals may be set through a process of public deliberation, and may have no inherent relationship to the market. It is then a pragmatic question to determine when market-based policies offer the best tools for achieving those goals, and when traditional regulation or other approaches are preferable. The answer naturally differs from one issue to the next.

If, on the other hand, the market is the blueprint of society's objectives, then there is little scope for pragmatism and pluralism of political strategies. From this perspective, what matters above all is "getting the prices right," i.e. adjusting selected prices as necessary to reflect the true valuation of environmental costs and benefits. Once the prices are right, the market automatically produces the right allocation of resources and the appropriate level of environmental protection; the less additional intervention, the better the market outcomes will be. On this view, public deliberation about environmental objectives is unnecessary or even harmful; society should do no more than endorse the mechanisms that allow the market to work.

The blueprint offered by the market is spelled out in general equilibrium theory. Under a series of idealized assumptions, a competitive economy is guaranteed to have an equilibrium which is Pareto-optimal, and every Pareto-optimal outcome is an equilibrium for some set of initial conditions. These well-known "fundamental theorems of welfare economics" are ultimately the foundation for the common idea that market outcomes are efficient. Yet the relevance of these abstract theorems is doubly limited, both in theory and in practice.

In the abstract, even if the assumptions of general equilibrium theory are accepted, its results remain mathematically problematical. There is no guarantee that the equilibrium of a general equilibrium model is either unique or stable. Intensive theoretical analysis has found no way around this problem, and in fact has found that the dynamic behavior of small (i.e. mathematically manageable) general equilibrium models is not necessarily a guide to the behavior of related, larger (i.e. more realistic) models (Ackerman 2000).

In reality, the assumptions of general equilibrium theory are inconsistent with what we know about people, firms, and technology. The neoclassical behavioral model and its assumptions of well-informed, narrowly defined maximization clash with the results of most social sciences—and with common sense (van den Bergh et al. 2000). Major firms routinely fail to be as small and competitive as the theory requires; oligopoly and monopoly are obvious, persistent facts of life. Path-dependent technologies, involving "learning by doing" and network effects, further undercut the presumption that market outcomes are reliably optimal or efficient (Arthur 1994).

In short, the equilibrium of a market economy is not necessarily an ideal outcome, either in theory or in practice. Our central argument is that *the market is a reasonable policy tool but not a reasonable blueprint for society's goals*. The market as blueprint fails because there are significant public purposes that cannot be achieved by prices and markets alone. There are many instances in which getting the prices right becomes a narrow or meaningless objective; in such cases, society may intentionally and appropriately choose to "get the prices wrong" in order to pursue more important goals.

Five Forms of Failure

There are at least five general reasons why market-based policies fail to address some of the most basic environmental objectives.

1. Large, irreversible damages must be prevented.

The market does not guarantee that producers will always do the right thing; it only ensures that those who do the wrong thing too often will go out of business. In the textbook model of perfect competition, every surviving producer is forced to adopt the most efficient, least-cost technology, because those who do not keep up with the state of the art will be undersold and driven out by those who do. Implicit in this model is a process of trial and error in which unsuccessful producers may do the wrong things (produce things that are needlessly expensive, or that fail to meet consumer desires) for a while before giving up and trying a different line of work.

This is a useful way to make many resource allocation decisions—*if* there is no great social cost or lasting harm caused by a few failed experiments (Koopmans, 1951; Krutilla, 1967). It is hard to imagine a better way to choose which restaurants should serve your community; the economic and environmental impacts of unsuccessful restaurants are minimal. But the same process of trial and error is less attractive as a strategy for disposal of high-level radioactive waste, where it is essential to get it right the first time and every time. When the potential damages are large and irreversible, as with radioactive waste, then society cannot afford the experimental learning process that is implied by market competition. Reliance on market mechanisms in this case would be an abdication of the most basic responsibility for public health and safety.

Many environmental problems are more analogous to the urgent questions of nuclear waste disposal than to the benign issues of consumer preference and restaurant choice. Threats of extinction of endangered species, destruction of irreplaceable wildernesses and other ecosystems, and emission of toxic and carcinogenic pollutants, all involve large, irreversible damages. The market can safely play a role on these issues only in a firmly regulated context, intentionally constrained by high minimum standards that safeguard the interests of nature and humanity.

2. Outcomes far in the future are important.

Discounting, the standard method for comparison of costs and benefits that occur at different times, is indispensable for near-term decisions but nonsensical for the long run. Application of this form of short-run thinking to our environmental future repeatedly leads to the mistaken conclusion that we should do almost nothing on behalf of future generations.

Discounting is essential, and indeed commonplace, for many practical financial decisions. If offered an investment opportunity with a payoff a few years in the future, you can (and should) compare it to the return you would get by putting the same amount of money into a predictable, safe alternative such as a bank account or government bond. Why does this innocuous bit of accounting become nonsensical when applied to society's long-run choices?

The solutions to many environmental issues such as climate change involve sizeable costs now that have their principle benefits far in the future. For an investment with a ten-year lifetime, one individual can weigh her own initial costs against her own ultimate benefits. But there is no one who will personally experience both the cost of investments in carbon reduction made today, and the resulting benefit of mitigation in climate change 100 or 200 years from now. In fact, there is no way of knowing what value our far-future descendants will place on the environment; they could consider it either much more or much less important than we do today. The problem is that by accepting the use of a discount rate we have implicitly imposed a specific pattern of preferences regarding the relative welfare of present and future generations (Howarth and Norgaard, 1993).

Moreover, thanks to the magic of compound interest, benefits far in the future have a very small present value. At 5% annual interest, $1 left in the bank is worth more than $17,000 after 200 years, and more than $2,000,000 after 300 years. So if it costs as much as $1 today to prevent environmental damages worth $17,000 in the year 2200 or $2 million in 2300, economic theory says our descendants would be better off if we left $1 in the bank for them. As strange as it may sound, this argument is seriously advanced as a reason to go slow and minimize current spending on long-run environmental objectives (Hartwick, 1977; Solow 1986). The only reasonable conclusion is that economic theory does not offer a reasonable understanding of our responsibility to future generations (Bromley, 1998).

3. Many environmental values are not commodities that can be priced.

Economic theory usually assumes that environmental damages can be meaningfully measured in monetary terms. From this it is only a short step to calculating the prices that "should" be applied to clean air, clean water, and other values. The vision of the market as blueprint for environmental protection generally assumes such prices have been put in place, so that the market can balance supply and demand in order to achieve the optimal level of pollution reduction. That is, economists assume that environmental values can be treated as commodities like any others.

This approach is problematical on several levels. On a practical level, there are serious conceptual and technical critiques of the standard methods of monetizing environmental damages by economists and lawyers alike (Diamond and Hausman, 1994; Harvard Law Review, 1992). Economists frequently rely on "contingent valuation" surveys that ask people to place a hypothetical dollar value on some aspect of the environment; the question does not always produce a meaningful answer.

A subtler problem is that every unit of a commodity typically sells at the same price: three tons of steel are worth three times as much as one. However, for pollutants with threshold effects or critical levels, three tons of emissions may have vastly more than three times the impact of one ton. In contrast to traditional regulations, market-based policies such as emission trading are more prone to creating "hot spots" where critical levels of pollutants are exceeded.

On the most fundamental level, there are deep ethical, philosophical, and religious objections to assigning dollar values to human or other life (Anderson, 1993; Kelman, 1981). For many people, the protection of endangered species and unique natural habitats, or the prevention of avoidable deaths and injuries, involve a realm of fundamental principles that transcend the market. From this perspective, monetization of human life and health, or of the existence of other species, is either meaningless or degrading. It is important to talk about these principles and their policy implications, but that conversation cannot be reduced to purely monetary terms (Vatn and Bromley 1994).

4. Volatile market prices can cause wasteful misallocation of resources.

When prices change too fast, the investment that made sense yesterday may no longer be profitable today—as many people have learned the hard way in the stock market. This problem can also affect the environment, when volatile markets send mixed signals about the value of environmental policies and initiatives. Sky-high prices for recycled materials in 1995 inspired more than a billion dollars of investment in new recycled paper mills; by 1997 those new mills had closed, most of them bankrupt (Ackerman and Gallagher, 2000). High oil prices in the early 1980s drove the auto industry to retool for small car production, just before prices fell and consumers went back to buying big cars. More recently, as the restructured electricity industry increasingly relies on auction-style pricing to set electric rates, there have been cases where summer peak power has sold for hundreds of times the normal price. This is sure to be a misleading signal about the value of new generating capacity.

Day trading is not an example of the efficiency of the market. In a world with high, industry-specific sunk costs of both physical and human capital, there is a limit to the velocity at which people and businesses can sensibly respond to new price signals. When the market exceeds that speed limit, it leads to wastefully rapid, extreme changes. The government can improve matters by intervening in such markets, enforcing a reasonable speed limit and establishing a sustainable pace of change.

5. If it's not broken, don't fix it.

It is not always the case that market incentives are superior to old-fashioned environmental controls. There are substantial areas—protection of public health, provision of urban infrastructure, and emissions monitoring, among others—where traditional regulatory or public spending approaches remain more effective than market-based policies. The two strategies provide different benefits: the market minimizes consumer choice and creates incentives for cost minimization; the government can supply public goods, minimize transaction costs, and create a transparent standard of fairness. The relative importance of these contrasting strengths will differ from case to case.

Market-based approaches have much higher costs, and hence more limited advantages, in some circumstances than in others. Economists have analyzed the conditions under which market incentives are more or less effective; for example, when pollution approaches thresholds beyond which damages rise rapidly, the rationale for strict emission controls becomes stronger. There is also some evidence that market incentives, like any other policy, are less effective in practice than they were projected to be in theory (Gustafsson, 1998).

Finally, market incentives frequently involve taxes. (The principle alternative, emissions trading, involves high start-up and transaction costs, and is not appropriate in every case.) No one wants any new taxes; most politicians can't bring themselves to utter the word. Traditional regulation, involving rules that lower or prohibit certain emissions, may be more politically feasible—even if, in a theoretical world divorced from politics, market incentives might appear to be more efficient.

Two Cheers for the Market

Despite this catalogue of things the market cannot accomplish, there are things at which it does excel. Guidelines for the appropriate use of market incentives can begin with the negation of the five points listed above. Market-based policies should be used in cases where: there is little risk of irreversible damages; the relevant outcomes are relatively short-term; there are no fundamental ethical or philosophical issues at stake; prices are not excessively volatile; and traditional regulation is expensive or ineffective.

In more positive terms, the great strength of the market is that it decentralizes information processing and decision-making, allowing each firm to analyze and respond to the data that affects its operations. This is one of the key points of the economic critique of traditional regulation: regulators cannot possibly keep up with all the relevant information on complex, changing technologies, let alone the site-specific information about the relative cost of installing new technologies at each location. When there are complex technical choices, especially when the choices depend on site-specific information, it is more efficient to set broad standards and allow firms to choose the most cost-effective means of meeting those standards.

The allowance trading system for sulfur emissions under the 1990 Clean Air Act Amendments comes close to meeting these standards, although it has not been entirely free of problems. Sulfur emissions have been reduced more rapidly, and at lower cost, than anyone thought possible in 1990—though there are other factors that contributed to this happy outcome, such as the increased availability and lowered price of low-sulfur coal in the 1990s (Ackerman and Moomaw, 1997). Moreover, many observers have concluded that the allowances should have been auctioned by the government, rather than given away to the existing producers. Other changes could make the system more environmentally palatable: if the cap on total emissions was steadily declining, rather than constant, the trading system would not create a permanent "right to pollute."

Still, the process of emissions trading is an interesting innovation that has played at least some part in an environmental success story. Our suggested guidelines for the use of market incentives fit well in this case: the damage from acid precipitation appears to be reversible; it occurs promptly following emission; ethical issues about human life or biodiversity are no more prominent here than they are in any environmental issue; relevant prices are not unusually volatile; and traditional regulation, calling for scrubbers at all coal-burning plants, was indeed expensive and inflexible, while trading allowances between U.S. power plants is simple and fairly cheap to administer. There is a complex choice of strategies for sulfur reduction, in which the best choice depends on site-specific information.

Yet in the current climate of celebration of the market, it is important to stress that this is *not* to say that emissions trading is always a good idea. The proposed application of emissions trading to worldwide carbon emissions fails several of our criteria, and raises technical problems of coverage, administration, verification and enforcement. In general, there is far more danger of exaggerating than of overlooking the potential of market-based policies today. The greater need is to re-legitimize other approaches, and to open a broader dialogue about the full range of options for environmental policy.

References

Ackerman, F., 2000. Still dead after all these years: interpreting the failure of general equilibrium theory. GDAE Working Paper No. 00-01, Tufts University.

Ackerman, F., and Gallagher, K., 2000. Mixed signals: Market Incentives, Recycling, and the Price Spike of 1995. GDAE Working Paper, Tufts University.

Ackerman, F. and Moomaw, W., 1997. SO_2 emissions trading: does it work? *Electricity Journal*, August.

Anderson, E., 1993. Cost-benefit analysis, safety, and environmental quality. *Ethics in Economics*. Cambridge: Harvard University Press, 190–216.

Anderson, T., and Leal, L., 1991. *Free Market Environmentalism*. Boulder: Westview Press, 163.

Arthur, B., 1994. *Increasing Returns and Path Dependence in the Economy*. Ann Arbor: Michigan Press.

van den Bergh, Jeroen C. J. M., Ada Ferrer-i-Carbonell and Guiseppe Munda. 2000. Alternative models of individual behaviour and implications for environmental policy. *Ecological Economics* 32, 43–61.

Bromley, D., 1998. Searching for sustainability: the poverty of spontaneous order. *Ecological Economics* 24, 231–240.

Diamond, P., and Hausman, T., 1994. Contingent valuation: is some number better than any number? *Journal of Economic Perspectives*, v8, n4, 45–64.

Gustafsson, B., 1998. Scope and limits of the market mechanism in environmental management. *Ecological Economics* 24, 259–274.

Hartwick, J. M. 1977. Intergenerational equity and the investing of rents from exhaustible resources. *American Economic Review* 66, 972–974.

Harvard Law Review (unsigned editorial). 1992. "Ask a silly question...": contingent valuation of natural resource damages. *Harvard Law Review* 105, 1981–2000.

Howarth, R., and Norgaard, R., 1993. Intergenerational transfers and the social discount rate. *Environment and Resource Economics* 3, 337–358.

Kelman, S., 1981. What price incentives? *Economists and the Environment*. Boston: Auburn House.

Koopmans, T. C. 1951. Analysis of production as an efficient combination of activity. *Activity Analysis of Production and Allocation*. New York: John Wiley, 48.

Krutilla, J., 1967. Conservation reconsidered. *American Economic Review* 57, 777–786.

Solow, R. M. 1986. On the intertemporal allocation of natural resources. *Scandinavian Journal of Economics* 88, 141–149.

Stavins, R. N., et al. 1988. Project 88—Harnessing market forces to protect our environment: Initiatives for the new president (Senators Timothy Wirth and John Heinz, Washington D.C.).

Stavins, R. N., et al. 1991. Project 88 Round II—Incentives for action: Designing market-based environmental strategies (Senators Timothy Wirth and John Heinz, Washington D.C.).

Vatn, A., and D. W. Bromley. 1994. Choice without prices without apology, *Journal of Environmental Economics and Management* 26, 129–148.

POSTSCRIPT

Should Pollution Be Put to the Market Test?

For more than 30 years a massive effort has been put forth in the United States to advance environmental protection by using laws and regulation. At first, federal action was directed toward air- and water-pollution control; this was accomplished by issuing regulations and permits. The second set of initiatives focused on cleaning up hazardous waste dumps. This action was first authorized by the Resource Conservation and Recovery Act (RCRA) of 1976, which established a permit system for disposal sites and regulated underground storage tanks. Later initiatives in this area were authorized by the Comprehensive Environmental Response, Compensation, and Liability Act (CERCLA) of 1980. This act, known as Superfund, created a fund to finance the clean-up of hazardous waste sites.

What is significant is that throughout the 1970s and the 1980s, efforts to control, contain, and eliminate pollution and its effects were accomplished largely by traditional government regulation. Economists such as Blinder argued for policies that capture and utilize the strength of the market. By the 1990s their voices had been heard and the population witnessed a marked shift in public policy. Traditional regulation, which demands a uniform response from all who produce pollutants, was replaced with market-based regulation that invites firms to weigh the benefits and costs of their actions. Traditional regulation simply faded into the background.

This concerns Ackerman and Gallagher, who believe that the pendulum has swung too far. They argue that it is time to recognize that it may be best to return to the good old days of a "command and control" type of regulation. They assert that if the public does not take heed, private market interests could kill the goose that lays the golden egg and, in the process, deny society a perpetual stream of golden eggs.

For a review of the initial legislation in the air pollution area, see Richard H. Schulze, "The 20-Year History of the Evolution of Air Pollution Control Legislation in the U.S.A.," *Atmospheric Environment* (March 1993). For a discussion of some of the ethical issues surrounding pollution permits, see Paul Steichmeier, "The Morality of Pollution Permits," *Environmental Ethics* (Summer 1993). To see how important market incentives are to economists, examine the recent appeal to the Supreme Court signed by more than 40 prominent economists, who urged the Court to let the Environmental Protection Agency (EPA) consider the cost and consequences of clean air regulations. This can be found on the Brookings Institution Web site at http://www.brookings.edu/Comm/news/0007EPA.htm. At the far right of the political spectrum, visit the Regulation Home Page at http://www.regulation.org.

ISSUE 17

Has the North American Free Trade Agreement Been a Success?

YES: Joe Cobb, from "A Successful Agreement," *The World & I* (October 1997)

NO: Alan Tonelson, from "A Failed Approach," *The World & I* (October 1997)

ISSUE SUMMARY

YES: Joe Cobb, president of the Trade Policy Institute in Washington, D.C., asserts that the North American Free Trade Agreement (NAFTA) has been a success. He cites evidence that the average living standards of American workers have improved; that U.S. exports have increased; and that the average annual growth rates of the United States, Canada, and Mexico are greater than they otherwise would have been.

NO: Researcher Alan Tonelson negatively assesses NAFTA based on his contentions that the real winners were large U.S. multinational corporations, that median wages in the United States and Mexico have declined, and that the flows of illegal immigrants and drugs into the United States from Mexico are high.

$\mathbf{T}$ he North American Free Trade Agreement (NAFTA) was signed into law in the fall of 1993. The passage of NAFTA was no simple matter. Although the basic agreement was negotiated by the Republican Bush administration, the Democratic Clinton administration faced the challenge of convincing Congress and the American people that NAFTA would work to the benefit of the United States as well as Mexico. In meeting this challenge President Bill Clinton did not hesitate to use a bit of drama to press the case for NAFTA. He gathered together former U.S. presidents George Bush, Ronald Reagan, Jimmy Carter, Gerald Ford, and Richard Nixon and had them speak out in support of NAFTA. The public debate probably reached its zenith with a face-to-face confrontation between Ross Perot, perhaps the most visible and most outspoken opponent of NAFTA, and Vice President Al Gore on the *Larry King Live* television show. The vote on

NAFTA in the House of Representatives reflected the sharpness of the debate; it passed by only a slim margin.

In pressing the case for NAFTA, proponents in the United States raised two major points. The first point was economic: NAFTA would produce real economic benefits, including increased employment in the United States and increased productivity. The second point was political: NAFTA would support the political and economic reforms being made in Mexico and promote further progress in these two domains. These reforms had made Mexico a "better" neighbor; that is, Mexico had taken steps to become more like the United States, and NAFTA would support further change. Both of these two major points reinforced a third claim made on behalf of NAFTA: the improvements in economic and political conditions in Mexico might lead to a reduction in the flows of illegal immigrants and drugs into the United States. In fighting NAFTA, opponents in the United States countered both of these points. They argued that freer trade between the United States and Mexico would mean a loss of American jobs—Ross Perot's "giant sucking sound" was the transfer of work and jobs from the United States to Mexico. Opponents argued that the notion of passing NAFTA as a reward to the Mexican government was premature; the government had not done enough to improve economic and political conditions in Mexico.

Implementation of NAFTA began in 1994. But events in Mexico during 1994 and 1995 took an interesting series of twists. By December 1994 the Mexican economy faced a balance-of-payments crisis—and the peso began to depreciate. In order to prevent a collapse of the Mexican economy, President Clinton organized a $50 billion multilateral assistance effort that included $20 billion of U.S. credit. The Mexican government also took action, including making cuts in government spending and increases in interest rates. The net result of these events was a deep recession in the Mexican economy with a contraction of 7 percent during the first three quarters of 1995.

In assessing the impact of NAFTA, there are any number of different perspectives that can be employed. Should the focus be economic, political, or both? Should the evaluation concentrate on the benefits and costs to the United States, to Mexico, or both? Should Canada be added to the mix? How much of the economic and political history that follows NAFTA can be attributed to NAFTA, and how much can be attributed to other factors? When is the appropriate time for an evaluation?

Some of the difficulties of evaluation are captured in the following selections. Both were published four years after the passage of NAFTA and some three-and-one-half years after its implementation. Joe Cobb introduces a number of economic and political considerations to support his strong endorsement of NAFTA. Alan Tonelson also takes up economic and political arguments in presenting his equally strong rejection of NAFTA.

Joe Cobb  **YES**

A Successful Agreement

During the heated debate about the North American Free Trade Agreement (NAFTA) in 1993, many claims and counterclaims were made about job losses.

Ross Perot coined the famous sound bite "a giant sucking sound" to describe American jobs going south. Now the evidence is in. Hundreds of thousands of U.S. jobs have *not* been destroyed, and the U.S. manufacturing base has *not* been weakened.

Instead, U.S. exports and employment levels have risen significantly as total trade among the NAFTA countries has increased, and the average living standards of American workers have improved. The general unemployment rate declined to 5.3 percent in 1996 from 6.8 percent in 1993.

In 1996, U.S. global trade (exports plus imports) totaled $1.765 trillion —over 23 percent of U.S. GDP [gross domestic product], compared with 10 percent in 1970. The Office of the U.S. Trade Representative (USTR) has estimated that by the year 2010, trade will represent about 36 percent of U.S. GDP. Today, more than 11 million U.S. jobs depend on exports, 1.5 million more than in 1992. Roughly a quarter of U.S. economic growth during the Clinton administration has been due to export expansion.

Total North American trade increased $127 billion during NAFTA's first three years, from $293 billion in 1993 to $420 billion in 1996, a gain of 43 percent. Canada and Mexico are already the top two U.S. trading partners, but if the post-NAFTA increase in trade with them had been with a single country, it would make that country the fourth-largest U.S. trading partner.

In 1996, U.S. exports to Canada and Mexico, at $190 billion, exceeded U.S. exports to any other area of the world, including the entire Pacific Rim or all of Europe. Mexico and Canada purchased $3 of every $10 in U.S. exports and supplied $3 of every $10 in U.S. imports in 1996.

While NAFTA involves both Canada and Mexico, the controversy in 1993 was whether adding Mexico would have bad effects for the American worker. But obviously, the economic growth from increased trade with Mexico has not hurt. U.S. exports to Mexico are up 37 percent from 1993, reaching a record $57 billion in 1996.

From Joe Cobb, "A Successful Agreement," *The World & I*, vol. 12, no. 10 (October 1997). Copyright © 1997 by *The World & I*. Reprinted by permission of *The World & I*, a publication of The Washington Times Corporation.

During NAFTA's first three years, 39 of the 50 states increased their exports to Mexico, and 44 states reported a growth in exports to Mexico during 1996, as the pace of U.S. exports to that country accelerated.

According to the U.S. Department of Commerce, U.S. exports to Mexico in the fourth quarter of 1996 were growing at an annualized rate of $64 billion. Moreover, U.S. market share in Mexico increased from 69 percent of total Mexican imports in 1993 to 76 percent in 1996.

Total two-way trade between the United States and Mexico was nearly $130 billion. During this period, U.S. exports to Canada also increased by $134 billion, or 33 percent. Total two-way trade between the United States and Canada was $290 billion in 1996.

A close look at the numbers shows there is a U.S. trade deficit with both Canada and Mexico, but the success of NAFTA once again proves there is nothing wrong with trade deficits, as economists have taught for over 200 years. The combined U.S. trade deficit with Canada and Mexico increased from $9 billion in 1992 to $39.9 billion in 1996. But since 1992, the U.S. economy has created 12 million new jobs (net). Manufacturing employment grew from 16.9 million jobs in 1992 to 18.3 million in 1993, an increase of 1.4 million net new jobs.

The U.S. Department of Labor lists more than 110,000 U.S. workers as certified for training assistance under NAFTA's Trade Adjustment Assistance Program, which indicates that Perot was not entirely wrong. Those Americans lost their jobs because of NAFTA. But the negative impact of NAFTA each week must have been very small if only 110,000 jobs is the total after three years.

Although 110,000 families were hit hard by NAFTA, the job-loss rate in the United States, as reported by the number of new unemployment insurance claims, is normally about 350,000 every week. Moreover, the U.S. economy currently creates more than 110,000 new jobs (net) in about two weeks. On the positive side of the employment issue, U.S. exports to NAFTA countries currently support 2.3 million U.S. jobs, according to the USTR.

A study by economist Richard Nadler, who reviewed U.S. standards of living before and after NAFTA was launched in 1994, found that the rate of increase in personal wealth has more than tripled since NAFTA was implemented.

His review measured the improvement in three ways: First, growth in disposable personal income, adjusted for inflation, averaged 1.89 percent annually in 1994–95, compared with 0.25 percent annually 1990–93. Second, personal consumption expenditures grew by an inflation-adjusted 1.76 percent annually during 1994–95, compared with 0.56 percent a year in 1990–93.

Finally, inflation-adjusted GDP per capita grew by 1.79 percent annually in 1994–95, compared with only 0.23 percent during 1990–93. Of course, there was a recession in 1990–91, which slowed down the economy in the pre-NAFTA period, but perhaps NAFTA has helped prevent a recession since then.

Investment Boom

The major complaint against NAFTA by organized labor during the 1993 controversy over adopting the treaty was the fear that new investments would be made south of the border instead of in U.S. factories. There has indeed been an investment boom in Mexico, but the inflow has not seemed to have any depressing effect on the United States.

NAFTA has encouraged U.S. and foreign investors with apparel and footwear factories in Asia to relocate their production operations to Mexico. This diversion of investment from Asia to Mexico "saved the heavier end of clothing manufacture in the United States: the textile mills," according to Nadler.

NAFTA has been very good for the traditional southern textile states like North Carolina and Alabama, as well as for major U.S. agricultural states such as Montana, Nebraska, and North Dakota, whose politicians in Congress typically opposed it.

The investment boom in Mexico has been a major source of new demand for U.S. manufacturers of capital goods. The largest post-NAFTA gains in U.S. exports to Mexico have been in such high-technology manufacturing sectors as industrial machinery, transportation and electronic equipment, plastics and rubber, fabricated metal products, and chemicals.

A recent economic analysis published by the U.S. Federal Reserve Bank of Chicago concludes that NAFTA will lead to output gains for all three participant countries. The study concluded that, under NAFTA, the sustained annual growth rate of the three economies is permanently higher than it would be otherwise.

Mexico's GDP is predicted to rise by an added factor of 3.26 percent, U.S. GDP by 0.24 percent, and Canada's GDP by 0.11 percent. These gains are roughly twice as large as those predicted by previous forecasts of NAFTA's potential for accelerated growth in North American trade, output, and employment.

In general, bilateral Mexican-North American trade should increase about 20 percent as a result of NAFTA. This projected growth also means more U.S. jobs and a higher standard of living for American workers.

One of NAFTA's main purposes was to "lock in" the process of economic and political reform in Mexico, which started in the late 1980s. Mexico's membership in NAFTA, the World Trade Organization, the Asia-Pacific Economic Cooperation forum, and the Organization for Economic Cooperation and Development has created international commitments and linkages that politicians in Mexico cannot ignore.

Mexico's constitution was amended in 1996 to make the electoral process more transparent and independent of the government. These reforms had a dramatic effect on July 6, 1997, when opposition parties obtained a majority in Mexico's congressional elections for the first time. There can be no doubt that NAFTA is a major factor in Mexico's congressional elections for the first time. There can be no doubt that NAFTA is a major factor in Mexico's transformation toward a free-market democracy on the U.S.-Canadian model.

The proposals to expand NAFTA to include Chile and other countries of the Western Hemisphere are questioned by doubters, but the evidence is already clear. As a market for U.S. goods, the Western Hemisphere already is nearly twice as large as the European Union and nearly 50 percent larger than Asia. The Western Hemisphere accounted for 39 percent of U.S. goods exports in 1996 and was the only region in which the United States recorded a trade surplus in both 1995 and '96.

Moreover, while U.S. goods exports to the world generally increased 57 percent from 1990 to 1996, U.S. exports to Latin America and the Caribbean (excluding Mexico) increased by 110 percent during the same period. If current trends continue, Latin America alone will exceed Japan and western Europe combined as an export market for U.S. goods by the year 2010.

There should be no doubts about the success of NAFTA. Although only three years old, this international trade agreement has far exceeded the expectations of its advocates back in 1993. Even though three years may seem like too little time to reach any final judgments about NAFTA, it already is clear that critics of this agreement have been wrong on all counts.

Alan Tonelson  **NO**

A Failed Approach

In 1992, Bill Clinton won the presidency in part by making a very quotable, trenchant point about George Bush's economic record. Everything that was supposed to be going up, he and Al Gore emphasized repeatedly, was going down. And everything that was supposed to be going down was going up.

Five years later, a similar point can be made about NAFTA, the North American Free Trade Agreement completed by the Clinton administration in late 1993. In fact, few public policy initiatives in recent memory have so mercilessly and consistently mocked their champions' predictions.

Today, NAFTA supporters want to extend the treaty's terms to the rest of the Western Hemisphere, starting with Chile.... [T]he administration is expected to submit to Congress its request for fast-track authority for these and a series of other major trade talks. But the cracked crystal ball of NAFTA lobbyists in and out of government should call into question not only their credentials as analysts but their entire approach to economic globalization.

NAFTA was advertised as nothing less than a godsend to the United States, Canada, and Mexico—a boon not only to broad-based prosperity throughout North America but for social progress and political stability in Mexico in particular.

By the entirely reasonable Clinton-Gore up-down standards, however, NAFTA's results have been positively perverse—except for the big U.S. multinational corporations that dominate North American trade flows.

The impact of NAFTA and NAFTA-style globalization has been especially damaging in the United States and Mexico, whose recent trade record will understandably be the focus of Congress' upcoming NAFTA expansion debate.

Since NAFTA's late-1993 signing, median wages in the United States and Mexico are down, as is employment in manufacturing, which generates an economy's highest-paying jobs on average.

The U.S. trade deficit with Mexico, on the other hand, is way up. So are flows of illegal drugs and immigrants from Mexico into the United States—even though NAFTA was supposed to make Mexico so prosperous that its people would be able to earn a decent living by staying home and out of criminal activity. And despite NAFTA's ostensible national security dimension—preventing chaos on America's southern border—social and political instability in Mexico are way up, too, as is anti-Americanism.

NAFTA supporters point to two of their own rising indicators to score the agreement as a success: the simple post-NAFTA expansion of trade within North America and the continued healthy levels of U.S. exports to Mexico despite the peso collapse and subsequent Mexican depression.

Expanded trade, however, is at best a peculiar measure of economic policy success. In the first place, most of the U.S.-Mexico trade expansion has come in the form of rising U.S. imports from Mexico.

Rising imports, of course, can be a sign of national economic health, and bilateral trade deficits are not always bad or even important. But in America's current circumstances, the jump in imports from Mexico is adding significantly to a U.S. global deficit that sets new records every year. That deficit persists despite the vaunted competitive comeback of American industry during the 1990s, a historically weak dollar, and unimpressive recent relative growth rates.

Although macroeconomists have assured us that the gap would close, the Fed now judges the economy's overall growth rate is being cut by about a third. In fact, significantly reducing America's global trade deficit might actually enable the U.S. economy to grow fast enough to push up real wages for most Americans—something that hasn't happened on a sustained basis since 1973.

Just as important, expanded trade per se has no place as a major goal of U.S. foreign economic policy. It is simply a means to an end. The raison d'être of any economic policy is encouraging a healthy and sustained rise in living standards for the vast majority of Americans. Failure to meet this goal dwarfs any other economic achievements, whether low inflation, expanded productivity, rising stock markets, or even strong overall growth.

Intra-Company Trade

As for the levels of U.S. exports to Mexico, a look beneath the surface reveals how misleading such aggregate figures can be. According to a UCLA study commissioned by the Clinton administration itself, post-NAFTA U.S.-Mexican trade has been driven "almost entirely" by the growth of intra-company trade.

Such exports, which represent a large (more than one-third) and growing share of overall goods exports, do more to destroy good jobs than to create them. The reasons can be complex, but the export argument is so central to the pro-NAFTA case that they are worth examining in some detail.

Traditional goods exports—which consist of sales of finished products from U.S. companies to unrelated customers abroad—boost American employment by expanding a company's customer base and thus require increased production and often more employees to meet the new demand. U.S. intra-company exports, for their part, consist of the shipments of parts and components of finished products from individual companies' U.S.-based factories to their overseas factories.

These foreign facilities perform further manufacturing or final assembly work. From the standpoint of creating high-paying manufacturing jobs for

Americans, such exports are a growing problem, because in most cases the assembly or further manufacturing used to be done in this country.

Intra-company exports can still produce U.S. jobs in net if shipping some production abroad helps U.S. businesses increase final overseas sales or recapture markets at home—say, by enabling companies to customize their products to suit local tastes in new markets.

But much of the new U.S. manufacturing investment abroad is in countries like Mexico, whose people are generally too poor to buy what they make, and/or that are trying to export their way to national prosperity and thus artificially depress consumption. Moreover, the figures for U.S. industries like autos —where U.S. investment has been enormous—indicate that very little of what they produce in Mexico is exported outside North America.

Instead, much of the U.S. multinationals' foreign output gets sent right back to America for final sale. And since virtually no U.S. industries with big American payrolls have won back much domestic market share since NAFTA's signing, it's clear that intra-company trade amounts to America largely exporting to itself. This means that most of the new production in countries like Mexico is simply replacing production in the United States.

Exactly how much do U.S. multinationals produce abroad for eventual sale back to the United States? Only the companies and Washington know for sure. But the former want to keep this information secret—largely to avoid a public relations nightmare.

The latter simply swallows the corporate line about the need to protect trade secrets. In the case of Mexico, however, the scale of this ersatz exporting can be measured by looking at Mexican government figures. They tell us that, currently, 62 percent of all U.S. exports to Mexico are eventually reexported back to the United States—up from 40 percent before NAFTA.

When Vice President Gore debated Ross Perot in 1993 on the treaty's merits, he used booming new Mexican Wal-Marts as symbols for the huge new Mexican consumer market he claimed NAFTA would open for American companies and workers alike. A better symbol would be Mexican autoworkers performing sophisticated, highly productive manufacturing work that used to be done in America—at one-eighth the wage.

Mexico's Crisis

NAFTA supporters offer a superficially convincing alibi for Mexico's ills, blaming them entirely on the peso crash, not the trade treaty. But they conveniently overlook the role played by NAFTA-style economic liberalization policies in triggering Mexico's crisis—principally, hooking Mexico on inflows of foreign capital that the country's corrupt leaders could sustain politically only by overvaluing their currency and artificially increasing the average Mexican's purchasing power. In addition, any U.S. administration failing to anticipate such an extraordinary event is obviously not competent to make Mexico policy to begin with.

The NAFTA lobby also insists that without the treaty, high-paying manufacturing jobs would continue to flee overseas—only they would wind up in

East Asia, where manufacturers use far fewer U.S.-made inputs and therefore far fewer U.S. workers. They're right, but their point unwittingly indicts the broader globalization approach they favor.

In the world created by these policies:

- where the U.S. permits many of its biggest trading partners to shut out competitive American-made goods;
- where American companies therefore have little choice but to remain competitive by cutting costs through outsourcing to low-wage countries;
- and where the enormous U.S. market remains wide open to goods carrying American brand names but produced in countries where cheap and even child and slave labor is abundant, where unions are violently repressed, and where job safety and serious environmental-regulations protections are virtually unknown;

it is indeed better to use NAFTA to encourage production in Mexico rather than in China or Indonesia. Yet simply accepting these conditions ultimately condemns American workers and their foreign counterparts to a global race to the bottom in terms of wages and working conditions.

Replacing the failed NAFTA approach to North American trade alone will not turn globalization into a winner for workers at home and abroad. But with the fast-track debate looming this fall, it's the ideal place to start.

POSTSCRIPT

Has the North American Free Trade Agreement Been a Success?

Cobb begins his positive evaluation of NAFTA by stating that the NAFTA opponents' two major claims have been proven false: the U.S. manufacturing base remains strong, and hundreds of thousands of jobs have not been lost. Instead, for the overall U.S. economy, exports are up, employment has increased, total trade has expanded, and the average standard of living of American workers has increased. Cobb reports that during NAFTA's first three years the following has resulted: total North American trade increased by 43 percent, with 39 of the 50 states increasing their exports to Mexico; U.S. market share in Mexico increased from 69 percent to 76 percent; and U.S. exports to Canada increased by 33 percent. He accepts the U.S. Department of Labor's calculation of 110,000 American workers who qualified for training assistance under NAFTA but offsets this negative effect by stating that at current rates the United States creates more than this number of jobs every two weeks. He also states that U.S. exports to NAFTA countries support 2.3 million U.S. jobs. Furthermore, Cobb offers evidence to support his contention that living standards for American workers have improved, namely that "the rate of increase in personal wealth has more than tripled since NAFTA was implemented." With regard to investment, he agrees that NAFTA has created an investment boom in Mexico, but he argues that this has benefited the United States by increasing the demand for American-produced capital goods. As to political developments in Mexico, Cobb finds that NAFTA has produced positive outcomes in this domain as well.

Tonelson asserts, "Few public policy initiatives in recent memory have so mercilessly and consistently mocked their champions' predictions." He then offers empirical evidence to support his position: median wages in the United States and Mexico are down, as is employment in manufacturing; the U.S. trade deficit with Mexico is up; the flows of illegal immigrants and drugs from Mexico into the United States are up; and anti-Americanism and social and political instability in Mexico have risen. Tonelson also cites a Federal Reserve study that estimates that the trade deficit has cut the U.S. growth rate by about one-third. Citing a study done at the University of California, Los Angeles, that concludes that most of the increase in trade has been an increase in intracompany trade, Tonelson argues that the increase in intraindustry trade means that new Mexican production "is simply replacing production in the United States." Although he is willing to accept the argument that the loss of production to Mexico is better for the United States than the loss of production to the Far East, Tonelson believes that "simply accepting these conditions ultimately condemns American workers and their foreign counterparts to a global race to the bottom in terms of wages and working conditions."

For a taste of the debate before the passage of NAFTA, both pro and con, see *NAFTA: An Assessment,* rev. ed., by Gary Clyde Hufbauer and Jeffery J. Schott (Institute for International Economics, 1993); "Grasping the Benefits of NAFTA," by Peter Morici, *Current History* (February 1993); "The North American Free Trade Agreement," *Economic Report of the President 1993;* "The High Cost of NAFTA," by Timothy Koechlin and Mehrene Larudee, *Challenge* (September/ October 1992); and "The NAFTA Illusion," by Jeff Faux, *Challenge* (July/August 1993). For more recent assessments of NAFTA, see "NAFTA's Positive Impact on the United States: A State-by-State Breakdown," by John P. Sweeney, *The Heritage Foundation FYI No. 160* (November 6, 1997); "NAFTA's Three-Year Report Card: An 'A' for North America's Economy," by John P. Sweeney, *The Heritage Foundation Backgrounder No. 1144* (May 16, 1997); and *NAFTA: Experience and Fast-Track Authority* by the Century Foundation (1997).

Contributors to This Volume

EDITORS

THOMAS R. SWARTZ was born in Philadelphia, Pennsylvania, in 1937. He received his B.A. from LaSalle University in 1960, his M.A. from Ohio University in 1962, and his Ph.D. from Indiana University in 1965. He is currently a professor of economics at the University of Notre Dame in Indiana and a fellow of the Institute for Educational Initiatives. He and Frank J. Bonello have coauthored or coedited a number of works. In addition to *Taking Sides*, they have coedited *Alternative Directions in Economic Policy* (University of Notre Dame Press, 1978); *The Supply Side: Debating Current Economic Policies* (Dushkin Publishing Group, 1983); and *Urban Finance Under Siege* (M. E. Sharpe, 1993). He has also coedited or coauthored three other books. His most recent book is entitled *Working and Poor in Urban America*.

FRANK J. BONELLO was born in Detroit, Michigan, in 1939. He received his B.S. in 1961 and his M.A. in 1963, both from the University of Detroit, and his Ph.D. in 1968 from Michigan State University. He is currently an associate professor of economics and the Arts and Letters College Fellow at the University of Notre Dame in Indiana. He writes in the areas of monetary economics and economic education. *Taking Sides* is his seventh book. In addition to being coeditor on several publications with Thomas R. Swartz, he is the author of *The Formulation of Expected Interest Rates* (Michigan State University Press, 1969) and coauthor, with William I. Davisson, of *Computer-Assisted Instruction in Economic Education: A Case Study* (University of Notre Dame Press, 1976).

STAFF

Theodore Knight   List Manager
David Brackley   Senior Developmental Editor
Juliana Gribbins   Developmental Editor
Rose Gleich   Administrative Assistant
Brenda S. Filley   Director of Production/Design
Juliana Arbo   Typesetting Supervisor
Diane Barker   Proofreader
Richard Tietjen   Publishing Systems Manager
Larry Killian   Copier Coordinator

AUTHORS

FRANK ACKERMAN is a research assistant professor in the Department of Urban and Environmental Policy at Tufts University in Medford, Massachusetts. He is the author of *Why Do We Recycle? Markets, Values, and Public Policy* (Island Press, 1997).

ROBERT ALMEDER is a professor of philosophy at Georgia State University and a member of the editorial board of the *Journal of Business Ethics.* He is the author of *Harmless Naturalism* (Open Court, 1998).

RICHARD APPELBAUM is a professor of sociology and global and international studies at the University of California at Santa Barbara. He is also the founding editor of *Competition and Change: The Journal of Global Business and Political Economy.*

ROBERT A. BAADE is the James D. Vail Professor of Economics at Lake Forest College in Illinois.

DEAN BAKER is an economist with the Center for Economic and Policy Research in Washington, D.C., and coauthor, with Mark Weisbrot, of *Social Security: The Phony Crisis* (University of Chicago Press, 2000).

ERIC BATES is investigative editor of *Southern Exposure* and a staff writer for *The Independent* in Durham, North Carolina. He is coeditor, with Bob Hall, of *Ruling the Roost* (Southern Exposure, 1989).

ALAN S. BLINDER is the Gordon S. Rentschler Memorial Professor of Economics at Princeton University. He is a former vice chairman of the Federal Reserve Board and a former member of President Bill Clinton's Council of Economic Advisers.

MICHAEL J. BOSKIN is a senior fellow at the Hoover Institution and the Tully M. Friedman Professor of Economics at Stanford University. He is the author or editor of over 100 articles and books, including *Some Thoughts on Improving Economic Statistics* (Hoover Institution Press, 1998).

PATRICK J. BUCHANAN, who sought the 1996 Republican nomination for the presidency, is the author of *The Great Betrayal* (Little, Brown, 1998).

CHARLES T. CARLSTROM is an economic adviser at the Federal Reserve Bank of Cleveland. His principal field of research is macroeconomics, with a concentration on monetary economics and public finance.

THOMAS V. CHEMA is a partner in the law firm of Arter & Hadden LLP. He was also executive director of the Gateway Development Corporation of Greater Cleveland, a development agency.

JOE COBB is president of the Trade Policy Institute in Washington, D.C.

CHARLES CRAYPO is a professor of economics at the University of Notre Dame in Indiana. He is the author of *The Economics of Collective Bargaining: Case Studies in the Private Sector* (BNA Books, 1986).

WILLIAM A. DARITY, JR., is the Cary C. Boshamer Professor of Economics at the University of North Carolina. He is coauthor, with Samuel L. Myers, Jr., of *Persistent Disparity* (Edward Elgar, 1998).

JAMES DEVINE is a professor in the Department of Economics at Loyola Marymount University.

PETER DREIER is the Dr. E. P. Clapp Distinguished Professor of Politics and director of the Urban and Environmental Policy program in the Urban and Environmental Policy Institute at Occidental College in Los Angeles, California.

PETER J. FERRARA is an associate professor of law at George Mason University in Fairfax, Virginia, and an associate policy analyst at the Cato Institute.

MILTON FRIEDMAN is a senior research fellow at the Stanford University Hoover Institution on War, Revolution, and Peace. He and his wife are coauthors of several publications, including *Two Lucky People* (University of Chicago Press, 1998).

KEVIN GALLAGHER is a research associate on the Sustainable Hemispheric Integration Project in the Global Development and Environment Institute at Tufts University in Medford, Massachusetts.

ROBERT GREENSTEIN is the founder and executive director of the Center on Budget and Policy Priorities. He also served as administrator of the Food and Nutrition Service at the U.S. Department of Agriculture.

WENONAH HAUTER is director of the Critical Mass Energy Project for Public Citizen in Washington, D.C. Formerly the environmental policy director for Citizen Action, she was also a senior organizer at the Union of Concerned Scientists.

JAMES J. HECKMAN is the Henry Schultz Distinguished Service Professor of Economics at the University of Chicago and a senior fellow of the American Bar Association. He is coeditor, with Burton Singer, of *Longitudinal Analysis of Labor Market Data* (Cambridge University Press, 1985).

CATHERINE HILL is a study director at the Institute for Women's Policy Research. She was also an assistant professor at the University of Virginia.

ARTHUR L. KELLERMANN is a professor in the Departments of Internal Medicine, Preventive Medicine, and Biostatistics and Epidemiology at the University of Tennessee in Memphis, Tennessee.

NICHOLAS D. KRISTOF, a correspondent for the *New York Times,* served for 14 years as one of that newpaper's Asia correspondents. He is coauthor, with Sheryl WuDunn, of *Thunder From the East* (Alfred A. Knopf, 2000).

LESTER B. LAVE is the James H. Higgins Professor of Economics at Carnegie Mellon University in Pittsburgh, Pennsylvania. He is coeditor, with Arthur C. Upton, of *Toxic Chemicals, Health, and the Environment* (John Hopkins University Press, 1987).

PATRICK L. MASON is an associate professor of economics at Florida State University, where he is also director of African American studies. He is also an associate editor for the Southern Economic Association.

ADRIAN T. MOORE is director of economic studies at the Reason Public Policy Institute. He is also a policy analyst with Reason's Privatization Center and editor of the monthly newsletter *Privatization Watch.*

DANIEL D. POLSBY is the Kirkland and Ellis Professor of Law at Northwestern University in Evanston, Illinois. He has published many articles on a number of subjects related to law, including employment law, voting rights, broadcast regulation, and weapons policy.

GEORGE REISMAN is a professor of economics in the Graziadio School of Business and Management at Pepperdine University. He is the author of *Capitalism: A Treatise on Economics* (Jameson Books, 1996).

CHRISTY D. ROLLOW is a research associate at the Federal Reserve Bank of Richmond.

THOMAS RUSTICI is an instructor and head of undergraduate development at George Mason University in Fairfax, Virginia.

WILLIAM A. SAHLMAN is the Dimitri V. D'Arbeloff-MBA Class of 1995 Professor of Business Administration at the Harvard Business School, where he teaches entrepreneurial finance. He is coeditor of *The Entrepreneurial Venture,* 2d ed. (Harvard Business School Press, 1999).

ROBERT J. SAMUELSON writes a column for *Newsweek* and the Washington Post Writers Group, and he is the author of *The Good Life and Its Discontents* (Vintage Books, 1997).

NANCY SCHEPER-HUGHES is a professor of anthropology at the University of California, Berkeley, and a member of the International Bellagio Task Force on Transplantation, Bodily Integrity, and the International Traffic in Organs.

ISAAC SHAPIRO is director of the International Budget Project at the Center on Budget and Policy Priorities. He is coauthor of *The Personal Responsibility Act: An Analysis* (Center on Budget & Policy Priorities, 1994).

CYNTHIA POLLOCK SHEA is a senior researcher at the Worldwatch Institute and coauthor of the institute's annual *State of the World* publication.

TYSON SLOCUM joined Public Citizen's Critical Mass Energy Project in December 2000 and is currently working on electric utility restructuring and oil and gas policy.

MICHAEL TANNER is director of the Cato Institute Project on Social Security Privatization and coauthor, with Peter Ferrara, of *A New Deal for Social Security* (Cato Institute, 1998).

ALAN TONELSON is a research fellow at the U.S. Business and Industrial Educational Foundation. He coauthored *The New North American Order: A Win-Win Strategy for U.S.-Mexico Trade* (University Press of America, 1991).

SHERYL WuDUNN, a correspondent with the *New York Times,* has served for 14 years as one of that newspaper's Asia correspondents. She is coauthor, with Nicholas Kristof, of *Thunder From the East* (Alfred A. Knopf, 2000).

Index